THE
WHITE HOUSE
STAFF

INSIDE THE WEST WING
AND BEYOND

BRADLEY H. PATTERSON JR.

BROOKINGS INSTITUTION PRESS
Washington, D.C.

This book is dedicated to all those who,
serving the president,
serve the presidency.

Copyright © 2000
THE BROOKINGS INSTITUTION
1775 Massachusetts Avenue, N.W., Washington, D.C. 20036
www.brookings.edu

Library of Congress Cataloging-in-Publication data

Patterson, Bradley H. (Bradley Hawkes), 1921–
  The White House staff : inside the West Wing and beyond /
Bradley H. Patterson Jr.
     p.   cm.
  Includes bibliographical references and index.
  ISBN 0-8157-6950-4 (cloth: alk. paper)
  ISBN 0-8157-6951-2 (pbk: alk. paper)
  1. Presidents—United States—Staff. I. Title.
  JK552 .P37 2000   00-008802
  352.23'7'0973—dc21   CIP

(First softcover printing, November 2001)

9 8 7 6 5 4 3 2 1

The paper used in this publication meets minimum requirements of the American National Standard for Information Sciences—Permanence of Paper for Printed Library Materials: ANSI Z39.48-1992.

Typeset in Sabon

Composition by Oakland Street Publishing
Arlington, Virginia

Printed by R. R. Donnelley and Sons
Harrisonburg, Virginia

Contents

Preface to the Paperback Edition

The publication of the hardcover version of this book was timed to be useful during the 2000–01 transition. In 2001 a new president took charge of the White House; a new policy staff occupied the West Wing. Does this mean that a book about the White House staff published in 2000 is now out of date? Quite the contrary.

The modern White House is an institution with continuity as well as change. The change that comes with a new president is dramatic. Equally impressive, however, is the roster of White House elements that stay very much the same from administration to administration. This is a fact almost unknown to the public, who picture the White House staff as a small coterie that is reorganized and cleaned out by each incoming chief executive. That picture is wildly inaccurate.

The Organization and Structure of the White House

In 2000 there were 125 separately identifiable units in the White House staff. How many were Clinton creations? Seventeen. Principal among them were the National Economic Council, the National AIDS Policy Coordinator, an assistant for environmental initiatives, the President's Initiative for One America, the Special Envoy to the Americas, the Office for Women's Initiatives and Outreach, the Vice President's Office for Reinventing Government, and the First Lady's Millennium Council. All the other 108 offices have been in the White House for years—many dating from Eisenhower's time or earlier.

If President George W. Bush had wanted to, how many of those 125 could he, in theory, have disestablished by his own authority? All but one, the statutory National Security Council (NSC). Readers may be surprised to learn that, legally, the organization of the White House is almost entirely subject to the president's whim.

Was there a wholesale reorganization in 2001? By no means. How many of the 125 units did President Bush terminate? Sixteen. He *retained* the first two Clinton innovations mentioned above, disestablished the next six, and consolidated several NSC offices. The pool of volunteers was cut back and the number of White House interns greatly reduced.

President Bush then did what incoming chief executives typically do. Initially he established four new White House offices, which would focus on and dramatize his own priorities. These four were a Counselor for Communications, an Office of Strategic Initiatives, an Office of Faith-Based and Community Initiatives, and an additional Deputy National Security Adviser for International Economic Affairs. Vice President Cheney terminated Mr. Gore's Reinventing Government group but then added several new or newly identified offices on his own staff, including an Executive Director for National Energy Policy Development.

In response to the nation's needs so starkly dramatized by the terrorism of September 11, 2001, President Bush created three more new White House offices. He established a White House Office of Homeland Security and strengthened his NSC group still further by creating a third Deputy National Security Adviser/National Director for Combating Terrorism and a Special Adviser for Cyberspace Security. Result: the White House staff (as of fall 2001) comprises approximately 109 pre-existing offices and 21 new or newly identified ones—an overall total of 130. These are portrayed on pages 44–48 of this paperback edition, which has been revised to include the Bush emendations.

Any president can, in theory, dramatically reorganize and cut back the entire White House staff—but no president today would do so. Those 100-plus offices were created not merely for patronage, but to meet what each president considers are real needs. That has been the criterion for fifty years, is now, and will be in 2005 and 2009.

The Men and Women on the White House Staff

How many are there? Some 5,000. This number far exceeds what most of the public believe is the size of the White House staff.

I count only the White House group and (as explained on pages 4–5 of the Introduction) exclude institutions that are wholly in the Executive Office. The White House staff family, as I define it, includes the vice president's, first lady's, and NSC staffs; the Military Office; most of the Office of Administration; the White House support units of the National Park Service, the National Archives, the General Services Administration, and the Postal Service; the indispensable (and unpaid) corps of volunteers and interns, and the Washington-based Secret Service contingents directly involved in protecting the president and the vice president.

As is the case with the organization of the staff, all of those personnel serve—*in their White House capacity*—at the pleasure of the president. Just as he could restructure its offices, so, if he wanted to, he could discharge all the men and women in that White House staff community. That would be an egregious mistake. The crews that fly *Air Force One* or the *Marine One* helicopters, the Navy group who run Camp David, the 900 military communications professionals who, with the most advanced encryption equipment, keep the president in touch with his national security community, the Executive Clerk, the records and files professionals, the maids and butlers in the Residence, the librarians, the civilian telephone operators could all be given their walking papers; the highly skilled watch officers detailed to the NSC's Situation Room could all be sent back to their home agencies.

Did that happen in 2001? Of course not. As is expected, most of the nearly 1,000 people in the policy offices changed, as did almost all the volunteers (who tend to be adherents of the president's party). The reductions President Bush made in some offices, however, are being matched by increases in others; the new Homeland Security Office, for example, is authorized to use detailees from the cabinet departments; he will undoubtedly bring in significant numbers of them. But beyond the thousand new policy staffers, some four thousand others—nonpartisan, expert personnel in technical and support units—were invited to stay and to keep right on doing their professional jobs. Some of this group take enormous pride in thirty or even forty years of service (the record is fifty) not just to presidents, but to the institution of the presidency.

The new White House staff total may be 5,000—an educated guess, since (as explained on page 348 and accompanying footnotes on page 465) the U.S. Secret Service (a part of the Treasury Department) does not make public the figures for its uniformed and civilian White House contingents. Nor does the Military Office, which is estimated at 2,200, all on various payrolls of the Department of Defense.

The Senior Policy Staffs: Changing People, Unchanging Functions

The principal continuing value of this book lies in its full descriptions of what the various White House units *do*: what are the responsibilities of the major policy offices and how those senior personnel, men and women, go about discharging them. It is a striking fact that not only does the organization of the offices remain quite constant from one administration to the next, but so do the duties that the new office heads perform. For instance:

The incoming National Security Affairs Adviser continues with scooping up and sorting out the vast flood of vital diplomatic, military, and intelligence messages pouring into the White House, coordinating (in most cases, actually writing) the briefing papers for the president on the policy options he should consider, meeting with foreign visitors, and also making public appearances (while not ruffling the sensitivities of the Secretrary of State).

The new legislative affairs assistant moves straight into tracking pivotal legislation on the Hill, counting noses up there, twisting legislators' arms, alerting the president to phone calls that only he should make.

By election morning (if not before), the new Director of the Office of Presidential Personnel is wasting not an hour in the task of recruiting, vetting, selecting, and getting the presidential sign-off on the 3,694 presidential appointments that must eventually be made (including some 200 federal judges), and brusquely asserting his prerogative to clear the 2,128 political (Senior Executive Service and Schedule C) appointees that Cabinet members will want to be bringing immediately into their respective departments.

Vice President Cheney—just as did Vice President Gore—has a towering agenda of extremely high priority assignments from the president in both national security and domestic issues and has accumulated a strong personal staff to support him in this vital role.

The Counsel immediately fulfills the traditional role of advising the president on constitutional and ethical issues, vetting federal judges-to-be, guarding the president's executive privilege and instructing the White House staff on avoiding even the appearance of conflict of interest.

The Political Affairs office reaches out to the National Party headquarters and to the fifty State Party Chairmen and arranges to keep on developing polls for the White House leadership. The Scheduling Director, inundated with requests for the president's time, must, as always, say "no" 98 times out of 100. The Public Liaison head continues the White House practice of bringing in national opinion leaders for group briefings. The speechwriters must balance the drafting of world-shaking speeches with "Rose Garden rubbish." The Communications Director will take up the never-ending work of organizing all his opposite numbers in the Cabinet departments to amplify the president's message of the week. The Intergovernmental Affairs deputy will be repeating the tradition of planning for the president's participation in the next National Governors Conference. The Press Secretary will continue to seek presidential guidance on what to tell each morning's gaggle of newspeople and each noon's press conference. The Director of Advance will be phoning in from Moscow or Tokyo with recommendations on whatever will be the next presidential visits abroad.

The three counterterrorism offices will be potent new players in the White House environment, but even they will have to operate within time-honored restrictions. The Executive Order charter for the new Assistant for Homeland Security, for instance, gives that incumbent reach into nearly every part of every cabinet department, yet the incumbent must still operate without trashing cabinet-level sensitivities.

And the new Chief of Staff will have the same nineteen fundamental responsibilities his predecessors had (see pages 348–56). He will continue to be the boss of none but the quarterback of everything, the *system manager* for all the White House processes.

This, therefore, is the continuing scene in the modern White House, where the incoming officers will be very new people engaged in very old duties. Some functions will be modified, a few discarded; some will be added (and remain in White Houses of the future). This book describes these continuing responsibilities objectively and in depth. With surprisingly few exceptions, readers of this book in the Bush years—and those in the administrations that follow—can simply put different names over the existing doorways.

The Budget of the Modern White House

This remains the only book in the presidential literature to discuss the total budget of the White House—of all its parts. Naturally the figures given on pages 342–45 will vary with each year's appropriations, buried in the budgets of at least eleven agencies, but the categories of expenditures will continue with few changes. The estimated FY 2001 total of $730,500,000 will change, too—and, in the face of current emergencies, clearly not downward.

In Conclusion

In the White House, presidents typically decide that eleven-twelfths of the structures and two-thirds of the personnel should continue from administration to administration. This book portrays the structures of that institution, describes the continuing functions that the incoming officers inherit, and illustrates what the men and women who work there actually do. Its value to Washington officialdom, scholars, students, interns, and the public continues as well.

Acknowledgments

While this book has one father, it has a host of godparents. Authors of previous books are cited throughout the text; this work owes much to them and is itself but one more link in a chain of continuing research on the American presidency.

Some one hundred and thirty men and women, interviewed over the course of three years, were indispensable progenitors. Most had served in the White House; many are still there. Several were in departments or agencies that support the White House; a few were independent observers. The author cannot adequately express his debt to them, nor will the nation ever know how much it owes to their years of service in public life. Many are cited; some asked to remain anonymous. All spent hours with the author, sharing unmatchable experiences and unique memories. Many reviewed entire chapters, helping to guarantee accuracy and balance at a time when some writing about the White House has been overdramatic—even fanciful.

The author warmly commends the staff of the Brookings Institution Press: Director Robert Faherty, Managing Editor Janet Walker, Acquisitions Editor Chris Kelaher, Marketing Manager Rebecca Clark, and Art Editor Susan Woollen. He expresses his profound appreciation for the professional skill and personal commitment of copy editor Sandra F. Chizinsky. In addition, he would like to acknowledge the services of Carlotta Ribar, who proof-read the pages, and Julia Petrakis, who provided the index.

Like most of the author's undertakings, this book was a family enter-prise. Daughter Dawn Capron and sons Glenn and Brian Patterson aided in the research. Chief reviewer and tough critic, an experienced public administrator in her own right, and a full and energetic partner in this adventure—as in more than fifty-six years of marriage—was Shirley D. Patterson.

In the end the buck stops with the author; if there are mistakes, they are his. The views here are his as well, their roots growing out of fourteen years of White House service (1954–61 and 1969–76), and from twenty-three years of close observation of the work of the White House staff. The tone of these words stems from a respect for a place very few have known first-hand.

Introduction

Why a factual book about the White House staff? Because the 125 offices of the contemporary White House staff constitute the policy center of the executive branch of American government. There are books about individual presidents, the presidency, and presidential power, but it is the men and women on the president's personal staff who first channel that power, shape it, focus it—and, on the president's instructions, help him wield it. These 125 offices are the primary units of support as the president exercises executive leadership.

To most Americans the White House staff and its work are nearly unknown—largely because it is usually in the president's interest to keep them out of sight. Yet despite being curtained off within the presidency, the staff are public servants—and in helping the nation's foremost officeholder, they do the public's business. The public thus deserves an account of why the modern staff are there, how they are organized, and what they actually do. Scandalmongering and kiss-and-tell chronicles do not meet that need.

The curtain that screens most of the staff from view is thick with surprising contrasts, false stereotypes, and even paradoxes. For example:

—Despite providing essential support to the most visible person in America, almost all White House staff remain cloaked in anonymity (although a few key officers may be brought forward publicly to explain and defend the president's policies).

—The Constitution includes not a word about the White House staff, and they are barely mentioned in statute. Staff members have zero legal authority in their own right, yet 100 percent of presidential authority passes through their hands.

—A president or a presidential candidate typically pledges that he will have only a small White House staff and will rely predominantly on his cabinet officers for policy guidance. These pledges are not likely to be kept.

—The president's next inclination is to emphasize how few are his staff associates—when in fact they are numerous. Veterans of past administrations typically look at the current staff and cluck disapprovingly: "We did it with a third of that number." Stung by this criticism, a sitting president tries even harder to mask the size of his personal team, or makes a show (as did President Clinton) of cutting it back by some fixed percentage.

—Despite vows to cut back, presidents do just the opposite: they add to the menu of White House staff services. (Clinton's inauguration of the National Economic Council is an example.) Once created, many of the innovations turn out to be truly useful, and the added functions are carried over into succeeding administrations.

—Even if a cutback in staff numbers is instituted at the beginning of a president's first term, the staff's core responsibilities will remain undiminished. They will be met by requiring the remaining staffers to work unendurable hours, by adding detailees and consultants, and by bringing in volunteers and unpaid interns who are not included in White House budget totals. As the reelection campaign approaches, staff numbers again begin to creep upward.

—From afar, the White House staff appears to be a small group of broad-gauged generalists. A closer look reveals a different scene: forty-six principal offices engaged in specialized duties. Each of these units tells all the others to enter its guarded turf only with permission. The forty-six are aided by twenty-eight senior policy support groups.

—Supporting the forty-six principal offices and the twenty-eight subordinate groups—and invisible to the public—are fifty-one additional offices that contain the three-quarters of the staff who are nonpolitical professionals. These men and women serve not just the person but the office of the president—in effect, enhancing the presidency while aiding the president. Indeed, this dual loyalty—to the person and to the office—is found among the senior political assistants as well.

—The senior staff are partisans of the president. But their political commitment cannot be allowed to override the intellectual integrity that they must bring to their work. Contrary to public belief, sycophants and crusaders, if tolerated briefly, are not long welcome at the White House.

—Citizens might assume that White House staff members are cut from the same pattern, with common views on issues of public policy. Wrong. Differences in background, experience, age, sex, race, and especially party faction arc across the White House. The environment is an intellectually electric one, which is to the president's benefit—unless the internal arguments become ad hominem or are fought out in public.

—Although sometimes regarded as a barrier, walling off the president from people who advocate different opinions or from papers that present unconventional ideas, seniormost White House staff members often do just the opposite, insisting that dissenters be heard and challenging memorandums that tell the president only the welcome news.

—In the midst of the coterie composed of his own assistants, who serve entirely at the president's pleasure, are the vice president and the president's spouse: two key players whom the president cannot remove. *Their* large and energetic staffs work, on the one hand, with a sense of independence from the presidential group; on the other hand, they must be tied into the whole team—or else their principals may be embarrassingly out of step. (A third such player, of only somewhat less stature, is the vice president's spouse.)

—However intense the differences and distinctions within the White House staff may be, when a major presidential initiative gets underway, each of those specialized offices has to play its role *in coordination* with every other one. Does this happen effortlessly? No, and hell no. A set of unifying offices—and especially a tough, all-seeing chief of staff—operating precisely as the president wishes, is indispensable in guaranteeing the necessary teamwork.

—Shrouded, as most of them should be, by anonymity; protected, as they often must be, by executive privilege; and necessarily immersed in matters both delicate and confidential, staffers nonetheless do their work under the surveillance of an expert, unremittingly skeptical, and occasionally hostile press corps. Leaks are frequent; secrets are rare. Fortunately for our democracy, the White House is a glass house, with both light and heat streaming in.

—Within White House circles, the overriding ethical standard is so strict that it could be called unfair: the mere appearance of impropriety is itself the impropriety. A few White House incumbents, perhaps innocent in fact, have run afoul of that elevated criterion.

—The most exasperating paradox of all concerns a principle enunciated more than sixty years ago by Louis Brownlow, adviser to Franklin Roosevelt. Brownlow told President Roosevelt that White House assistants should never be "interposed" between the president and his department heads. But daily—yea, hourly—staff members fire questions, demand information, make pointed suggestions, summarize departmental views, add their own recommendations, and convey and interpret directives—about which the harried cabinet recipients may complain, "Usurpation!" What is often unknown to both the recipients and the public is that these staff actions are generally—and sometimes specifically—*at the president's own instructions.* This last and most pervasive "unknown" darkly colors the view that outsiders hold of the White House staff. In the eyes of the cabinet, the bureaucracy, Congress, the press, and the public, the staff are often accused of being unaccountable, out of control, pushing their own agendas. This is almost always a false view. Let there be a White House staffer who more than once (or maybe only once) misinterprets or subverts the president's wishes, and he or she will be found on the sidewalk outside.

Shrouded in this miasma of misperceptions, the White House staff is but dimly understood. Past and present scandals have strengthened the popular inclination to paint the staff deep purple, if not black, and to view the place as crawling with miscreants and misbehavior.

But hold on, dear readers. That's a bum rap.

Of course there have been staffers who were heavy-handed, boorish, immoral—even criminal. Some within the White House ring of power are so seduced by the privileges they are afforded and so oblivious to the public's watchful eye that they not only do foolish things but believe that their actions will go unnoticed. The nation is—and always has been—rightfully skeptical about how presidential power is used, and has become, properly, ever more attentive to the behavior of the president's agents.

Greatly outnumbering the dozens whose misdeeds have sullied their surroundings, however, are the hundreds who have served their presidents, and the public, with brilliance and with self-effacing commitment. No apologies are due to the miscreants, but the public's very watchfulness now calls for better illumination of the White House as a whole.

Just what is meant, in this book, by "the White House"? The author owes readers a clear delineation of the units that he regards as being within, and not within, that famous phrase.

Directly assisting the president, and separate from the line departments and agencies, is the Executive Office of the President, a collection of offices first created by Franklin Roosevelt in 1939. Not counting the president himself, these now number eleven. One of the eleven, formally referred to as the White House Office, includes the Executive Residence. Three other offices in the Executive Office of the President are so intimately tied to the work of the Oval Office that, for the purposes of this book, they have been included as de facto parts of the White House, broadly defined. These three are the Office of the Vice President, the Office of Policy Development (the president's domestic and economic policy staffs), and the National Security Council (here meaning the staff of the council, not the cabinet-level body itself).[1]

The other seven (the Council of Economic Advisers; the Council on Environmental Quality; the Office of Management and Budget; the Office of National Drug Control Policy; the Office of Science, Technology, and Space Policy; the Office of the U.S. Trade Representative; and probably half of the Office of Administration) are, in the author's judgment, Executive Office, but not White House, units and are therefore outside the focus of this book.[2]

The reasoning behind this delineation becomes clear if one keeps in mind the four cardinal characteristics that distinguish the White House units from the other institutions of the Executive Office.

First, except for the president and the vice president, no person in the "White House" parts of the Executive Office has any legal authority to *do* anything, other than to assist and advise the two principals. The other Executive Office institutions have specified statutory duties. Second, with a few exceptions, all those who serve in the White House units do so at the pleasure of the president; none have any tenure in their White House jobs (those on detail may of course have tenure in their original agencies).[3] Below the layer of politically appointed officers, employees of the other Executive Office units have career civil service status. Third, any papers generated by the four White House institutions are presidential records and subject to the provisions of the Presidential Records Act,[4] whereas the papers of the Executive Office units are agency records and come under the provisions of the Federal Records Act.[5] Finally, there is a strong tradition, rather strictly adhered to, that no persons serving in the White House are to appear before congressional committees and testify about their actions: nor do they, except in connection with criminal investigations (for example, Watergate, Iran-Contra) or allegations of wrongdoing that would create great political embarrassment for the White House if they refused to appear.[6] (White House staff may and often do, of course, visit individual legislators informally.) Heads of the other Executive Office units routinely give formal testimony.

Important as they are, these four distinctions are almost never clarified in public discourse, neither by the president nor by knowledgeable journalists. This lack of clarity about the distinction between the White House and the Executive Office has enabled President Clinton, for example, to say that he "cut the White House staff by 25 percent" when much of the cutting was done in the Office of National Drug Control Policy. No wonder the public is confused about what constitutes "the White House."

A final word of clarification: the White House that has just been defined in this introduction—and that is described in the first twenty-one chapters of the book—is the group of relatively small offices that serve the president in substantive policy areas; these offices are the first forty-six on the list that appears at the end of the introduction to part 2. In chapter 21 and part 3, the author introduces the broader concept of the "White House staff community," which includes the professional and technical support staffs for the presidency. In this wider, much more numerous, but indispensable "community" are the White House Military Office and the White House components of the Secret Service, as well as men and women from the National Park Service, the National Archives and Records Administration, and the General Services Administration. Hundreds of career employees are indeed in these ranks; hundreds more are interns and part-time White House volunteers. The public knows little about them; they belong, though, to the White House family—and they are therefore included in this volume.

How does this book differ from the author's 1988 work, *Ring of Power: The White House Staff and Its Expanding Role in Government*?

Perhaps for the first time in the history of presidential literature, readers will be given an encyclopedic look at the contemporary White House in its entirety, with its 125 separately identifiable offices. Parts 1 and 2 fully portray each of the White House's forty-six major policy offices (one such office, made up of the staff of the National Security Council, encompasses nineteen subsections; another, the National Economic Council, is a new outfit) and treat more briefly the twenty-eight units that immediately support the principal forty-six. A new chapter discusses the never-before-described office of the spouse of the vice president. The eighteen separate physical facilities of the modern White House are identified and described.

Part 3 illumines in greater detail the fifty-one professional and support offices of the contemporary White House, in which 87 percent of the staff do their indispensable work for the president and the country in almost complete obscurity and anonymity. Two of these offices are 135 years old; several were instituted only in the Clinton years. This book describes the newly enlarged White House intern program as well as the National Park Service's recently published *Comprehensive Design Plan for the White House and President's Park*.

Part 2 and portions of part 3 not only describe the functions of the various White House offices and offer recent examples of their work but also analyze the problems and issues that each policy unit needs to address in the long term. The final chapter of part 2 addresses two aspects of the White House characterized by both controversy and concealment: the full size of the White House staff community, and the total White House budget; the latter is set forth for the first time in any publication about the White House.

Part 4 looks ahead. President Bush (1989–92), in managing national security affairs, and President Clinton, more generally (particularly during his second term), seem to have succeeded in dampening the old animosities between the cabinet and the White House staff. Will the animosities resurface? How much real freedom will the president of 2001—and those in the years beyond—have to make changes in the White House? What is the real limit on White House staff size, and what governs its accountability? Is anonymity still the universal desideratum? What new physical facilities are on the drawing board for the White House of the future? Part 4 addresses these questions.

Although this book draws some examples from presidents of the more distant past, it concentrates on the changes in White House operations that occurred during the Bush and Clinton administrations. The focus here is not on the president but on the staff; the emphasis is not on what the presidents did but on how the staff supported them. The objective here is not to judge the wisdom or success of any president's policies: many other critics and historians are taking up that challenge.

This new work is designed—and timed—to be of help to the most immediate newcomers: the White House staff of 2001 and other presidencies of the near future. Sad to say, in a presidential transition, White House file cabinets and bookshelves are typically devoid of any such guidance. Unless there are White House veterans among them, the incoming team rushes in to find nearly a tabula rasa when it comes to White House operations and procedures. The book also aims to be of interest and benefit to students, to scholars, to public administrators, and to the public at large.

The author spent fourteen years on the White House staffs of three presidents and was close to the staff of a fourth. What follows is not a kiss-and-tell account, a personal memoir, or an exposé. Readers will need to turn to other sources to obtain an exhumation of the Lewinsky affair or other scandals or to revel in breathless, blow-by-blow accounts of who said what in inner White House conflicts.

This is the professional view, not of a theorist, not of an outsider looking in, but of a White House practitioner—a public administrator with an intimate knowledge of how the entire White House really works. Joined with the author's voice are those of some 130 others whom he interviewed during the past three years—and who have also lived through the heat and tension, the frustration and exultation, of White House service. Some interviewees have held positions in other agencies but have worked closely with the White House; a few are distinguished journalists, veteran observers of the White House scene.

In the interest of accuracy, balance, and professionalism, the author not only submitted the attributed quotations for confirmation but also invited many of the interviewees to review the entire chapters in which their work is described. Many of the interviews were conducted in situ—in operating areas of the White House that are necessarily out of the public view, but adding new depth to the author's own previous experience in the halls of that institution.

The author's nonpartisan aim is to illumine public administration at the apex of government, at the center of policy: to open up the White House gates and describe what is within.

PART ONE

Outside and Inside
the White House

The modern White House is now sixty-one years old, and so is the environment that sired it. The twin sources of turmoil—domestic economic disaster and world conflict—that formed the background for the early development of the White House staff, under Franklin Roosevelt, have evolved into even more complicated challenges for the ten presidents who followed him.

At home, the action centers of our social and economic system are so interdependent and tightly interwoven that our government's highly variegated storehouse of aids and subsidies—1,412 separate domestic assistance programs—must be employed with exquisite coordination on the part of their cabinet managers. Abroad, the days have utterly vanished when America's national security resources—diplomatic, military, intelligence, public information, economic—could be kept in separate compartments. Vanished, too, are whatever boundary lines ever existed between domestic policy and foreign affairs, or between policy and politics. The president today acts in a gigantic theater-in-the-round: he is an omnidirectional executive.

The support institutions for the modern presidency reflect this changed domestic and foreign policy environment. The president is not only a leader in public policy but is now the chief coordinator of a potent and intricate executive branch: potent because its annual outlays have reached $1.8 trillion, intricate because the multitudinous and competing interests of contemporary society are now duplicated within the government's own ranks. The "cabinet government" has not grown in total size—in fact, it has shrunk a bit in recent years—but has exploded in complexity.

But what began to be true in Roosevelt's time is even more true today: it is the White House that must supply the required leadership and coordination. The evolution that was required fully to implement that principle has taken place over sixty years, and has occurred on two fronts. First, the departments and agencies have gradually come to accept the primacy of the White House in executive branch policy work; second, the White House staff itself has emerged as the lead engine of both policy development and interdepartmental coordination.

In researching and writing first the 1988 book, *Ring of Power,* and now this one, the author's convictions have evolved. Although the subtitle of the 1988 volume referred to the White House staff's "expanding role in government," the author's research over the past three years has led him to a fundamental thesis that reaches beyond his conclusions of a dozen years ago: on almost all important foreign and domestic issues today, the formulation, coordination, articulation—and, in some cases, the implementation—of policy are being drawn away from the line departments and centralized in the White House and in its large and energetic staff. This development has occurred gradually in the course of recent years, but is now clearly the case.

Does this mean that the departments are out of the loop? Of course not. In contrast to the White House, the agencies and the cabinet departments have vast resources: specific authorities granted in hundreds of statutes; expert personnel—the repositories of continuity and institutional memory—spread throughout the country and the world; the ability to buy and build big things; and years of time. But what no one line agency has is the reach—much less the authority—to give instructions to any other one, or even to extract sensitive information from another. What no department or group of departments has is the presidential perspective: the overarching vision of goals and priorities, the acute political sensitivity to opportunities and limits. It is predominantly in the White House that these unique abilities reside.

In every case? On every issue? No. A rare cabinet secretary (Clinton's Robert Rubin, for instance) will have such a close relationship with the president that the two see eye to eye. But that is the exception to the general thesis that is being advanced—and which the chapters in this new volume will attempt to demonstrate.

Are there risks in this centralized mode of governance? There were when Richard Nixon and Henry Kissinger pushed Secretary of State William Rogers into the shadows. An impressive feature of the Clinton years, in contrast, is that even with national security policy centralized in the White House, the historic tension between the White House and the State Department was minimized. Nevertheless, there are indeed risks, and these will be examined.

The purpose of the book is not to pontificate about what is right or wrong but to describe what is in fact happening. Such strength at the presidential center, it can be observed, does no offense to the Constitution, in which Article 2 makes it clear that "the executive Power is vested in a President" who "shall take Care that the Laws be faithfully executed."

The objective of these two opening chapters is to position the readers atop the White House gates: to survey first the tumultuous environment outside, then the ways in which, within the perimeter, all the postwar presidents have strengthened their White House staffs to counterbalance the cacaphony without.

"Cabinet government"—in which each agency manages its own affairs, with the president as general supervisor—is shibboleth, not reality. It is the White House staff that, under close presidential direction, superintends policy development, directly manages policy coordination, governs the flow of information to the president, and monitors the implementation of presidential initiatives.

Readers are the jury. The case begins in the White House front yard.

CHAPTER ONE

Outside the Gates: A No-Consensus Society

A zeal for different opinions . . . an attachment to different leaders ambitiously contending for preeminence and power . . . have . . . divided mankind into parties, inflamed them with mutual animosity, and rendered them much more disposed to vex and oppress each other than to cooperate for their common good.

JAMES MADISON

BRING US TOGETHER!

SIGN HELD BY A TEENAGE GIRL IN DESHLER, OHIO, DURING THE NIXON CAMPAIGN OF 1968

This pair of admonitions brings to life the central dilemma of the American presidency. At 1600 Pennsylvania Avenue sits a unitary executive in the midst of a raucously pluralistic nation. Beyond the White House fence, the machinery of presidential policy is surrounded on all sides by noisy nationwide disagreement on every imaginable policy issue.

The American Mosaic

Today's presidents are charged with the "common defense" and "general welfare" of nearly 300 million Americans and are directly accountable to the 193.7 million who are registered voters—a moving, pulsing, mosaic of needs, dreams, interests, and pressures. Nowhere in that mosaic, however, can one detect consensus as to how best to provide for the common defense or how to allocate most equitably the resources for the general welfare. Merely describing the mosaic reveals the reason for the policy tumult.

Of the total American population, some 224 million are non-Hispanic whites, 34.4 million are African American, 30.3 million are Hispanic, 10.5 million are Asian, and 2.3 million are Native American or Inuit. Our nation encompasses dozens of nationalities, speaking 140 languages, and nearly 20 million Americans are foreign born. Nearly 35 million Americans are over sixty-five, and more than 70 million are under eighteen. Over 17 million live in families with a net worth of more than $100,000; over 36 million Americans live below the poverty line. Cities of over 100,000 are home to 210 million; 57 million live in nonmetropolitan areas. Phi Beta Kappa members number 650,000, while 25 percent of Americans twenty-five years of age or older have less than a ninth-grade education. In the work force are 724,000 doctors, over 4.5 million teachers, 2.5 million truck drivers, 1 million police officers, and 574,000 miners. There are 1.8 million federal civilian employees, 875,000 postal employees, 1.8 million members of the armed forces, and 16.7 million state and local government workers.

Nearly 1 million business firms have annual receipts of $1 million or more, and there are nearly 3 million small businesses with annual receipts under $100,000. In 1992–93, some 564,000 new firms with fewer than 500 employees were created, and 34,700 failed. During the same two years, 411 new companies with more than 500 employees were started. Disabled workers number 17.4 million, 43.7 million Americans draw social security benefits, and 685,000 are in hospitals. Fifteen percent of the American public reportedly leans "strong Democratic," 19 percent "weak Democratic," 13 percent "independent Democratic," 10 percent Independent, 12 percent "independent Republican," 15 percent "weak Republican," and 16 percent "strong Republican."[1]

From this phantasmagoria of varying individuals arises—as our Federalist designers explicitly anticipated—a correspondingly dizzying welter of views on every imaginable economic and social question. Many are not merely "views"; they are quarrels.

"So strong," wrote Madison, "is this propensity of mankind to fall into mutual animosities," that many disputes erupt into litigation. In 1997, 36.6 million (nontraffic) cases were filed in state and local courts. More pertinent to the White House, however, are the conflicts being brought to the federal courts: in 1998, 314,478 cases were filed in the ninety-four district courts and 53,805 in the thirteen courts of appeals; 8,083 were petitioned to the Supreme Court. On a typical day, over 100,000 lawsuits are pending against the federal government itself.

Another measure of the pluralistic character of our country is the number of centers of political power across the nation. Beyond the White House gates are 50 state governments encompassing 3,043 county governments, 19,372 city governments, 16,629 townships, 13,726 school districts, and 34,683 special districts, to which one must add 558 federally recognized Native American tribes and groups—a total of 88,061, in addition to the federal government itself.

Instruments of Influence

Three hundred million Americans and 88,061 subunits of governing power: on issues of federal public policy, how do they weigh in? They organize.

In 1997, national nonprofit institutions numbered 22,901, an increase of 8,000 since 1980. Most of these organizations were formed, in part, to press their views on the federal executive and legislative branches. These groups act through 17,000 Washington representatives—regular habitués of the White House neighborhood.

Armadas of warring interest groups form around every issue of public policy. Indeed, the emotions surrounding policy conflicts can become so inflamed that leaders of opposing organizations who so much as sit down in the same room to discuss compromise risk being repudiated by their own memberships.

New technologies have increased the ability of advocacy groups to wield pressure. "Blast-fax" equipment—often used at night, when circuits are free—can spew thousands of facsimile messages at a time; the National League of Cities (NLC) has an electronic mail system that can in five seconds send an alert to hundreds of city halls, galvanizing NLC members to make phone calls or write letters of complaint.

Mirrors of Pluralism: Congress and the Laws

Congress is the closest target for the cascade of pressures from interest groups; both its structure and its actions mirror the society that elects it. Reflecting the nation's multiplicity of needs and concerns, Congress today is subdivided into some 44 committees and 157 specialized subcommittees. Members also adhere to unofficial advocacy task forces and to voluntary, organized associations of members called caucuses (for example, the Iron and Steel Caucus, the Wine Caucus, the Congressional Black Caucus, and the Hispanic Caucus); there are currently 172 caucuses in all.

The raw material of public opinion—millions of letters and telegrams a year—inundates the Capitol. If a controversial issue is pending, one million letters a day will flood into the House alone. The vast winnowing work of the legislative process need not be detailed here, but its products—the laws—reflect, in two important respects, the factionalism that Madison described long ago.

First, statutes enacted at different times in our history either create the possibility of or directly induce conflict between the federal agencies that must carry them out. Considered separately, each such statute mandates actions that help a particular sector of American society; taken collectively, however, these laws mandate grief for the president, who must straddle their contradictions. For example, a 1938 law directs the secretary of agriculture to pay price supports to tobacco growers, while a 1965 statute requires every package of cigarettes to carry a health warning from the surgeon general. Both laws—bearing their inconsistent instructions—are still in the federal code.

A second and more common reflection of sharp policy differences—both within the nation, and, by extension, within Congress—is the ambiguity deliberately incorporated into some of our laws. Vague language masks deep splits in legislative purpose but permits the necessary compromises to be struck among quarreling congressional partisans. The resulting legislation, with its key provisions fuzzy and subject to conflicting interpretations, is then deposited on the president's doorstep with the expectation that it will be "faithfully executed."

Former presidential assistant Henry Kissinger dissected the series of congressional enactments that, over the course of four years, both authorized and limited U.S. aid to the Nicaraguan contras. Summing up, Kissinger noted: "Clearly Congress provided neither continuity nor criteria to which even the most scrupulous administration could orient itself. . . . Of such stuff are institutional crises made."[2] In struggling to interpret ambiguous statutes, the president and his cabinet colleagues are in fact wrestling with the original and continuing uncertainties of Congress, which faithfully represents its constituents' conflicting priorities. A no-consensus society produces a no-consensus Congress.

Mirror of Pluralism: The Executive Branch Itself

The other targets of the drumfire of bewilderingly conflicting public pressures are the president and his executive branch. The president being singular, is it not here that pluralism should come to an end? With executive power "vested in a president," does not the language of Article 2 imply that despite faction and dispute elsewhere, the executive branch is to be a unified environment? Alexander Hamilton certainly thought so:

> No favorable circumstances palliate or atone for the disadvantages of dissension in the executive department. Here they are pure and unmixed. There is no point at which they cease to operate. They serve to embarrass and weaken the execution of the plan or measure to which they relate, from the first step to the final conclusion of it. They constantly counteract those qualities in the executive which are the most necessary ingredients in its composition—vigor and expedition, and this without any counterbalancing good.[3]

But no. In this arena, Publius's advice has been passed by. In the two centuries since Hamilton wrote, the executive establishment has developed in contradiction to his warning.

On the morning after their inauguration, the newly elected presidents of 2001 and the years beyond will peer over the White House fence, surveying the executive branch over which they will preside.

What will they see out there? Not unity, but a vast plurality: seventy-one permanent, full-time agencies. Of these, forty must be set apart: as regulatory commissions (such as the Federal Reserve Board) or independent, multiheaded bodies (such as the Tennessee Valley Authority), they are insulated from White House intervention in their decisionmaking. That leaves thirty-one departments and agencies. Through his power to appoint and remove and through the exercise of personal leadership, the president will have a principal influence over these institutions. Yet, as he looks at them on January 21, gauging that future influence, what does he notice?

They have the status of age. The departments of State and Treasury, the War Department (later subsumed in the Department of Defense), and the post of Attorney General date back to the beginnings of the Republic. Constituent pieces of even the "new" departments have a history: the Department of Education had its beginnings in 1867, and the atomic energy part of the Department of Energy in 1946. The originating statutes of these agencies convey more than authority: they radiate a sense of mission.

"Leave [the national parks] . . . unimpaired for the enjoyment of future generations," the Park Service was instructed in 1916. The Environmental Protection Agency's mission is to "create and maintain conditions under which man and nature can exist in productive harmony and . . . fulfill the responsibilities of each generation as trustee of the environment for succeeding generations."

In agency after agency, age and mission combine to create a pervasive culture of commitment. In the Forest Service, begun in 1905, careerists proudly claim that they wear "green underwear." In the National Park Service the password is "green blood": there are now park service rangers who are the grandchildren of rangers. In the words of a retired superintendent, "The programs of the National Park Service are our faith and heritage, our trust and my task."[4]

New classes of Foreign Service officers are sworn in under the portrait of Benjamin Franklin. Every person who walks into the Diplomatic Entrance at the Department of State is confronted by the two large wall plaques that list the names of the 186 employees who lost their lives while on duty.

At the Central Intelligence Agency (CIA), graven into the right wall of the white marble foyer are seventy-seven stars representing the men and women of the agency who were killed in action; on the left wall is engraved a passage from the Bible: "For ye shall know the truth and the truth shall make you free." When President Eisenhower laid the cornerstone of the building in 1959, he said of the CIA's responsibilities, "No task could be more important."

In the Pentagon's Alcove of Heroes are listed the winners of the Congressional Medal of Honor. The Army battle flag at the Pentagon bears 169 campaign streamers—most recently from Bosnia, but dating back to Yorktown.

At the Air Force Academy in Colorado Springs, an emphasis on institutional pride is part of the daily routine: at lunchtime, the cadets form squadrons and, with the chapel and the Rocky Mountains towering overhead, march into the dining hall, past the colors, in step to the "Air Force Hymn." In the principal classrooms, Air Force generals' pictures line the walls, each with the implicit message "Emulate me!"

Throughout the entire executive branch, agencies and services—military and civilian alike—are infused with a sense of history, mission, and commitment. Award and retirement ceremonies reinforce the pride and dedication that motivate the great majority of the nation's public employees. Most of the presidents help strengthen that dedication; in return, they are incredibly well served by the men and women who work with such enthusiasm.

But the line between loyalty and parochialism is a thin one. Referring to the need, emphasized by many presidents, to develop joint service capabilities and to damp down interservice rivalry, former Marine commandant P. X. Kelly said, "Asking a man to be as loyal to the other services as to his own is like asking him to be as loyal to his girlfriends as he is to his wife."[5]

As he surveys the executive branch, the president cannot help but notice the twenty-four separate federal personnel systems that, in effect, ensure that agency parochialism remains ironclad. These distinct administrative cages were stuck into place as if Article 2 had never been written. Outside the White House staff, there is no such thing as a presidential service: even the president's political appointees belong to the departments—and only the departments hire, evaluate, promote, and fire the 1.8 million civilian and 1.8 million military personnel who work for them. The Senior Executive Service claims to facilitate the efficient and flexible use of top-level civil servants, but the president has no role in determining career assignments, and most transfers occur within the walls of a given agency.

Ask a federal employee "For whom do you work?" and the answer will always be "for the Bureau of Land Management"—or the FBI, or the IRS, or the Navy—never "I work for the president."

Taking an even closer look at the elements of the executive branch, a president would see within each department a mind-boggling array of specialized bureaus, divisions, and units, an alphabet soup of acronyms: more than three thousand, for example, in the telephone directory of the Department of Health and Human Services alone.

But this array is not surprising. Like Congress, these thousands of micro-offices within the executive branch mirror the diversity of Americans' wishes, needs, hopes, and dreams.

In fact, that's how they got started.

In the course of two centuries, needs communicated strongly enough became laws, laws authorized money, money paid for public employees, employees were organized into bureaus (or minibureaus), and the work of government proceeded, often under the attentive eyes of the advocates who had fought to have the needs met in the first place.

Consider the federal program to develop outdoor recreation trails. Needled by public-spirited advocates of increased outdoor recreation resources, in 1958 Congress expressed its official concern and created a study commission. As a consequence of the commission's 1962 report, Congress established by law the Bureau of Outdoor Recreation within the Department of the Interior. In 1965 President Johnson proposed "a national system of trails," and in 1966 the bureau produced a response: Trails for America. Two years later Congress created the National Trails System, which now consists of 8 National Scenic Trails, 12 National Historic Trails, and 790 National Recreation Trails. A president looking closely at the Department of the Interior will find several "trails desks" within the National Park Service; in the White House, the mail room is likely to hear directly from the more than 170 regional, state, and local organizations keenly interested in this one area of public policy: among these are the Chugiak Dog Mushers Association, the Concerned Off-Road Bicyclists Association, the Driftskippers Snowmobile Club, the Friends of the Pumpkinvine National Trail, the Georgia Blind Adventurers, the International Llama Association, the National Horse Lovers Association, the Okie Dirt Riders, the Rails-to-Trails Conservancy, and the United States Snowshoe Association. One can imagine from their very names that the letters from these outfits will pressure the government with conflicting advice about what kinds of trails should be built and how they should be used.

Multiply this example by perhaps twenty thousand, and the contentious environment of the executive branch is revealed in its almost incomprehensible variety.

The bureaus of the executive branch, furthermore, don't just sit still outside the White House perimeter: they move, pulse, vibrate.

Impelled by eloquent statutory injunctions, inspired by decades of tradition, stung by congressional surveillance or fired up by advocacy groups, government officials are usually the very opposite of the stereotypical "do-nothing bureaucrats." They want to attack the nation's problems, and they press for the resources to move ahead with their mandates. "We are the punta de la lanza," boasted the early Peace Corps staffers, and from director Sargent Shriver to the lowliest typist, they glowed with zeal.

Whether a venerable Forest Service or a new AmeriCorps, the agencies of the president's executive branch are driven by strong and independent traditions. Although each executive agency's duty is to help the president, an agency's varied program mandates often impel it in directions that go beyond White House priorities.

Through patronage and through the use of White House staff (detailed in succeeding chapters), a president has some—but only limited—control over what is constitutionally his own executive branch.

The Pluralist Planet

There is, of course, one circle of institutions within the Washington scene where the president's constitutional reach is zero.

The United States recognizes some 191 foreign nations; of these, 167 have embassies in Washington and reciprocal U.S. representation in their capitals.

Their sovereignty renders foreign nations unique. The decisions of foreign governments are subject to persuasion, bargaining, and even pressure. But in the absence of conquest, their policies are their own: neither the U.S. president nor Congress can command them.

The 191 coexist in a world community where military, economic, and environmental challenges require multinational responses. U.S. attack warning systems depend on bases in Greenland and Australia. Closing down the traffic in illegal drugs will be impossible without the cooperation of Latin American and Asian governments. Reducing U.S. unemployment depends on the purchase of American goods by foreign consumers, and the prosperity of American farms relies on other nations' willingness to lower the barriers to trade.

Much of a president's so-called domestic agenda, therefore, is in reality a menu for the persuasion of sovereign governments elsewhere in the world. Unless they accede, he will fail to achieve some of his own domestic political goals. Each of the 191, however, has its own priorities and desires, about which the American president and his associates must bargain.

The Warfare of Washington

The landscape beyond the White House fence, then, is less a pastoral scene than a battlefield, a war zone. Long-range institutional artillery sends shells screaming in from state and local governments. Missile batteries fire throughout the Capitol. The Big Berthas of the judiciary alternate with grenades hurled by advocacy groups. Every cabinet agency bristles with rocket launchers; minefields are sunk along Embassy Row. Many of the projectiles are smoke and chaff, intended to confuse and mislead, and policy battles are sometimes clouded with the poison gas of personal vindictiveness.

Strange battlefield, though! The lines of combat shift. Alliances form and disband; allegiances fluctuate constantly. Hundreds of different banners are unfurled, and bugles sound their clarions to herald an ever-changing panoply of objectives. Surprise attack is almost unknown; enemies today are friends tomorrow. Perhaps the most vital pieces of military equipment are not guns but binoculars: every unit watches the others. Thousands of spotting-scopes peer to discover who is accumulating too much power, or whether anyone is stepping outside recognized boundaries.

One last feature of the field: it is illuminated day and night. Star shells and flares from the nation's—the world's—print and television media throw a rude light across every meadow, into bedroom and Cabinet Room alike.

There are practically no secrets; information is as all-permeating as the smoke in the air, and there may be more spies afoot than soldiers. There are occasional victories and sometimes defeats; more often, there are merely truces and compromises, many of which last only until new forces have been mustered to fight again.

Former secretary of state George Shultz described the Washington war zone to Congress: "Nothing ever gets settled in this town. It's not like running a company or even a university. It's a seething debating society in which the debate never stops, in which people never give up, including me, and that's the atmosphere in which you administer."[6]

Precisely as the writers of our Constitution foresaw, the struggles never end. This policy warfare of a heterogeneous, free society pauses only momentarily while a new president marches for the first time through the White House gates. It then resumes—and, as the new chief executive looks back over his shoulder, he may begin to reflect on that "cabinet government" that some of his predecessors admired, and to wonder whether he should, instead, strengthen the countervailing resources within the White House perimeter.

Bring Us Together?

Beyond the White House fence is a kaleidoscopic country, a judiciary swamped with conflicts, a narrowly divided Congress, an executive branch of thousands of program offices, and 191 independent nations—the lot of them in unending and rancorous debate about resources and priorities. Within the White House is a president who feels the full force of all those needs, dreams, interests, and pressures—and who is himself a warrior ready for battle.

"Bring Us Together!" urged the teenage girl in Deshler, Ohio—but Madison and Hamilton give us cause to wonder whether the president can do it.

CHAPTER TWO

Inside the Gates: Alternatives for Organizing a White House

A President is not bound to conform to the advice of his ministers. He is even under no positive injunction to ask or require it. But the Constitution presumes that he will consult them, and the genius of our government and the public good recommend the practice.

ALEXANDER HAMILTON

We could always go out and find an expert on meat prices or special education or health economics to help our people analyze and understand a specific issue. But loyalty, versatility, and reliability were Nixon's first criteria, and he counted on his own campaign people to take charge of his major projects.

JOHN D. EHRLICHMAN

On the morning after inauguration, a new president will review the list of issues awaiting his attention. Still echoing from his inaugural address—as well as in his party's platform, in his acceptance oration at the convention, and in a hundred campaign speeches—are goals that have been set and promises that have been made. Environmental degradation, illegal drugs, gun control, budget surpluses, civil rights, trade deficits, homelessness, relations with China and Russia: the gravity of these and at least a dozen other issues is outweighed only by the realization that in just four short years, the same questions will likely appear first on the presidential reelection exam. Now the president searches for the swiftest and most effective way to address these issues—to mobilize the brainpower and resources of his executive branch to help him develop creative initiatives.

Back in December, he may have made the standard promise—pledging, as he introduced his cabinet, to rely on its members and on their institutional strengths. But taking that menu of momentous issues in one hand, and holding up the organization chart of the executive branch in the other, the newly elected president is struck by the disparity. There is no correspondence: not a one of his top-priority problems fits within any single cabinet box on the diagram. None can be confined inside the walls of an existing department. To no one cabinet officer can the chief executive point a finger and say: "The trade deficit—you, Secretary Smith, will be responsible for attacking that problem. I believe in delegation; this assignment is yours; you run with it." If Smith were, for example, the secretary of commerce, he or she would run but ten yards before crossing into the jurisdictions of State, Treasury, Labor, Agriculture, Transportation, Energy, the Central Intelligence Agency, the Export-Import Bank, the International Trade Commission, the Council of Economic Advisers, the National Security Council staff, the Office of Management and Budget, and the Office of the U.S. Trade Representative. The expertise of every one of those institutions will need to be mined, their analyses and recommendations solicited.

Being peers, none of the cabinet-level officers will defer to Secretary Smith; few of them will even agree on which questions should be studied; and most of them will come up with different sets of facts. One or two will secretly feel that they, rather than Smith, should have been given the lead in the first place.

Here is the earliest conundrum that confronts modern presidents: how to organize for analysis, for policy development, for interagency coordination, for decision, for public communication, and for action when the range of cross-cutting issues is so thoroughly at odds with the traditional and rigid structures of the executive branch. There are a number of possible solutions: (1) reorganize the structures; (2) create supersecretaries; (3) convene cabinet meetings; (4) designate one cabinet department as the "lead agency" to coordinate the others; or (5) concentrate policy development leadership within the White House, giving the assignments to the president's own senior White House assistants.

Two other supplementary approaches are (1) to ask the first lady to get deeply involved in one or a few issues and to coordinate the job of preparing—and even publicly defending—recommendations and legislation and (2) to task the vice president with responsibility for organizing and direct-

ing interagency staff work on several principal policy initiatives. But these
two options—each of which is described separately in chapters 18 and 19—
both have the same drawback: they lay responsibilities on the shoulders of
persons who are outside the direct line of executive authority that starts
with the Constitution and runs through the president and downward.

All of the first five techniques have been used by recent presidents. What
have we learned from these attempts?

Reorganize

If areas of presidential concern keep crossing departmental boundaries, why
not change the boundary lines? If trade, for example, is one such interagency
policy puzzle, create a department of trade and sweep the trade-related functions of other agencies into the new department. Then the new president
can point to one cabinet officer and say, "You're in charge!"

The choice seems so elemental and appealing that a president is tempted
to try it. Perhaps he has even made campaign promises to do so—or to establish a new "Hoover Commission." (Established in 1948 by President Truman
and chaired by former president Herbert Hoover, the commission proposed
wholesale executive branch reorganization.) As former presidential assistant Joseph Califano has explained, "If he can reshape the government
departments and agencies into sensible functional organizations, then he
will have gone a long way toward consolidating his power over the executive branch and providing himself with department heads who can truly and
fairly be held responsible for program areas, like manpower training or the
development of natural resources."[1]

President Nixon put it this way:

> The executive branch of the government should be organized around
> basic goals. Instead of grouping activities by narrow subjects or by
> limited constituencies, we should organize them around the great pur-
> poses of government in modern society. For only when a department
> is set up to achieve a given set of purposes, can we effectively hold
> that department accountable for achieving them. Only when the
> responsibility for realizing basic objectives is clearly focused in a spe-
> cific governmental unit, can we reasonably hope that those objectives
> will be realized.[2]

"Human Resources," "Community Development," "Economic Affairs,"
"Natural Resources"—advisers to Lyndon Johnson, Richard Nixon, and

Jimmy Carter all proposed or seriously considered unscrambling the older agencies and re-sorting them into new departments with broader functions.

All these initiatives encountered strong opposition. Congress and its sub-committees, the affected bureaus and their bureaucracies, and advocacy groups joined hands and drowned such menacing presidential ideas in a swamp of parochial goo. Johnson's "Department of Labor and Commerce" never got into hearings; Nixon's 1971 recommendations for four new superdepartments went nowhere in Congress. The Senate Governmental Affairs Committee forced Carter's reorganization brain trust to promise that it wouldn't even come near Congress with a "Department of Natural Resources" proposal or "anything resembling it."[3] A statute creating a new "Hoover Commission" has been proposed several times but never approved. After arduous negotiations, Congress and President Clinton did agree to combine the foreign assistance agencies with the Department of State, but no other major reorganization measures were enacted or even attempted in that administration.

An easier way to reorganize is to establish new agencies or to upgrade old bureaus into new cabinet departments: create a Peace Corps, a Corporation for National and Community Service, or an Office of Economic Opportunity; remake a Housing and Home Finance Agency into a Department of Housing and Urban Development, a Federal Energy Administration into a Department of Energy; elevate the Office of Education or the Veterans Administration to cabinet status. Such actions are easier because they involve minimum remodeling of older agencies and no demolition of cabinet-level skyscrapers. (A proposal to upgrade the Environmental Protection Agency to a cabinet-level department has been floated but not adopted.)

But by increasing the number of the departments or agencies, what is a president really achieving? He may indeed be accumulating political gains among advocacy groups and adding a star to agency epaulets, but he is making his own work as chief executive harder. Instead of simplifying the management of the executive branch, he may be magnifying his own burden of coordination: the larger his cabinet and the greater the number of agencies under the president's direction, the more power centers will be in place for the White House to manage. (The argument that an upgrade to "cabinet department" status will ensure the erstwhile agency head easier access to the president is specious. In a well-run White House, such access is linked not to the protocol status of the requester but to the importance of the issue to be discussed.)

In the cool light of the day after the inaugural morning, and irrespective of presidential campaign promises, thoroughgoing cabinet-level reorganization will be revealed to be an option not worth the effort. It is the president's own office, and not the cabinet, that must be strengthened. Califano concluded: "Inevitably, Republican or Democrat, conservative or liberal, [the president] will perceive a substantial and powerful White House staff as the best means of exercising presidential power to achieve his public policy objectives and render responsive the erratically organized executive branch over which he presides."[4]

Create Supersecretaries

Although President Nixon's 1971 proposals to create four new superdepartments were never enacted, he still believed that his cabinet agencies should be regrouped into more rational structures. Just before his second term started, Nixon created by fiat what Congress would not give him in law: he established three new counselors to the president—for natural resources, human resources, and community development. The three new supersecretaries were, in effect, to spend half of each day in the White House and the other half in their respective departments. Each was to chair a cabinet committee; suites were reserved for the new counselors in the Old Executive Office Building.[5] No statutory reorganization was needed: three existing cabinet officers were simply given White House titles; new, cross-cutting responsibilities; and presidential office space.

Are supersecretaries—half White House, half cabinet—the answer to the enduring conundrum of how best to organize the executive branch?

At least in the domestic arena, the nation will have to wait longer to find out; Nixon's supersecretary experiment ended after only four months, when the Watergate scandal erupted in May of 1973 and Chief of Staff Bob Haldeman and domestic policy head John Ehrlichman were forced to resign. The obvious pitfall of the approach, however, is the distinctions that the supersecretary designation creates within the cabinet: some cabinet officers become less equal than others. Nixon's experiment would have made the secretaries of Commerce, Labor, and Transportation appear to be cabinet members second class.

The experiment did continue, however, in the area of national security affairs. Henry Kissinger was named secretary of state and wore two hats—as both head of the State Department and as White House national security adviser—for two years. He reflects: "It did not work. . . . For two years I was exposed to the charge that I had an unfair predominance over the policymaking process. . . . My dual position was, in fact, a handicap and a vulnerability."[6]

President Ford ended the last trial of the supersecretary idea in 1975, turning the position of national security adviser back into a distinct and full-time White House post.

Convene the Cabinet

Only one president in recent history—Dwight D. Eisenhower—has made systematic use of the cabinet as a collectivity: that is, to discuss specific policy issues addressed in formal cabinet papers. He convened his cabinet 236 times to consider 1,236 agenda items (including 112 circulated papers): the result was 160 records of action that Eisenhower personally initialed. (His use of the formal National Security Council machinery was even more systematic.)

This mode fitted Ike's style. The meetings (which the author attended as the assistant cabinet secretary) had twofold value for the president. First, he benefited from hearing advice about issues to which his cabinet members, as departmental chieftains, brought their institutional expertise. Second, and of equal value, Ike's cabinet, like all cabinets, was made up of former governors, legislators, university presidents, business executives, and religious leaders—people who have much to say about our nation and the choices it faces. Thus, they also contributed wisdom from their broad experience in public and private life. Their advice was given openly, for all to hear and debate. At the cabinet table, the members directly witnessed a president wrestling with tough choices: they faced his questions; heard him state his doubts, his objectives, his priorities; and saw him make his decisions. Such sessions bred a special collegiality.

Readers are reminded, however, that this was no "cabinet government." All three of the key elements in Ike's cabinet process: the agendas, the records of action, and the follow-up—were the products of the White House staff.

No president since Eisenhower has used the full cabinet in this fashion and to this extent.

The cabinet group is larger now, and succeeding presidents have concurred with the judgment even of Nixon—who sat opposite Ike for those eight years—in considering cabinet meetings "unnecessary and boring." Recent presidents have met with their full cabinets occasionally, but the sessions are often show-and-tell affairs.

During the Clinton administration, "cabinet briefings" were convened, but they were chaired by the White House chief of staff, with the president either absent or perhaps dropping by briefly. These sessions were aimed at keeping cabinet members informed of major administration initiatives and imminent enterprises. The teambuilding benefit perhaps continued, but the question arises whether such sessions were worth the time of the entire group, especially when the president was not attending.

While cabinet meetings have greatly diminished, the White House's Cabinet Affairs office has not; this unit and its current responsibilities will be described in chapter 21.

Designate a Lead Agency

In the spring of 1977 President Carter embarked on an initiative to improve the quality of life in urban America. Ideas and resources would be required from twelve departments and agencies. He initially instructed six of them to form a working policy group on urban and regional development. In Carter's words, "The purpose of the group will be to conduct a comprehensive review of all federal programs which impact on urban and regional areas; to seek perspectives of state and local officials concerning the role of the federal government in urban and regional development; and to submit appropriate administrative and legislative recommendations."[7]

White House aides Jack Watson and Stuart Eizenstat were requested to "facilitate and support your collective efforts," but Patricia Harris, secretary of Housing and Urban Development (HUD), was designated to lead the enterprise. Secretary Harris established the Urban and Regional Policy Group (URPG), which convened for the first time in the Roosevelt Room of the White House.

Even at that first meeting, it soon became obvious that each URPG department had its own agenda—often one that was at odds with those of other departments. Treasury was not enthusiastic about the urban policy initiative if it meant changing the tax code. Secretary of the Treasury Michael Blumenthal liked the idea of a new "Urban Development Bank" (to be located in Treasury) but thought that the more "conservative" Department of Commerce should have been given the urban policy lead in the first place. Commerce, for its part, would gladly have taken the lead: its Economic Development Administration (EDA) could offer expert advice and experience on development issues. But Commerce thought that the Urban Development Bank should be under its own purview—not that of Treasury.

HUD, in turn, insisted that any such bank be within *its* turf and saw Carter's new urban initiative as an opportunity to increase its own development assistance programs—but in the distressed Frost Belt metropolises, not in the more rural areas that were EDA's focus. The Office of Management and Budget (OMB) was on guard against any "noxious new programs." The first lady put yet another finger into the stew: outside lobbyists pushed her to support "volunteer efforts," and she herself wanted "urban" funds put into the arts.

Some members of the URPG alleged that Secretary Harris's personal style was abrasive—"brassy." In spite of the president's memorandum, there were occasions when she cut Eizenstat and Watson out of interagency meetings. Her attitude was, "This is *my* project." Privately, she told the White House that she "could not be perceived as coming out of this exercise weaker as a department than she went in."[8]

The active agents in the enterprise—those who attended the URPG meetings—were the departmental assistant secretaries. Many had Capitol Hill origins and had been selected not by the president but by their cabinet superiors; thus, their loyalties were not to the White House but to congressional friends and to the programs within and the constituencies outside of their departments. As one former White House staffer commented, "Carter . . . put foxes to guard the chicken coops." Another added: "All of these activists, with ambitious spending plans in their pockets, saw the urban policy enterprise as a boat to jump on." As soon as the URPG study was announced, they headed for Capitol Hill and tipped off friendly legislators. Next they passed the good word to the thirsty advocacy groups. "Expectations exploded," said a third observer ruefully. Another summed up: "The whole exercise turned out to be executive branch logrolling."

In the late fall, Secretary Harris telephoned White House domestic policy chief Eizenstat. He was supposed to "facilitate," wasn't he? Above all, he was the president's agent. "I can't do this," she complained. "I give those other departments instructions and they won't follow them. I call meetings and they won't come. I need help. A strong president would back up the chairperson. *You* must get involved!"

Eizenstat assured Secretary Harris that he would help out. From then on, the urban policy development project was in large part a White House staff enterprise. Eizenstat hired additional experts in his own office to help. Then to each of his several domestic policy assistants he assigned one or more of the URPG subgroups for monitoring. And he chaired the URPG meetings—all of which were held in the White House.

The first urban policy report, which went to the president in December 1977, reflected the pluralistic character of the undertaking. To his disappointment, Carter's "cabinet government" gave him not an integrated urban policy statement but a set of departmental wish lists—stapled together, no less—that merely proposed add-ons to existing programs. Eizenstat's notes from Carter's review of the report underscore a presidential request: "It needs a common thrust and theme."

After a second report was compiled, Eizenstat sent the package to the president along with a six-page personal note. Carter scribbled comments and approvals. Two more months of work were required, now completely led by White House staff and climaxing in an all-night session among representatives from HUD, OMB, and the White House. The final product was a 200-page Harris-Eizenstat memorandum accompanied by a 13-page Eizenstat-OMB "road-map." The concluding actions were a White House announcement, a press briefing, and a message to Congress on the very day of the president's final approval.

Staff veterans of that period later agreed with the observations of David Broder, a *Washington Post* columnist: "Harris' interdepartmental . . . committee proved mainly to be a device for protecting every program of every agency represented. . . . And in his kind of Cabinet government, with a weak White House staff, even as able an aide as Eizenstat has little authority to crack the whip on the president's behalf. . . . None of the 160 recommendations call for eliminating any single existing program—despite the almost universal acknowledgement that some of them are real losers."[9]

Assign Policy Leadership to White House Staff

Of the five options laid out at the beginning of this chapter, the assignment of policy leadership to White House staff is the one that, after forty years' experience, has now become the presidential preference. One particularly good example can be drawn from the Clinton administration's efforts to address the future of affirmative action.

In the wake of the 1994 elections, Charles Canady, a Republican Congressman, and Senate Majority Leader Bob Dole had introduced identical House and Senate bills which, if enacted, would have put an end to all preferences based on race, color, national origin, or gender.[10] The Senate bill was never reported out of committee. Whether preferences of any kind were ever justified—and if so, how they should be used—was an issue that divided the country, had been in and out of the courts, and was being presented

daily to every agency conducting federal programs.[11] It was time for the
president to speak up, to clarify what he believed to be the mandates—and
the limits—of affirmative action. What position should he take?

The president turned to his senior White House staff to conduct and
closely manage a wide-ranging policy review. Christopher Edley, on a leave
of absence from his position as a professor at Harvard Law School, was just
winding up his tenure as an associate director of OMB; George Stephanopoulos was the president's senior adviser for policy and strategy. The president
pulled Edley into the White House and instructed the pair of them to spear-
head the enterprise. For Edley it was a full-time assignment. Their first job
was to dig out information as to what practices the various federal agencies were currently following; they were then to develop a presidential policy.

Why did Clinton not assign this task to the Department of Justice? Edley
gives three reasons:

> First, this was the kind of policy issue that ultimately would very much
> reflect the president's personal assessment of the values, interests, and
> vision at stake. . . . I think the president's interest was personal, and
> the need was to make the policy consistent with Bill Clinton's take on
> America. . . . Second, this was an issue in which you had multiple
> actors spread around the bureaucracy, and their views and their activ-
> ities had to be woven together into a whole. You had disputes about
> priorities, disputes about vision . . . and there had to be a mechanism
> for reconciling those—and that requires somebody at the center. The
> agencies simply are not going to defer, even to so powerful an officer
> as the attorney general and the Justice Department. It just doesn't hap-
> pen. . . . If it ever was the culture of the executive branch, it definitely
> was not the culture of the late 1990s—or of the early 1990s for that
> matter. . . . Third, this decision had to move at a pace that is simply
> inconsistent with the ordinary pace of agency decisionmaking. It was
> being driven by a pace that was determined by the president. . . . It's
> just unthinkable that you could turn it out to a bunch of agencies and
> say, "We'd like you to study affirmative action and come back to us
> as soon as you can." They just wouldn't—that would not work. We
> knew that we had to crack the whip in a very aggressive way.[12]

The White House pair organized a sub-cabinet-level steering committee of
agency representatives (including Justice, of course), chaired by
Stephanopoulos but more often by Edley, because the former was frequently
detained by other duties. The committee held eight or ten sessions and

always met in the White House. There were many gatherings of lower-level departmental representatives; these meetings produced some twenty thick ring-bound notebooks that described the affirmative action practices of the respective agencies.

From Edley's analysis of this mountain of factual material and from steering committee discussions came ideas for option papers. What questions should be posed to the president that would help in the evolution of his thinking? Which hypotheticals—about hirings, firings, layoffs, contracting—were going to be the most profitable to debate with him? Edley described the standards he imposed for the material to be presented to the president: "We made the calculation that striving to be intellectually honest was the best *political* strategy—whereas many of the civil rights agencies themselves had a very different view. In the light of their constituencies, it was a full-bore defense: 'Don't yield an inch!' 'We're not doing anything wrong!' 'We're doing this right, just give us more resources!' But of course we knew that to be incorrect."[13]

Edley and Stephanopoulos met with outside groups with a vital interest in affirmative action: the Congressional Black Caucus, the Hispanic Caucus, the Leadership Conference on Civil Rights, the NAACP Legal Defense Fund—as well as with the Democratic Leadership Council and the "Blue Dogs," a group of conservative Democrats on the Hill. Distilling ideas from all these sources, Edley drafted the option memorandums, which he and Stephanopoulos signed jointly. A handful of senior people (usually including the vice president and the White House chief of staff) would then meet in the Oval Office to discuss these papers; a few sessions were held with a larger group in the Cabinet Room.

The ninety-six-page final report was made up of a policy section—most of which Edley wrote—followed by the agency-by-agency program descriptions, parts of which were taken from the original departmental submissions. The *Affirmative Action Review* was dated July 19, 1995, and phrased in the first person plural: "We . . . "—meaning Edley and Stephanopoulos. Why this style? Edley explained:

> We wanted to give the president our candid assessment of what was going on. We did not want that assessment to be blunted, blurred, compromised, by trying to reach a bureaucratic consensus among all the agencies. We wanted it to be *our* thing. We wanted it to be a document from us, rather than from the president, because we wanted to frame this in the posture of presenting the president with an analysis

and with a set of recommendations. His response was then going to be in the speech that he gave, and in the directive.[14]

What happened was just as Edley and Stephanopoulos had intended. On the same day that the review was turned over to him, the president issued a succinct directive emphasizing that

> [We] will seek reasonable ways to achieve the objectives of inclusion and antidiscrimination without specific reliance on group membership. Where our legitimate objectives cannot be achieved through such means, the Federal Government will continue to support lawful consideration of race, ethnicity, and gender under programs that are flexible, realistic, subject to reevaluation, and fair. Any program must be eliminated if it (a) creates a quota; (b) creates preferences for unqualified individuals; (c) creates reverse discrimination; or (d) continues, even after its equal opportunity purposes have been achieved.[15]

Also on the same day, the president journeyed to the Rotunda of the National Archives and Records Administration and delivered a full and eloquent speech about the history of civil rights in America. Clinton had written the speech himself, after receiving information and recommendations from White House communications and speechwriting assistants as well as from Edley and Stephanopoulos.[16] (Chapter 17 includes a description of further steps the Clinton White House took—in part to follow up on the *Affirmative Action Review*—in the areas of race relations and civil rights.)

Recent years offer many more examples of presidential policy reviews that illustrate the five options discussed in this chapter. It is the conclusion of the author that the fifth here is the mode most fitting and most likely to be chosen by the presidents of today and tomorrow. The chapters that follow will reinforce this conclusion.

The Not-So-Bashful Bureaucracy

The two chapters of part 1 introduced the cacophony of a no-consensus society—and served as reminders that some of that cacophony echoes within the president's own executive branch. Troubled by what he perceives as the din of advocacy in the bureaucracy, and not finding—even among many of his top political appointees in the departments and agencies—enough sensitivity to his own personal goals and priorities, a president tends to rely for policy development less and less on his cabinet departments and more and more on his White House staff.

What is the contemporary White House staff? What are its core functions? What are its major and its lesser offices? News accounts and some scholarly works throw light on one or another aspect of the White House, but *what is the whole picture?*

In the White House of today are 125 identifiable units: forty-six principal policy offices, twenty-eight supporting policy and operations offices, and fifty-one professional and technical units. The purpose of part 2 is to describe the principal forty-six. (Nineteen of these, plus the office of the national security adviser, constitute the National Security Council staff group and are dealt with collectively in chapter 3.) The twenty-eight subordinate policy and operations offices that are attached to the senior group are listed at the end of this introduction, as are the fifty-one professional and technical outfits (described in part 3). Although each new president has the flexibility to design—and redesign—the entire White House organization, this never really happens in the sense of wholesale revision. Other than the posts of president and vice president, only one White House office is actually established by statute: the National Security Council (which, for its first two years of existence, was simply ignored by Mr. Truman).

All White House offices are subject to being juggled or combined, their lines of supervision redrawn; they can appear or disappear as presidential priorities wax or wane. If those priorities become enduring, so may the offices. Since 1939, when President Franklin Roosevelt began with his "six anonymous assistants," additional core functions have been identified, found to be indispensable to the presidency—and, *for that reason*—included in each succeeding administration. President Clinton's National Economic Council, which may well be continued by future administrations, fits this description. It is the author's contention that the presidents of the future will build upon, rather than uproot, the White House structure of today.

Some innovations take the form of "special assistants for special purposes"—less permanent, perhaps, but nonetheless a category of staff assistance that is typically created by every president. (See chapter 17.) Others—such as President Clinton's Office of National Service, created in 1993—may be temporarily located in the White House until a statute creates a new agency. One or two—such as the assistant to the president for the year 2000 conversion and Mrs. Clinton's Millennium Council—have built-in time limits. And a few—for example, Mr. Bush's Points of Light office—are judged by a succeeding president not to be needed, and are eliminated.

Core Functions of the Contemporary White House

The modern White House staff manages more than a dozen principal presidential functions. The following brief introductions to each of these functions lay the groundwork for the more detailed discussions of part 2.

Integrating National Security Policy and Operations

The national security adviser and his nineteen-unit domain make up the collective organism that ensures the interlinking of the largest of the president's executive branch communities: that is, our worldwide diplomatic, military, intelligence, overseas information, and foreign economic complex. (Other issue areas—such as agriculture, commerce, finance, law enforcement, science, and space—are inescapably parts of this network.) Within this complex, the president, who is both commander in chief and chief diplomat, can tolerate no wild-card moves: coordination is tightly held at the White House.

Developing and Overseeing Domestic Policy

Areas of domestic policy include welfare reform, health care, social security, the tobacco settlement, education, and domestic law enforcement. The issues are contentious, and the participating departments are many.

Coordinating Foreign and Domestic Economic Policies

Economic policy coordination has bedeviled many a White House organizer because it cuts across almost the entire cabinet. The new National Economic Council is the latest attempt to effect this integration and to bridge both its foreign and domestic elements.

Providing Legal Advice to the Chief Executive

White House legal advice has a twofold purpose: to represent the president's own official legal interests and to protect the constitutional prerogatives of the presidential office for the long term. Since almost every issue in the White House has a legal component, the counsel to the president must be everywhere: assessing investigative requests and subpoenas; reviewing presidential speeches and statements, enrolled bills, veto messages, proclamations, executive orders, pardons, and treaties; and guarding executive privilege.

Managing Legislative Affairs

Legislative affairs management involves building and maintaining the connection between two constitutionally separate entities—the executive and legislative branches—on issues of presidential concern. This work includes supporting presidential legislation, negotiating compromises, threatening vetoes, defeating overrides, winning appropriations, and securing the ratification of treaties and the confirmation of presidential appointees. Legislative affairs is the carrot-and-stick office of the White House.

Informing the Press

The press secretary is the authorized, on-the-record spokesperson for the president, preparing the president for his own press appearances and taking full advantage of off-the-record opportunities as well. With a press office in every department and agency, the White House has an enormous task in trying to ensure that they all speak with one voice.

Overseeing Communications

In the theater called the White House, the Office of Communications is the lens that focuses the diffuse luminescence of a multitude of White House activities into an attention-getting beam that spotlights the president's purposes and goals—and keeps the president illuminated in his starring role. The publicity-generating resources—not only of the White House itself but of all the departments—are marshaled to amplify whatever is the president's message of the moment.

Speechwriting

The speechwriters' pens give the president his voice, and the president's voice is potentially a unifying force in a cacophonous nation. World leaders and peoples listen, too. Be it "Rose Garden rubbish" or the State of the Union address, White House speechwriters aim for a masterly blend of facts, persuasion, and eloquence.

Building Alliances with Constituency Groups

For the leaders of the 23,000 national organizations whose representatives knock at the White House gates, the Office of Public Liaison is the entrance foyer to the presidency. The Business Roundtable is in that throng, as are lobbyists for civil rights groups and advocates for disabled people. All need (and can distribute) information, and all deserve a hearing; some carry crucial weight in Congress. Occasionally, their views merit personal sessions with the president. President Clinton, for example, created the White House Office of Women's Initiatives and Outreach within the Office of Public Liaison.

Scheduling

The president has four years—1,461 days—to make his mark on history. Endless thousands of requesters will vie for some 8,000 weekday hours. To which will the president accede? Will he fill those hours with significant achievements or with mere activities? The Office of Presidential Scheduling helps him balance and choose.

Collaborating with State and Local Governments

Most of the issues in the White House directly affect several—or many— of the 88,000-odd state, local, and tribal governments of our nation. Governors, mayors, county executives, and tribal officers, all partners in the American federal system, can be cooperative or hostile. Because presidential policy initiatives nearly always require their support to succeed, these leaders will expect to be consulted as initiatives are being developed; the Office of Intergovernmental Affairs staff are the facilitators for this consultation.

Keeping President and Party in Harmony

As head of his party, the president has obligations to its one national and fifty state organizations, to numerous political action committees, to his financial contributors, and to hundreds of local volunteer groups. He also has reciprocal debts and credits with his party's elected officials. The White House Office of Political Affairs helps the president keep the ledgers and acts as ombudsman for those on the "plus" side. When the president runs for reelection, his real campaign headquarters is in the White House.

Recruiting and Appointing Noncareer Officers

A president can make or control over 6,400 appointments to the executive and judicial branches. Much of his own reputation will ride on the quality of these men and women, 1,800 of whom will be subject to scrutiny and confirmation by the Senate. The president will, in addition, want his White House staff to oversee closely the choice of some or all of the 2,148 full-time, noncareer jobholders appointed by his cabinet and agency heads. By vetting the candidates, balancing the pluses and minuses, the Office of Presidential Personnel helps prepare the chief for his decisions.

Advancing Presidential Trips

If only for security reasons, impromptu public appearances have disappeared from the president's life. While his hours in the White House afford him some flexibility, any venturing beyond those eighteen acres demands extraordinary preparations. Organizing a presidential trip means dealing with dozens of local hosts, each of whom has his or her own agenda for the chief executive's time. The staff of the Advance Office plan every last detail, keeping themselves discreetly in the background and the president's own priorities in the forefront.

Support for Special Purposes

Extraordinary and consuming national issues may require extraordinary presidential responses: the regular governmental machinery will be deemed insufficient. On such occasions the president will create special offices—

whose heads are often colloquially referred to as White House "czars"—to dramatize his concerns and to galvanize old interdepartmental efforts with new presidential energy. There are currently six such offices: the Office of National AIDS Policy, the Special Envoy to the Americas, the Office of Environmental Initiatives, the assistant to the president for the year 2000 conversion, the Office of the President's Initiative for One America, and the Senior Adviser to the White House Chief of Staff for Native American Affairs.

Support for the President's Spouse

The office of the first lady is a copy, in part and in miniature, of the president's staff. Giving speeches, making press appearances, hosting White House conferences, traveling within the United States and abroad, handling correspondence, visiting members of Congress, writing a weekly news column, campaigning in support of friendly candidates, supervising the extensive White House social responsibilities—the preferences and priorities of each first lady vary, but she needs staff of her own to support her activities.[1]

Support for the Vice President

Until 1961, the Office of the Vice President was on Capitol Hill: his (or her) principal headquarters is now in the White House itself. President Clinton not only invited his vice president to join in most policy meetings but also gave Mr. Gore an impressive list of assignments to undertake, both at home and abroad. The Gore staff was a mini–White House, but with a difference: their boss was planning to be president. Gore's staff members were responsible not to the Oval Office but to the vice president—yet, like their chief, they were part of the White House environment. (Gore's personal campaign staff is a separate group.)

The spouse of the vice president not only assists the vice president but aids the president as well, in the spouse's areas of special concern and expertise. The spouse is afforded office space and official staff within the White House complex. Very little scholarly work, however, has been done about this fourth member of the two "first couples" who make up a visible and active foursome at the apex of the executive branch.

Tying the Place Together

If this highly plural—and somewhat centrifugal—set of White House domains is going to serve a singular president effectively, there must be a countervailing set of centripetal White House offices to integrate the lot of them. Five of them, in conjunction, perform this holistic function.

Superintending the President's Paper Flow

The staff secretary asks, "Is this document ready, in every sense, for the president to see? Have the right internal staff offices (the counsel, the press secretary, legislative affairs, scheduling, or others) concurred or voiced their objections?" A draft of every presidential speech is circulated for comment as well. For all the papers heading toward, or coming out of, the Oval Office, the staff secretary is the unpopular but indispensable controller.

Keeping the Bridge Open to the Cabinet

The Cabinet Affairs office still assists in setting up such rare meetings of the full cabinet as may be convened, but it now has wider duties. From weekly submissions that are required from each line department and agency, the cabinet affairs staff sift out essential excerpts and incorporate them into a Cabinet Report to the president. Under Clinton, Cabinet Affairs also helped to coordinate the agendas of the three policy councils—domestic, economic, and national security—ensuring that there was no overlap in agenda items and that no important issues fell through the cracks.

Running the White House Efficiently

The assistant to the president for management and administration controls White House personnel and finances. Are staff resources being properly allocated to meet the president's requirements, and are their numbers being kept within the ceilings? Are expenditures consistent with budget limits? Is the Intern Program well run? Besides handling these and similar issues, the presidential assistant supervises the Military Office, the largest single group in the White House staff family.

Meeting the President's Hour-to-Hour Needs

The president's Oval Office Operations team—his personal secretaries and the presidential aide—bring order to the immediate swirl of telephone calls, papers on the desk, briefing memos, visitors coming in and out, and the minute-by-minute schedule commitments, so that the events of each day are—hopefully—synchronized rather than chaotic.

Is the Whole System Working?

Is the system working precisely as the president prefers—no tighter, no looser than his personal wish? Have the protagonists in a policy debate met around a table first, to tighten their arguments before taking their issue to the president? What issues must be brought into the Oval Office even if everybody agrees about them? Which staff people need to meet with the chief executive? What presidential guidance is there to pass on to staff? Are any people or operations getting out of hand?

The chief of staff is system manager. Without his superintendence—and the president's strong and evident support of it—the other forty-five "mini-worlds" fly apart, and the White House is chaos. The chief of staff function has been combined with that of president (Kennedy, Johnson, Carter), but it was Eisenhower who asked: "Do I have to be my own sergeant major?"

In 1833, this, allegedly, was the "system":

> The Gineral [President Jackson] says he likes things simple as a mouse-trap.
>
> There is enuff of us to do all that's wanted. Every day, jest after breakfast, the Gineral lights his pipe and begins to think purty hard, and I and Major Donaldson begin to open letters for him; and there is more than three bushels every day, and all the while coming. We don't git through more than a bushel a day; and never trouble long ones, unless they come from Mr. Van Buren, or Mr. Kindle [Amos Kendall] or some other of our great folks. Then we sort 'em out jest as Zekel Bigelow does the mackerel at his Packin Yard. . . . We only make three sorts and keep three big baskets, one marked "not red" another "red and worth nothin" and another "red and to be answered." And then all the Gineral has to do is to say "Major, I reckon we best say so and so to that," and I say "Jest so," or not, as the notion takes me—and then we go at it.
>
> We keep all the Secretaries, and the Vice President, and some District Attorneys, and a good many of our folks, and Amos Kindle, moving about; and they tell us jest how the cat jumps.

And as I said afore, if it warnt for Congress meetin once a year, we'd put the Government in a one-horse wagon, and go jest where we liked.[2]

What is the White House of today?

Part 2 presents analytic descriptions of the forty-six principal policy offices (and their twenty-eight supporting units) that carry out the core functions described in this introduction. These chapters contain some basic history, describe the present, and look a bit into the future.

The chapters of part 2 are preceded by (1) a diagram and key showing the organizational structure of the contemporary White House (the White House does not issue any such chart itself, presumably because the arrangements change frequently; the author therefore takes responsibility for what is portrayed); (2) a list of the 125 separately identifiable units of the White House; (3) a list of the eighteen separate physical facilities that house the offices of the White House staff community.

The White House Staff

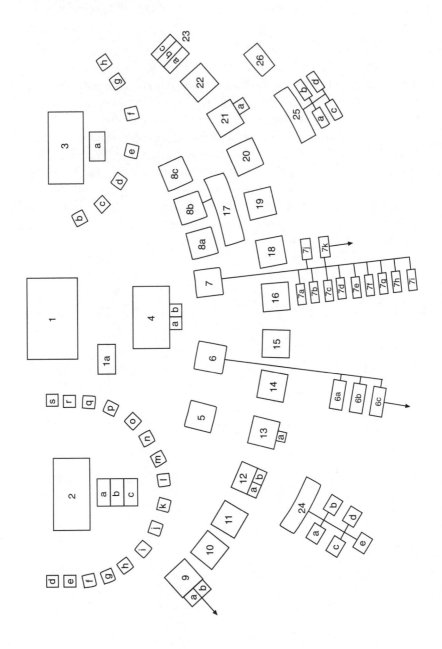

Key to the Organization Chart of the White House Staff

1 President
1-a Director of Oval Office Operations, the presidential aide, the president's secretaries, and the West Wing receptionist

2 Vice President
2-a Chief of Staff
2-b Deputy Chief of Staff
2-c Executive Assistant
2-d Counselor for Public Affairs
2-e Press Secretary
2-f Speechwriter
2-g Scheduling Office
2-h Advance Office
2-i Deputy Assistant for National Security Affairs
2-j Domestic Policy Adviser
2-k Executive Director, National Energy Policy Development Group
2-l Counsel
2-m Legislative Affairs Office
2-n Deputy Assistant for Operations
2-o Correspondence Office
2-p Photo Office for the Vice President
2-q Military Aides to the Vice President
2-r Residence Manager and Social Secretary
2-s Spouse of the Vice President

3 First Lady
3-a Chief of Staff
3-b Special Assistant
3-c Press Secretary
3-d Director of Correspondence
3-e Director of Projects
3-f White House Social Secretary and Social Aides
3-g Director of Scheduling and Advance
3-h Speechwriter

4 White House Chief of Staff
4-a Deputy Chief of Staff for Policy
4-b Deputy Chief of Staff for Operations

5 Secretary to the Cabinet

6 Staff Secretary
6-a Executive Clerk
6-b Office of Records Management
6-c Correspondence Office (includes ten specialized units)

7 Assistant to the President for Management and Administration
7-a White House Management Office
7-b Intern Program
7-c Photography Office
7-d Telephone Service
7-e Travel Office
7-f Visitors Office
7-g White House Conference Center
7-h Personnel Office
7-i Support services from the Office of Administration (database, libraries)
7-j Service Delivery Team of the General Services Administration
7-k White House Military Office (eleven units, including the White House Communications Agency, the Medical Unit, Camp David, *Air Force One*, *Marine One*, food service, transportation, Ceremonies Coordinator)

8-a Senior Adviser for Policy and Strategy
8-b Counselor for Communications
8-c Office of Homeland Security

9 National Security Adviser and three Deputy National Security Advisers
9-a Executive Secretary
9-b Situation Room (plus fifteen specialized NSC Senior Directors and staffs)

10 Assistant for Economic Policy

11 Assistant for Domestic Policy

12 Assistant for Legislative Affairs
12-a Deputy for Legislative Affairs (Senate)
12-b Deputy for Legislative Affairs (House)

13 Counsel to the President
13-a Security Office

14 Director of Political Affairs

15 Director for Intergovernmental Affairs

16 Director of Presidential Personnel

17 Director of Communications/Media Affairs

18 Press Secretary

19 Director of Public Liaison

20   Director of Speechwriting

21   Director of Presidential Scheduling
21-a Presidential Diarist

22   Director of Advance

23   Special Assistants for Special Purposes
23-a Office of Strategic Initiatives
23-b Office of Faith-Based and Community
      Initiatives
23-c National AIDS Policy Coordinator

24   White House units of the U.S. Secret
      Service
24-a Presidential protective detail

24-b Vice Presidential protective detail
24-c Technical Security Division
24-d Protective Research Division
24-e Uniformed Division

25   Chief Usher and the staff of the Execu-
      tive Residence
25-a Curator
25-b Family Theater
25-c White House Liaison Office of the
      National Park Service
25-d Graphics and Calligraphy Office

26   President's Commission on White
      House Fellows

Units of the White House Staff

Principal Policy Offices

Chief of Staff
Vice President
First Lady

National Security Affairs (National Security
      Council)
   National Security Adviser
   Deputy National Security Adviser
   Deputy National Security
      Adviser/National Director for Com-
      bating Terrorism
   Deputy National Security Adviser for
      International Economic Affairs
   Executive Secretary
   Special Assistants to the President and
         Senior Directors for
      African Affairs
      Asian Affairs
      European and Eurasian Affairs
      Western Hemisphere Affairs
      Near East/North Africa Affairs
      Defense Policy and Arms Control
      Democracy, Human Rights, and
      International Operations
      Intelligence Programs
      International Economic Affairs
      Transnational Threats

   Proliferation Strategies, Counter-
      Proliferation, and Homeland
      Defense
   Special Adviser for Cyberspace
      Security
   Legislative Affairs
   Press and Speechwriting
   Legal Adviser

Senior Adviser for Policy and Strategy
Counselor for Communications
Office of Communications
Office of Homeland Security
Economic Policy (National Economic
      Council)
Domestic Policy (Domestic Policy Council)
Counsel to the President
Legislative Affairs (Director, and Deputies
      for House and Senate)
Political Affairs
Intergovernmental Affairs
Presidential Personnel
Press Secretary
Public Liaison
Media Affairs
Speechwriting
Scheduling
Advance
Management and Admininstration

Cabinet Affairs
Staff Secretary
Special assistants for special purposes:
    Office of Strategic Initiatives
    Office of Faith-Based and Community
       Initiatives
    National AIDS Policy Coordinator

SUBTOTAL: 48

Supporting Policy Offices

Oval Office Operations and the Presidential
    Aide

Office of the Chief of Staff, including
    Deputy Chief of Staff for Policy
    Deputy Chief of Staff for Operations

Office of the Vice President
    Chief of Staff
    Deputy Chief of Staff
    Executive Assistant
    Counselor for Public Affairs
       Press Secretary
       Speechwriter
    Scheduling office
    Advance office
    Deputy Assistant for National Security
       Affairs
    Assistant for Domestic Policy
       Executive Director, National Energy
          Policy Development Group
    Counsel
    Legislative Affairs Office
    Deputy Assistant for Operations
    Correspondence Office
    Photo Office for the Vice President
    Spouse of the Vice President
    Military Aides to the Vice President
    Residence Manager and Social Secretary

Office of the First Lady
    Chief of Staff
    Special Assistant
    Press Secretary
    Director of Correspondence
    Director of Projects
    White House Social Secretary and the
       social aides
    Director of Scheduling and Advance
    Speechwriter

SUBTOTAL: 31

Professional and Technical Offices

National Security Council
    Situation Room
    Administrative office
    Records and Access Management
    Systems and Technical Planning

White House Management Office
    Intern Program
    Photography Office
    Telephone Service
    Travel Office
    Visitors Office
    White House Conference Center
    Personnel Office

Support staff from the Office of
    Administration
    White House database
    Main libraries and law library

Presidential diarist (Scheduling Office)

White House branch of the U.S. Postal
    Service

White House Military Office (director's
    office)
    White House Communications Agency
    Camp David
    Military aides to the President
    Presidential Food Service (White House
       Mess and the Presidential Watch—
       mess service to the president)
    White House Transportation Agency
    Presidential Contingency Programs
    Ceremonies Coordinator
    Air Force One group
    Marine One group
    White House Medical Unit

Secret Service
    Presidential Protective Division
    Vice presidential Protective Division
    Technical Security Division
    Protective Research Division
    Uniformed Division

Executive Clerk

Records Management
Correspondence Office
    Agency Liaison Unit
    Comment Line
    Greetings Office
    Mail Analysis Unit

Gift Office
Presidential Personal Correspondence
Presidential Messages and
    Proclamations
Student Correspondence
Volunteer Office
Presidential Support Unit

Chief Usher and Executive Residence staff
    (including the Family Theater)
Graphics and Calligraphy Unit

White House Curator

White House Liaison Office of the National
    Park Service

President's Commission on White House
    Fellows

Service Delivery Team, General Services
    Administration

SUBTOTAL: 51

OVERALL TOTAL: 130

White House Facilities, Properties, and Offices

The White House staff community, and its multitude of offices, are to be found not only at 1600 Pennsylvania Avenue, but in a group of some eighteen dedicated facilities and properties in and near Washington, as listed below. Unless otherwise noted, facilities are located in the District of Columbia.

Executive Residence and grounds (18.08 acres)

East and West Wings

Eisenhower Executive Office Building (two-thirds of the building is assigned to the White House)

New Executive Office Building (a few White House offices and a reception and screening facility for mail that is hand-carried to the White House)

Jackson Place row (a series of buildings accommodating a number of White House offices, including those of the Office of National AIDS Policy, the White House Conference Center, and a townhouse for former presidents to use when visiting Washington)

White House Visitor Center (in the Commerce Department Building)

White House Communications Agency Headquarters, Washington Navy Yard
Secret Service Headquarters

White House Emergency Relocation Center, Virginia

Vice President's Residence, Naval Observatory grounds

Camp David, Catoctin Mountain Park, Maryland (221 acres)

White House Museum Storage Facility, College Park, Maryland

White House Grounds Division Nursery, Oxon Hill, Maryland

White House Grounds Division Greenhouse

White House Remote Delivery site, Washington Navy Yard (for mail arriving via the U.S. Postal Service)

Marine One Hangar, Washington Navy Yard

Air Force One Hangar, Andrews Air Force Base, Camp Springs, Maryland

White House Garage

CHAPTER THREE

The Assistant to the President for National Security Affairs

Within the area of foreign affairs, I believe . . . the Secretary of State [should] be your vicar for the community of Departments.

ALEXANDER HAIG

The National Security Council is, by far, the most dominant entity in foreign policy making in this administration. . . . [Samuel] Berger and [his deputy] really are the source of most policy development and most policy coordination in this administration.

TWO FORMER SENIOR OFFICIALS IN THE CLINTON WHITE HOUSE

The fifty-three-year-old statutory language establishing the National Security Council (NSC) and authorizing a staff for it—a mere handful in 1947—still stands, but it masks a dramatic transformation. The formal council almost never meets, and the staff—an integral part of the White House—now numbers nearly two hundred.

The purpose of this chapter is not to retrace the history of this transformation but to describe how, today, the assistant to the president for national security affairs and his associates serve the council members and the president in achieving a mission that has remained unchanged from the council's earliest existence: "the integration of domestic, foreign and military policies."

The centerpoint for national security policy is still the president—the decisionmaker. And the old challenge is still present: the multiplicity of agencies whose work must be interwoven—State; Defense; the intelligence community; the United States Information Agency; frequently Justice; and often Treasury, Commerce, Energy, and the National Aeronautics and Space

Administration as well. What have been transformed are, first, the facilities and processes that support presidential decisionmaking; second, the methods contemporary presidents employ to govern America's national security operations.

A Transformed Facility and Its Processes: The Situation Room and the Flow of National Security Information

Information in the White House is like arterial blood in the body: the indispensable nutrient. The ventricular center of the national security affairs staff is the Situation Room—the "Sit Room"—in the basement of the West Wing.

The departments and agencies of the national security community generate some 500,000 communications each day between Washington and U.S. diplomatic, military, and intelligence posts abroad. This torrent of electronic traffic, constrained in the first instance by its passage through the decryption processes, is then controlled for distribution in Washington by operations centers located at the top level of the responsible agencies: State, Defense (including all four armed services as well as the National Security Agency), and the CIA. It is these operations centers, working according to criteria handed down from cabinet-level authority or higher, that determine who will receive these communications—and how quickly. Special code words identify degrees of secrecy and urgency: the caption "CRITIC," for example, immediately warns any op center that a crisis is occurring.

Before the Kennedy administration instituted the White House Situation Room, messengers from the various agencies would trot across town, hand-carrying into the White House envelopes that contained paper copies of a few selected cables. The transformation since those years has been dramatic. Today the various op centers—established in the sixties—have systems that almost automatically skim off the most urgent and important national security messages and relay them immediately and electronically to the Sit Room. Around the clock, these thousands of communications flow into the White House filters. From the Department of State, for example, some 1,500 especially important and urgent incoming and outgoing diplomatic cables each day (4,000 a day during a crisis) are instantly transferred to the White House, where they are displayed on a bank of silently glowing computer screens in a semidarkened alcove behind the Sit Room.

The Situation Room staff can move the intake threshold up or down, vacuuming in hundreds of messages from a crisis area or raising a stricter standard to eliminate those deemed routine. If the Sit Room staff spot incomplete data, they will tell a distant post to wake up and produce more, in order not to expose the president to misleading information. To help guarantee responsiveness to the president's priorities, the Sit Room prepares and distributes to the national security departments a weekly checklist identifying the topics that will be of special interest to the White House in the forthcoming days.

The Sit Room staff never forget, however, that presidents come before systems. If the boss says, "Get me everything," he will get it: the whole pile. President Johnson at times demanded: "I want that report—NOW!"—and he would be given it—raw. Presidents can—and do—manipulate their institutional systems, or bypass them altogether.

Like the Sit Room, all the op centers are staffed twenty-four hours a day by skilled intelligence and watch-officer teams. Connected by secure conference lines, they check back and forth with each other constantly, supplementing their ultrasophisticated equipment with their own sensitive judgment. Neither the ambassadors who dispatch the cables nor the assistant secretaries who will act on them can limit their relay to the Situation Room; the telegrams may be marked "NODIS" (very limited distribution), but that does not deter State's op center from sending them to the White House. From Defense, both strategic and tactical military communications pour into the Sit Room, especially if American armed forces are in action anywhere in the world. In addition to the classified cable traffic, 2,500 international news briefs come in daily on the tickers. A resource file of 15,000 items can be tapped for reference.

The experienced Sit Room staffers know precisely whom in the White House to notify, and how quickly. They alert the White House national security adviser to messages that are of presidential significance. (When a cable from an American ambassador is brought to the attention of the president, the secretary of state is notified, so that he or she can be prepared for a possible presidential phone call.) The hundreds of other messages are distributed, according to subject, to the NSC senior directors, who scrutinize them minutely.

Just as the torrential flow of electronic information can overwhelm the humans on the receiving end, the computers' power can be harnessed to help channel that same flow: the intake or search instructions can be programmed to admit or select out communications that contain certain words, names, or phrases, or to create a personalized "profile" for a senior recipient, ensuring that only messages within defined categories will come through.

The twenty-five-person, round-the-clock Sit Room duty staff do more than simply receive messages: they compose an early-morning summary for the president, the vice president, the national security adviser, and the NSC senior directors, with updates at nine and twelve in the morning and three in the afternoon. The summaries of the Sit Room staff dovetail with the special morning reports from State and the CIA—which are, in turn, used by the national security adviser in his daily intelligence briefings with the president.

Although State, Defense (and its National Security Agency), and the CIA share some of their messages and reports with each other, no one of them gets everything. Only at the White House does it all come together.

No student of the presidency should underestimate the significance of the Sit Room operation for American public administration. It is impossible to overstate how dramatically the transformation of this one office illustrates not only the emergence of the president as the absolute center of national security policy but also the burgeoning importance of the White House national security affairs staff in supporting and strengthening the president in his central role. Because of this facility and these procedures, the members of the White House staff—and, through them, the American president—can be privy to every detail, tactical as well as strategic, of the national security environment and operations. If the president can be that aware, he can be that much in command, just as the Constitution provides—a matter discussed later in this chapter.

The Development of National Security Policy

In the Bush and Clinton administrations, issues of national security were first addressed in interdepartmental working groups (IWGs)—but the chairmanship of those teams was most frequently assigned to an NSC senior director rather than to a departmental officer. Meetings were almost always held in the White House—in the Old Executive Office Building or, for highly classified gatherings, in the small, simple, but elegantly paneled Situation Room itself. Occasionally these sessions were conducted remotely, through secure videoconference facilities that allowed seven separate minigroups to participate (as well as others, if needed, on audio-only hookups). A special chamber next to the Sit Room could project onto seven separate screens all seven sets of participants simultaneously. One veteran IWG participant pointed out an additional advantage of using the remote system: it's more private. The press outside the West Wing doorway can't count the cars driving into West Executive Avenue or figure out which VIP is arriving at the White House.

Literally dozens of IWGs were created and disbanded to meet ever-changing needs. Papers were drafted, exchanged by secure fax, and hashed over in incessant meetings. When the issue was ripe for higher consideration, it was the chair—the NSC senior director—who would compose the summary option paper, sometimes including departmental contributions as attachments.

The deputies meetings—the most regularly used element of the policy machinery above the level of the IWGs—were attended by the number-two officials of the participating departments and were under the chairmanship of one of the two deputy assistants to the president.

The deputy assistant set the agenda, assigned whatever papers had to be readied, and held the meetings in the White House. Twice a week was the usual frequency—far oftener when there was a crush of issues. The vice president's national security adviser attended, as did the White House chief of staff or his deputy. One of them observed: "Me. Did they want me there? Hell no. Did the State Department want me there? No. Did I go to all the meetings? Yes. Was I there to ask 'dumb' questions? Yes."[1]

In both the Bush and Clinton administrations, the next step up in the decisionmaking hierarchy were the principals: the cabinet heads and the CIA director. The meetings were chaired by the national security adviser, and the NSC staff—after combing through memoranda and intelligence information from the national security agencies—would draft the key papers for discussion.

Principals meetings were often attended by the "principals plus one" (the cabinet member, for example, could be accompanied by the responsible assistant secretary)—but not by the president. Bush's national security chief, Brent Scowcroft, explained why principals meetings were used in this fashion: "It was without the president, and was a much more informal kind of a session, to try to hash out where we were, try to get more agreement, or highlight the points of disagreement, so we could go to the president and didn't waste his time. We could be more candid with each other, without worrying about people carrying stories back to their departments."[2] A Clinton NSC veteran observed: "The advantage is that people perhaps speak a bit more freely. You can do a little bit more in depth on an issue.... It makes sense to have these meetings without him, and then to refine, often on paper, your options, and then staff them up to him."[3]

Did principals meetings ever include the president? Of course—in both administrations—when the issue was ripe. The group that convened was then called the foreign policy team. And the origin of the papers that were discussed? An NSC senior staff member replied: "It depended on the issue. Sometimes, if it was a big enough issue, it would have supporting memoranda from the other members of the cabinet. But most of the time these were memos which were homegrown here in the NSC."[4]

The end results of meetings with president Clinton were sometimes presidential decision directives (PDDs)—formal documents signed by the president—but decisions were often communicated informally.

And what has become of the traditional, formal "National Security Council"? It has fallen into desuetude, apparently—in part because a formal meeting of the council carries with it the implied obligation to have numbered papers, minutes, numbered records of action, and a press briefing afterwards. The Clinton style was to steer away from such formalities; as of this writing, Clinton had not convened even one formal NSC meeting in his second term.

NSC Support for the President's Personal Role in National Security Affairs

The words in Article 2 that specifically describe the president's national security functions are scanty but puissant: "Commander in Chief of the Army and Navy . . . by and with the Advice and Consent of the Senate . . . make Treaties . . . appoint Ambassadors . . . and Consuls . . . receive Ambassadors and other public Ministers." From these and the other less specific admonitions of Article 2, however, has arisen the imposing panoply of modes by which the chief executive exercises personal governance of a great deal of the work of his national security community. Some of those modes are venerable, but a few are quite new in style—and potent in their requirements for staff support.

VIP Visitors in the Oval Office

A meeting in the Oval Office between the president and a foreign leader doesn't happen without a written schedule proposal from the NSC—a proposal that then has to be defended against a plethora of competing requests. "I spent a lot of my time dealing with the scheduling people, fighting for time on the president's calendar," sighed one NSC officer. Clinton's first national security adviser was almost too adroit at getting people onto the president's schedule. "The president doesn't have to see every general and deputy foreign minister that comes through town," lamented a Clinton scheduling official. "One of the things that made my life miserable [was that] things got on the schedule because Tony Lake put them there—but they didn't have any fingerprints on them."[5]

Material for the necessary briefing memorandums was collected from State or Defense, but the memorandums themselves were written by NSC senior directors, then rewritten by a demanding and fastidious security adviser. As President Clinton became more familiar with foreign policy issues and needed only captions to remind him of substantive matters, even the memorandums were reduced to 5" x 7" cards. When President Reagan needed memorandums on foreign policy issues, State would produce them. "We don't even go through that fiction any more. We don't ask the State Department for cards; we produce them here," explained a Clinton NSC staffer. When the door to Clinton's office opened for a foreign visitor, it was a restricted meeting—but it nonetheless included the secretary of state; the vice president; the president's national security adviser, Samuel (Sandy) Berger; the vice president's national security adviser, Leon Fuerth; the White House chief of staff; and an NSC senior director, who was the note-taker.

President Bush enjoyed a unique form of Oval Office session that might be described as "Seminars with the President." National security adviser Brent Scowcroft would invite a mix of people with different views—scholars, authors, think-tank researchers—to sit down with the president and engage in a leisurely but penetrating discussion of a foreign policy issue. Bush wanted to be exposed to experts from outside government in an environment free of any pressure for decisions. At least four such meetings were arranged: on the Soviet Union, on China, on Iraq, and on the Middle East.

Summit Sessions

The Constitution's well-worn wording was an early indication that the American president might one day become chief diplomat as well as commander in chief. In the years since American presidents made historic journeys to Versailles, Yalta, and Potsdam, that is precisely what has occurred. Summit conferences are now routine—as are presidential trips to nearly every continent on the globe. As chapter 16 will describe, summit meetings are major productions, the presidential preparations advanced and managed almost wholly by the White House.

In preparation for face-to-face meetings between chiefs of state, it is the NSC staff that compiles the enormous briefing books. One of its senior staff officers described the process: "We solicit raw material from the State Department. It comes in and it is usually completely rewritten by the NSC staff. And then, the book that we give the president before the trip is usually just the beginning point. We go on the trip, and every night—before the next day's meetings—we go back to what we have done, and very frequently rewrite it, sometimes dramatically."[6]

Why was departmental material so routinely redone? A State Department senior staffer with previous White House experience explained:

> If you ask the State Department for a document . . . you get something that comes much too late, that's much too long, much too convoluted, much too down-in-the-weeds—because people there are dealing with their own day-to-day problems. It's very hard for this department to put itself in the shoes of the president and to say, "Now, this is what *he's* going to want to know." . . . If you are the president, you want a very different kind of a memorandum from what naturally arises from the bowels of this building. . . . There is a great line in the movie *The American President* where a guy comes in and says, "Some governor wants to see you. He wants to talk about X." The president says, "Trust me; he really wants to talk about Y." That's what presidents think when they see foreign leaders: "What does he want from me? What do I want from him? Can I give him what he wants? If so, with what limits? And what can I get from him that will help me—that is part of *my* agenda, not the [agenda of the] State Department country director?"[7]

Some summit encounters, however, have been more extemporaneous. Attending the funeral, in Amman, of Jordan's King Hussein, President Clinton found himself in the midst of a rare assemblage of the world's kings and prime ministers, all confined in the palace for a lengthy period. Clinton's personal style coincided with the unbeatable opportunity: "He was like a kid in a candy shop," recalled the NSC staffer who tried to keep up with him. "It was unstructured, rapid-fire, kinetic diplomacy . . . completely freeform."[8] Clinton had cordial—and effective—"corridor conversations" with a dozen of his counterparts.

Summit meetings were often followed up by personal correspondence—drafts of which from State were, as an NSC staff officer explained, "cross-hatched over here. . . . We rewrite many of those because they are, frankly, not very well done."[9] Not infrequently the president would take a personal hand in such correspondence. When a human rights activist took refuge in the American embassy in Beijing and the Chinese responded with obstructionist tactics, President Bush wrote a lengthy letter to Deng Xiaoping. "I wanted a letter straight from my heart, so I composed it myself," Bush later explained.[10]

The President on the Telephone

The president-as-chief-diplomat does not wait for episodic face-to-face sessions to keep in touch with his opposite numbers. Foreign events move too quickly, and sensitive situations may arise that require immediate and direct personal contact. In another evolutionary development of tremendous significance, the American president gives twenty-first-century meaning to that original constitutional empowerment: he uses the telephone to communicate personally with other chiefs of state around the world.

A practice that began with Eisenhower, use of the telephone to communicate with foreign chiefs of state has now become a favorite means of presidential diplomacy. President Bush made and received over a thousand such telephone calls, many of them during his efforts to garner support before the Gulf War. President Clinton had 750 such phone conversations in his first five years in office; in 1998 he spoke by telephone with British prime minister Tony Blair an average of once a week. An impressive example of the value of such personal presidential telephone diplomacy was reported near the end of 1999: "After private diplomatic exchanges that included more than a dozen phone calls between President Clinton and Syrian President Hafez Assad since August, both sides will enter the [forthcoming Shepherdstown] talks with a clear understanding of the other's requirements on issues relating to territory, timing, security and the nature of diplomatic, cultural and trade relations . . . officials said."[11]

Sometimes the national security adviser takes the initiative and submits a schedule proposal explaining the pressing need for a presidential telephone call. Or the president himself may start the process. Explained Scowcroft: "He would be reading either the morning intelligence report, or perhaps just the morning newspaper, and exclaim, 'Well, you know what Mitterand just did! Why don't I call him about that?' I would go back, call in my appropriate staff officer, and say, 'The president wants to talk to Mitterand; give me a little background and some talking points.' Sometimes—he had so many friends—he would say, 'I think I'd just like to find out what's going on in Europe; I'm going to call . . .'"[12]

Before the call was put through, the national security adviser would submit the talking points and personally brief the president. The Situation Room would contact the U.S. embassy abroad and ask embassy staff to have the foreign ministry make the arrangements and confirm the date and time. The White House Communications Agency would make the connection and ensure the security of the call; interpreters (if needed) would be on hand on both sides; the security adviser or another NSC staff officer would listen in, take notes, and write up a memorandum for the record. "The bureaucracy doesn't like this calling business," Scowcroft commented. "They hate it because it's too hard to script."[13]

If a call was to be initiated by the head of a foreign government, the Sit Room would notify the NSC and a staff member there would check with State or with other sources to try to determine what was on the caller's mind. After one disturbing experience—when a foreign caller hoaxed the White House and actually succeeded in getting the president on the phone—the White House practice has been to decline to take incoming calls, and to guarantee the caller's authenticity by calling back from Washington through preestablished channels. Telephone diplomacy unquestionably requires White House staff resources: briefers, communicators, interpreters, notetakers. But this relatively new requirement of the nation's chief diplomat is well worth it.

Many presidential calls, of course, are of the lightweight variety: checking in, exchanging information, wishing happy birthday. The more substantive calls may carry a double disadvantage. First, the U.S. ambassador abroad may not have been notified of the call—and nothing is more embarrassing than to have the leaders of the host government exclaim, "But we just talked to your president!" Second, negotiation via presidential telephone bypasses—and thus may deprive the United States of the benefits of—what ambassadors are paid to do: engage in robust, in-depth discussions of policy issues. "Let's probe this some; let's get some more facts; let us give you our counterarguments. . . . "

President Bush, nonetheless, makes a strong case for personal relationships:

> There are actually commonsense reasons for an American president to build relationships with his opposites. If a foreign leader knows the character and the heartbeat of the president (and vice versa), there is apt to be far less miscalculation on either side. Personal relationships may not overcome tough issues dividing two sides, but they can provide enough goodwill to avoid some misunderstandings. This knowledge helps a president formulate and adjust policies that can bring other leaders along to his own point of view. It can make the difference between suspicion and giving each other the benefit of the doubt— and room to maneuver on a difficult political issue.[14]

Scowcroft echoes this view: "President Bush invested an enormous amount of time in personal diplomacy—and, in my opinion, it was indispensable to the success of our foreign policy. His direct relationship with his counterparts had a tremendous effect upon them—most were immensely flattered. They would no longer be strangers, having only occasional formal contact. . . . As a result, foreign leaders tended to be there when we needed them, often only because they knew, understood, and empathized from having spoken with him on so many occasions."[15]

Scowcroft goes on to rebut the concern of the professional diplomats:

Foreign ministries had their own ways of viewing issues, sometimes quite different from those of their current head of state or government. The Quai d'Orsay (foreign ministry) in France, for example, had a reputation with the State Department as adversarial and obstinate. It was enormously helpful to [Secretary of State] Jim Baker that the various foreign ministries knew that, if they were disposed to be negative or simply drag their feet on an issue, they might receive an inquiry from their head of government—stimulated by a Bush phone call.[16]

On February 16, 1994, in a message to Swedish prime minister Carl Bildt, President Clinton inaugurated an even newer method of personal diplomacy: e-mail. Clinton's note concluded: "I share your enthusiasm for the potential of emerging communications technologies. This demonstration of electronic communications is an important step toward building a global information superhighway. Sincerely, Bill." The prime minister's reply ended: "It is only appropriate that we should be among the first to use the Internet also for political contacts and communications around the globe. Yours, Carl."[17]

The President as Tactical Commander in Chief

The first section of this chapter described the NSC's Situation Room and the streams of information that flood into its computers and appear on its monitors. During a national security crisis—especially when U.S. armed forces are threatened by or engaged in combat—the Situation Room is capable of pulling in highly detailed tactical intelligence from the distant crisis area. Thanks to small, unmanned Predator planes, which produce live digital videos, and big J-STARS (Joint Strategic Airborne Reconnaissance System) 707s, which use Doppler radar to detect anything moving, the White House, should it choose, can even observe a battlefield in real time.

Top-ranking military professionals, however, traditionally adhere to the dictum of Sun-tzu (a Chinese sage who lived some 2,500 years ago): "He will win who has military capacity and is not interfered with by the sovereign." Echoing Sun-tzu, national security leaders under Bush and Clinton strongly voiced their opposition to any White House attempts at battlefield management. Referring to a Reagan-era "command center" on the second floor of the Old Executive Office Building—an office that he dismantled—Brent Scowcroft explained: "I'm not going to use it; I'm never going to take the president into that building. I don't want him to see the disposition of forces; I don't want him to see all those things. That's not what he is designed to do. He has to make the big decisions. I don't want his mind cluttered up with all this stuff. This is not the SAC [Strategic Air Command] command post; this is not the Pentagon. I like the Situation Room, where the best thing you have is a clock."[18]

Photographic intelligence, however, has a special appeal to presidents. Reagan looked at photos often, and news accounts described President Clinton's scrutiny of videotapes from Predator planes over Bosnia.[19]

Scowcroft reflected further:

It's a tough issue. In these limited kinds of conflicts—like Vietnam, for example—you have to trade the knowledge that the battlefield commander has on the scene of what the tactical situation really is with the strategic knowledge of vulnerability that a president has, in Washington. The tactical commander knows what's on the scene, but he doesn't know what kind of trouble he could get his commander in chief into if he does A instead of B. So, whenever there is that kind of decision to be made, any commander in chief is going to want to be in on it. Because if there is going to be a disutility it is better to have it in the field than in Washington, and have a big disaster. So that's the balance you have to keep. And it's not always an easy one.[20]

Not infrequently, the commander in chief will at least want to engage in battlefield management in advance: to inspect tactical military plans before the engagement begins. President Bush reportedly did this before the initiation of Operation Desert Storm: "[Secretary of Defense Richard] Cheney also reviewed the target list with the President, to make sure Bush was aware of potential points of controversy. He wanted Bush to be happy with all of it. The President was concerned about one set of targets and asked that it be dropped. It included statues of Saddam, and triumphal arches, thought to be of great psychological value to the Iraqi people as national symbols."[21]

A quite recent—and very impressive—example of the dilemma that General Scowcroft describes took place during the spring of 1999, during the seventy-eight-day NATO bombing operation in Kosovo. The question of which targets to strike was not merely a military but a political decision. The "quints"—the foreign ministers of Britain, France, Germany, Italy, and the United States—acted as a "management committee" and "held a five-way conference call almost every day." But above the foreign ministers were the presidents themselves:

> [French president] Chirac asked to review any targets in Montenegro, a small republic of Yugoslavia that had remained democratic and was trying to stay out of the war. [British prime minister] Blair wanted a veto over all targets to be struck by B-52 bombers taking off from British soil. And all three leaders wanted to review targets that might cause high casualties, such as the electrical grid, telephone system and buildings in downtown Belgrade.
>
> All agreed on [these] . . . new guidelines. . . .
>
> At a morning intelligence briefing, [General Wesley K.] Clark was informed that Yugoslav artillery in Montenegro was shelling northern Albania. . . . "Hold off on that," he said, "I'll get French permission."
>
> Within hours, Clark and three of the Clinton administration's top players—[Secretary of State Madeleine] Albright, national security adviser Samuel R. "Sandy" Berger and defense secretary William Cohen—dialed their counterparts in Paris. By the next morning, Clark had political approval for the strike. . . .
>
> After the internal military review, the target approval process passed through the White House, the British prime minister's office and the French presidential administration. During the first 45 days, Gen. Henry H. Shelton, chairman of the Joint Chiefs of Staff, was at the White House every day, seven days a week, with targets that needed the president's approval.
>
> From Shelton's perspective, the White House process was expeditious. Clinton and his top advisers were quick to make decisions, and there was never a logjam of targets waiting to be approved. In the field, though, the wait sometimes seemed long and mystifying.[22]

Months later, U.S. leaders had second thoughts about this lengthy and involved political clearance arrangement for military operations. Testifying before the Senate Armed Services Committee in mid-October of 1999, General Shelton acknowledged that "the NATO target approval process was slow. Obtaining consensus before striking highly sensitive targets proved the most challenging."[23]

Defense Secretary Cohen added:

I think that we have to really have greater thought given to the target approval process in the future. . . . [We] have to decide in advance what sort of latitude and leeway our military commanders who are charged with carrying out the operation have, and set these forward in a fairly straightforward fashion, so we do not have to have questions raised during the course of the campaign: is this something that must necessarily be kicked up to the higher political authorities for their judgment? . . . At what point does the need for allied cohesion tend to be outweighed by the military effectiveness of an operation? . . . I do not think you are ever going to have a situation in which the elected leaders of a democracy are going to say we are turning it over to the military; we do not care what you do, you can make a desert and call it peace, and you can wipe out an entire population as long as you succeed in your military objective. I think the military itself would object to that, and surely a democratic society would object to that, and so what we need to do is to evolve into that process, and see if we cannot speed up and improve the process in the future. We will never eliminate it, and we do not want to.[24]

Readers will immediately appreciate the significance—and the potential consequences—of this debate for the future functioning of the national security affairs office at the White House.

The National Security Adviser and His Staff

Former President Bush emphasized the importance of the officer whose formal title is assistant to the president for national security affairs: "The President should make clear that in all but title the NSC adviser is like the Chief of Staff for foreign affairs. Clearly the Chief must be included in discussions and decisions on major foreign policy or security matters; but it is important that the NSC adviser be seen as the President's powerful National Security principal on all NSC matters. If this does not happen the NSC adviser will be bypassed not just by staff and Cabinet, but by diplomats as well."[25]

Besides managing the policy development process and supporting the president's personal national security role, the security adviser and his staff have important additional responsibilities.

In the Security Adviser's Office

In recent years foreign representatives, recognizing that the White House is the locus of national security decisionmaking, have beaten a path to the

West Wing door of the national security adviser himself, but only a few have succeeded in getting a spot on his notoriously crammed schedule. Most are welcome in the White House but are referred to whichever NSC senior director follows the affairs of their particular country. Some only want to make a courtesy call; others carry "eyes-only" messages for the president. Refused a meeting with Clinton's national security adviser, one ambassador whined directly to the Congress that he couldn't get into Berger's office. Explained Brent Scowcroft: "Ordinarily I would see them when we wanted to put a White House twist on something—either really impress them that the president was serious about something, or make them feel good, coming to the White House. . . . You know, it is useful to use the White House as a part of diplomacy; it's like underlining a word in your sentence."[26]

Richard Haass, Scowcroft's senior director for the Middle East, observed:

> In normal times, we didn't do a lot of it. But during crises we did a bit more, particularly with the Kuwaiti ambassador, with [Saudi ambassador] Bandar, with the Israeli ambassador. That's because the White House is the center. . . . [You] know when you have a crisis, it's no longer just diplomacy; it's no longer just State. In normal times, State is first among equals. But in a crisis, the White House becomes the hub of the wheel; State just becomes the end of one of the spokes. You have the Pentagon and others, so you [in the White House] end up doing more of it yourself."[27]

The members of the national security staff are careful to keep their colleagues in the Department of State informed about such visits.

In addition to ambassadors, international luminaries with some notoriety—such as the Dalai Lama, author Salman Rushdie, and Irish partisan Gerry Adams—were received in Sandy Berger's office. To preserve the subterfuge that such visitors were not accorded a formal or official Oval Office appointment, the president would then drop by—a strategy that helped forestall accusations from the Chinese, the Muslims, or the British that the American president was, in some official way, sanctioning their enemies.

Under Clinton, the national security adviser was especially involved when the president was preparing to meet with a foreign chief of state, as the following excerpt (from a March 1997 White House press secretary briefing) indicates: "The National Security Adviser, Samuel Berger, met with Egyptian President Mubarak this morning at Blair House, in preparation for the working visit on Thursday with President Clinton. They had a good discussion, which focused mostly on the current state of the Middle East peace process."[28]

In the evolution of White House dominance of national security affairs, one of the most significant steps was taken by Henry Kissinger when he arranged to install a direct, secure telephone connection to Bonn, Paris, and London—not to the U.S. embassies, not to the foreign ministries, but to his counterparts: the national security advisers in those three countries. (Kissinger also made heavy use of back channels—via the CIA station chief— to reach the heads of foreign governments; in this fashion, he would send policy messages personally that bypassed the American ambassadors.)

Scowcroft continued Kissinger's "drop-line" system; he could simply pick up the proper phone on his desk and it would ring on the desk abroad. Members of Clinton's national security staff similarly relied on a network of telephones that linked them to their opposite numbers in certain foreign countries. These links were made secure through a portable encryption gadget that could be plugged into any senior staff member's phone—whether at home or at the office—and that worked in tandem with a companion piece that had been lent (sealed up, of course) to the appropriate office abroad. There was even such a link to the Zhongnanhai headquarters of the Chinese leadership in Beijing.

Why are such connections useful? If a foreign country is being run by a coalition government, the prime minister and the foreign minister may be of different parties—or, even within the same party, not the best of friends. It can be assumed that the national security advisers abroad, like those in the United States, serve as close personal assistants to the heads of their respective governments. For the White House, that is the connection that counts.

The Bush and Clinton national security advisers eschewed the back-channel approach to communications, in which instructions were issued to U.S. embassies without the knowledge of the secretary of state. As one State Department staffer commented: "I think the Iran-Contra escapade put that to rest. Too many people got burned: Where were you taking instructions to or from? Now there is quite a rule about that. NSC staff may call an embassy to ask, 'What is going on?' but Tony Lake and Sandy Berger would limit themselves to suggesting to the secretary of state that *she* might send some instruction out to X."[29]

NSC Staff for Legislative Liaison

Congress being the control gate for every national security action that requires statutory authorization, for every dime that is spent to carry out such actions, and for the approval of every international treaty, the national security adviser and his colleagues watch the Hill intently. In fact, one of the senior directors of Clinton's national security staff was specifically assigned that task.[30]

The NSC legislative assistant worked under dual oversight: he or she was part of the NSC group and attended NSC staff meetings; but because the assistant's duties also came under the jurisdiction of the White House director of legislative affairs, he or she participated in those staff meetings as well. For the NSC, this assistant snared all incoming congressional mail on national security matters, assigned it to the right experts on the NSC staff, and got the responses cleared with both the national security adviser and the White House assistant for legislative affairs. A collaborative triad—the NSC legislative assistant and his or her counterparts in State and Defense—kept in sync through daily conference calls, bringing in Justice, the CIA, and other agencies as needed. One incumbent composed a nightly report about any actions or events on the Hill that might affect national security matters.

With a TV monitor on the wall carrying continuous live floor debate, the four members of the legislative assistant's staff could split their time between the Hill and their White House desks, all the while concentrating on their principal task: taking the lead in arranging briefings for the Senate and House leadership on pending national security issues. The cabinet departments were expected to work with their respective congressional committees, but the White House dealt with the congressional leadership—knowing that if necessary, it could call in the heaviest support: phone calls from the president.

Having worked on the Hill earlier in his career, security adviser Berger was at home in the Capitol; he needed no reminder of the intimate connection, in national security matters, between the legislative and executive branches; nor did he need to be reminded how essential it was for him, as the head of the national security affairs office, to consult often with legislators. "If I told Sandy, 'I really need you on this,' he would do it," explained Bill Danvers, who served nearly four years in the liaison post. "We would do nose counts; we would do it interagency; we would work with the leadership; we would go to whip meetings."[31]

It was not unusual for the national security adviser to be on the Hill as often as four times a week, and on the telephone to members between three and six times a day. During the contentious debate on the Chemical Weapons Convention, for example, Berger headed an administration team that—at the request of majority leader Trent Lott, and with a strict deadline impending—negotiated with nine senators to iron out a set of conditions and assurances (which would accompany the ratification resolution) sufficient to persuade several reluctant conservatives finally to agree to passage.

On issues like this, Bill Danvers emphasized, there was not much horse trading between White House and Congress; indeed, there was little to trade. It was a matter of persuading senators and representatives to support the president's policy.

NSC's Own Legal Staff

In 1985, hunting for legal advice that would support their desire to supply the Nicaraguan contras with arms, NSC deputy assistant John Poindexter and staff member Lieutenant Colonel Oliver North went not to the junior officer who at that time was responsible for giving legal advice to the NSC staff but to "an odd source":[32] a lawyer working for the president's Intelligence Oversight Board, a group that is independent of the NSC. According to that officer, the restrictions in the Boland Amendment did not apply to the NSC staff. This was the advice they wanted—and the rest is history. One disaster and two years later, the President's Special Review Board recommended "that the position of Legal Adviser to the NSC be enhanced in stature and in its role within the NSC staff."[33] As a result of that recommendation, the NSC staff came to include a legal adviser and three deputy legal advisers.

National security policy questions are steeped in legal issues: the limits of congressional oversight, the proper wording for presidential findings to authorize covert actions, the boundaries of presidential war powers, the interpretation of conditions imposed on treaty ratifications, the judgment as to whether or not a space interceptor would be permitted under the Anti-Ballistic Missile Treaty, and so forth.

One particularly difficult legal issue that arose between the CIA and the FBI concerned terrorist attacks against Americans in foreign countries. The CIA uses its resources abroad to track down the perpetrators; the FBI wants to bring them to the United States for trial. But obtaining a conviction at an open trial would likely require disclosure of the CIA's sources and methods. To reconcile intelligence and law enforcement objectives, the NSC arranged to create a high-level coordination group consisting of representatives from the two agencies—which, in former times, had barely been in communication with each other. An NSC staff officer sat with this group to track its work, and to call in White House intervention if required.

Departmental general counsels are the first level of review for interagency national security issues, but they can and do disagree—in which case the NSC legal adviser steps in to oversee a review. If a departmental general counsel is under pressure, for policy reasons, to concur with the proposed action of his or her own agency, it has become the duty of the NSC legal adviser to stiffen the departmental counsel's spine—and, if legal problems have been passed over or left unresolved, to blow the whistle. The NSC legal office provides "the last legal review of all documents going to the president in the national security area with 'legal effect,'" that is, "presidential determinations, reports to Congress, executive orders and Presidential Decision Directives."[34]

Like the NSC legislative assistant, the NSC legal adviser works under dual oversight: as part of the staff of the national security adviser but closely linked to the counsel to the president—and sits in on the staff meetings of both groups. He asks for the White House counsel's concurrence if there are significant legal issues in a national security paper going to the president. (President Bush's counsel, Boyden Gray, actually chose the person who served as the NSC legal adviser.)

The legal assistant will often ask the Office of Legal Counsel (OLC) at the Justice Department to aid in unsnarling interdepartmental legal disputes that are critical to national security policy decisions. (If the disputes are irreconcilable, it is the OLC, not the NSC legal adviser, that has the authority to adjudicate.)

Is it indispensable for the national security assistant to have his own legal adviser? The Clinton administration thought so. But General Scowcroft, who signed the 1987 review board report but who then served as President Bush's security adviser, changed his mind, indicating that he thought it better for the NSC to rely on the White House counsel. However, that office's almost total preoccupation, in 1998–99, with the Monica Lewinsky scandal and with its aftermath—the impeachment imbroglio—is a signal that this question has two sides to it.

NSC Press Relations Staff

Another dual arrangement: like the White House itself, which has a press secretary and assistants, the Clinton NSC had its own "press and communications" group: a senior director (who also had the title of deputy White House press secretary) and a small staff.

Each morning, the first task of the NSC press group was to equip the national security adviser to answer questions or make comments at the White House senior staff meeting. The staff accomplished this task by combing through the thick stack of photocopied press articles—which had been delivered to every White House office—and alerting the adviser to any stories, editorials, or op-ed columns about national security issues.

The NSC press group's next duty was to help prepare the White House press secretary for his daily press briefing. To do so, the press staff tapped a variety of sources. They would approach the NSC senior directors, who would already have been in touch with their policy counterparts in State and Defense. For any current issues, the senior directors would compose talking points for the press secretary that incorporated just the right language, the right nuances: What could the press secretary say about a given situation? What could he say about actions the U.S. government was taking? What should he avoid saying? State and Defense, meanwhile, would have developed guidance for their own press staffs; the NSC press group would obtain copies of these materials, and ensure that any disparities were reconciled before the press secretary appeared in the Briefing Room. The NSC press group also perused the CIA's *National Intelligence Daily* and obtained copies (from the Sit Room) of State's pertinent cable traffic. Finally, the NSC press officers would listen in—and chime in as needed—to the White House press secretary's hour-long daily conference call with his opposite numbers at State, Defense, the CIA, and the U.S. Mission to the United Nations.

The product of all this research was a summary paper from the NSC press office to the White House press secretary that covered the national security questions that might come up during the early-afternoon press briefing. At the briefing, some members of the NSC press group would sit along the side of the room, alphanumeric pagers at the ready; meanwhile, other members of the press group would watch the press briefing on closed-circuit monitors. If an unexpected query was thrown at the press secretary, he would likely answer, "I'll get back to you on that"—whereupon the NSC press office staffers (who were watching the monitors) would dig out the answer, ring up the pagers, and dictate a short response. An NSC press staffer would then scribble the answer onto a card and slip it to the rostrum. This quick-reply technique was not often used, but in case the press secretary needed information, misspoke, or used inappropriate terminology, the correction could be made on the spot—before the press conference ended and before any damage was done.

After the press conference, members of the NSC press staff would return to their office, where follow-up calls were piling up: typically seventy in a day.

NSC Speechwriting Staff

In the spring of 1989, President Bush decided to make a set of four speeches: his debut pronouncements on foreign policy. The first, concerning Eastern Europe—especially developments in Poland—would be delivered in Hamtramck, Michigan, a blue-collar community vibrant with Polish-Americans, thereby adding a domestic political coloration to the occasion.

Who would write these speeches? The national security staff had the experts—the senior directors, whom Scowcroft trusted; but the White House speechwriting office, supported by Chief of Staff John Sununu, had a knack for dramatic political rhetoric. There was an astringent division of opinion in the White House. The speechwriters' view of the NSC product? It would tend to be written "in an academic and 'heavy' style . . . too difficult to fix." Scowcroft's view of the speechwriters' product? "Their texts seemed to be marked by a choppy political-campaign style, designed for applause at rallies but hardly befitting a serious discussion of important policy issues."[35]

Scowcroft believed that in order to get the substance exactly right for the international as well as the domestic audience of a major presidential address, his NSC staffers should always do the first draft; the professional speechwriters could add the catchy phrases later. Miffed by the implication that they were no more than technicians, the speechwriters insisted that they could fully absorb the substance and explain it lucidly. In practice, portions of some drafts were created jointly by the NSC and the White House speechwriters. But, adds Scowcroft, "there were instances of competing NSC and speechwriter drafts."

During the Bush presidency, the debate was never really settled. "It remained a major irritant, with a negative impact on the quality of the president's foreign policy speeches throughout the administration."[36]

Things were different, however, under Clinton, as a senior NSC officer made clear: "We write the speeches now. Any foreign speeches, we write . . . from soup to nuts. And not just the speeches, obviously, but what is called the 'toppers'—which, although [they precede] this administration—[are] a favorite device now. If the president is going to an event, say an AIDS event, but if something newsworthy is going on in the world, he will say, 'Before I talk about AIDS, permit me to . . . ' And then he will issue a warning about Kosovo, or something like that."[37]

Clinton had a five-person NSC speechwriting staff. Security adviser Berger—himself a former speechwriter—worked heavily on any major foreign policy speech. Only when Berger said "Go" was the draft released for comment to the White House speechwriting office, to a few other senior White House advisers, and to the secretary of state. "Then the slings and arrows would begin," an NSC officer said with a smile. "If the suggested change is from 'happy' to 'glad,' our NSC speechwriters will take it. If it's something that cuts to the core of an argument, they will check with Sandy. Sandy closely controls the speechwriting process; he rewrites heavily."[38]

From the point of view of the State Department, NSC drafts invariably arrived with too tight a deadline. The direct copy that came from Berger was "never too early from our perspective," acknowledges a senior State officer. "It's always a last-minute thing. If we only get it at ten to five, we have to work all night."[39]

Reciprocally, State sent the secretary of state's speeches to Berger in advance, for comments and a green light.

Given their unbeatable credibility, national security advisers are always in demand to appear on the Sunday TV talk shows. In fact, the White House press secretary hoped that all the administration's knowledgeable senior national security officials would follow Berger's practice and blanket the Sunday roundtables. Although under Clinton there was almost always an understanding with the president that such appearances were acceptable, even encouraged, in the past some presidents had insisted on giving specific advance approval. Brent Scowcroft and Tony Lake were very conservative about going public; Sandy Berger did so with gradually increasing frequency and became expert at it.

But no national security leader ever wants to be surprised by the TV appearances of any of his colleagues. It was the practice of the Clinton team that if any appearances were scheduled, a conference call would be arranged ahead of time so that all the senior national security players would know who would be saying what.

Expanded NSC Leadership for Counterterrorism

President Clinton and the national security community were deeply concerned that the United States was vulnerable to rogue or foreign-state–sponsored terrorism in the form of chemical, biological, radiological, or nuclear attack here on our own soil.

The Oklahoma City and World Trade Center bombings and the sarin gas episode in the Toyko subway were warning signs of potentially even more catastrophic events. Local governments would be the first line of response to a domestic attack, but federal resources to "manage the consequences" would be needed immediately, and from some agencies—such as Agriculture (which would have to oversee food safety) and the General Services Administration—that are not accustomed to working with the national security community.

"We must have the concerted efforts of a whole range of federal agencies," explained the president, "from the Armed Forces to law enforcement to intelligence to public health."[40] Clinton designated the NSC staff as the centerpoint for mobilizing such efforts. On May 22, 1998, President Clinton signed Presidential Decision Directive 62, which established, within the NSC organization, the Office of the National Coordinator for Security, Infrastructure Protection and Counter-Terrorism. The coordinator is to "oversee the broad variety of relevant policies and programs" and to "report to the President through the Assistant to the President for National Security Affairs and produce for him an annual Security Preparedness Report."[41]

The national coordinator was promptly appointed: one of his first efforts was to work closely with the director of the Office of Management and Budget to review the budgets and programs of the ten most relevant domestic federal agencies—identifying duplications, gaps, and weaknesses that would need to be addressed in order for the planned special-defense efforts to be effective. The objective was to create a unified antiterrorism budget while fully recognizing that despite the superintendency of the White House national coordinator, it would be the federal domestic agencies themselves—with their staffs and resources in the field—that would provide the primary support for local governments in the event of a terrorist attack that used weapons of mass destruction.

NSC Relationships within the White House

The NSC staff participates heavily in many enterprises that cut across internal White House boundaries, yet it also needs to be fenced off somewhat, both for security reasons and to ensure that it remains insulated from partisan political manipulation. For these reasons, President Clinton and national security adviser Berger designated the NSC executive secretary as the exclusive "bridge" between the NSC staff and all White House and Executive Office units (except for the chief of staff; the counsel; and the legislative, press, and speechwriting shops.)

After the Roger Tamraz and campaign coffee-klatsch embarrassments, national security adviser Berger, in June of 1997, issued a set of instructions entitled "Appropriate Contacts."[42] According to this document, any staff office—other than the NSC itself—that plans to invite any foreign visitor to meet the president, the vice president, or either of their spouses is required to request clearance for such a visit from the NSC executive secretary at least three days in advance. The executive secretary then checks the name with State, the CIA, and NSC staff, and makes a recommendation to the White House chief of staff, who is to make the final decision. If other senior staff officers want to meet with foreign visitors, similar checks are required. The instructions caution NSC officers about meeting with any outsiders, prohibit them from having contact with officials of any political party, and warn them never to show favoritism when American businesses are competing for foreign contracts.[43]

The NSC Staff

The title of this chapter is something of a misnomer. Clearly the tasks and responsibilities that have been described thus far cannot be undertaken by one national security adviser—even with the assistance of two deputies.

The staff of the NSC has become the largest policy group in the White House. Indeed, its combination of skill and size is a measure of the ascendancy of the White House in executive-branch policy development and policy coordination. As noted earlier, NSC staff members in 1948 numbered barely a handful; today they number nearly two hundred.

In the Clinton White House, nineteen regional and functional senior directors (listed at the end of the introduction to part 2 of this volume) supported the top offices of the assistant and the two deputy assistants. These nineteen, in turn, were supported by the White House Situation Room, described at the beginning of this chapter, and by three auxiliary offices: for systems and technical planning, records and access management, and administration. Each of the NSC senior directors has carried the additional title of special assistant to the president, marking them formally as officers of the White House staff.

The security adviser has had the latitude to create new staff units as necessary and to cut back or disband others; he has also had great flexibility in hiring and terminating staff members, all but a very few of whom serve at the NSC at the pleasure of the president.[44] In fiscal year 2001, the internal White House "ceiling" for NSC staff "slots"—that is, those salaried by the government—was 155. Of those, 60 were paid from funds appropriated to the NSC (the number given in the personnel summary of the NSC staff that was reported to Congress in the fiscal year 2001 budget). Of the other 130-plus, most were on detail from State, Defense, or the CIA; the others were "non-counters" against the ceiling of 155: full-time consultants whose salaries were being paid by the universities from which they had come. Finally, there were usually a few interns at the NSC (who also did not count against the ceiling).

The fiscal year 2001 budget request for the NSC was just over $7 million. As a member of the White House staff, the national security adviser is exempt from the duty to defend that budget in congressional appropriations subcommittee testimony; that job is handled by the director of the Office of Administration.

The Historic Tension: The National Security Adviser and the Secretary of State

This chapter has so far described the principal duties and operations of the assistant to the president for national security affairs and his colleagues. Every hour—indeed, every minute—these duties and operations directly affect the Departments of State and Defense—State in particular. As is to be expected, differences of opinion arise on virtually every foreign policy issue; many of these differences are both profound and sharp. But whereas policy arguments can be resolved at whatever level is needed—and can be brought to an end by conclusive answers—conflicts about jurisdiction tend to linger, suffusing the entire interdepartmental environment. It is in the area of jurisdiction that the greatest changes have occurred in the White House in the years since 1948.

During that span of time, the NSC staff has been transformed from a small group performing primarily secretariat functions into a major policy shop that generates its own substantive views. In its initial years, the NSC staff simply reproduced and distributed policy papers from State and Defense; now it writes its own—and sends them to the president. NSC staffers once merely took notes at interagency meetings; now they chair the meetings. NSC staff used to depend on State's "desk officers" to share whatever information they received from embassies abroad; now all the important raw cable traffic comes directly to the NSC staff, who read it themselves. The secretaries of State and Defense used to send memorandums to the president; these are now most likely to end up as attachments to memorandums from the security adviser. Our nation's most sensitive matters in England, France, Germany, and China were once handled as part of our ambassadors' visits to the foreign ministries; now the White House national security adviser is in direct telephone contact with his counterparts in London, Paris, Berlin, and Beijing. The president formerly used his ambassadors to conduct crucial diplomatic relations; now he often telephones the foreign chiefs of state and conducts them himself—with an NSC staffer listening in. The

president once depended on his secretary of state to journey overseas to negotiate the most sensitive agreements; now he convenes personal, face-to-face
summit meetings. It was the practice that foreign ambassadors accredited
in Washington transacted their business with assistant secretaries of state;
now they bring many of their most delicate concerns to the NSC staff. The
relationship between the White House and the State Department is indeed,
to borrow a phrase from Messrs. Bush and Scowcroft, a world transformed.

These transformations have been bumpy, or worse. Many readers will
remember how acrimonious—and degrading to the Department of State—
were the relations with the White House during the Nixon, Carter, and
Reagan presidencies. They will recall the anger of the chief of naval operations at the White House management of the 1962 naval blockade of Cuba.
During the Bush and Clinton administrations, however, the historic tensions
were at least contained, if not damped down almost entirely. How come?

The answer is clear: security advisers Brent Scowcroft, Tony Lake, and
especially Sandy Berger assiduously reached out to the secretaries of State
and Defense, using constant and open communication to forge strong institutional and personal connections. These connections were reciprocal, and
pertained at all staff levels. If the president had a substantive telephone conversation with a foreign chief of state, the secretary of state was either
notified orally or received a copy of the memorandum of conversation—the
gist of which, in most cases, was also cabled to the U.S. ambassador. If a
foreign ambassador had a serious talk with an NSC senior director, the latter promptly informed the responsible assistant secretary in State. If Sandy
Berger took an official trip abroad, a State Department officer accompanied
him; if Secretary of State Madeleine Albright or Secretary of Defense William
Cohen traveled overseas, an NSC staffer went, too.

Berger convened a weekly "ABC" luncheon with Secretaries Albright and
Cohen, plus a weekly breakfast with Albright, Cohen, CIA head George
Tenet, Joint Chiefs Chairman Henry Shelton, and the U.S. ambassador to
the United Nations. Albright and the president talked very frequently on
the phone. Berger and Albright—who typically spoke on the telephone
thirty times a day—were especially careful to check with each other if either
was considering making a speech or appearing on a Sunday roundtable.
Similarly, Scowcroft recounts, "I never went on a TV show that I did not
say, 'Jim [Baker], is this OK with you?'"

There are, of course, endemic differences in perspective between any cabinet officer and any presidential staffer: the secretary will appreciate getting
as much personal praise as possible from a successful action, while the

White House staff member will want to turn the credits toward the president. Personal factors affect the mix as well: Madeleine Albright and Sandy Berger, for example, had known each other, worked together, and been friends for many years by the time she was elevated to the cabinet and he was appointed national security adviser.

Mindful, then, both of the tensions of the past and of the enormity of the fifty-year transformation of the relationship between State, Defense, and the NSC, the three "ABCers" worked out the "four rules for not killing each other":

1. No friendly fire: we don't criticize each other publicly.

2. Walk ourselves back: rather than say, "Well, Berger doesn't know what the hell he is talking about," Berger himself walks back and says, "Maybe I overstated it."

3. Presumption of innocence: "Before you accept the fact that your colleague has been engaged in some kind of mischievous, dishonest effort, you pick up the phone and talk it through."

4. No policy by press conference: "We ought to agree to things before we make policy."[45]

The American people can hope that these four rules—and the open communication practices that have accompanied them—will endure long into future administrations.

CHAPTER FOUR

"To Summarize and Analyze ... Refine the Conflicting Views": The Domestic Policy Staff

[Shortly before inauguration, Nixon] exhorted his Cabinet to work hard, seize their departments from the dastardly bureaucracies. . . . The President made it sound as if he intended to give his Cabinet full freedom to run their departments without White House interference. At the time, that might have been Nixon's real intention.

JOHN D. EHRLICHMAN

[Kennedy] could not afford to accept, without seeking an independent judgment, the products and proposals of departmental advisers whose responsibilities did not require them to look, as he and his staff looked, at the government and its programs as a whole. He required a personal staff, therefore—one that represented *his* personal ways, means and purposes—to summarize and analyze those products and proposals for him, to refine the conflicting views of various agencies, to define the issues which he had to decide, to help place his personal imprint upon them, to make certain that practical political facts were never overlooked, and to enable him to make his decisions on the full range of *his* considerations and constituencies, which no Cabinet member shared.

THEODORE SORENSEN

The title *council* seems to be a favorite in White House organizational nomenclature. By using that moniker to denote assemblages of cabinet officers, the president helps to create a picture of a chief executive formally chairing solemn plenary synods of cabinet secretaries. In addition to the existing National Security Council, Nixon established two such councils, Reagan created seven, and Bush and Clinton each had two.

The picture is more fakery than fact. The formal assemblages, chaired by the president, rarely assemble. Principals meet as teams, often without the president; deputies get together frequently; working groups abound. It's the top staffs of the councils—senior White House officers—who supply the leadership, scope out the questions, draft the papers, and call the meetings. Even the final sessions of cabinet folks and White House staffers in the Oval Office are not the grinding of formal "council" machinery but informal decisionmaking clusters.

The previous chapter described how today's National Security "Council" actually works; eschewing ritualistic trappings, the White House domestic policy development bodies—the Domestic Policy Council and the National Economic Council—likewise use less formal processes. This chapter deals with the domestic policy development body; the economic council is discussed in chapter 5.

"Domestic Council," "Domestic Policy Council": whatever the title, within the contemporary White House this is the staff that helps the president set priorities on his agenda of domestic issues and takes the lead in developing solutions—executive actions or legislative proposals to Congress. This domestic assignment is about the broadest in the White House, requiring the domestic policy head to reach out across twelve of the fourteen cabinet departments plus the Environmental Protection Agency (EPA). Some of the domestic policy chiefs have come straight from the presidential campaign staff (Nixon's John Ehrlichman, Carter's Stuart Eizenstat, Clinton's Carol Rasco and Bruce Reed); others have come from experience in the executive branch (Johnson's Joseph Califano) or academe (Bush's Roger Porter).

Bush's Domestic Policy Council

In the Bush administration, the de jure chair of the Domestic Policy Council was Attorney General Richard Thornburgh. The assistant to the president for economic and domestic policy was Roger Porter, who had a staff of some thirty-five, but the executive secretary of the council was part of the staff of the secretary to the cabinet. This last arrangement, initiated under Reagan, consolidated the executive secretaries of both the domestic and economic councils under the Office of Cabinet Affairs.[1] It was Porter, however, working closely with Chairman Thornburgh, who managed the council's substantive policy development work.

Porter's time and energy were devoted to a long string of major issues, such as crime, education policy, health care, environmental protection, and product liability reform. Two examples are illustrative: drafting a new Clean Air Act and trying to come up with a more explicit definition of wetlands.

Revisions to the Clean Air Act

In July of 1989 President Bush submitted proposals to Congress to revise the Clean Air Act of 1970. By November of that year the Senate Environment and Public Works Committee had reported out its version of the revisions, which was much more costly than the administration's proposals. The pollution controls in the committee's revised bill were allegedly so burdensome for heavy industry—including auto manufacturing and utilities—that senators who represented those interests were threatening to filibuster the amendments.

After he had spent three months superintending the contentious interagency effort to produce the original administration position, it became Porter's additional duty to try to break the impasse between the parties on the Hill. He led five administration officials (including one from EPA) into three weeks of closed meetings of the "Group of 15": majority leader George Mitchell, four Democratic senators, minority leader Bob Dole, and four Republican senators. The sessions—125 hours of negotiations—were held behind closed doors, but continuing leaks spurred industry and environmental lobbyists into making frenzied efforts to protect their interests. The administration representatives, mindful of Bush's threat to veto any bills that were too expensive, insisted upon—and succeeded in getting—tentative agreement from the congressional negotiators on a less expensive set of amendments than the Senate Environment and Public Works Committee had first approved.[2]

Reaching agreement on auto pollution controls and on actions to curb acid rain required yet another week of intense negotiation between Porter and the senators—but resulted in a front-page news story and Senate passage of the Clean Air Act revisions. (The House passed a different version, and it was not until the fall of 1990 that the Senate-House Conference Committee produced a final piece of legislation for the president to sign.) This brief story is simply one example of how far beyond the formal title of "domestic policy adviser" the White House job actually extends.

Wetlands

In his 1988 campaign for the presidency, Vice President Bush, promising to be "the environmental president," had pledged that during his time in office there would be "no net loss of wetlands"—the swamps, bogs, and marshes that filter bay and river water, help control floods, and provide habitat for migratory birds and other wildlife. According to federal legislation then in effect, if property was found to be a wetland, the owner could neither build on it nor disturb it. The issue was: How was a wetland defined?

A 1989 interagency technical manual contained broad and ambiguous criteria. In 1991 several federal agencies proposed revising the manual to provide a more explicit and relatively liberal definition—one that environmentalists preferred. But a White House task force chaired by one of Porter's assistants suggested more restrictive criteria that would meet the mounting demands of property owners, developers, oil-well drillers, and other business leaders. What had appeared to be a scientific question became a hotly contested political issue—with the White House in the middle of it.

Porter and his staff spent from May to August of 1991 crafting a definition that the president finally approved.[3] Both Porter and the president hoped that the definition represented the best attainable compromise between the opposing sets of demands. Porter reflected:

> There was, and remains, a wide range of scientific opinion on many policy questions. Scientific findings are rarely able to resolve issues definitely. Many in policy deliberations would like to assert that the weight of science dictates a particular course of action. In most instances, that is simply not the case. The nature of these debates is such that no matter what set of procedures you follow, you will have differing views. Neither side is able to convince the other side that its evidence is superior and should prevail. Everyone will have his or her own experts and will emphasize those studies which support his or her own position.[4]

Clinton's Domestic Policy Council

President Clinton waited seven months before formally establishing his version of a domestic council.[5] Although his executive order specified that the president and vice president were to be chairman and alternate chairman, respectively, the council met as a formal body perhaps only six times in as many years. The second alternate council chair—the actual force behind the council's work and the head of its staff—was the assistant to the president for domestic policy, Carol Rasco. At the outset, Ms. Rasco was supported by a staff of some thirty-three, including interns and at least one White House Fellow;[6] in the second Clinton term, Bruce Reed, who had replaced Rasco, had a staff of twenty-seven. The fiscal year 2001 budget for what was called the Office of Policy Development—that is, the staffs of both the Domestic Policy Council and the National Economic Council—was $4,032,000.

Both of Clinton's domestic policy advisers maintained a special linkage to the first lady's office: one or two people whose salaries were paid by the Domestic Policy Council actually sat in the first lady's nearby suite and attended the meetings of both staffs. Whenever the first lady participated in events that had a domestic policy element, these staff members would brief her; if the domestic policy office was the lead office for an issue in which she was also interested—for example, child care or the AmeriCorps initiative—they would serve as a bridge between the two offices.

A novel example of this bridging arrangement—and of White House staff taking the lead on policy issues generally—was Clinton's structuring of a cabinet committee to study and improve collaboration between the federal government and private nonprofit organizations. When he created the Interagency Task Force on Nonprofits and Government, Clinton directed that its three co-chairs all be senior White House officials: the assistants for domestic policy and economic policy and the chief of staff to the first lady.[7]

Rasco and Reed sent both the president and the first lady a short weekly report on the activities of the domestic policy unit—covering, for example, unusually interesting people they had encountered, "hot" issues coming around the corner. Both Clintons would respond with comments and suggestions.

Two contentious issues—agricultural pesticides and welfare reform—illustrate the work of the Clinton domestic policy staff.

Agricultural Pesticides

Early in the Clinton administration a group of federal executives from the Department of Agriculture, the EPA, and the Food and Drug Administration (FDA) approached William Galston, deputy assistant for domestic policy, with a simmering problem: farm pesticides. Citing the extremely strict Delaney Amendment to the federal Food and Drug Act, a federal court was about to ban the use of dozens of widely used pesticides—an action that would cause near-chaos in the entire farming community.

Knowing that because of his Arkansas roots President Clinton was interested in farm legislation, Galston suggested to the president that an interagency group was needed to undertake a fresh review of this contentious issue, which had long divided farmers and environmentalists into bitterly warring factions. Galston established and chaired a working group of representatives from the affected federal agencies: Agriculture, the Council of Economic Advisers, the EPA, the FDA, and Health and Human Services (HHS). First, as he later explained, he had to persuade all the players to "map the terrain . . . figure out what the questions were. There were twenty to thirty policy judgments that would have to be made; we spent months working through those, one by one."[8]

Word soon got out that this review was in process, and Galston's office was promptly inundated with visitors: advocates from growers' organizations, environmental groups, grocery stores. So controversial were those twenty or thirty issues and so strongly held were the opposing views that Galston's policy development process was agonizingly slow. He kept the chief of staff and the president informed, but he knew that the president would not want to get drawn into the individual dogfights. Galston laid down the law to the warring protagonists: "Look, this debate has been going on a long time. One side is not going to persuade the other. We have different, legitimate interests here; we are going to have to find a way of bringing them together in a fashion which is mutually satisfactory. I can't tell you how to do that; all I can tell you is that it has to happen."[9] On the particularly intractable issues, Galston set up subgroups, telling the factions: "You pick one person from subgroup A, one person from B, and one from C. . . . You know what your job is: to get some resolution of this issue, because we're all going to lose—and your constituencies are going to lose— if we remain divided."

On one or two occasions Galston stepped in, telling the members of the working group what the compromise should be: "'I think we are going to cut the line here, and this is the way I think we are going to have to cut it.' I tried to do this in such a way that the different parties would not be so dissatisfied as to go back to their bosses and inspire them to appeal. . . . The deputy secretaries themselves were at the table, but I didn't allow anybody to veto anything."[10]

Galston still did not believe that he needed to insert the president into the detailed issues. He did know that the president wanted a strong and prosperous agricultural sector, that he did not want to be seen as an antienvironmental president, that he did not want public warfare in his administration, and that he did not want the federal courts to take actions that would have serious negative consequences. This knowledge gave Galston all the White House leverage he needed.

Briefs of the Solicitor General

The solicitor general, a presidential appointee in the Department of Justice, serves at the president's pleasure and speaks for the administration: literally so, for he argues in person before the Supreme Court. The solicitor general's briefs to the Supreme Court or the appellate courts are thus given special attention to ensure that they reflect the president's views.

The more sensitive and controversial a case before the higher courts, the more significant for the president are the solicitor general's views and arguments. While the solicitor general himself generally takes the position that he is "above politics," many a White House domestic affairs chief has insisted on White House review of any brief that involves a major policy question. When an important environmental case reached the Court in July of 1977, domestic policy head Stuart Eizenstat, Cabinet Secretary Jack Watson, and White House Counsel Robert Lipshutz together wrote to President Carter: "There are a few conflicts, however, whose resolution entails significant policy choices for the Administration. The question is how the White House can assert the legitimate Administration interest in such matters without in any way compromising the integrity of the Justice Department. We recommend that you authorize us to contact the Attorney General and request that no legal brief be filed before a policy decision has been made at the White House level, and that Stu coordinate the policy analysis."[1]

President Carter agreed.

Eizenstat and Lipshutz had to repeat the maneuver two months later, when the Court considered the Bakke case, a wrenching example of the affirmative action controversy. Here it was not only the solicitor general but Attorney General Griffin Bell himself who wanted to keep the White House out of the business of reviewing briefs. When Bell brought the Justice Department's draft brief with him to discuss the Bakke case with the president, Carter asked that Lipshutz, Eizenstat, and Vice President Mondale look over Justice's wording—and the text soon leaked to the *New York Times*. Bell later reflected that bringing the brief with him to the White House that day was

> perhaps my greatest mistake with regard to the power centers at the White House. Nowhere is the tug of power between the White House and a Cabinet department more apparent than in a dispute between the Justice Department and the President's staff over what

is law and what is policy. If the staff had its way, no doubt every major issue that naturally fell to the Justice Department would be considered policy rather than a legal matter. Then the White House would be making all the decisions, because it is the White House where policy is made.[2]

Whether expressed in the Eizenstat-Watson-Lipshutz memorandum or in Griffin Bell's rueful recollection, the point is precisely the same. The president is policymaker in chief, and the leaders of those thirty-one departments and agencies that are under the president's authority are constitutionally required to have him—not themselves—decide the administration's position on sensitive and controversial questions. Mr. Bell's gripe notwithstanding, law and policy are inseparable.

The Bush and Clinton administrations adhered to the same principle. Although it was not an everyday occurrence, both Bush and Clinton reached out to review—and, if necessary, to alter—Justice Department briefs to make them conform to the president's policies.

In 1991, the Department of Justice and a group of black Mississippians challenged the state's system of higher education, charging that Mississippi was not doing enough to desegregate its colleges and universities. The Justice 'brief' argued that the objective was to end duplication in curriculum and resources, not necessarily to provide equal funding; the state did not have to spend extra money to raise the historically black colleges up to the standards maintained at the predominantly white schools. After a meeting with black educational leaders, who told him that such a position would cripple publicly supported black colleges, President Bush told White House counsel Boyden Gray to instruct Solicitor General Kenneth Starr to change the government's brief and to push for eliminating the financial disparities. Starr inserted a footnote into the altered brief: "Suggestions to the contrary in our opening brief no longer reflect the position of the United States."[3]

In another case, a lower court in Minnesota had ruled that an evangelical church was required to give up the tithe that it had received from a couple that had declared bankruptcy for business reasons; the court instructed the church to turn the money over to the couple's creditors. When the church appealed the decision to the Eighth Circuit Court of Appeals, the Justice Department brief argued that the Religious Freedom Restoration Act (which Clinton had signed the year before with much

continued

fanfare) prohibited the government from supporting the church—and accordingly supported the creditors. Clinton, in response to criticism from the evangelical community—and being convinced that this interpretation of the act was too narrow—instructed Justice to withdraw the brief entirely and get out of the case.[4]

1. Stuart Eizenstat, "Memorandum for the President," July 18, 1977 (Washington D.C., National Archives, Papers of Stuart Eizenstat).
2. Griffin B. Bell with Ronald J. Ostrow, *Taking Care of the Law* (New York: Morrow, 1982), 29–30.
3. Ruth Marcus, "Bush Shifts Stand on Aid to Black Colleges," *Washington Post*, October 23, 1991, p. A6.
4. Pierre Thomas, "Clinton Stops Justice Department from Seeking Forfeiture of Tithes," *Washington Post*, September 16, 1994, p. A8.

The whole process took a full twelve months—a year when the Clinton presidency was in continuous crisis over a number of issues: health care, the crime bill, gay men and women in the military, the economic stimulus package, the North American Free Trade Agreement—and then the 1994 elections. Draft comprehensive legislation went to the Hill but no action was possible before November. Galston left the government in 1995, saying to himself, "Well, hell, nice try. . . . "

Surprise: in August of 1996 Galston received a call from the White House—an invitation to a signing ceremony in the Old Executive Office Building. The president praised the vice president and officials from Agriculture and the FDA, then signed into law the Food Quality Protection Act of 1996. Galston's efforts had paid off.

Welfare Reform

Even more contentious than agricultural pesticides was the issue of welfare reform. Some thought had been given to assigning this issue to the vice president, but in view of his own considerable experience with welfare as governor of Arkansas, Clinton decided to task his personal domestic policy staff with responsibility for policy development on this matter.

In the typical first step, a working group was established, but this one had three co-chairs: Bruce Reed; Mary Jo Bane, assistant secretary for Health and Human Services (HHS); and senior adviser David Ellwood, also from HHS. "This was a large-systems issue," commented Carol Rasco. The working group was composed of thirty-two people from eight departments (the thirty-two included some from the Office of Management and Budget and eight from the White House staff). The three co-chairs sat down with HHS secretary Donna Shalala and outlined the issues that were to be explored. Subgroups were then formed—so many that White House meeting rooms were at a premium.

As specific proposals were developed, the White House Office of Public Liaison arranged briefings for outside advocacy groups, and the Office of Intergovernmental Affairs assisted in sponsoring sessions with governors, mayors, and state legislators. The president was kept informed, and in his January 1994 State of the Union message, Clinton made a promise and set a deadline: "This spring I will send you a comprehensive welfare reform bill."[11] Clinton's words were a much-needed forcing mechanism.

"We went through an agonizing process of developing legislative specs," remembered Reed, "meeting on every single issue, sometimes at HHS, sometimes here in the White House." Decision memorandums went to the president: all were drafted in the domestic policy office, but each carefully set forth the various agencies' views—a requirement that Reed insisted on and that the White House staff secretary enforced. Reed recalls, "It was very cumbersome, and in the end I think it just prolonged the agony. The hard decisions had, ultimately, either to be made by the president or not made— and a group that large wasn't going to narrow the options enough for him. . . . The process was riddled with leaks. I don't think that anybody involved in it looks back on it as the fondest months of their lives. We came out with a less than perfect bill. It was only with a lot of pressure from here that we got it done at all."[12]

Reed and company barely made the deadline: the proposed Work and Family Responsibility Act of 1994 was sent to Congress under a presidential message (which Reed wrote) on June 21, the last day of spring.[13] Even before the bill went up, Reed—together with his two co-chairs—had begun wearing out shoe leather on the Hill, trying to sell the president's package to Congress—a task that White House policy staff members are often pressed into undertaking.

The timing was unfortunate: the administration's health care bill was getting its going-over on the Hill at the same time, so any action on welfare reform would have to wait until the new Congress took office.

The second Clinton push for welfare reform legislation, in 1995, was even more "White House centered"—and, according to Reed, with "dwindling participation" in the number of players. This time around the effort involved more negotiations with the Republican-dominated Congress, while within the administration, "all the major decisions happened around Leon Panetta's table. . . . Whenever there was a difference, he would bring everybody in there."[14] (Panetta was now White House chief of staff.) To coordinate the communications and presentation efforts, a very small strategy group—including the White House legislative and intergovernmental liaison officers and the HHS legislative affairs assistant and press secretary—met weekly in Reed's office. Again, Reed himself spent hours meeting with legislators: consulting with Democratic allies, working out compromises with Republicans.[15]

When, in 1996, Congress finally sent over a finished bill for the president's signature, a profound policy divide was exposed within the administration: should the president sign the bill or veto it? A kind of cabinet meeting (a rarity) was convened so that all the domestic department secretaries could present their views to the president. Secretary Shalala argued for a veto; in her view, the bill was too harsh. Reed led the arguments for signature, and his views won the day. The president's signature occasioned the resignation of two senior HHS officers: Mary Jo Bane and Peter Edelman.

Looking back, Reed reflected on the dual role that a White House policy officer must play to perfection, at once gathering the views of cabinet members and other protagonists and presenting his own opinions: "That is a constant tension for the person in this job . . . because the president wants us to do both. He wants us to be honest brokers, and represent everybody's points of view. You can't run an effective process if you are cutting corners, or shortchanging somebody's point of view. On the other hand, the president, I think, feels that we share his point of view, and that we can frame decisions for him. We know . . . we've been with him long enough; we know his inclinations."[16]

A Summing-Up: Three Reflections on the Development of Domestic Policy

Thinking about her experience on Governor Clinton's staff in Little Rock and in the 1992 presidential campaign, Ms. Rasco summed up the advice she would give to those who aspire to be White House policy officers:

> You need to get out there and get your hands dirty working in a major, direct program in the field that you're going to be handling as policy. If you haven't done that, quite frankly, I don't want to be surrounded

with people who have never been out there. If your policy field is welfare reform, but if you have never visited with welfare mothers, have never been in their homes, have not walked in their shoes, have not walked into an agency or worked fairly directly with the agency that is carrying the policies out . . . [you are missing something essential]. My second piece of advice: whether you like it or not, you need to work in a very tough campaign—because it will give you an appreciation for why you are going to have to take some of that into account in the policy process. If you totally ignore those political advisers, then I don't care how good a policy proposal you come up with, if you have not paid attention to them as to how you'll go about presenting it, or building the base that is needed to get it enacted, you may go nowhere.[17]

Ms. Rasco's advice echoes the admonition given to the author twenty-two years earlier by John Ehrlichman, Nixon's domestic policy chief. Ehrlichman was at that time doing his legal penance by working in a remote section of the Navajo Reservation in Arizona. He had called in to ask whether the General Services Administration could perhaps locate a spare Jeep that could be used as an ambulance in that rough, inaccessible country. He later observed: "If I had it to do over again and was hiring a policy assistant for the White House I would tell him: 'Now you go get your ass out to the farthest possible end of the so-called service delivery system of the federal government—live out there for six months, and see what comes out at the end. Only then come back and take up your policy duties in the White House.'"[18]

Clinton domestic policy assistant Reed concluded:

I think it is very important to center decisions in the White House. Presidents pick their cabinets for lots of different reasons but policy development tends not to be one of them. I think there is an inevitable tension between the White House and the agencies, but that tension will be diminished to the degree that presidents fill their cabinets with people who see the world the way they do. A lot of the time that doesn't happen; they pick their cabinets to meet other needs or fill other gaps. . . . I think that we've been able to establish a good working relationship, where we can tap the best ideas in the agencies. But it really took a good three years. . . . Some people would say it wasn't until the second term that we really developed those channels.[19]

CHAPTER FIVE

The National Economic Council

[As Ford took office] the composition of the new [Economic Policy] board, and the appointment of the Secretary of the Treasury as its chairman, reflected the President's desire to return cabinet members to a greater role as presidential advisers. It demonstrated his commitment to incorporating departments and agencies more fully in presidential decision making. Creating the Board redressed some of the morale problems of cabinet officers who felt that the Nixon administration had excluded them from much of the White House decision-making process.

ROGER PORTER

Obviously we [the White House staff] see the president more times a day than a cabinet member, when you consider the frequency of quick, five-minute briefings. If we use that five minutes to advocate our opinions on contested issues, then cabinet members would look at us as a threat. On the other hand, if, for example, a department has come up with its own tax incentive ideas and we run to the staff secretary saying "No way—that memo can't go to the President until we've had a fair process involving Treasury and other agencies," then we become their protector, and the guardians of a fair process. If all cabinet secretaries and agencies believe we will be their protector against process fouls, then we have the trust we need to make the NEC [National Economic Council] work.

GENE SPERLING

The coordination of economic policy—meaning both domestic and international economic matters—is a challenge that has vexed presidents for several decades. Because coordination in this area involves so many domestic issues, the National Security Council (NSC) has not been viewed as either interested in, or capable of, undertaking it; other mechanisms have been tried.

From Nixon to Bush

Toward the end of the Nixon administration, George Shultz had served simultaneously as secretary of the treasury and assistant to the president for economic affairs. President Ford, by executive order, created the Economic Policy Board (EPB) to "provide advice to the President concerning all aspects of national and international economic policy; oversee the formulation, coordination and implementation of all economic policy of the United States; and serve as the focal point for economic policy decision-making."[1]

The Ford executive order named the secretary of the treasury as chairman and made the assistant to the president for economic affairs the executive director. In his seminal work describing the functioning of the Economic Policy Board during the Ford years, EPB executive secretary Roger Porter detailed executive director William Seidman's comprehensive role as policy manager but stressed that Seidman "consciously and consistently" avoided being either an advocate or a public spokesman: "Rarely did he identify with a particular option or alternative. Even on matters within his own technical expertise, such as tax policy questions, he generally refrained from advocacy."[2]

Seidman and Porter were located in the West Wing of the White House but had a staff of only ten (five professionals and five support people). As Porter explained, "Seidman was convinced that EPB member departments and agencies would view a relatively large staff in his office as a competitor—resulting in less cooperation."[3]

Approximately the same structure lasted throughout the Reagan and Bush administrations: the secretary of the treasury retained the chairmanship and the staff was located in the White House. The word *board* in the unit's title was changed to *council*, and under President Bush the staffs of both the economic and domestic policy councils were grouped under the Office of Cabinet Affairs. This arrangement meant that Cabinet Secretary David Bates (later Edith Holiday) attended council meetings and was a link in the chain of paper-flow from the council to the president. White House Chief of Staff John Sununu was also present at most council sessions.

The Bush Economic Policy Council used working groups and meetings of deputies as well as of cabinet principals; meetings with the president were scheduled as needed (which turned out to average once every five weeks).

Chairman Nicholas Brady and the council's executive secretaries—first Lehmann Li and later Olin Wethington—worked out a common-sense division of jurisdiction with national security adviser Brent Scowcroft and the National Security Council in which one of the NSC's top staffers was a senior director for international economic policy. Most of the background papers for the council, and all the decision memorandums for the president, were drafted in the White House, usually jointly by Wethington and Porter—who, in the Bush administration, had been elevated to the post of assistant to the president for economic and domestic policy.

The Bush council did not address either global warming—which was receiving increasing attention in the press—or any overall budget policy issues, and the famous Bush decision about raising taxes was as much of a surprise to the council members as it was to everyone else.

Clinton's Innovation

What changes did President Clinton make in the arena of economic policy coordination?

In his 1992 campaign Mr. Clinton said that he wanted to create an "Economic Security Council" that would be similar to the National Security Council; later, however, he dropped the word *security* to avoid the possibility that security considerations might be seen as overriding trade and economic goals in dealings with nations such as Japan, Russia, or China.

Following his inauguration, Clinton promptly made good on his promise. On January 25, 1993, he signed Executive Order 12835, and the National Economic Council (NEC) came into being. The NEC bore similarities to the economic policy arrangements under Bush but also reflected significant evolutionary changes. The actual chair of Bush's Economic Policy Council had been Secretary of the Treasury Nicholas Brady; the council's staff support had come from two points on the White House staff: from the Office of Domestic and Economic Policy (later the Office of Policy Development) for overall policy issues, and from the executive secretary of the council, who was part of the staff of the secretary of the cabinet.

Clinton shifted the chairmanship of his new National Economic Council into the White House, placing it in the hands of an assistant to the president for economic policy, who also headed the entire council staff. The president named Robert Rubin, a distinguished Wall Street financial expert, to this position; Rubin was succeeded in 1995 by Laura D'Andrea Tyson, who had been chair of the Council of Economic Advisers (CEA). Tyson was succeeded in 1996 by Gene Sperling, who had been Rubin's deputy from the beginning. The staff numbered thirty.

Questions of relationship—with the CEA, with the Office of Management and Budget (OMB), with the NSC—were inevitable. Rubin and CEA Chair Tyson worked out their respective roles: each would create and maintain the kind of staff that would support their slightly different missions. Tyson would, of course, continue to have her council produce the annual *Economic Report of the President*; she also wanted to maintain the CEA's long-standing reputation as the purveyor of hard, factual economic data—gathered, analyzed, and distributed without any bending to political considerations or need for "spin." In fact, such basic material would be an indispensable ingredient at the beginning of any policy dialogue.

The division of labor between the NEC and OMB was reportedly as follows: the NEC would not invade the traditional OMB function of reviewing and marking up expenditure requests from individual agencies, but the council could—and did—discuss any and all major issues of budget, tax, and fiscal policy. If the State of the Union address impended, the NEC would be the forum for the discussion of what the administration's priorities should be—from jobs to entitlements to the environment. Determining overall economic priorities was not a narrow, OMB-type question; it was a government-wide issue for presidential judgment.

Arrangements between the NEC and the NSC resulted from a preinaugural conversation between the NEC's Rubin and the NSC's Tony Lake. Lake said, "On these international economic issues, instead of my having a staff and your having a staff, let's have just one staff which reports to both." "That," recalled Rubin, "is what we did. We had a deputy at the NEC, who handled all the international economic issues, and the staff that supported him reported to both the NSC and the NEC. These issues got co-chaired."[4] The NSC staff was larger, however, and its processes more formal.

In each of these relationships, the key to effective cooperation was not so much institutional arrangements but personal trust and respect—which must undergird whatever workaday channels of process are agreed upon. "Some issues," commented Rubin, "got taken out of the regular process. [Policy concerning] Russia, for example, was run by Strobe Talbott; it wasn't run through the regular NSC process. Health care was run by the first lady from the very beginning, but what happened with health care is that as time went on, the economic agencies—Treasury, OMB, CEA—all of them got very much involved, although we did it as a part of an independent process; it was never run through the NEC."[5]

But those were the exceptions. In its six-and-one-half years of existence, the NEC—not unlike its predecessors in the two previous administrations—was the combination flour mill and bakery for literally dozens of the most complicated and contentious domestic and foreign economic concerns of the Clinton presidency, grinding the raw seeds of ideas into the finished loaves of legislative proposals: from limiting steel imports to encouraging investments in the nation's pockets of poverty.

There is space to mention only a few illustrations here.

"Look at this table here," said Gene Sperling, sitting in his office,

> virtually every social security meeting, every medicare meeting, happened here. We drive things, but the policy decisions are made through a team effort. Instead of Treasury just deciding tax policy, or OMB just deciding budget policy, they are instead the lead presenters in an NEC process where the decisions are made as a team, with differences being fairly taken up for decision by the president. In the NEC system, everyone gives up being the sole ruler of his or her specific area for the benefit of being an integral decisionmaker in a vast and varied array of economic and budgetary decisions.[6]

In the fall of 1997, preparing for the January State of the Union message, the NEC focused on a triad of overlapping objectives: cutting taxes, allocating the budget surplus, and bolstering social security. Because it would be too revealing to refer to any of these three issues in the titles assigned to meetings or papers, the three sets of meetings—all held in the Sperling conference room—were referred to by a code designation: "Special Issues."

There were meetings about the opposition's plans to propose tax cuts. How were they to be countered? There were meetings about the surplus. Would there be one? (They had never dealt with that before.) If so, how should it be allocated? There were meetings on social security. How much of the surplus should be reserved to protect social security?

In the end, the three strands of discussion converged. Sperling sifted through everything that had been said, stirred in calculations on whether an expensive highway bill would blow away the hoped-for surplus, considered adding still another ingredient—a national debate on how to allocate some of the surplus—and wrote option papers for the president. "We did go into the Oval Office, and I did do the presentation to the president, but my presentation was what everybody had agreed on, and had worked on together," Sperling emphasized. "Treasury came in and presented its part; OMB came in and presented its part."[7]

Climate change was an especially difficult issue for the NEC because it was so controversial. Agencies all over town were affected: domestic, environmental, international, scientific. The econometricians looked at their tables and predicted that if the nation placed strict curbs on pollutants dumped into the atmosphere, the prices of gasoline and coal would skyrocket, industry would be crippled, and the economy would be dragged down. The environmentalists looked at their thermometers, saw the melting glaciers, calculated the size of the ice packs in Greenland and Antarctica, and predicted that without worldwide reductions in greenhouse gas emissions, coastal cities all over the globe would be drowned out. The "techno-optimists," as Sperling called them, predicted that technological improvements could be—were being—found that would let the world slip between Scylla and Charybdis. Commented Sperling, "It was almost like people speaking different languages."

Sperling put together a small internal working group: the vice president's chief of staff and representatives from State, Treasury, and the CEA, the EPA, and the NSC. Those not in that inner circle were promised, "Nothing is going to go to the president of the United States until you see it. No option will go to the president of the United States without your giving him your recommendation."[8] Negotiations were "tortuous" —but four or five options finally emerged.

At a small meeting held in the Oval Office, the president reminded the participants that on the one hand, the status of the U.S. economy was, after all, one of his biggest accomplishments as president—but at the same time, he was not in the thrall of the econometricians. He cared how the United States would look in the eyes of other countries—countries that we were trying to persuade to reduce their own levels of air pollution. At the forthcoming Kyoto conference of the United Nations Committee on Climate Change, could we not join in an agreement to reduce our greenhouse gas emissions to meet a fixed target by a certain date? If we signed on to the Kyoto Protocol, would we have any wiggle room in the future—or would these be binding treaty commitments? The NSC lawyers were called in.

After the small session there was a larger meeting attended by almost the entire cabinet; extra chairs had to be stuffed into the Roosevelt Room. Sperling, who chaired the meeting, admonished the nervous group by—as he said—using Rodney King's language: "We just have to get along here!" Sperling warned the group that everybody had to show *flexibility*.

In the end the president decided that he did not want the United States to be an environmental pariah. With technological change continuing as it had been, and with the right kind of leadership, we and the world could cut down the flow of pollutants. But no mandatory caps would be imposed: we would use tax incentives, and there would be world trading in emissions allowances. In 2008 we would assess where we were, but our goal would be to achieve—by 2012—a net reduction in greenhouse gas emissions of 5.2 percent from the 1990 level.

It was a decision that didn't make everybody happy. It was a cautious decision: it included five-year reviews and used market incentives rather than mandatory regulations to reach the goal. Vice President Gore carried the U.S. position to the Kyoto assembly, and the president issued a statement at the conclusion of the conference.[9]

The whole policy coordination enterprise was managed by the White House staff from start to finish. Reflecting on that fact and on his years at the White House, former NEC head Robert Rubin commented:

> I don't see how else the agencies are going to work together. . . . I think the problem comes when the White House becomes more than a coordinator, and either gives undue weight to the view of the person who is doing the coordination, or becomes operational. What I did when I was secretary of the treasury—in all the four-and-one-half years that I was there—any time there was an issue that involved a number of agencies I would always call the staff leader of the NEC and say, "Look, here is this issue; we want to bring it to you; why don't you arrange the meetings and we will all come." The key was to produce a memorandum for the president which stated the various options in a fair and neutral and balanced fashion. . . . I think where the process gets distorted is if the chairperson of the process takes advantage of being the chair to, in some unfair way, get an edge in presenting his or her views to the president. . . . There is nothing wrong with the head of the process having very strong views. But as long as the person has those strong views, he must also be fair-minded enough to make sure that he does not take advantage of his chairmanship to present his views in a way which gives him an advantage over everybody else.[10]

Sitting at his well-worn table, Sperling added:

> I have seen the most vigorous debates, and if people thought that the process was fair, that they got to see the memo ahead of time, if they thought that the NEC was representing things well, or if they thought, at the meeting, that they got to present their case, the president could

trounce them and they would walk out of there and be team players. But have one time when somebody felt that the memo was slanted, or that they were kept out of the room, and a year and a half later people will still feel bitter about it. Trust in a policy process is as fragile as in a personal relationship; it doesn't take much to break it, and it takes a vigilant commitment to fair process to keep it strong. Any NEC director must never forget that.[11]

Implementation of National Economic Policy: A White House Role

Section 4(a)(4) of the executive order establishing the NEC states that among the "principal functions of the Council" is "to monitor implementation of the President's economic policy agenda." Much like the policy development and policy coordination roles just described, this, too, is a function often centered in the White House staff. A striking example of this strong White House role occurred in November 1999, when NEC chief Gene Sperling accompanied trade representative Charlene Barshefsky and her team to Beijing, to help negotiate with the tough and stubborn senior Chinese government officials the terms of China's possible entry into the World Trade Organization. Would China allow the United States access to its telecommunications and textile markets? Ms. Barshefsky took the lead, but from the NEC table to the Zhongnanhai conference room the White House staff was at work as well.

Enthusiastic about the NEC's work, President Clinton said in November 1997 that he believed "the time has come to elevate [the NEC] to the level of stature that the National Security Council has had. . . . It works like the NSC does. We try to get everyone together, reach a common policy, and then all back it. Sometimes we don't quite get there, but we've had a remarkable amount of success, and I think that it is the single most significant organizational innovation that our administration has made in the White House."[12]

In a cogent summing up, Sperling declared, "What I say is: the National Economic Council is not a set group of people; it is a fair-process commitment."[13]

CHAPTER SIX

The "Just-Us Department": The Counsel to the President

If the president wants to play a role in his own administration, he will need to have staff resources. If he wants to play an effective role in the evolution of constitutional law, he will need to have a sizeable and capable White House Counsel's Office.

JEREMY RABKIN

We certainly did not want some young, faceless, twenty-five-year-old White House staffer taking issue with the attorney general of the United States, who was an officer nominated by the president and confirmed by the Senate, and then taking the issue to the president in a memo which might set forth two paragraphs and "Mr. President, check the box below."

A FORMER MEMBER OF THE JUSTICE DEPARTMENT'S
OFFICE OF LEGAL COUNSEL

For nearly six decades—since 1941—each president has set up in the White House what Eisenhower counsel Gerald Morgan called the "Just-Us Department": an office on his immediate staff that could give him advice directly—and independently of the institutional resources of his cabinet. Over at the Justice Department, attorneys general and their associates have been skeptical. "The attorney general views *himself* as the president's lawyer," was the warning that Truman's attorney general passed on to Edward McCabe, Eisenhower's newly appointed special White House counsel.[1] "They are not equipped to do painstaking legal research over at the White House; they tend to skim the surface," commented one former Justice officer. "In Justice, nobody is over-awed by our environment, nor are we subject to the kinds of pressures which abound at the White House. Some of those younger White House lawyers have views of their own which can color their legal judgment." Justice vet-erans are afraid that presidents may "shop around" for the legal advice they prefer—resulting in inconsistencies in the administration's judgments.

The view from the White House is different. The Department of Justice is "too remote," "twenty blocks away." White House legal staffers know that they must answer the "How do I do this?" question with a speed that matches the president's urgency. "Nothing propinqs like propinquity," for-mer counsel Lloyd Cutler observed.[2] The attorney general, preoccupied with administering a department of 123,000 people, is rarely available to take part in the daily White House meetings at which the White House coun-sel identifies legal issues and refers them to Justice Department lawyers "who might never hear about the problem but for the White House Coun-sel's intervention."[3]

More to the point: the Watergate, Iran-Contra, and Clinton scandals of the seventies, eighties, and nineties have so directly and personally involved the presidents in primarily political and legal—rather than institutional and legal—firestorms that the Department of Justice has had neither the capac-ity nor the desire to step forward into the infernos of investigations, subpoenas, grand juries, and impeachment hearings. The White House counsel—along with private personal attorneys—has had to be the rescue squad.

Outer and Inner Relationships

Even in normal times, what are the first steps that a White House counsel takes?

A White House–Justice "treaty" is usually agreed to: each White House counsel renegotiates it with each new attorney general. Advance consulta-tion is promised in both directions. The White House typically pledges not to exert improper pressure on Justice (especially when prosecutions are involved), agrees that all White House calls to the department will come only through the counsel's office, and promises to exempt the attorney gen-eral from campaign politicking.

In addition to the talents of his own immediate staff, which currently numbers close to forty, the White House counsel can draw upon a well of legal brainpower—and, more important, institutional memory—unique in the executive branch: the Office of Legal Counsel (OLC) in the Department of Justice. This elite staff, particularly expert in constitutional law, has the capacity not only to present recommendations on current issues to the president and the president's counsel but also to reinforce its conclusions by researching precedents from previous administrations.

White House staff, with their nearly empty bookshelves, cannot compete with this kind of institutional memory. Nevertheless, presidents and their chief counsels may or may not choose to rely on the OLC. The office of Bush's counsel was "joined at the hip" with that unit, but the relationship suffered in the Clinton administration. The OLC lacked a confirmed head, and White House dependence on OLC staff reportedly greatly diminished—a serious mistake, in the eyes of some White House veterans.

The counsel's resources are not limited to White House and Justice circles: he establishes links to every agency. Each department has its own general counsel—and each of these officers, before being appointed, has an interview with the presidential legal staff. In this fashion, and through regular meetings and constant telephone calls, the White House counsel has a hand on the legal network of the entire executive branch.

An early step the counsel takes within the White House is to try to establish exclusive turf, not for selfish reasons but to ensure orderly conduct. To enforce his treaty with the attorney general, the counsel notifies all other White House offices early on that he will be the only channel from the White House to the Justice Department. Nevertheless, there are large holes in that barrier. On basic social, legal, and political issues—such as civil rights, crime, drug-law enforcement, Native American affairs—one or more of the domestic, economic, or specially appointed White House advisers will also play a central role.

The counsel's next task is to send a second warning to his White House colleagues: stay *away* from the independent regulatory commissions and any other agencies that perform regulatory or adjudicatory functions. His injunction may bring to mind Sherman Adams's grief in 1958.[4] Even today, a few Washington veterans remember that incident.

The counsel will raise the same caution with respect to investigative agencies (such as the IRS and the FBI) and procurement offices: "to avoid the appearance of conflict and subsequent embarrassment," not even "status" inquiries are allowed.[5] Finally, the counsel will warn that the intelligence community is off-limits to everyone in the White House except the national security adviser and his cohorts. This quadriad of sober admonitions echoes down the years; the counsel's warning memorandums are the same, almost word-for-word, in each presidency.

Ethics

For a newly elected president and his new White House counsel, ethical issues represent a minefield with which they are likely to be unfamiliar. The counsel is the "ethics officer" for the White House staff, and almost all incoming staff are novices in the federal environment. A few examples show how treacherous is this passage.

When President Clinton asked the first lady to take charge of developing a new health care initiative, was the cabinet task force that she chaired subject to the Federal Advisory Committee Act (FACA)? Under the FACA, unless all task force members were full-time government employees, task force papers would have to be made public. In response to a legal challenge demanding that the task force be held to FACA regulations, the White House counsel argued that the first lady was the "functional equivalent" of a government employee. The U.S. District Court of Appeals later agreed with that categorization, thus immunizing the task force from the FACA requirements.

But did Hillary Rodham Clinton's status as the functional equivalent of a government employee make her a "special government employee": that is, someone who is "retained [or] designated . . . to perform . . . temporary duties?"[6] If so, she might have been subject to the conflict-of-interest laws and could have been criticized for her holdings in Valuepartners—an investment partnership with investments in health care–related companies. The White House counsel, supported by the Office of Government Ethics, ruled that because the health care legislation with which Mrs. Clinton was concerned was so broad, it was not a "particular matter" relating to her investment interests—and that the conflict-of-interest statute was therefore inapplicable in her case.[7]

Was the first lady's health care working group—of some six hundred government employees and outside consultants—subject to the FACA? The White House counsel helped senior staff assistant Ira Magaziner prepare a sworn deposition stating that "only federal government employees serve as members of the interdepartmental working group."[8] The White House's release of the working group's papers rendered the original lawsuit moot— but not a related complaint that Magaziner had committed perjury and that the government had failed to correct the false statement about the working group. District court judge Royce Lamberth was so exasperated by the false-hood and by the government's disingenuousness that he issued an order holding the government, and Magaziner, liable to pay plaintiffs' fees of nearly $300,000.[9]

Beginning early in his administration, President Clinton used the services of a number of outside political consultants, especially Paul Begala, James Carville, Stanley Greenberg, Mandy Grunwald, and Harry Thomason. All had White House passes and attended White House meetings frequently; Thomason had a White House office and phone. A series of congressional inquiries and press stories raised the question of whether such consultants were "special government employees" subject to the financial disclosure and conflict-of-interest rules. As pass-holders, had they undergone the drug test-ing and full-field FBI investigations ordinarily required?

The White House counsel had to help the chief of staff clarify the rules and procedures: these political consultants were not to be considered employ-ees, but as of September 1993 they were to "receive counseling regarding the limits of their roles as political advisers and potential areas of conflict of interest."[10] By July 1, 1994, those who continued to hold White House passes would be required to file disclosure reports. In the spring of 1994, the White House informed the House Appropriations Committee that prospective pass-holders would be given a preliminary security check, a drug test, and a full-field FBI investigation, which the counsel would review before recommending that the Secret Service issue a permanent pass.[11]

Besides advising White House staff about questions of ethics, the White House counsel's office serves, in effect, as the patrol team for all appointees in the executive branch who serve at the president's pleasure. If any of these officers break the ethics rules, the counsel will judge whether the president's displeasure—that is, removal from office—is to be invoked.

The ethics rules, which apply to all federal employees, were first pro-mulgated by President Kennedy in 1961, restated by President Johnson, and again reissued by President Bush.[12] In all three cases, the presidential exec-utive orders required that employees not only adhere to the rules but also avoid even the appearance of violating them.

It was this elevated criterion that was the basis for President Clinton's decision to force the resignation of Secretary of Agriculture Mike Espy in 1994. Four years later, a district court jury acquitted Espy of thirty corrup-tion charges (for acceptance of gratuities) that had been filed against him by Independent Counsel Donald Smaltz. In 1999 the Supreme Court went further and affirmed the acquittal of one of the gift-givers of criminal charges, agreeing with a court of appeals decision that had ruled that there was insufficient proof of an "official act" by Espy that would have benefited the giver.[13] No matter. The mere fact that the gifts had been accepted created *the appearance of impropriety*—and on those grounds alone, Espy was forced out of the cabinet.

Presidential appointees are always giving speeches out of town. Can they accept travel or accommodations if the host is a company "regulated by or doing business with the appointee's agency"? No, and the counsel drafts a White House statement telling them so.[14] Under what conditions may a cabinet secretary or senior White House staff officer use government military aircraft, helicopters, or even limousines? After Chief of Staff Sununu used poor judgment in this regard (and was forced to resign), the White House counsel was tasked with the assignment of ruling on the proprieties.

One other ethical dimension received President Clinton's early attention: postemployment activities of his senior appointees. On the very day of his inauguration in 1993, Clinton issued an executive order requiring any such presidential appointee to sign a four-part pledge: (1) no lobbying of the employee's agency for five years; (2) for former Executive Office employees, no lobbying, for five years, of any government agency on any matter for which the employee had Executive Office responsibility; (3) no lobbying for a foreign government during the employee's lifetime; and (4) for those who had participated in trade negotiations, no giving advice, for five years, to any foreign government or business concerning any current U.S. governmental decisionmaking. The president may waive these requirements for an individual if he finds it "in the public interest" to do so.[15]

A question arises: Will such restrictions discourage potential appointees from accepting political positions in government? A Yale law professor comments, "People who have been in the private sector would have to think a long time before making that kind of foreclosure on their professional involvements."[16]

Vetting Presidential Appointees

One White House aide who constantly looks to the counsel for advice is the director of the Office of Presidential Personnel (OPP). When a presidential appointment is pending, two streams of sensitive data about each top candidate converge at the counsel's desk: financial disclosure statements, including tax returns, and FBI full-field investigation reports. Is everything in order? Has the potential appointee come out reasonably clean from the background investigation, paid all income taxes, paid the required social security tax for household workers? Are there any potential conflicts of interest between the candidate's investments and the prospective federal responsibility? How did the candidate reply to the question, "Is there anything in your past which might embarrass the president?"

It is the counsel who will give the green, yellow, or red light to the OPP. Personnel Office recruiters may feel a certain "pride of authorship" in the candidate they have found; the counsel must be arm's-length and neutral.

Even with FBI reports, the counsel's office is not passive. If a file contains questionable data, the counsel may call in the candidate and give him or her a chance to rebut: some informants pour mere personal spite into their statements to bureau agents. The candidate may supply such convincing exculpatory rejoinders that the counsel will instruct the bureau to include them in its file.

In advance of confirmation hearings, a member of the counsel's staff will, if necessary, hand-carry the FBI reports to the Capitol, and show them to the chairman and ranking minority member of the confirming committee.

Judicial Selection

Some 200 of the 868 federal judgeships typically become vacant during a presidential term. The Office of Presidential Personnel looks to the White House counsel to handle the substantive staff work for selecting nominees for these judgeships (a procedure described in chapter 15). It was President Carter's counsel that initiated this process—essentially a White House group review of nominees. Attorney General Griffin Bell later termed it "such an outrageous intrusion into the prerogatives of the attorney general and such a politicization of the process of selection that I thought of resigning."[17] But the practice went forward anyway, and each succeeding White House has repeated—and solidified—the precedent.

A president's Supreme Court nominations demonstrate, if demonstration is needed, that for such judicial positions, politics and policy are inseparable. The president must be able to depend on his personal staff to help him ascertain not only what kind of legal philosophy he is underwriting in making judicial nominations but also what the confirmation politics are likely to be.

Congressional Actions and Presidential Powers

The counsel is at both ends of the legislative pathway. The office reviews all presidential messages to Congress and particularly inspects any draft statutes that are to be sent up in the name of the president. At the other end of the process, when enrolled bills are sent to the White House, the counsel (along with the Office of Management and Budget and the affected departments) is on the short list of reviewers who, within the ten-day deadline, must examine the bills before the presidential decision to sign or veto. A veto message must, of course, pass the counsel's scrutiny.

If the president agrees to sign the bill, there may be a signing statement, which the counsel must review. When a bill is generally acceptable but contains a provision that the counsel and the president consider to be invasive of presidential constitutional prerogatives, the president may sign it but issue a formal statement giving his judgment that he considers the offending provision to be unconstitutional. For example, when he signed a defense authorization bill late in 1999, President Clinton singled out several constitutionally objectionable sections and defiantly declared, "To the extent that these provisions conflict with my constitutional responsibilities . . . I will construe them where possible to avoid such conflicts, and where it is impossible to do so, I will treat them as advisory. I hereby direct all executive branch officials to do likewise."[18] The counsel scrutinizes each such instance with exceptional care.

Does such presidential recalcitrance deserve judicial or congressional deference? The counsel and the Department of Justice support the chief executive's practice of simultaneously signing a bill and proclaiming that he intends, on constitutional grounds, not to comply with portions of it. The lawyers argue that such statements represent appropriate guidance to implementing agencies. A memorandum to the White House counsel from the head of the OLC concluded: "A signing statement that challenges what the President determines to be an unconstitutional encroachment on his power, or that announces the President's unwillingness to enforce . . . such a provision, can be a valid and reasonable exercise of Presidential authority."[19] A constitutional scholar agrees, especially if the objective is to "protect executive autonomy" or when the subject is foreign affairs.[20] Democratic Congressman Barney Frank, however, called such statements "the gravest usurpation of legislative prerogative I can think of."[21]

Always present is the issue of presidential power. For the two centuries since the Framers first wrestled with the question, Congress, the courts, and the White House have verbally assaulted one another in the course of ongoing disagreements about the extent of presidential authority. How far can it be stretched? More recently, the question has become: What are its proper limits? Outranking perhaps all the counsel's other duties is this one: to represent the office of the president in that continuing constitutional debate.

Before the Supreme Court ruled the legislative veto unconstitutional in 1983, such veto provisions were perennially inserted into bills for the president's signature.[22] Counsels would occasionally recommend presidential vetoes; at other times the chief executive would say, "I am signing this bill but disagreeing with the legislative veto contained in it."

A recurring constitutional debate for contemporary presidents concerns their commander-in-chief role. The 1973 War Powers Resolution was vetoed by President Nixon—who criticized it as unconstitutional—but passed by Congress, which overrode the presidential veto.

Now, under the War Powers Resolution, whenever U.S. forces are to be in action overseas, the White House counsel immediately convenes the general counsels of State and Defense and representatives from Justice and the National Security Council staff. Are the forces being introduced into "situations where imminent involvement in hostilities is clearly indicated by the circumstances"? If so, the president is supposed to notify Congress, and a sixty-day clock (extendable to ninety days) begins to run: unless Congress passes authorizing legislation in the meantime, the troops must be removed before the sixty (or ninety) days have elapsed. (Congress, acting alone, can force the removal of the troops at any time.) State usually argues in favor of notification; Defense almost always opposes. The counsel will try to widen the area of presidential flexibility. If notification must be made, the president's letter to Congress may say that he is acting "consistent with" rather than "pursuant to" the War Powers Resolution—a signal that the White House continues to have reservations, on constitutional grounds, about that 1973 enactment.

President Bush's advisers were divided about whether he should seek congressional sanction for the use of U.S. forces in the Desert Storm engagement. His White House counsel, Boyden Gray, along with Vice President Quayle, argued that the president had an obligation to request congressional backing. Bush believed that he should get an expression of congressional support but that formal congressional authorization was not constitutionally necessary. The measure he fought for—and got—was a sanction of the use of force pursuant to the United Nations Security Council's resolution, which called upon member states to "use all necessary means to . . . restore international peace and security in the area."[23]

Presidential Pardons

The Constitution gives the president the power, with practically unlimited discretion, to commute sentences and grant pardons for those convicted of federal crimes (a pardon restores the rights to vote and hold office). Papers associated with this routine but ancient responsibility fill up every counsel's in-box.

The hundreds of applications—which are usually not even accepted until five years after a lawbreaker's sentence has been completed—are sent first to the Department of Justice, where the pardon attorney makes the first-cut analysis. Priority is given to nonviolent offenders convicted of minor crimes who can demonstrate that they have been law-abiding citizens since their release. An assistant attorney general gives a second review, and for each case sends a "letter of advice" to the president, accompanied by a three- to fifteen-page summary of the background. The counsel's staff considers every case that makes it to this level. The White House usually follows the recommendation from Justice, but on occasion reverses it in favor of denial, "to protect," in a former counsel's words, "the reputation and integrity of the office of the president."

In his first six years in office, President Clinton received nearly 4,000 petitions but granted only 77—or 2 percent—compared with Truman's 42 percent. A president of course bears responsibility before the public for his decisions on pardons. Some are newsworthy; a few—such as Ford's pardon of Nixon and Bush's pardon of six Iran-Contra figures—raise widespread outrage.

Presidential Disability

Any illness of the president creates a quiver on the counsel's voltmeter. If the president should be gravely ill, or if surgery with general anesthesia is in prospect or under way, the question that must be immediately addressed is whether, under the Twenty-fifth Amendment to the Constitution, the president is or will be "unable to discharge the powers and duties of his office." If it is determined that the answer is yes, either the president must transmit a written declaration to this effect to the Speaker of the House and the President Pro Tempore of the Senate, or the vice president and a majority of the cabinet must do so.[24]

Reagan counsel Fred Fielding had started to compile an "emergency book" to cover the contingencies of presidential illness, but it had not been completed by the fateful day of March 30, 1981, when the president was shot during an assassination attempt. "When I mentioned the Twenty-fifth Amendment I could see eyes glazing over in some parts of the Cabinet," Fielding recalled.[25] Readers will remember the sorry confusion that then ensued. Thereafter the counsel promptly finished the book, and its value was apparent when, three years later, Reagan underwent abdominal surgery and invoked the amendment for the first time. At 10:32 on the morning of July 18, 1984, he signed the following letter to the Speaker and the President Pro Tempore:

> I am about to undergo surgery during which time I will be briefly and temporarily incapable of discharging the Constitutional powers and duties of the office of the President of the United States.
>
> After consultation with my counsel and the Attorney General, I am mindful of the provisions of Section 3 of the 25th Amendment to the Constitution and of the uncertainties of its application to such brief and temporary periods of incapacity. I do not believe that the drafters of this Amendment intended its application to situations such as the instant one.
>
> Nevertheless, consistent with my long-standing arrangement with Vice President George Bush and not intending to set a precedent binding anyone privileged to hold this office in the future, I have determined and it is my intention and direction that Vice President George Bush should discharge those powers and duties in my stead commencing with the administration of anesthesia to me in this instance.[26]

At 7:22 the same evening, Reagan signed a letter to the same addressees, reclaiming his presidential powers and duties. The counsel, presumably closely in touch with the vice president, the attorney general, the president's physicians, the chief of staff, and the first lady, was intensely involved in the preparation and dispatch of these two letters.

During the Bush administration, Counsel Boyden Gray and other White House associates elaborated on the emergency book so that it became a "very comprehensive road map" that goes through "every significant hypothetical, from a president being killed to having a hernia operation." It offers step-by-step guidance on who should be called, by whom, in what order; who should take over what duties; at what point power should be passed temporarily to the vice president; and which procedures to follow to accomplish all that needs to be done.

Copies were placed in the safes of the White House chief of staff, the White House physician, the White House counsel, the vice president's chief of staff, the head of the Secret Service, and a few others. When Bush left office, copies were given to Clinton officials; Clinton adopted the Bush procedures.[27]

When President Bush went to the hospital with a thyroid problem in May of 1991, "the whole thing went very, very smoothly," said Gray.[28]

Defending the President

In the Clinton administration, the counsel's priorities were forced into a narrow and terribly time-consuming quarter: defense of the president, the first lady, and the White House as an institution against a six-year-long avalanche of subpoenas from independent counsels, grand juries, and congressional investigating committees. The counsel also represented the president during the impeachment proceedings.

The business of defending Clinton did more than gobble up 75 percent of the White House counsel's time and human resources: it resulted in three significant victories but four important losses for the president in cases before the judiciary and Congress. These victories and losses bear directly on the functioning and operation of the White House.

The first victory was on the question of whether the well-established protection of executive privilege for presidential communications applied only to documents that the president had personally seen or whether notes and papers merely exchanged among his staff advisers were also privileged. A unanimous panel of three in the District of Columbia Court of Appeals ruled in favor of the wider privilege:

> These predecisional documents are usually highly revealing as to the evolution of advisors' positions and as to the different policy options considered along the way. If these materials are not protected by the presidential privilege, the President's access to candid and informed advice could well be significantly circumscribed. . . . If presidential advisors must assume they will be held to account publicly for all approaches that were advanced, considered, but ultimately rejected, they will almost inevitably be inclined to avoid serious consideration of novel or controversial approaches to presidential problems. . . .

Given the President's dependence on presidential advisors . . . we conclude that limiting the privilege . . . would indeed impede effective
functioning of the presidency.[29]

The first loss was in a case decided by a divided Eighth Circuit Court of
Appeals in May of 1997. The question was whether notes made by two
White House associate counsels in a meeting with the first lady concerning
the Whitewater affair (allegedly a criminal matter), for which the independent counsel had issued a subpoena, were covered by the equally
well-established attorney-client privilege or should be handed over to a
grand jury. In its ruling against the White House, the court said:

> We believe the strong public interest in honest government and in
> exposing wrongdoing by public officials would be ill-served by recog-
> nition of a governmental attorney-client privilege applicable in crim-
> inal proceedings inquiring into the actions of public officials. We also
> believe that to allow any part of the federal government to use its in-
> house attorneys as a shield against the production of information rel-
> evant to a federal criminal investigation would represent a gross misuse
> of public assets. . . .
>   An official who fears he or she may have violated the criminal law
> and wishes to speak with an attorney in confidence should speak with
> a private attorney, not a government attorney.[30]

The second victory came during the investigations of the Monica Lewinsky affair. The independent counsel argued that the White House claim of
executive privilege for conversations between two senior White House officers and the president "applies only to communications regarding official
presidential matters." At the outset of its opinion, the district court recalled
that "no court has ever declined to treat executive communications as pre-
sumptively privileged on the grounds that the matters discussed involved
private conduct," and negated the independent counsel's narrow position,
citing a Nixon-era case: "A President's communications and activities encompass a vastly wider range of sensitive material than would be true of any
'ordinary individual' [and] it is therefore necessary in the public interest to
afford Presidential confidentiality the greatest protection consistent with the
fair administration of justice."[31]

The district court later went on to overrule the executive privilege defense
on other grounds, but since neither side appealed that first finding in the
opinion, it stands—and provides a significant additional protection to inter-

nal White House communications.[32] In the same case, the court ruled against the White House on its second claim—of attorney-client privilege—and the White House did appeal that part of the opinion.

This appeal resulted in the second loss for the White House, in the District of Columbia Court of Appeals in July of 1998, before a divided panel of three. The question was whether a "government attorney-client privilege" can shield a White House attorney from answering a federal grand jury's questions about possible criminal conduct by government officials. The court said that it cannot, and reminded the White House that government lawyers, unlike private attorneys, bear not the responsibility of defending clients against criminal charges, but bear, like "all members of the Executive Branch," the constitutional duty to "take care that the laws be faithfully executed." The court concluded: "A government attorney, even one holding the title Deputy White House Counsel, may not assert an attorney-client privilege before a federal grand jury if communications with the client contain information pertinent to possible criminal violations."[33]

The third loss was when the Supreme Court refused to consider both of the cases just described, in spite of the fact that three former counsels to the president and two former attorneys general submitted an *amicus* brief for the second of the two. Their brief stated that if the Eighth Circuit decision were allowed to stand, "government officials will be uncertain as to the confidentiality of such communications and will be less willing to seek full and frank legal advice from government lawyers concerning official government business."[34]

But that Eighth Circuit decision stands, and the White House must now live in this environment of legal ambiguity.

The fourth loss occurred when the Supreme Court refused to hear the government's appeal of two lower court rulings that the Secret Service agents in the president's protective detail could not, under present law, invoke a "protective function privilege" and could not refuse to tell a grand jury about private presidential conversations that they may have overheard or private actions that they may have witnessed. The White House had appealed, out of concern that if the rulings stood, a president might be inclined to distance himself from his bodyguards and thereby diminish the essential physical protection he requires. The Secret Service may propose a statute that it hopes will remedy this deficiency. (Part 3 includes further discussion of this subject.)

Looking back at the chain of unfavorable decisions, a Republican veteran of the OLC wondered aloud whether the Court's "evident distrust" of the Clinton administration will be long-lasting. And a *Washington Post* columnist wrote of the "attenuation of presidential privilege" in a column entitled "Will the Presidency Ever Be the Same?"[35]

Distinguished former counsel to the president Lloyd Cutler opines that, in effect, it may not:

> The temptation of the president and his political advisers is, even though you could refuse to produce these documents on the grounds of executive privilege, since they *do* constitute advice and communications with the president—and that would be better for the institution as a whole—the short-term political consequences of doing it are so adverse—"He's covering up!"—that "executive privilege" has virtually disappeared. One result is that few if any people now give written advice to the president. And the president doesn't make notes himself or request much advice in writing. . . . But even if he talks to you now . . . he has to be circumspect, because it is not only notes and memos that are now subject to examination, at least by a grand jury or an independent counsel, but also the recollections of a person in the White House about what the president told him or asked him or what he said to the president. . . . I will bet the farm no future president is going to keep a diary!
>
> The subpoenas and demands have just grown exponentially and have not only caused an enormous increase in the number of people in the White House counsel's office, but this has also brought the White House counsel into a free-fire zone, where he is criticized no matter what he does. . . . That is a challenge to the professional ethic of the White House counsel and his staff. That is a new phenomenon; it wasn't true in my time, in the Carter administration, when we only had six people.
>
> What it amounts to . . . is that there is now a camera—a television camera, for all practical purposes—in every room, in the Oval Office, and the rest of the West Wing.[36]

The author was assistant cabinet secretary under Eisenhower. Every Monday morning the approved record of action from the Friday cabinet meetings was circulated to all the departments. In this way, all the cabinet secretaries and their top staff members knew the substance of the president's views and what their own assignments were. In eight years, there was only one leak— and no subpoena for a record of action was ever issued. Today no such decision memorandums are circulated outside of the White House, and fewer and fewer within it—a circumstance that has arguably diminished the effectiveness of presidential public administration.

Miscellaneous Duties

The counsel is among the senior White House staffers who are regularly asked to review draft presidential speeches. Here, deadline clocks tick insistently: a new version will arrive even before the counsel staffer has finished inspecting the one before. "Those speechwriters aim for soaring rhetoric," smiled one staff veteran. "We want to minimize error."

Hundreds of gifts pour in to the first family from Americans and from abroad; counsel staff advise on the proprieties of acceptance.

In selfish calculation or in innocence, entrepreneurs and advertisers will use the president's name or some official-looking White House label as a magnet to attract sales. A catalogue features T-shirts emblazoned with the American eagle motif, surrounded by the words *Presidential Flight Crew: Air Force One*. Even though the shirts do not display the prohibited presidential seal, the White House counsel is nonetheless likely to notify the merchant that his goods are at or over the line.

During a presidential reelection campaign, the legal binoculars are trained on the connections between the reelection committee and the White House staff: Which one pays for the plane ticket when a staffer delivers an out-of-town speech? How are the expenses of *Air Force One* to be apportioned between campaign and government ledgers? Any misjudgment could mean a dangerous political embarrassment.

Demonstrators and protesters stream into town and head for the White House gates, petitions in hand. Should White House staff members invite them in for a confab? In previous administrations, protesters who were allowed within the White House gates had ended up staging sit-ins. In an advisory to his colleagues, a former chief of staff required that the counsel be informed in advance of the petitioners' arrival so that staffers could be briefed about the group's background if necessary, and Secret Service or other law enforcement teams could be forewarned.

The White House is hypersensitive about criminal matters. If any federal law enforcement agency has a suspect under investigation, the counsel tries to ensure that the suspect doesn't appear on any White House invitation lists. If a staff member is alleged to have committed a criminal transgression, White House counsel can be of no help because a statute requires all government lawyers and law enforcement officers to report any knowledge of crimes to the attorney general. The staffer must usually obtain—and pay for—outside private counsel.

If a flood decimates a county's bridges or crops, petitions for federal disaster relief roll in. The counsel reviews them before any presidential action is taken.

When they prepare briefings for outside groups in support of presidential legislative initiatives, White House public liaison officers will ask the counsel how far they can go to try to convert audience enthusiasm into pressure on Congress. There is a statutory prohibition on spending appropriated funds to engage in such pressure, and the counsel will warn the White House staffers that they must temper commitment with caution.[37] Lists of "targeted legislators" have sometimes been drawn up—but not on White House letterhead.

Policy issues—many of them heavy with political as well as legal tonnage—demand the counsel's attention. Boyden Gray was expert on, concerned about, and deeply involved in the major legal questions inherent in the civil rights and environmental disputes that arose during the Bush presidency, although initially his time was mostly taken up with untangling the backlog of presidential appointments. Eventually, Gray had the time, as well as the president's support, to immerse himself in policy development and may have done so more than any White House counsel before or since.

At the end of a presidency, the White House counsel's office retains a very limited number of documents that are passed on to the next administration. These include the emergency book, memorandums regarding ethics, the proprieties governing contacts with regulatory and investigative agencies, and the rules about what are and what are not "official records." Also preserved is a collection of the most significant opinions from the Office of Legal Counsel on constitutional issues affecting the presidency.

No one counsel uniform fits all, nor can one chapter describe all. The "Just-Us Department" is a flexible resource: each president will employ it in infinite variation. White House Counsels Leonard Garment and J. Fred Buzhardt defended Nixon in the Watergate litigation. Lloyd Cutler was asked by President Carter to play a role in the negotiations for the Strategic Arms Limitation Treaty, and Cutler spent uncounted days in the international financial footwork that preceded the release of the U.S. hostages from Iran. During the Senate impeachment trial of President Clinton, Counsel Charles Ruff and Deputy Counsel Cheryl Mills personally carried the case for the president's defense on the floor of the upper body.

Some presidents short-circuit their lawyers: the Reagan Iran-Contra enterprise was not checked with the president's counsel at all. Although the counsel function is a fifty-year-old tradition, it is still supple, still "very unstructured," as Cutler observed, and always subject to the president's management style.

The counsel is an intergenerational person: protecting the sitting president, summoning past precedents to do so, and serving as a steward for the presidency of the future. As noted earlier, however, the presidents of tomorrow may find themselves operating in a very different—and more constrictive—legal environment than the presidents of the past.

CHAPTER SEVEN

Legislative Affairs: "An Ambulatory Bridge across a Constitutional Gulf"

White House special counsel Lanny J. Davis stood in the middle of the House committee room making one venomous accusation after another. Republicans investigating campaign finance reform were "abusing their subpoena power" in a "hypocritical exercise" designed to "bankrupt" the Democratic Party, he said. "This investigation cannot be taken seriously as a search for the truth."
GUY GUGLIOTTA AND SUSAN SCHMIDT, IN THE *Washington Post*

By nightfall, the president had sent a team of defense, diplomatic and legal aides to meet with senior Dole staff members, who quickly narrowed differences to such critical issues as whether any legally binding restraints could be put on Clinton's constitutional powers as commander in chief. White House congressional lobbyist Howard Paster virtually lived at the Capitol for the next two days as the two sides gradually came together, working both with Dole and key Democrats.
HELEN DEWAR, IN THE *Washington Post*

The gulf between the Capitol and the White House is not always the constitutional one. As the epigraphs to this chapter reveal, it yawns within the White House itself. Fire across—or reach across—the partisan boundaries?

The winners in this venerable debate are usually the president's legislative affairs leaders—the "ambulatory bridge," as the late and respected Bryce Harlow, an Eisenhower assistant, called them. As long as Congress is

114

closely divided—and especially if the party opposing the president controls either house—the system can't work without two-way cooperation. Every federal program must have the imprimatur of Congress; every dime the executive branch spends must pass congressional muster; hundreds of senior appointees and dozens of treaties require Senate approval. The White House is engaged in a never-ending process of persuasion.

The weight of this fact is not brought home by any campaign experience, however. "Congressional relationships are almost nonexistent in a campaign," commented one presidential aide.[1] The importance, therefore, of building effective relationships with legislators must be recognized—and hopefully quickly—as the White House staff is shaped during the frantic preinaugural days.

The Office of Legislative Affairs

Ever since the Eisenhower administration, the White House has had a special office that supports the president in his efforts at legislative persuasion. The Office of Legislative Affairs has been headed by an assistant to the president with, typically, a staff of up to thirty-five, including interns and volunteers. Its director has occupied treasured space in the West Wing. In addition to the ability to call on the president's personal participation, what are the other resources of the Legislative Affairs Office, and how does it use them?

The office has historically been divided into those who work with the Senate and those who work with the House; one staffer concentrates on getting nominees confirmed by the Senate (some eighteen hundred have to run that gauntlet within the course of a presidential term). The Clinton legislative affairs staff included a "special events" person who made sure that the right members of Congress were invited to presidential ceremonies on the South Lawn or in the Rose Garden—and that when the president traveled, the appropriate senators or representatives either had seats on *Air Force One* or were included in the VIP group that greeted the president on his arrival. ("CODELS"—congressional delegations that undertake "inspection" trips abroad—are ensured proper reception and "handling" by the often over-burdened American diplomatic posts in the countries that are visited.)

Further specialization within the Legislative Affairs Office has been in accordance with either the congressional committees being covered or the issues that were pending. The legislative affairs officers are not strangers to those issues: by sitting in on White House policy meetings and budget reviews, they will have provided the administration's policy planners with "reality therapy." And their warnings—"This will not fly"—will usually have been heeded.

When it was clear that there would have to be a vote in both the Senate and the House on the Desert Storm engagement, the Department of State warned the White House that opposition on the Hill was so strong that it might prevail. The White House legislative office disagreed with that estimate, and a bipartisan meeting with the House leadership was arranged in the chief of staff's office. Compromise was reachable: after the meeting, Bush legislative affairs director Nick Calio recalls, "We went over into the Roosevelt Room and sat down with [Democratic] representatives Robert Toricelli and Stephen Solarz and some of our people and basically drafted the authorizing resolution. Working with them, we created an ad hoc Democratic work group."[2]

At the Capitol the White House legislative liaison staff try to cover all the strategic bases. In Calio's words, "The most important thing was, we were on Capitol Hill all the time—I mean, all the time. We became familiar sights; people on both sides of the aisle were very comfortable with seeing us; they expected to see us. They consequently would talk to us, all the time. You didn't have to bargain to get a conversation, to find out what somebody was thinking. You would assimilate the information and thus keep your finger on the pulse and sense the mood and have a feel for what was going on."[3]

Calio's White House agents were assiduous: "We hung out all over; we would place ourselves all over the Capitol. When the bells went off, the call was: Who's taking elevators? Who's taking subway? Who's taking stairs? We would cover all of them. We also could get into places where most lobbyists couldn't get. On the House side we had people at the top of the steps, right where members come in; we had other people at the bottom, where the elevators were, then down by the subways where they were coming across. We covered all the doors. We would catch 'em everywhere."[4]

Why such a race to buttonhole members in person? It is a lesson long learned by White House legislative affairs staff: it's the only way to get an accurate advance vote count. They must relay a very precise estimate back to the team at home base so that last-minute presidential or cabinet calls can be made in time to those members considered amenable. When fence-sitters are identified, the legislative affairs officers want to go past the members' staffs and talk directly with the senators or representatives. Only thus can the legislative staffers be confident that their head counts are accurate and can be relied upon when the time comes for last-minute personal persuasion of the dissenters. If it is a cabinet member who is to make the phone contact, the call will be placed through the White House switchboard: the first voice the member hears will say, "The White House calling."

The White House has no office of its own at the Capitol, so the liaison group—equipped, of course, with pagers and cell phones—uses the vice president's suite on the Senate side, and the offices of their party's leadership at the House, as temporary command centers. In both places, television monitors provide live coverage of the floor action in both chambers, so the White House staffers can, if need be, follow every speech and every vote. In these command centers and from other "Hill rats" (congressional staffers with long-standing Capitol ties), legislative affairs staff can pick up scuttlebutt, rumors, even what congressional insiders call "minute notices"—that is, advance word that the opposing party leader is about to come onto the floor and make some sudden, important announcement. This gives the White House agent about one minute to call home base and tell White House colleagues to pay attention to the C-SPAN House or Senate monitors (which are going live in the White House legislative affairs suites as well)—and avoid being caught napping.

Clinton legislative affairs chief Pat Griffin, highly respected at the Capitol because of his former service with the Senate Budget Committee and his experience as secretary to the Democrats under Senator Robert Byrd, was invited to attend Democratic Whip meetings—closed-door sessions where legislative strategy was hammered out. Griffin recalls: "I had a relationship with them; they knew I was leveling with them. They knew what my job was, and I had enough respect for them to face them and tell them, 'Well, we can't do that,' or 'We're not going to do that.' And sometimes they were rude, and sometimes I was rude, I guess. But I think all involved knew what they had to do."[5]

For the legislative affairs staffers, the end of the day in Congress is only another beginning. Their East Wing offices then become an "elves' factory" where they produce briefings and bios of members scheduled to meet the president in the near future, write up one-pagers as background for presidential phone calls, and query agencies about the status of an issue or project.

One brand of White House pressure is called "the hotfoot." If a legislator in the president's party is "leaning against" the president, calls may be made back home—to the state party chairperson and to the offending lawmaker's major contributors. The message is: "Look what your man is doing to our president! You'd better counsel him." Early in his administration, after one of his handball partners complained about the practice, President Bush gave firm orders to his public liaison, political, and legislative staffs to cease and desist using such methods in the grass roots. They did—until close votes came up on issues such as Desert Storm, capital gains, and "fast track" trade agreements legislation—at which point every last vote was pursued. The Clinton agents tried this technique during the health care debates, but the current legislative affairs director observed, "We had varying success because it was real easy to make it too 'hot' where the thing would blow up against you. Core majorities were so thin."[6]

At the end of each week, the legislative affairs director and his staff typically composed a succinct weekly report for the president, with copies to the White House senior staff. As he did with the other reports that came to him, President Clinton would scribble all over his copy, marking items to be sent to cabinet officers ("Did you know about this?") and to staff associates ("Why aren't you following this more closely?" or "I want you to work harder on this!"). He would make substantive comments as well, which provided his legislative affairs squad leaders with extra guidance for their encounters during the coming week.

The President as Persuader in Chief

Seniormost stroller across that ambulatory bridge is the president himself, on both formal and informal occasions. President Bush (who was a former congressman) would go up to the Capitol to play handball with former colleagues on the indoor court, and never missed the regular "gym dinners" where the athletic senators and representatives shared steak, baked potatoes, and small talk. President Clinton made several trips to the Hill, meeting informally with both friends and opponents. The Family Theater affords the president the opportunity to invite legislators to view the very latest releases, and the relaxing scenery of Camp David is occasionally used as a balm for legislative soreness.

The principal, more formal, and usually more common bridge-crossings occur when the president hosts meetings in the Cabinet Room of the congressional leadership: either sessions with his party leadership on domestic questions or bipartisan consultations on foreign affairs issues (most of Clinton's were of this type). The legislative affairs staffers sniff out the agenda from cabinet, Capitol, or White House sources and prepare briefing memorandums for the president.

Another type of meeting combines a group of supporters with some fence-sitters; the supporters are "seeded to say specific things," remembers one former officer, "so it wasn't only the White House doing the advocacy."[7] Even before the session is convened, White House liaison staffers will confer on the Hill with selected attendees, to help ensure that when the meeting breaks up the president's supporters will communicate the "right message" in front of the press microphones outside the door. At Eisenhower's every-Tuesday-morning congressional leadership meetings, private minutes were taken. That practice has ended. "We don't create paper trails," noted a recent staffer.[8]

If a close vote impends in the House or Senate, the legislative affairs chief will alert the president and provide talking points for phone calls to key members. Given a list of, say, ten names, President Clinton would make the calls late at night from the Residence—but he so enjoyed some of the encounters that he would spend forty-five minutes on just one of them. The next morning, Betty Currie, Clinton's personal secretary, would let the liaison office know which calls the White House operator had placed.

Sometimes the vote is so close and the need for a call so intense that it can't wait until evening. It is then that the legislative staffer's most treasured asset is tested: immediate access to the president. This is the indispensable attribute that a very few White House staffers must have: without it, the liaison office lacks full credibility on the Hill.

The Whole White House as a Persuasion Resource

The Legislative Affairs Office doesn't work all by itself: the entire White House team can be enlisted to help.

The chief of staff is unavoidably entangled in the relationship between the president and Congress. Senators and representatives, calling on highly important matters, may often be unable to reach the president on the phone but will then wish to talk directly to the chief of staff as the next-best alternative. But how often can a chief of staff—whose job is to manage the whole institution of the White House—let himself get drawn into doing the work of any one part of it? As the Bush legislative affairs director warned,

> Every chief of staff learns on his own that he needs the interposition of other people between him and the Hill, because, quite frankly, if members can call the chief of staff all the time, they will never call the head of legislative affairs. And if they can get to the president, they'll

never call the chief of staff. There were some times when John Sununu did, and later Sam Skinner tried to interpose themselves in areas where they were not needed. I think each learned in his own way that this was not a good idea.[9]

President Clinton's first chief of staff, "Mack" McLarty, espoused a somewhat different view:

> I don't think that some engagement, and hands-on interface, in certain areas where you have some value to add, is at all inappropriate for a chief of staff. . . . For me not to be active in economic matters with the business community, or with members of Congress whom I had known . . . would have been unnatural. . . . When you had a [Senate majority leader] George Mitchell calling you, saying "Mack, it looks to me that you can meet with Boren and Breaux and Lieberman and get more done than I can. We need you in this meeting," you're crazy not to respond.[10]

Chief of Staff Leon Panetta spent hours on the Hill negotiating budget agreements with the Republicans. He had been director of the Office of Management and Budget (OMB), and before that, he had been chairman of the House Budget Committee. Panetta knew budget issues inside and out—and knew that these were the biggest issues on the president's agenda. Before meeting with members of Congress, Panetta would convene OMB and White House policymakers in his office to clarify just where they thought the administration might compromise and where it could not. He would present the choices to the president and ascertain exactly what Clinton's preferences and priorities were—and where he would not yield. Members on the Hill, in turn, knew Panetta well: he had forged bonds with many of them. At the White House Panetta had two strong deputy chiefs of staff to manage his in-house duties. And every step he took on the Hill was coordinated with the legislative affairs director.

As a result of this close cooperation, legislative affairs chief Pat Griffin could say, "At first I didn't know how it was going to work—whether I would be squeezed out. It turned out that, based on the trust that developed, I welcomed him [Panetta] and this relationship empowered me in some ways. . . . I also had my own relationships on the Hill, before Leon. I actually had a much stronger relationship with the Senate than he did. . . . So together it turned out to be a real team effort."[11]

The relationship between Chief of Staff Erskine Bowles and his legislative affairs director, John Hilley, was similar: they would check back and forth with each other constantly. Either or both would call majority leader Trent Lott; either or both would call Speaker Newt Gingrich. As Bowles learned more and more of the budget details, he grew more and more expert and ended up handling budget negotiations on the Hill personally, much as Panetta had done. Like Panetta, Bowles had two experienced deputies in his chief of staff's office.

This three-way relationship will always be a tender one—to be negotiated anew among president, chief of staff, and legislative affairs director. The Clinton triad created a model to be emulated.

Like the chief of staff, other senior White House policy officers almost never testify at congressional hearings.[12] Also like him, however, they consider it part of their normal duty to meet informally with key committee chairs, members, and staff to explain and defend the president's proposals. National security advisers, such as Brent Scowcroft and Samuel (Sandy) Berger; and domestic policy heads, such as Roger Porter, Bruce Reed, and Gene Sperling, had the expertise and the credibility to explain and interpret the president's objectives in the programs they were shepherding. Often the issue would concern the specific language of a bill or a resolution: by suggesting acceptable amendments, the White House policy officers would help members and staffers on the Hill shape and draft compromises.

Legislative liaison staff members went with the senior policy officers or were informed about the meetings ahead of time and filled in afterwards. Pat Griffin comments: "I didn't try to control. . . . I encouraged people to go up; I encouraged cooperation; I didn't have enough staff. . . . We wound up being able to utilize folks, often with and in cooperation with my folks, but they always reported back, because if they wanted to be in the loop, they had to come back through me anyway."[13]

There is one danger, however: Scowcroft and Berger were in one category, but as veteran White House legislative assistant Tim Keating warned, there were younger White House assistants—"what we jokingly used to call 'junior legislative affairs staff,' meaning anybody who had ever worked on the Hill, even as an intern"—who would have drinks with a legislative assistant and would then say, "'Heck, I can go and lobby Congress!' That was a source of great frustration, because people like that don't realize that they can do damage. They are not speaking for the administration. That's *our* job."[14]

Mail from the Hill

In the Clinton White House, as was typical in past administrations, congressional mail to the president was snared in a special net—a legislative correspondence office, which was part of the legislative affairs staff. The mail was logged into computers, acknowledged, summarized for the president, and then routed for response. If a letter raised an important question about administration policy, got into budget territory, or dealt with a matter that was likely to end up in the courts, a special procedure was used. The legislative office would make a recommendation on who should sign the response (the president, the chief of staff, the director of the OMB?), whereupon it would usually be referred to OMB's own Office of Legislative Affairs. If the subject raised in the letter was a bill that had finished with the congressional committee process and was already on its way to the floor of either house, a careful substantive reply would be drafted, then submitted to several White House senior officers: one of the policy directors, the counsel, the legislative affairs head, the vice president, or the chief of staff. In the case of internal controversy, the chief of staff would host a meeting, or a conference call would be arranged to reach agreement. The president, even if he would not be signing the letter, would review and approve the final response. Less complicated queries would be handled more informally, but all congressional mail would be answered. President Clinton was a stickler for promptness on this score.

Help from the Vice President

The vice president is a resource for the White House Office of Legislative Affairs. Except for Spiro Agnew and Nelson Rockefeller, all vice presidents since 1944 have had experience serving in Congress. Every vice president also, of course, has a special constitutional link to the Senate (giving him the privilege of one or two office suites on Capitol Hill).

The legislative affairs director typically enlists the vice president's help. Vice President Quayle, for instance, regularly attended the Tuesday Republican caucus luncheons—"real bitch sessions," one participant recalls—giving Quayle very useful information about gripes and priorities: "We used Dan Quayle a lot. He didn't publicly get the credit, but Dan had real good political sense, and had good relationships with a lot of members. He was also willing to get his hands dirty in the sense of talking with people, making calls, doing anything he could. We did use him as a resource."[15]

Clinton legislative assistant Keating describes Gore similarly: "The vice president is about as good on the telephone as anyone I've seen. He is direct; he is very to the point. He's got an edge when he wants to get something done. He is very intense—a great lobbyist."[16] Griffin remembers Gore's technique on the phone: "What we need is this. Are you with me?"

Help from the First Lady

At the beginning of the Clinton administration, the first lady—as will be described in chapter 18—played a starring role on that ambulatory bridge to Congress. Even on issues other than health care, she was attentive to congressional interests: making congratulatory or condolence calls, including members in events she sponsored at the White House, notifying members when she traveled to their districts. Her interests in the Gulf war veterans' illnesses and in children's health took her to the Hill frequently, often without publicity.

Political Appointments: How Important?

Senators and representatives are naturally interested in patronage: they have friends who are on the hunt for executive branch political appointments. When it comes to appointments, the White House lobbyists find themselves being lobbied—caught between Congress and the White House Office of Presidential Personnel. The horse trading, however, may turn out to be of limited value to either side. Keating comments:

> Have I helped members of Congress place people? The answer is yes. They call up and say it is important, and you work it and get it through the system. We try to help them out. Sometimes the answer is no if they were trying to peddle someone who was just not qualified. . . . I don't think I have ever had a member say, "I will vote with you if you get X person a job." I don't think there is anybody who has ever had that big a priority. They might list patronage as one of three or four things they needed help with but I think the key was just, "Help me."
> . . . If they believe you will truly help them you don't have to deliver right away, on anything.[17]

In the final two years of the Clinton administration, the issue with Congress was less one of selecting appointees than of securing Senate confirmation for those who had been nominated. Much of the trading was between the Senate Judiciary Committee and the White House: "We will hold hearings on your nominees if you send us up an appointee that we like."

And from Every Corner of the White House

From other principal offices in the White House come favors, privileges, goodies, and benefits—which, carefully controlled, can be distributed to bolster the efforts of the legislative affairs staff.

The Office of Public Liaison, for example, can dovetail its constituency briefings with whatever are the legislative priorities: if a member has an important group coming to Washington from the home district or state, special briefing sessions can be arranged in the White House Indian Treaty Room. The visitors are impressed and the congressional sponsors grateful.

If, after a chat with the president, a representative or senator who is "leaning favorable" makes the jump to open support, the Press Office will shepherd the member into the White House Briefing Room, there to have his endorsement confirmed on camera—and to lock in the commitment.

The staff secretary will see to it that the speechwriters invite the legislative affairs staff to comment on the drafts of presidential addresses.

The legislative affairs deputy will sit in on scheduling committee meetings so that presidential events can be designed to support legislative initiatives. A half hour (or even an hour) every month may be routinely reserved for photo opportunities for lawmakers and the president. The Legislative Affairs Office will determine which members will be so favored and will brief the president beforehand to put in a persuasive word after the photographer has finished shooting.

The White House Social Office will normally reserve several places at each state dinner for couples from Congress. "You can't *imagine* how important that is to senators and representatives," exclaimed a legislative veteran. The Legislative Affairs Office recommends who the lucky invitees are to be. "That was tough," commented another. "State dinners and all that; I was always fighting for my share." For his part, Bush's legislative affairs chief Calio remembers:

> There is a whole range of things you have to negotiate with the Social Office, because it tries to be strict about what you can do: receptions, and who can be invited. The Congressional Picnic, for instance: we were told we could only have one person from each leadership office.

I just invited whom I wanted and checked them in an hour and a half early "for a meeting" in my own suite. The Social Office knows what its job is; it has a certain aspect of the presidency to protect. You have disagreements, but you talk it out and you get it done amicably.[18]

As was mentioned earlier, a small group of seats will be saved on *Air Force One* for favored members of Congress—sometimes even from among the opposition—to accompany the president when he travels. A legislative affairs officer joins the advance teams that plan those trips. The Secret Service, Calio remembers, did not want to permit the legislative office to give out advance word on the Hill of presidential travel, but there was usually a leak and the press would telephone a surprised member of Congress: "We understand the president is coming to your district. You'll be on the plane, won't you?"

"It was the hottest thing I experienced in the whole time I was there," smiled Griffin, recounting the time he had to choose between two desirous representatives: the one who was running for a Senate seat got the nod. Things were easier when the occasion was the funeral of Prime Minister Itzhak Rabin, in Israel. Two extra planes were added, to follow the president: one the Legislative Affairs Office filled with members of Congress, the second the Political Affairs Office filled with political supporters. Still, all the invitees really wanted to fly only on *Air Force One*.

Each of the three Kennedy Center halls has a presidential box, complete with anteroom and stocked refrigerator (the theater box seats twelve, the others eight). Kennedy Center seats are a perk relished by presidential friends all over town. Staff in the Legislative Affairs Office are often given control over those seats, and will escort members of Congress (with their spouses) who have been especially helpful in moving the presidential program. "I have seen *Phantom of the Opera* about ten times," recalls Keating, "and *Guys and Dolls* almost as often. But that is part of doing your job."[19] "I had the president's box every week," explains Griffin, "on Thursday evenings. It didn't 'deliver the goods,' but if you are building relationships, it helped!"[20]

On the occasion of meetings and conventions, the president may be asked to send a personal greeting; the White House has a special unit in the Correspondence Office that produces such messages (see part 3). The text may be merely pro forma or a flowery encomium for a member of Congress who is present. The Legislative Affairs Office will have a hand in arranging for the latter.

Legislators' offices are also allocated tickets to the special guided tours of the Residence that are arranged by the White House Visitors Office (described in part 3). The members almost invariably ask for an increased number—which prompts the legislative affairs staff to recalculate what favors are to be bestowed on whom. Legislators may sometimes be offered showings of the Oval Office and the Cabinet Room, but only on weekday evenings. "I can tell you, I have given tours, even at night, of the West Wing," Keating admits.[21]

Support from the Cabinet Departments

Like the White House counsel, the White House legislative affairs director is the hub of a wide circle: the assistant secretaries for legislative affairs in all the departments. These officers are presidential appointees; all have been picked by the White House—and almost all by the White House legislative affairs chief personally. Keating recalls:

> Right off the bat they know that they are reporting, not only to their secretaries, but . . . to someone within the White House. We implemented a weekly meeting with the [departmental] legislative affairs staffs. Every assistant secretary came in once a week. We had a roundtable; everybody knew what everybody else was doing. Everybody gave a report: "Here's what our top people . . . " You found out that when people talk to one another, you could see *(a)* people working at cross-purposes or *(b)* the opposite: people were trying to get the same thing done but didn't know it. Now all of a sudden we had a coordinated effort.[22]

Because many of these departmental legislative affairs specialists have come only recently from the staffs of senators or representatives, they provide vital additional entrée to their former employers. At the weekly or biweekly meetings, or in conference calls among departments that share common concerns, cabinet secretaries and senior departmental officers are given assignments to undertake on the Hill to help move the president's program. The Clinton legislative affairs staff required a monthly "agency report" from each of these departmental liaison offices.

Keating remembers that during the 1993 budget act debate, "It was all hands on deck; everybody was working on it." But for all such emissaries the fundamental rule was the same: Don't make promises up there on the Hill without the OK from the White House Legislative Affairs Office. Griffin was unrelenting: "Once we lost control of the Congress [in 1994], our strategy was to bring our legislative decisionmaking and priorities into the White House. I did not want anybody up there who was off-message. What I was concerned about was that the agencies were beginning to negotiate their own deals with the new committee chairs. I would say to cabinet secretaries, 'What the hell is going on here? We have our agenda here; this fits here, not there!' and we would go toe-to-toe sometimes."[23]

From his experience during the Bush years, Nick Calio adds: "There were certain agencies where we could work very well; with them I was high on their ability to count votes and get in the mix. Others were really not very good at all. There were other times when an agency would get in there . . . and we would have to go clean up after them where they had made a member or group of members really mad about something."[24]

The White House occasionally uncovered internal cabinet rivalries: at the request of one member of the cabinet, a senator or representative had put a "hold" on a piece of legislation—but it was legislation that was needed by another cabinet member. Commented Griffin, "If people were getting away from us, they would be snapped back into line—on the big issues."[25]

A recurring complaint from the president's supporters in Congress is the lack of advance notice when cabinet secretaries or other agency political officials take trips into members' states or districts. "They would fail even to pick up the phone and invite the member to show up at the event," recalled one White House assistant. "Our normal rule is: the member of Congress should know about any trip to the local territory being scheduled by any presidential appointee."[26]

In the total legislative ballgame, scores are kept. They are not "enemies' lists" but factual counts: Who voted how? Who supported the president how much of the time? Did the Bush legislative office keep track? "Yes, we did!" Nick Calio emphasized: "I was paranoid about putting it on paper . . . so I kept it in my head. Absolutely, you know: we would do rankings, at the end of every session, for the president—how members voted for us. . . . In that way the president would know, and we would know. . . . It would be tour tickets or seats at the Kennedy Center. We once yanked Kennedy Center tickets from one member, he had so often refused to vote with us."[27]

Adds Clinton legislative chief Griffin: "We kept track of everything we did for them. We didn't ever write down what they did or didn't do for us, but we would know the votes; we could pull up a vote in a minute. And then you had your own knowledge: we walked around with so much in our heads. People would say, 'You've got to screw this guy!' You know, if you're leaving town and that was the last act, that's fine but *we'd* be back tomorrow and the next day and the next day. You never made enemies; you tried never to make enemies."[28]

Being in the middle of that ambulatory bridge, do the legislative affairs directors sense that theirs is a dual role: faithfully to represent the president to the legislators while faithfully representing the legislators to the president? Do they feel a divided loyalty? "No," affirmed Clinton legislative affairs chief John Hilley. "It's a big mistake not to know who your boss is, and whose interests you are serving."[29]

With every cabinet department needing to create and maintain good working relationships with Congress, why does the White House have such a central role? Hilley reflected:

> I would say, honestly, of the domestic-based issues, those were almost exclusively run out of the White House. So while, yes, Interior might have an issue now and again, and Energy might have an issue now and again, for the 90 percent of the issues that counted, those were directly mediated out of the White House, with the direct participation of Treasury and OMB. . . . Since the eighties, we have had two decades where the budget has dominated the domestic debate. It just has been pervasive. So, one of the reasons why you have that central focus is that the budget has been the unifying thing in domestic policy. . . . You thus basically capture 90 percent of the domestic side of the government. . . . Just look at how the Congress works now: the budget process is very concentrated—leadership based, White House based—and you see all that stuff in the reconciliation bill.[30]

It was Larry O'Brien, legislative affairs director for Kennedy and Johnson, who perhaps best summed up the White House legislative experience: "It becomes a way of life in which you are engaged in human relations and constantly working out compromises. You listen to and solicit support from everybody on the Hill. You cajole, urge and plead. There's always the hot breath of opposition; don't resent it, understand it. You have to appreciate that at times there are those, even among your friends, who can't go along with you, that there is a line they can't cross. Just remember: there's always tomorrow."[31]

CHAPTER EIGHT

Equidistant in an Adversarial Relationship: The Press Secretary

[Critics say] the journalists were not just hostile to conservative governments. They were hostile to all governments. The news media had become so habituated to criticism, so steeped in antagonism, so besotted with power that they are making it impossible for anyone to govern the United States. No President would get a fair chance; the moment he assumes office, the media sets about the task of destroying him. Automatically. Mindlessly.

JAMES DEAKIN

My job is to challenge the President, challenge him to explain policy, justify decisions, defend mistakes, reveal intentions. . . . I don't believe there's any such thing as a bad question, only bad answers.

SAM DONALDSON

Newly retired press secretary Mike McCurry explained the geography outside his White House doorway: fifty feet in one direction was the Oval Office; fifty feet in the other was the West Colonnade Briefing Room—two institutions in an "increasingly . . . acrimonious relationship. The press secretary," McCurry said, "is there to explain one side of the equation to the other and then to try to balance out the interests."[1] Always a difficult assignment, and now getting a lot harder. Why?

The News Business: Thirty Years of Change

The demand for news, which was once modulated into segments—morning, evening, late night—has become constant and unending throughout all of the twenty-four-hour day. CNN's Headline News starts afresh every half hour: that's forty-eight times a day that CNN reporters are looking for "top stories." MSNBC likewise. Searching equally assiduously are the three major television networks (ABC, CBS, and NBC) plus Fox News and the four wire services (AP, UPI, Reuters, and Agence France Presse). Competing along with everyone else in the White House newsroom are the nation's major daily newspapers, eight radio networks (serving hundreds of talk-radio stations), and the principal weekly news magazines—not to mention domestic specialty publications and the rest of the foreign press. Photojournalists from anywhere snap pictures on their digital cameras—and in minutes the photos are on the World Wide Web.

"Information moves around the globe instantaneously, and we have a proliferation of outlets competing for the same stories," commented former press secretary Dee Dee Myers. "You can't fill twenty-four-hours-a-day with new facts."[2] McCurry agreed: "That becomes a voracious animal with an insatiable appetite for headlines on the hour. The only way you can feed that is to comment on every single sparrow that falls from the tree. . . . To me, future Presidents are going to need two press secretaries, one for the day and one for the night."[3]

The advent of twenty-four-hour cable news has had two results. First, it has forced the network news producers to alter their formats. In earlier years they saved their best tapes for their prime-time evening newscasts. Now, if a story breaks during the day and CNN airs it immediately, what is left for the evening shows is either less important or warmed-over news—or a higher percentage of commentary, opinion, and entertainment. Second, the unremitting pressure to be on the air immediately may, in a crisis, squeeze White House decisionmakers into feeling that they have less time for reflection. Myers observed:

> The most troubling thing to me is that when the Cuban missile crisis broke, John F. Kennedy had three days to decide what to do. He sat in the Oval Office; he conferred with the Joint Chiefs; he talked to his advisers; he prayed. If that happened now, Bill Clinton would have about 30 minutes, and [CNN reporter] Wolf Blitzer and everybody else would be standing out on the North Lawn of the White House

demanding action, or saying "The president is indecisive." So I worry that the time allowed leaders in crisis to make good decisions is compressed. That's a troubling development.[4]

Technological change has likewise contributed to this compression. When news photographers used chemical film, the reporting team for an afternoon event had until the next day to file. With the advent of digital cameras, videotape, and minicams, all it takes is a dash to the nearest microwave outpost. CBS reporter Lesley Stahl remembers the changeover: "That time became almost instantaneous, meaning that in a crisis, so did the time for our news judgments. . . . Now our time to reflect on the events we covered, to put them into context, and figure out what was important and what was not, was disappearing. This was obviously a momentous change, but little thought was given to the consequences."[5]

Ken Walsh, of U.S. News and World Report and the former president of the White House Correspondents Association, discusses those consequences: "Anything that happens around the world can be shown on America's television screens instantaneously, at any time of day or night. This means the mainstream media are constantly groping for ways to move a breaking story forward rather than cover it in depth, and too often the result is sensational, superficial, or negative coverage. Just as important, television has greatly accelerated the velocity of White House decision-making and increased the difficulty of governing."[6]

Other profound changes have also been taking place. The press's skepticism has been turning to hostility. The younger journalists have become convinced that investigative reporting is the heart of their calling. Walsh recalls that early in his career, "We felt that to do our jobs properly as watchdogs for the public, we had to be adversaries of all government officials and never give them the benefit of the doubt."[7] Stahl, too, remembers: "Watergate changed journalism forever. . . . The assumption would be: government officials skirt the truth. Presidents had been protected by newsmen: Franklin Roosevelt's wheelchair and John Kennedy's women had gone unreported. Watergate brought an end to the protections; thereafter, presidents would view the press as a squad in a perpetual adversarial crouch, always ready to pounce."[8]

In his thought-provoking book about how a newly elected president moves from campaigning to governing, political scientist Charles Jones observes that at the very beginning of an administration, the press presents a kind of "gift" to the new chief executive. Jones quotes a transition veteran: "During the transition, they [the press] are willing to say 'Well, you're a new president. We'll give you a chance to see if it works. . . . If you don't take advantage of that opportunity, you've wasted it.'"[9]

For their part, both Clintons came into Washington reciprocating the hostility of the fourth estate—especially since the press, during the 1992 primaries, had carried stories about Bill Clinton's philandering during his Arkansas years. One of the earliest moves the new White House made was to wall off the press secretary's office from the press corps—a decision that was later rescinded after outraged protests from press corps veterans. It was reported that the president and the first lady even gave serious thought to moving the entire press operation out of the White House and into the Old Executive Office Building across the street, but that the plan was abandoned as being too provocative. By late spring of 1993 "there was damn near a war going on," commented one insider. He added: "There was a view early on—in my judgment it was a mistake—that came out of the campaign, that people should go around the White House press corps and that you could aim your message: that you could rifle-shoot to the people you cared about, and the hell with the rest."[10]

A Still Tense—But Better Organized—Relationship

The president and the first lady realized the degree of acrimony and wanted to ameliorate the antipathies. Assigning him the title of counselor to the president, the Clintons brought in David Gergen—skilled and sophisticated in the communications arts—to mediate and advise. But it was not until January of 1995 that Mike McCurry, an experienced press officer who was also no newcomer to politics, was appointed White House press secretary.

Before McCurry took office, he met with Marlin Fitzwater, his predecessor in the Bush White House—and heeded Fitzwater's advice. Ranking high on Fitzwater's list was to glue in a guarantee of complete access to the president. As Fitzwater put it, "My basic decision had been that I would go to any meeting on the president's schedule if I needed it to do my job. I would never wait for an invitation. If I was ever asked to leave, then I would consider resignation. Fortunately, in six years with two presidents I was never asked to leave a meeting."[11]

To signify, right from the start, that he was part of the White House inner circle, McCurry began showing up at senior staff meetings. When he came on duty in January of 1995, changes were made in a hurry. Relying on candor, humor, and an unquestioned ability to speak for the president, McCurry

The White House Correspondents Association

As a bridge between the White House press corps and the press secretary, the White House Correspondents Association aids in the dialogue between two institutions so often at odds. Founded in 1915 to give credentialing advice and thus help the White House to control unregulated requests for places on the White House beat, the association later became best known for its sponsorship of the annual White House Correspondents Dinner. Its nine-member board, elected from the various media constituencies, undertakes to represent the press corps in continuing negotiations with the press secretary's office about pools, passes, access, credentials, travel arrangements, and press conference rules. The Clinton Press Office had a management deputy who handled those matters.

began to whittle away at the press's resentment. Observing how the members of the White House press corps were cooped up most of the day in their tiny cubicles, McCurry opened more presidential events to more of the corps, rather than limit press attendance to restricted pools. He educated the president and the president's schedulers to notify the Press Office of the details of the president's movements so that the press corps could coordinate their day-to-day planning with that of the president. McCurry met privately with many of the correspondents, searching out their suggestions for improving relationships. He instructed his staff not only to be courteous to reporters but also to answer their phone calls before their deadlines expired and to provide them with timely copies of presidential remarks. He clarified who else on the White House staff would be expected to deal frequently with the press—and managed a coordination process to ensure that they hewed to the same message. He arranged private, informal "deep background" sessions with the president for senior correspondents. He made, as Ken Walsh observed, "a fresh start."

The Press Secretary's Daily Round

Every working morning, the press secretary asks himself three complementary questions: First, what are the current headlines? Second, what is the president going to be doing today? And third, what should the White House message be about the first two? After glancing at the thick stack of photocopied pages in the overnight White House News Report and the National

Security Council's intelligence take, the Clinton press secretary typically attended a rapid-fire series of staff meetings—with the White House chief of staff and senior colleagues, with Communications Office heavyweights, and with his own staff team—and was then ready for his first session with the press.

Some thirty or more reporters—especially those from the fast-breaking news contingent—squeezed into McCurry's office for what had come to be known as the "gaggle" (a gathering perhaps not unlike the word's original meaning: a bunch of cackling geese). This was the opportunity for the press secretary to lay out the president's schedule, to give a few answers to especially hot questions, to pour cold water on an unfavorable story—and to emphasize a politically helpful one. In other words, to engage in an ostensibly informal and free-form meeting that was in reality the beginning of a thoroughly planned communications operation. The gaggle evolved from similar morning sessions that had been convened by earlier press secretaries; in recent years it has, like other White House innovations, become an established part of the institution's traditions.

Next came the preparations for the more formal press briefing, which was usually held in the early afternoon in the Briefing Room, adjacent to the West Wing. White House staff were all warned: "Don't leave the press secretary out on a limb, uninformed and thus embarrassed, about anything going on—good or bad, top secret or wide open—that might in the near future become newsworthy or in any way touch the presidency." Special care was taken to coordinate with the press staffs of the vice president and the first lady. As one representative from each of those staffs, respectively, explained:

> We would try never to surprise Mike. . . . We always made sure, if the vice president was doing anything new—any new announcements— that Mike had paper before his morning meeting with reporters; we would never want him to get blindsided by anything. . . . Mike would decide if there were certain matters about which he would say, "I'm not taking any questions on that." He was just going to refer them to me.[12]

> We in the first lady's office and they in the White House press office all talked to each other every day. . . . We depended on each other. . . . They helped us when we were doing events in the Residence, and we helped them when we could. . . . If I called McCurry he took my call

immediately, or if I walked over and . . . was told that his door was closed, I could walk in. There was a very good relationship.[13]

When sensitive national security operations are involved, the press secretary may have to push especially hard to ensure that he is informed. President Bush's press secretary, Marlin Fitzwater, encountered at least one instance in which another White House office had failed to keep him informed about a particular matter—and the press attacked Fitzwater for misinforming them. He recalled: "I used to joke with fellow staff members that in the White House everybody lies to everybody most of the time, meaning that nobody ever told you everything they knew about everything. It wasn't lying, really. But if you are a press secretary, whose every statement must withstand the media honesty test, you soon learn to question everything you are told in the White House."[14]

In the Clinton White House, the late-morning preparations would accelerate. The press secretary conducted conference calls with his opposite numbers in the cabinet departments, especially the national security agencies: What news was just around the corner? Which stories would the departments handle and which would the White House take over? (Answer: the White House would grab off whatever was good news.) For every anticipated question, written guidance was demanded from the cabinet department—then ruthlessly pared down to a single page. The total briefing package might range from twenty to fifty pages, which the press secretary would have to study minutely before he stood up at the Briefing Room podium.

The Clinton White House has issued nearly two thousand press passes—many of course to equipment technicians—but the Briefing Room has only forty-eight assigned seats, each labeled with a small brass plaque. (The regulars treasure their up-front privilege and pass their seats on, like mini-inheritances, to their successors.) Some sixty to eighty journalists cover the White House as their principal occupation. The actual number attending the daily briefing varies from under forty to over seventy, depending on the urgency of the day's news. Television cameras are set up at the rear of the Briefing Room—plus a few at the right front, which the networks use to record face-view shots of their own senior correspondents dutifully badgering the press secretary with their most dramatically tough questions.

The press secretary would begin with some routine announcements—perhaps telling of the president's future overseas travel plans. Then, for sometimes as long as an hour, the cluttered, often raucous scene would offer up a minidrama the likes of which is not played out in any other government headquarters in the world: the serrated edge of America's free press, sharp and rough, met the hard bread (sometimes rock) of presidential officialdom. Irreverence collided with imperturbability.

But in the Clinton years the press briefing was rarely the setting for major pronunciamentos. White House press strategy was to reserve those for carefully prearranged events at which the president would star but at which press questions would be either outlawed or limited.

At the typical White House press briefing, with the initial minima out of the way, it would become the journalists' turn—and, at least in this setting, there would be practically no limit to their inquiries. International affairs; military matters; the economy; congressional actions or inaction; issues of law, science, or politics; technical details of the president's health: no subject or person would escape interrogation. If a national security crisis had just taken place, reporters would vie to push the press secretary into a "tick-tock" mode: recounting the events breathless minute by breathless minute. Controversial statements or actions on the part of executive branch officials would merit special focus. Those officers are the president's people; the press secretary would be asked: Does the president agree with what they are saying and doing?

Stories of White House scandal may of course take up overwhelming amounts of time, and here press secretaries are cornered. Do they know the truth themselves? Veteran reporters remember Ronald Ziegler's Watergate admission that all he had said earlier was "inoperative." When the Lewinsky story broke in January of 1998, Clinton's Mike McCurry made an unshakable personal decision: he would simply not ask the president to tell him what the truth was—so that, pleading ignorance, he could never be accused of misinforming the press.

McCurry had another reason for taking this stand: "If Clinton answered the incriminating question, McCurry would be a potential witness, who might have to testify on the Hill or before a grand jury. . . . What the president needed was a lawyer to gather the facts, someone who would be covered by attorney-client privilege. Then McCurry could cite the lawyer's findings to the press without being personally exposed. He made a practice of taking few notes, just scribblings on his phone-message slips and throwing them away each day. Notes could be subpoenaed."[15]

McCurry referred all Lewinsky questions to the lawyers, one of whom (at first Lanny Davis, later Jim Kennedy), was specifically hired to handle them. One unsympathetic observer characterized this ploy: "By directing all scandal questions to the lawyers, McCurry could stay on the high road while Lanny Davis shoveled the shit."[16]

Besides informing the nation and the world, the daily press briefing can serve another vital and specific purpose: it can be used to inform the rest of the White House staff what the official message is on any current topic—and how to play it. To underscore this purpose, the later Clinton press secretaries inaugurated two new practices: First, immediately following the briefing, they distributed the full texts of their own press-guidance packages to their White House colleagues, which showed the whole staff what each of their respective offices had contributed; second, with the help of a video-camera installed on the Briefing Room ceiling, they televised the briefings, permitting the proceedings not only to be displayed on the internal White House screens but also to be broadcast to the public by C-SPAN or other networks. The likelihood, now, of such nationwide live TV coverage of the briefings has spurred both the interrogators and the press secretary to inject a more partisan "edge" into their exchanges. (The president and the first lady could—and sometimes did—turn on their personal monitors and watch their press secretary in action.)

In the Clinton White House, beginning in the early morning and through-out the day, background factual materials would be dropped into the hopper near the reporters' cubbyhole offices: transcripts of the Briefing Room pro-ceedings or of any presidential remarks, information about the day's presidential events, copies of presidential messages to Congress, lists and biographies of appointees. One day's pile could include fifteen releases, per-haps sixty pages. All this was the product of many hands on the White House staff, but collected and distributed through the press secretary's office, which simultaneously handled in the neighborhood of one thousand telephone calls a day. It was a dizzying maelstrom of responsibilities, even for a staff of forty.

When McCurry said his farewells on October 1, 1998, after forty-five months of service, he had given 539 press briefings.

The President at the Podium

The greatly changed news environment has wrought still another alteration in the press activities of the White House: the diminishment of the presi-dential news conference. These occasions, once the scene of reporters sprinting for the doorway, breathless with startling news of world or national or presidential developments, had become, by the closing years of Clinton's presidency, rather subdued rituals, dressed in the same trappings but with much less substance. What had once been given prime-time coverage, broadcast simultaneously by all the national networks, was relegated to second-rate status. ABC and NBC, for example, simply declined to carry live the news conference of April 18, 1995: they didn't think it would be newsworthy. CBS did carry it, and its Nielsen rating was 6.5—compared with 14.7 for NBC's "Frasier" and 15.8 for ABC's "Home Improvement."

Why? The principal reason is that twenty-four-hour news cycle. Significant announcements are no longer held in reserve for presidential press conferences: they are let loose when ready. Usually—as noted earlier—they are made in the context of carefully scheduled events, or mini-events, during which press questions are limited or even prohibited. The president may make a brief statement, then walk back into his office. But the news itself does not wait for even the most ad hoc presidential appearance: it has already been flashed worldwide from the CNN minicam on the ground in Kosovo or the CBS-TV pickup in the North Atlantic Treaty Organization (NATO) headquarters in Belgium.

For example, on June 25, 1999, Clinton made two public appearances: a lengthy speech at a local university in the morning and a press conference in the afternoon. The next day, the *Washington Post*'s front-page banner headline said that President Clinton was dropping his plan to propose a means test for medicare benefits: but the article cited "White House sources," and the president's own news conference—silent on the means-test issue— was merely excerpted on page ten of the *Post*.

Commented a *Washington Post* staff writer: "President Clinton's news conference yesterday was limp, reflective, meandering—taps rather than reveille, a lion in winter. . . . Clinton's exchange with reporters lasted an hour and a quarter and rambled over a stupefying range of questions, from the highly personal to the tediously obscure . . . . Zzzzzzzz."[17]

Not that President Clinton was closemouthed—really just the opposite. Pages upon pages of the Weekly Compilation of Presidential Documents laid out the texts of his hundreds of speeches. But whatever magnetism his occasional press conferences might have had was simply overwhelmed by the sheer volume of his statements elsewhere. Presidential scholar Fred Greenstein has been quoted as saying that "President Clinton's own volubility has diluted the effect of his words." "Instead of focusing like a laser," Greenstein said, "the Clinton White House has landed with a splat." Another distinguished presidential scholar—Martha Joynt Kumar, of Towson University—is more philosophical: "The White House doesn't have the same kind of allure for the media that it once had. It used to be the president was the initiator in national politics. Everything flowed through him."[18]

It may of course have been that the diminished substance of, and lessened interest in, President Clinton's news conferences were the inevitable concomitants of the winding down of his presidency. It must also be recalled that during practically all of 1998, presidential press conferences were scrubbed because of the Lewinsky and impeachment uproars. Even taking that hiatus into account, Clinton held some 180 formal press conferences in his first seven years as president (close to the 177 that Eisenhower conducted during the same number of years). For each of them, however, there was no diminishment in the press secretary's preconference responsibilities. Likely questions were identified in advance; "gooser sheets" were sent out to responsible White House and cabinet officers, assigning the preparation of suggested answers; and "prebriefings," as they are called, were scheduled with the boss prior to his meeting with the correspondents. Like the seats in the press briefing area, the chairs in front of the president's podium—in the East Room or wherever—were labeled. The president was given a seating chart showing who was where, accompanied by an occasional reminder: "It's been some time since you've answered a question from the *Dallas Morning News*," or "Take a question from the *Chicago Tribune* because you are about to announce something involving Bill Daley. . . ."

The press secretary will occasionally persuade the president to permit private interviews with one or a small group of reporters. These are on deep background, meaning that there can be no disclosure of what is said—but the seasoned journalist can often manage to weave together a story that conveys the president's mood and general thinking without violating the rules of the meeting. The attribution will be, "the president has told friends" or "the president is known to believe. . . ." In 1997, returning from a trip to Israel aboard *Air Force One*, McCurry invited reporters to have an informal session with the president—with a new twist. The interview was "on psych background," which one correspondent defined as "meaning that reporters could pretend to tap into the president's brain without attributing any comments to the Big Guy." The interview lasted a full three hours.[19]

The Press and Presidential Travel

Whenever the president travels, a press pool accompanies him. Places are rotated so that the pool is not made up of the same media people all the time. If the president goes jogging or out to dinner, an "in-town pool" of about eight tags along: a representative from the wire services, a network correspondent, a daily news reporter, plus a camera crew. If he flies, there is the *Air Force One* pool, which numbers about a dozen and includes three correspondents from the wire services; one correspondent each from the newspapers, the magazines, and the radio; the photographic contingent; and a press office representative. The White House will, on occasion, ask for an "expanded pool," meaning that many other reporters are given access, or for a very small "family pool," to protect the first family's privacy. At a major domestic event the motorcade will include four network vans, a van for wire reporters, and a van for photographers—positioned so that they can scramble out to snap the scene right as it happens.

When presidential trips are being planned, the advance teams invariably include a Press Office representative. On a major overseas trip, a press plane follows *Air Force One* and its Air Force backup plane. A journey abroad is always a major event in White House communications strategy: it requires a press plan—written up in military detail—specifying who in the party will meet with the press, who will do the "backgrounders" beforehand and the talk shows afterward, who will brief reporters during the conference overseas—and, on the return home, who will talk to the correspondents on *Air Force One.*

The Press Office works out this document with all the players; the last step is a sign-off by each of them: Defense, State, the National Security Council (NSC), and other senior White House officers. The aim is to have a minimum of misunderstandings, missed signals, and punctured egos. When a major presidential journey is undertaken, such as President Clinton's trip to China in June of 1998, the total press contingent, from all over the world, numbers over five hundred.

Beyond the Briefing Room

When VIPs meet with the president, the long-standing practice of Oval Office photo-ops continues. The Reagan-era "Deaver Rule"—"just pictures, no questions"—has been discontinued: the networks now refuse to send a mini-cam into the Oval Office without an "editorial presence," and President Clinton was prepped to handle the almost inevitable question from the likes of CBS's Bill Plante or UPI's Helen Thomas.

At times the press secretary had news that he wanted to get "into the bloodstream" quickly, without waiting for the daily press briefing. On the North Lawn's Pebble Beach (named for the gravel that had been spread over the grass), outside his White House doorway, stood sixteen cameras and an ungainly forest of wires, lights, and microphones. The press secretary needed only to signal to a wire-service correspondent or to the CNN reporter, and his hot story was likely to be put on the air instantly.

Or it may have been the other way around: *Washington Post* reporter Howard Kurtz recounts that Press Secretary George Stephanopoulos "used to run onto the lawn after a live shot and berate [CNN correspondent] Wolf Blitzer if he broadcast something that offended administration sensibilities."[20] Press Secretary Joe Lockhart was equally quick to fire off a complaint to a reporter and had absolutely no hesitation about doing so: "I do this every day. It's part of my job. People don't notice as much when a deputy press secretary calls. They notice when a press secretary does. . . . Sometimes circumstances dictate a more aggressive stance."[21]

Members of the White House press corps are well aware that the major policy issues of concern to the nation—and consequently to the president—are also being kneaded and shaped by the president's immediate economic, national security, and domestic policy advisers. Any correspondent covering such an issue in depth, therefore, will not be content to listen only to the press secretary but will seek interviews with the knowledgeable White House senior staffer.

Some past presidents (Lyndon Johnson and Richard Nixon, for example) disliked such freewheeling behavior and instructed their press secretaries to control reporters' access to all other White House staff and to inform the Oval Office whenever a request was made. Even before the inauguration, the Clinton administration issued the same edict: a December 28, 1992, memorandum from "transition headquarters" to all cabinet and senior appointees warned that "requests for interviews . . . can be best handled by the press/communications office. . . . According to transition communications director George Stephanopoulos, interviews with you or your family members should be granted only after they have been cleared through this system."[22]

Such strictures have usually been in vain. There is a symbiosis between senior White House assistants and veteran journalists. Their contacts are legion; they share information constantly.

After being in office for a while, the Clinton White House was more relaxed about such interviews. The press secretary preferred to be notified when other senior staff talked to the press, but he realized that it happened often. Provided that they kept "on message," senior White House policy officers were encouraged to meet with reporters—and they did so willingly and frequently. Such interviews are essential components of a well-planned communications strategy.[23] National security advisers Brent Scowcroft and Samuel (Sandy) Berger made themselves available on background; Clinton aides Gene Sperling and Bruce Reed did likewise, and often on the record. If the requests are many and the senior policy officers are submerged in work, the press corps will organize "tongs": groups of journalists with similar interests and expertise who conduct the interviews collectively.

What used to be considerable tension between the NSC staff and the White House Press Office has been ameliorated. The NSC's senior director for press and communications is also a White House deputy press secretary; other senior policy directors, such as the NSC's expert on arms control, often joined the White House press secretary at the Briefing Room rostrum when a complicated, sensitive subject like missile defense—requiring the NSC officer's special expertise—was discussed. When the president was engaged in an important telephone conversation with a foreign chief of state, the press secretary was sometimes permitted to assign one of the deputy press secretaries to go down to the Situation Room and listen in—unless the subject was extraordinarily delicate. This arrangement obviated a time-consuming later debriefing and guaranteed that the Press Office would have an accurate account of what would likely be a newsworthy exchange.

So solicitous, in fact, was the White House about media coverage of national security matters that in October of 1993 President Clinton dispatched White House communications assistant Jeff Eller to Somalia to shepherd the official pool of eighteen American reporters covering the operations of U.S. troops in Mogadishu. The reason given? To provide the press with "technical assistance" and "make sure they got access that they needed." But President Bush's former press secretary, Marlin Fitzwater, sniffed that the presence of a staff person from the White House "would tend to . . . politicize the conflict. It sends a signal that you're sending political people over there to handle the press and the message and the image."[24] CNN's Washington bureau chief added, "When you put a White House micro-manager in there, it implies media manipulation at the highest level."[25]

There are times when unhappy news must come out. Here, the experienced press secretary keeps three things in mind. First, pick the best day to release it: Fridays. Why? The Saturday papers are likely laid aside in favor of family outings; the television sets are left off; Congress is out of town. Former White House counselor David Gergen observed, "There's a tradition that goes back to the Dark Ages, which says that the best time to release bad news is Fridays after 4 pm. . . . Some of us have called that [time period] the Bermuda Triangle of news because anything that goes in never comes out." Adds McCurry: "This is a time-honored technique. . . . [Bad news often] loses its steam over the weekend."[26]

Second, bad news should, if possible, be made to come out in the newspapers rather than through television. In his book about White House spin, veteran reporter Howard Kurtz recalled an occasion when press secretary McCurry steered an unfavorable story to the *Wall Street Journal* rather than confirm an earlier scoop by a CBS news reporter: "McCurry would much rather take a hit in a newspaper story, where at least there would be ample space for his side, than in a TV report that flashed by in a minute twenty. Television tended to paint things in black and white and most stories were actually rather gray."[27]

The third concern about bad news is that it trumps good news. Presidential scandal at home will overwhelm even presidential summitry abroad. In May of 1997, President Clinton was in Paris meeting with NATO leaders and Russian president Boris Yeltsin to sign the agreement bringing Poland, Hungary, and the Czech Republic into NATO. The White House press office paged McCurry with the notice that the U.S. Supreme Court had just ruled, 9 to 0, that Paula Jones's sexual harassment suit against Clinton would go to trial—even though it was against a sitting president. Clinton managed to dodge reporters for several days, but the headlines at home undermined the good news from Paris.[28]

When the day is over—well, it's not really over. The White House and NSC press deputies typically share a duty rotation system: a week on at a time. They know that at about 11:30 P.M., when the first editions of the major East Coast newspapers hit the streets, one of them will be firing an aggrieved inquiry at the White House: "That story in the other paper—is it right? Where did it come from?" "The worst day is actually Sunday," explains a former White House deputy press secretary, "You can, on Saturdays, find people at the White House to answer questions, but they aren't around on Sundays—and it's just then that the news media are preparing for Monday morning. They have just seen the network talk shows; you end up going all day long."[29]

The White House News Report

An auxiliary service that the Clinton Press Office provided to the entire White House staff was begun during the Nixon administration: furnishing copies of news stories from the day's papers. When Nixon first initiated the practice, there was an actual news summary composed by a special unit that was intentionally independent of the Press Office itself. Reagan's team added the weekly "Friday Follies," a collection of the most pungent political satire of the week, and the Bush White House continued this supplement.

The Clinton White House tucked the News Report unit under the Press Office. At first, a news summary was again prepared, but the summary idea was subsequently dropped: instead, the Clinton news analysis group cut selected stories from nine different dailies, put a one-page list of headlines on top, then stapled together an enormous compendium (168 pages on a typical day), leaving it to staff assistants in the individual offices to mark up those items that their bosses should notice. The Clinton news analysis staff also circulated "Clintoons: A Week in Review." CNN Headline News is available all day long on the White House internal TV system—which, commented one aide, "makes you work a lot harder, because there would be no excuse not to know anything."[30]

News Facilities at the White House

Neither the original White House nor the West Wing, added in 1902, was designed to meet the needs of the world communications center that the White House has become. Many of the forty-odd correspondents—a number of them nationally known and representing the largest and wealthiest media businesses in the country—are sardined into cubbies the size of telephone booths, their work space for telephones, TV monitors, personal computers, and laptops measured in cubic millimeters. These windowless minicaves were scooped out of the area that once held the White House florist shop and indoor swimming pool.

When a briefing was being conducted, trunks of equipment took up space while the floor was strewn with spaghetti heaps of electrical cables. When a major event was scheduled in the Rose Garden or in the Residence's stately, historic East Room, it might require three hours' advance notice to set up the mikes, lights, and cameras amid the snakes of wires. Could the East Room be hardwired—with cables and lights pre-positioned? Not without threatening the architecture and decor of that famous chamber.

In January 1999, after seven years of study by twelve cooperating federal agencies, the National Park Service released the Comprehensive Design Plan for the White House and President's Park (described and discussed further in part 4). Featured in the plan is an upgrading of the present west colonnade press space plus a new, 9,700-square-foot underground briefing room and correspondents' office immediately beneath the West Wing drive. There will be a separate entrance for reporters and equipment; audiovisual rooms; areas for interviews, camera operations, photographers, and storage; vending machines; and rest rooms. Gone will be that forest of tripods that litters the Pebble Beach segment of the White House North Lawn—as unsightly to look at as it is useless in bad weather. The plan envisages a twenty-year development timetable. In the author's judgment, it can't come too soon. The press secretaries and journalists of tomorrow deserve much better than the facilities of today.

CHAPTER NINE

The Continuing Campaign: The Office of Communications

[Modern presidents] must try to master the art of manipulating the media, not only to win in politics but in order to further the programs and causes they believe in; at the same time they must avoid at all costs the charge of trying to manipulate the media. In the modern presidency, concern for image must rank with concern for substance.

RICHARD M. NIXON

We want to repeat what worked in the campaign. We want to make sure we use the broadest array of technology and resources available to us. . . . We have to make sure we coordinate activities so the administration is speaking with one voice and building support for the president's policies.

GEORGE STEPHANOPOULOS

The White House propaganda machine has become an increasingly effective instrument. For . . . years the president and his agents have clearly been winning the battle. . . . The White House has . . . enhanced the power of the communicator-in-chief. And it has raised to even greater importance the unmet challenge to provide an alternative, non-propagandistic view of the presidency.

DAVID BRODER

The election campaign does not end on election night. The morning after the win it just starts up again—for a somewhat different purpose but in much the same form. To be sure, the first task of persuasion has been successful: the president has been elected. Now begins the second task: to persuade the nation—and the world—that his actions are right.

It was a divided electorate that went to the polls. The same folks are out there, still divided. The follow-on campaign is designed to convince them that the new president is in fact meeting their needs, fulfilling their hopes, and improving their futures. There was raucous competition—strong, competing voices—in the first campaign. In the new campaign the competition is even more cacophonous.

Six months after his inauguration, President Clinton bemoaned to Larry King:

> The thing that has surprised me most is how difficult it is, even for the president, if you're going to take on big changes and try to make big things happen, to really communicate exactly what you're about to the American people.
>
> Mr. King: And why is that hard?
>
> The president: I think because there's so much else in the atmosphere, first; and secondly, because when you do something like this big economic plan we're pushing, only the controversy is newsworthy . . . the sort of yelling and screaming back and forth. . . . I have lost the ability to make sure everybody knows the things I want them to know.[1]

In the election campaign, every device, every resource, every voice that could be organized was commandeered and concentrated on the effort. A communications-conscious president—Mr. Clinton, for example—will likewise marshal the energies of all the cabinet agencies and his entire White House staff to focus them on the new task: to defend, explain, and extol the actions that he, the chief executive, is taking.

The grand chieftains of this second, and continuing, campaign are the White House chief of staff and the director of the Office of Communications. The press secretary, described in the preceding chapter, is a captain in this effort, but the Press Office itself is preoccupied with its day-to-day dialogue with the White House press corps. More than that: the press secretary and the communications chief operate under different rules of engagement. The press secretary sees his job—and wants the press to see it—as that of "an honest broker between the president and the press," while the director of communications is viewed as "the strategist, the propagandist, the counselor who could not be completely trusted to tell the truth" because he has taken sides.[2] The two offices will work side by side and will coordinate their efforts, but they will be separate organizations in the White House community.

Unexpectedly but frequently, their efforts may be forced out of sync. As a former deputy press secretary observed, "There is a natural tension, because the Communications Office will come up with some wonderful education event on the same day that India blows up a nuclear bomb. It's very hard, sometimes, for the Press Office to explain to the Communications Office that nobody is going to be concentrating on child care today."[3]

The Office of Communications: Connecting the President with the Country

In the Bush White House, the Office of Communications was large and included the speechwriting, intergovernmental, and public liaison units (described separately in other chapters) as well as the media relations group (described later in this chapter). In the Clinton organizational schema, the White House Office of Communications was small: a headquarters office, the speechwriting staff, and a research unit. But however subdivided, the whole White House organization is a multifaceted communications operation. There is not a person on the staff or an event on the calendar which—if the planning is done right—is not a piece of a public relations drama, carefully crafted to send a "message of the day." Indeed, this book could have been titled "Communications Central at 1600 Pennsylvania Avenue." What are the instruments of White House communications operations?

The director of the Office of Communications starts by conceptualizing its mission, which is vastly more broad than just managing the daily news cycle. "We say, 'What is it that we [this presidency] are here to do? Where do we want to be six months from now—or a year from now?' And we must then begin working back from that end, so that we can try to accomplish it. If there are certain things that we have to do, for whatever reason, how do they fit into our larger purpose?"[4]

The principal White House communications resource is the president himself: his persona, his voice, his words. The challenge to the White House communicators is how to bring that presidential presence—either in person or electronically—to the attention of the nation, unfiltered by the limiting decisions of TV producers or network editors. "Excerpts from" and "stories based on" are insufficient; the president's White House impresarios want him out there, unedited. They search hungrily for opportunities to reach out to the grass roots, over the heads of Washington or New York media controllers. What are these opportunities and techniques? How have recent presidents used those that are there? And what new ones have they invented?

The State of the Union Message

The State of the Union (SOTU) message is Opportunity One. It is as old as the Constitution and as recent as last January. The chamber of the House of Representatives is a magnificently theatrical setting for the president on that dramatic night. What takes place is also one of the very few high rituals of the American nation. Senators, the justices of the Supreme Court, the foreign ambassadors, the military chiefs, the cabinet: all are dramatically announced and solemnly take their seats in the well of the House. The first lady and some special guests are in the front row of a prominent balcony, where they will be featured for a "TV minute" when the president, as he usually does, makes specific reference to his wife and to the laudatory or heroic accomplishments of her guests. Up on the dais the vice president and the Speaker await the president's ascent to the rostrum. Whereas Eisenhower would come up to the Hill at high noon, recent presidents have seized the unmatchable opportunity of a nationwide television broadcast in evening prime time. It is a communications director's golden hour.

The SOTU message is, next to the president's one or two inaugural addresses, the principal and prize package of each year's presidential initiatives. (A close second is the annual budget message.) An adept communications strategy will spread the munificence of those two packages over much more than the one night and the one day of their respective releases. For the month of December and nearly all of January, Congress is out of town. The field is thus wide open for the president, day after day preceding the messages, to lay down enticing pieces of his program, whetting appetites and gaining almost unobstructed news coverage.

Said a January 6, 1999, *Washington Post* story:

> The Roosevelt Room announcement was the latest in a flurry of formal announcements and orchestrated leaks coming from the White House about its budget. The goal, say White House aides, is for these flurries to accumulate into a fresh blanket of domestic policy initiatives between now and Clinton's State of the Union address, planned for Jan. 19, and the official release of his budget on Feb. 1. . . . Profiting from the release of the budget is one of the advantages of incumbency. And White House officials said it only makes sense for them to maximize that profit by releasing the details over time, rather than putting them all into public view in one news cycle.[5]

Less Formal Presidential Remarks

Perhaps next in communications value are the presidential press conferences—*when* they are carried live on network television. For reasons
discussed in chapter 8, however, the Clinton press conferences, beginning
in 1999, had become increasingly subject to excerpting or had been omit-
ted from live coverage entirely. Where else does a president appear?

On Larry King's program, as in the example quoted earlier. No producer
interferes, no television anchor squeezes out excerpts: the president is connected directly with his listeners. In a 1993 article, journalist Sidney
Blumenthal (later a White House assistant) reported: "By March 18 . . . the
new President had held twenty-five sessions of one kind or another with
representatives of the provincial media, but he had not held a single press
conference. . . . The President was hardly embarrassed or apologetic. 'You
know why I can stiff you on the press conferences?' he asked. 'Because Larry
King liberated me by giving me to the American people directly.'"[6]

"Now the talk show campaign has given birth to the talk show presidency," commented *Washington Post* reporter Howard Kurtz.[7] The Clinton
communications technique of reaching out over the heads of the national
media networks was severely criticized by some, however. Kenneth Walsh,
former president of the White House Correspondents Association, approv-
ingly recounted Republican media consultant James Lake's advice to Clinton
press secretary Mike McCurry: "You guys have done some things right and
some things wrong, but this is the dumbest thing you've done so far. Every
White House tries to circumvent the mainstream press corps, but we never
bragged about it. In the end, . . . the mainstream media will always drown
out the regional or alternative media."[8] Thousands of requests for meetings
with and speeches to important conventions and groups flood into the White
House schedulers' hoppers. The problem is to choose: to select the strategic occasions and the most influential audiences. Howard Kurtz describes
the work of Ann Lewis, Clinton's communications director: "It was Lewis'
job to help decide what events Clinton should attend in the coming months.
Should he speak to the Boy Scouts? The Council of Chief State School Officers? A coalition working for free air time for candidates? Deliver a series
of Blue Room lectures on the presidency? Schedule was strategy."[9]

In the Clinton White House, the chief of staff, the communications director, and a small group of others met regularly with the president's scheduler,
looked ahead six weeks and asked themselves: What policy themes should
the president emphasize in the near future? The next question was: What
events could be seized upon and used to lay out those themes? Actually,

some planning can be done as much as a year ahead; in addition to January's major messages, national holidays and certain periodic international summit sessions (with Japan, Canada, the Group of Eight) predetermine opportunities to highlight pertinent accomplishments and objectives. If a policy initiative is pending but needs an event and an audience, both can be arranged—as is described in chapter 12.

The participants in the calendar meetings then narrowed their focus, concentrating on the upcoming week: How would each day's schedule be precisely tailored to dramatize specific themes and prevent them from being overshadowed by lesser White House or cabinet activities? As the plethora of requests were scrutinized, the discipline was intense: Which to accept? The answer had to be not what the president could do, nor what he should do to court the requester, but what would further the president's own great national goals. Former speechwriter Don Baer ruefully observed that in 1994, President Clinton had delivered over five hundred sets of remarks—"more than any other president in history." "We would go and ask, 'What is this event for? What is supposed to be happening here? How does this fit?' And no one would know; the answer would be, 'Go ask the group that he is speaking to: what would they want to hear about?' Bassackwards? Exactly."[10]

When he later took over as director of strategic planning and communication, Baer not only insisted on more stringent criteria for scheduling events but also used his influence to bring about a shift in some of the policy themes that had been identified earlier by the White House leadership. (Some acrimonious internal White House conflicts occurred during this period.)

Radio

If it is not feasible to produce the president's face in person, audio opportunities are investigated. President Carter inaugurated an addition to the communications enterprises of the presidency: a series of audiotapes called the *White House Press Office Radio Actuality Line*—and the tradition Carter had begun continued in the Clinton years. Audiotapes were made of important statements by the president or others; in addition, the staff would write up questions about policy issues and the president or his cabinet officers would record their responses.

At first, radio stations across the nation were given toll-free numbers to dial into any one of five identical tape machines. The opening message was, "Here's what happened at the White House this morning" or "We have three feeds for you today," whereupon the stations could select whichever they wanted. The five machines combined usually took a thousand calls a day. Later the dialers pressed 1 or any of six other options to pick up the subject of their choice. The Actuality Line became a standard feature of the White House communications apparatus.

"The day is coming," predicted one communications expert, "I think there may soon be *TV Actualities* . . . but I am opposed to television *Actualities*. I am worried that the trend line is toward the government's producing spots."[11]

Again employing audio, President Reagan inaugurated the weekly radio address, which was usually delivered from the Oval Office. The address was made available to hundreds of radio stations nationwide, and its text was published as a White House document. Bush did not copy this approach, but Clinton did. In Clinton's time, the delivery of the radio address became a VIP gathering, witnessed in the Oval Office by a sizable group of guests. A "protocol order" of sorts determined who could be invited: presidential friends, White House staff, cabinet secretaries, and senior appointees. Applications had to be submitted two weeks in advance. Readers may reflect: did Clinton start what may become a new White House tradition?

The White House Studio

The Executive Residence and the Oval Office can be made into appealing backgrounds for television, but only after hours of setup and despite unsightly snakes of cables. In 1989 President Bush asked, "Why don't we have our own TV studio?" That query started a modest construction project in Room 459 of the Old Executive Office Building. Now the White House has its own television facility, with built-in lighting and sound, and even lead-lined walls to keep out the wails of any passing sirens. Half of the studio is furnished as if it were the Map Room, the other half as if it were the Residence library.

Assume that a convention of thousands is assembling in Phoenix, that a group of women business leaders is meeting in Miami, and that Native American tribal heads are gathering in Missoula. All these events would present exceptionally favorable opportunities for presidential policy statements, but the chief executive's schedule makes personal travel impossible. The president need only travel to the fourth floor of the Old Executive Office Building, take a seat in the "virtual White House Map Room," and live coverage is arranged via satellite for direct television "narrowcast" of a separate speech to each of the three audiences. (The sponsoring organizations may be asked to help defray the modest production costs.) "We could drop him into any major event around the country," explained Bush communications innovator Barrie Tron.

As noted earlier, Clinton used this technique repeatedly. On July 30, 1993, for example, he gave two satellite interviews from Room 459: one to the Arizona media and a second to the California media. He went at it for two hours: the printed text takes up thirteen and one-half single-spaced pages.[12] On October 22, 1999—this time using the East Room itself—President Clinton and the first lady hosted a conference on philanthropy. It was carried live on several public-access TV channels and simultaneously narrowcast to "one hundred sites across the country, where groups held their own philanthropy conferences. Many public television stations were able to air the conference in subsequent weeks."[13] Room 459 is in use continuously, often for more than one production a day.

The Internet and the "Streaming" White House

The disadvantage of conventional radio, TV broadcasting, and narrowcasting is that the receivers are passive. Technology has now changed that. A further Bush innovation was to add an audio (and later a video) link coming back from the distant audience, so that after watching the president on television, viewers could send questions to the president in return (the White House communicators had anticipated the questions and supplied presidential briefing in advance).

President Clinton contributed still other innovations to the White House communications capability. He had his staff create a White House Web site (www.Whitehouse.gov). Within an hour of their delivery, full transcripts of the president's press conferences, Rose Garden remarks, or weekly radio addresses—as well as briefings by the press secretary—were put online, where they could be downloaded by any computer user. A listserve function was also established: by subscribing, individual citizens or organizations could automatically receive e-mails on specific topics that they selected from a menu of available White House materials. If for example, one had signed up to receive all the policy speeches and press briefings on foreign policy, the texts would be automatically e-mailed out to be read at one's leisure. The Web site menu currently has eight options to click on, including

—The President and Vice President: How to Send Them Electronic Mail
—White House History and Tours
—The Virtual [White House] Library
—What's New at the White House

—The Briefing Room—Today's Releases and Hot Topics
—The White House for Kids.

In Clinton's seventh year, the White House introduced a further innovation: cybercasting. Not only were presidential remarks electronically injected into the White House Web site for storage and retrieval, but they were also "streamed" onto the Internet as live productions. The first live White House cybercast took place on November 8, 1999; it was prospectively described as an

> on-line chat, fielding real-time questions in a format that will allow computer users to watch the responses on live video. . . . During the 90-minute session, from 7 to 8:30 p.m. EST . . . 15,000 people who make it into the virtual auditorium (www.townhallmeeting.excite.com) will have the chance to fire e-mail questions at Clinton. (An additional 35,000 can watch but not participate.) Clinton will respond verbally, not at a keyboard, but those whose computers lack video or audio capability will be able to read an up-to-date transcript . . . if the Webcast is successful. . . . The Democratic Leadership Council [the host of the program] hopes to schedule one with British prime minister Tony Blair.[14]

At the beginning of the cybercast that evening, the president commented: "The first presidential townhall meeting on the Internet taps the most modern technology for old-fashinoned communication between the American people and their President. Tonight's event is exciting not only because of the technology involved in its execution, but, on a larger scale, for the unbridled potential it represents."[15] During the one and one-half hour "townhall" cybercast, the president answered twenty-five questions. According to a news story the next morning, the "organizers called it a great step for a democracy that prizes close links between citizens and elected officials."[16]

As the system gets perfected in the future, school classes, for instance, will be able to "come into" the White House, be "present" at exclusive assemblages in the East Room or the Rose Garden, and "speak up" with e-mailed questions—which, with the proper screening, can be answered immediately by the president or whoever is hosting the event. Cybercasts were available not just in America but worldwide; during one recent production, a question came in from Mogadishu, prompting some White House staff to wonder: should its Internet contributions be multilingual?

The White House "streaming" expert reflected:

> This truly is a new platform for reaching people. What is so exciting about the Web in particular: it allows people to choose the informa-

tion that they want. We are not only pushing the information out, but people then have the opportunity quickly to find the exact information they are interested in. . . . People need to realize that the Internet is not just a print medium. Nor is it merely a multimedia creation. It can provide services. . . . One of the focuses I wanted the White House Web site to have was: What are the unique services that the government can provide? How can the White House highlight those? At a time when this administration has been aiming at doing more with less, that is an incredibly valuable tool. . . . It's the notion of how do we make government more accessible to the people.[17]

Jeff Eller, the original Clinton media manager, was quoted as dreaming, as far back as 1993, of a "C-SPAN–like channel to broadcast White House events around the clock": "B.C.[Bill Clinton]-TV," Eller called it.[18]

Welcome indeed to the White House of the twenty-first century!

As to the effect all this electronic innovation may have on executive branch public administration, the young Bush communications veteran mused, half-jokingly, "The White House of the future? Why do we have to have all these buildings around here where different cabinet departments are off the compound? Maybe they will all be in the EOB [Executive Office Building]!"[19]

Media Relations

While the press secretary concentrates on dealing with the White House press corps, the communications managers are very much aware that local and specialty publications require attention and "feeding" as well. There are thousands of them: *Cow Country News, Farmers Weekly Review,* the *Jewish Herald,* the *Lesbian News,* the *Minority Business Entrepreneur, Mundo Hispanico, News from Indian Country.* When the White House is taking actions that may affect their interests, all are potential conveyers of presidential information.

A media relations unit (sometimes a part of the Communications Office, but in the Clinton White House attached to the press secretary's operation) has long been an element of the continuing campaign. Just after President Bush had announced his proposals to amend the Clean Air Act, a convention of business writers happened to be in Washington. Attendees were invited to the White House, given a briefing by Environmental Protection Agency Administrator William Reilly and Chief of Staff John Sununu. The media relations staff provided each participant with a "media kit": fact sheets about what the amendments would accomplish and a copy of the president's speech.

The Clinton media affairs office had four regional press secretaries who covered the nation from their desks at the White House. Sidney Blumenthal describes how they operated: "Within each region, local radio stations, television stations, and newspapers are called daily to see if they'd be interested in an interview with an Administration figure. (There is a thick loose-leaf media book for every state. 'These are my bibles,' said Kim Hopper, who handles the Western region.)"[20]

A supporting element of the Clinton Communications Office was a five-person research unit—a resource available not only to the communications head but to the chief of staff and other White House senior staffers, to help produce backgrounders and undertake similar special projects. One researcher was specifically attached to the speechwriting operation, which is discussed in the next chapter.

Mobilizing the Cabinet

There are some three thousand political appointees in the cabinet departments and agencies, over a thousand of whom are Senate-confirmed, top-level officials, and between twenty and thirty of whom are agency heads—who travel, make speeches, and issue press releases. Nearly every one of them can be enlisted in the continuing communications campaign. Each agency has "in mini" what the White House has "in macro": its own office of communications. The White House reaches out and ties them all into the common purpose.

Every Monday morning at eleven the departmental communications directors in the Clinton cabinet were hooked into an "amplification" conference call originating from the White House: the director of the Office of Communications, the president's scheduler, and the deputy secretary to the cabinet were the joint callers. The vice president's office was included in the confab since there was strong, administration-wide interest in his activities as well.

Within half an hour after the amplification call, the basic agreements and assignments were faxed out to the participants. All were alerted: "Here's what's going to happen in the White House during the next five days." "This is what the president is going to be trying to talk about." Would Health and Human Services Secretary Donna Shalala be speaking in Chicago? She was expected to call attention to the president's just having signed an education bill. And "on Friday, Madame Secretary, kindly send us the Chicago news clips so that we can see how things went." Was the secretary of transportation dedicating a bridge in Ottumwa? He was told to include an emphasis on the president's highway safety initiative. Commerce would report: "Secretary Daley did media interviews in Omaha, Des Moines, and Dubuque."

Referring to such stories in the local press, former deputy cabinet secretary Steve Silverman observed: "The smaller the newspaper the better! . . . If I could see that Transportation Secretary Rodney Slater was interviewed in the local Ottumwa paper, I would give him a high five. . . . We were always trying to find the best way to use our time and our resources."[21]

By reviewing the material that came in from the departments for the weekly Cabinet Report, the Office of Cabinet Affairs could jump on any opportunity to maximize the benefits of a cabinet officer's travel—or even to promote such travel, if a key event could use the extra jazz that a cabinet secretary's presence might supply. Some cabinet members, however, were less than sanguine about such promotional orchestration. In his book on his years in the cabinet, former secretary of labor Robert Reich recounted a diary entry:

April 29
"The White House wants you to go to Cleveland," [Reich's secretary announces] . . .

"Houses don't make phone calls. *Who* called?"

"I don't know. Someone from Cabinet Affairs. Steve somebody. I'll schedule it."

"How *old* is Steve?". . .

"What difference does it make? They want you to go to Cleveland. You're going to Cleveland." . . .

"I'll bet he's under thirty. . . . Some *twerp* in the White House who has *no clue* what I'm doing in this job. Screw him. I won't go." . . .

Orders from twerps in the White House didn't bother me at the beginning. Now I can't stomach snotty children telling me what to do. From the point of view of the White House staff, cabinet officials are provincial governors presiding over alien, primitive territories. Anything of any importance occurs in the imperial palace, within the capital city. The provincial governors are important only in a ceremonial sense. They wear the colors and show the flag. Occasionally they are called to get their next round of orders before being returned to their outposts. They are of course dazzled by the splendor of the court, and grateful for the chance to visit.[22]

The amplification calls were nonetheless a staple of the Clinton communications operation.

Were the cabinet members expected to work up these initiatives from their own resources? Not in the Clinton administration. A daily e-mail entitled "Talking Points" issued from the White House Communications Office. This message went not just to cabinet heads but to two thousand of the political appointees. From time to time the departmental communications officers were assembled in the White House to compare notes in person and smooth out any kinks in their interwoven processes.

Should a cabinet member or senior White House staff officer be invited to participate in one of the Sunday talk shows, the response was expected to be, "I'll get back to you." Like many previous administrations, Clinton's followed a rule: the White House controls such acceptances—and governs them according to the president's own communications priorities.

Here the press secretary plays an active as well as a reactive role, taking the initiative to suggest to a TV producer that a given cabinet secretary or administration spokesperson would be (1) available and (2) useful to cover a particular theme on a particular show. There is a steel hand behind the friendly offer: while negotiations may be undertaken, it is clear that the White House preference can be made binding. Indeed, a cabinet officer may be instructed to decline a media invitation in order to "steer" that invitation to a different cabinet officer whom the White House would prefer to be the current center of the public relations effort. In July of 1978 a senior White House staffer under Carter circumvented the control system—and was forced out of office.

Organizing Rebuttals

In instances of what they consider to be proper defense of their presidents, White House communications staffers have not shrunk from quick and direct personal intervention to rebut what journalists or TV reporters are writing or saying. In the Reagan years, communications assistant David Gergen would watch Dan Rather's evening news broadcast on Baltimore's CBS television station at 6:30 P.M. If he spotted a story he considered clearly unfair to the administration, he would telephone CBS to try to persuade Rather to change the story before the program aired in Washington at 7. When veteran *Washington Post* columnist David Broder wrote a piece in February of 1993 criticizing Clinton's economic program as "bad politics as well as bad economics" and describing the president's tactics as "dangerously wrong," Clinton's young assistant George Stephanopoulos called him up to argue with him.[23] During the August 1997 Senate hearings concerning allegedly improper White House fund-raising activities, White House "rebuttal spokesman" Lanny Davis posted himself outside the Senate hearing room, looked over the shoulder of the Associated Press reporters who were writing up their story, and tried (in vain) to get them to rewrite it on the spot.[24] This approach might be called the Code Red style of White House communications operations.

Communications at the White Hot: The "War Room"

The chapter epigraph quoting George Stephanopoulos was both a historical summing-up and a prediction. Unmentioned but implied was that this peculiarly hyperactive, Clintonesque communications enterprise that had been used in Little Rock during the 1992 campaign was going to be reemployed in the White House. And it was.

In today's large, specialized, and diverse White House, coordination is the sine qua non (more about this in chapter 21). But coordination comes hard: staffers are overworked, preoccupied with their specialized duties, protective of the turf of their assignments, and not inclined to share information or to dovetail their activities. Based on his obviously successful experience with the campaign headquarters at Little Rock, Clinton established a coordinating center—a "war room"—for each of the big, early initiatives: the economic program, health care, and the North American Free Trade Agreement.

Rather than just hope that the frantically busy staffers would keep in touch, by telephone or by e-mail, with each other and with the departmental specialists, the Clinton managers commandeered a large room on the first floor of the Old Executive Office Building, set up two horseshoe-shaped table arrangements, and crammed twenty or more staffers into one hyperkinetic, face-to-face mix. "A roiling caldron," as one reporter described it: "People crammed side by side, urgently answering phones, purposefully passing each other sheaves of paper, jumping up from their seats to confer with one another, tapping the keyboards of their computer terminals." At one desk, "cabinet members and other surrogates" are being scheduled for "television and radio appearances around the country"; at another, "rapid responses" are being shot out to counter opponents' charges; at still another a senior White House staffer is writing out manifestos. The Democratic National Committee chairman was delighted to see this "boiler room operation, where people can sit across from one another and shout at one another.

... It provides a greater sense of urgency, with everyone there cheering each other on and keeping each other accountable."[25]

"The theory is a simple one," explained a veteran of the health care initiative:

> You have everybody working toward the same goal; you have all these different elements, and you need to have them communicating with each other. The best way to do that was to put them all in the same damn room ... people from our press staff, public liaison, legislative affairs, intergovernmental affairs, scheduling, political affairs, the first lady's office, people from the departments of HHS [Health and Human Services], Treasury, VA [Veterans Affairs] and Labor. . . . We needed to be coordinated; we needed to be responsive to the Congress when they asked; we needed the substantive people so they could answer questions; we'd be on press out of that room. . . . We had twenty people stuffed in there. It was coordination by proximity. . . . And the president would drop by; he'd come in and ask, "Hey, how're you doing?!"[26]

Looking back, though, another White House veteran expressed reservations about using war rooms: "I think it was overused as a technique. It tends to compartmentalize the White House. . . . It undercuts the legislative office; it undercuts the press office. You don't have an integrated view of governing. In fact, it divides the White House into mini–White Houses—people who will then start competing with one another. . . . You need some captain of the effort, but this became so draining. . . . People who were working on one project didn't give a damn whether the other project got passed or not."[27]

The war room technique was not used in the later Clinton years, and former chief of staff Leon Panetta explained why:

> If you have a good staff operation you don't need a war room. People ought to be capable of working on an issue without having to put them all in one room. If it's a high-level effort that is really high profile and you think it's a better way to coordinate, then it might make some sense. But I would be very cautious about doing a war room because it really undermines the morale of other people that are not part of the staff operation. . . . It makes people think they are exclusive, and then the war room becomes a policymaking operation, and that is the last thing you need.[28]

"My role as communications director," former director Don Baer summed up, "was to try to be a 'creative director of the White House' . . . a 'strategic director'—not merely doing a public relations job." The task was "to help the president and others to try to assert to the country that this presidency was *about* something."[29] Another former Clinton counselor looked back at the frantic melange of communications activities and judged them to be "so excessive that they have changed the character of the presidency, have gone way too far." He added, "I think there are too many people in the PR game in the White House . . . too much attention given to what is of immediate impact—what will be in the press tomorrow—as opposed to what is of real impact. More emphasis is paid to politics . . . than to governance."[30]

CHAPTER TEN

Judson Welliver and His Successors: The Speechwriting Office

The man who writes the President's speeches runs the country.
THOMAS E. DEWEY

Speechwriters aren't supposed to make policy!
ROBERT C. MCFARLANE

His title was "literary clerk" when Judson Welliver, the first presidential speechwriter, began his White House service under President Warren G. Harding on March 4, 1921. Ever since, the president's staff has included a speechwriting person or unit. And continuously since, that office has expanded and its output has exploded.

In his first six and one-half years in office, President Eisenhower's speeches, written statements, press conferences, addresses, and remarks filled 6,618 pages of the *Public Papers of the Presidents*. In the comparable period in his presidency, President Clinton filled 15,669 pages.

The contemporary White House is, in fact, a high-speed prose factory. Presidential speeches and statements come in long and short sizes—some of them rating worldwide attention, a few of them sheer miscellany.

The Variety of Presidential Speeches

Every presidency starts with a speech—the inaugural address—with phrases designed to be memorable. Ronald Reagan wanted us to believe that "gov-

ernment is not the solution to our problem, government is the problem."
George Bush asked that we, as a people, "make kinder the face of the nation
and gentler the face of the world," but cautioned that "we have more will
than wallet." In 1993 Bill Clinton declared that "we must do what America does best: offer more opportunity to all and demand more responsibility
from all."

Of principal importance for celebrating a president's past accomplishments and setting the tone of his future objectives is the State of the Union
(SOTU) message. Each January the president delivers this message in person to a joint session of the House and Senate. Like the inaugural, the SOTU
address is broadcast simultaneously to a national television audience. As
mentioned in chapter 9, it is delivered in prime time and preceded by what
has become an impressive national ritual.

This message makes the year's greatest demand on a presidential speechwriter: summing up the president's recent success, cataloging the challenges
of the present, introducing the president's vision of the months to come. It
is here that program initiatives are unveiled, needed legislation requested.
For a president with a heavy agenda of new proposals, the SOTU message
may become, as one speechwriter described it, "a kind of a list, with nice
sentences at each end." The speechwriter for that address usually starts writing in October.

At the lesser end of the scale is "Rose Garden rubbish"— slang for greetings and pep talks to special groups that are invited to gather at the Rose
Garden steps. Here the president accepts (and pardons) a live turkey just before
Thanksgiving, congratulates a winning athletic team, or celebrates the resur-
gence of the bald eagle. (In July of 1999, an impressively large specimen of
that species, tethered as a prop, aimed a hard peck at the president's fingers.)

The Speechwriting Process

The authors of much of the 2,500-odd pages produced each year (which
include the president's weekly radio addresses and the hundreds of video
messages to favored organizations) are the White House speechwriting and
research staff. Like other principal White House actors described in this
book, the speechwriting director operates on a rule of exclusivity: for all the
president's spoken words, the speechwriters are the guardians of his style,
his syntax, and his accuracy. Other staff units may suggest draft language,
but the speechwriting office demands—with one exception—a monopoly
over the crafting of the president's addresses.

That exception is foreign affairs speeches. Particularly under Bush and Clinton, speechwriters on the staff of the National Security Council (NSC), closely supervised by the national security adviser, drafted the president's foreign policy addresses. They called in materials from State or Defense and would show the White House speechwriting office a nearly final draft for a last once-over, but the NSC staff controlled the foreign policy speechwriting process "from soup to nuts," as one Clinton NSC officer described it.[1]

Campaign consultant Dick Morris had a disdainful view of the NSC's exclusivity. The NSC's contributions to the 1995 State of the Union message "arrived on stone tablets," he sneered—a further example of the acrimony (described in chapter 3) between the two sets of speech drafters.[2] With Samuel (Sandy) Berger's advent as national security adviser, the animus between the speechwriters and the NSC drafters moderated. "You say a blooper in a domestic speech," observed a Clinton senior staffer, "and your ratings sink five points, or the stock market goes down fifty. You say a blooper in a foreign affairs speech and you could start a war!"[3]

"We speechwriters are translators," emphasized one Republican-era wordsmith, "not translating Spanish into English but translating the bureaucratic into the poetic, the legalese into the elegant, the corporatese into the conversational, the complex into the simple. . . . The job of the writer is to zap the jargon with which academics or bureaucrats couch their proposals. . . . If a president were ever to deliver a televised address in the same form that some department functionary sent over to the White House, it wouldn't be a 'Fireside Chat' because it would put out the fire."[4]

How does a presidential speech get written in today's White House?

At the beginning of the Clinton administration, the sheer number of speeches was so staggering (some seven hundred were made that first year) that advance notice was slight. One speechwriter remembers: "The first year was like the campaign: you might be called on Friday about a speech on Monday. The scheduling was not done far in advance at all, and it was all very often changed. It was run like a campaign: 'The president is going to be in three different places on Thursday, and we won't know until Tuesday, and we'll change it on Wednesday.' And you don't know the message; they would be moving from a shopping mall in Milwaukee to a factory in Detroit."[5]

Scheduling procedures, as chapter 12 relates, were tightened and improved after that early period. For major addresses there were finally longer lead times; but, as another writer added, "If I had two or three days to work on a speech, that was a luxury. I was often writing a speech a day just to keep up with the next day. . . . There were occasions, on some foreign trips, where I was only asleep an hour a night, or two hours a night, literally. You never really recover; you are just exhausted."[6] A third recalled: "For something like a radio address, he might not see it until just before he gave it. He was incredibly adept at working through something very fast, or reading something quickly, committing to memory the parts that he wanted to remember, and then extemporizing on the other parts."[7]

When a speech is scheduled, a team is usually formed: one from the writing staff and one from the research unit. Bush had seven in each unit; Clinton had five speechwriters but only one researcher, although interns helped out on the research side. Before the speechwriting begins, the researcher prepares a "site memorandum" describing the event in which the president will participate: its history, background, and setting.

The speechwriter soaks up this story and prepares an initial draft, but the draft's first routing is back to the research unit for a fact check. Is there a single statement that cannot be substantiated? Speech authors, suggested one observer, tend to regard even their initial prose as "graven in marble"; the research staffer is expected to suggest alternative language if the factual record requires it. Is there a historical reference that didn't happen, a quotation without a source? Speechwriters, the observer commented, have been known to make up quotes that they would like to believe that somebody said.

To back up the research unit's checking system, the White House has access to the Office of Administration's libraries in the Old Executive Office Building, and through those libraries the full use of the Library of Congress as well as computer access to commercial data banks of every variety.

Speechwriters, Policymakers, and the President: How Distant or How Close?

As White House writers contemplate the substance of any piece they are shaping, they are aware of the two severe criticisms that have been leveled at them during most contemporary administrations: (1) they are divorced from policymakers and (2) they have little contact with the president.

In 1979, Theodore Sorensen, who served Kennedy as both counsel and major speechwriter, wrote of his concern: "Alas, the poor speechwriter. I knew him well. Once he was a presidential collaborator . . . a Sam Rosenman, a Clark Clifford, participating in the decisions he helped to communicate, exchanging ideas with the President as well as phrases. . . . In the last three administrations . . . he has typically not been a policy adviser but a professional wordsmith, isolated from decision-making and from personal contact with the decision-maker."[8] The same sentiment appears in a 1997 book on White House speechwriting: "Presidential relegation of speechwriting to wordsmiths who are not essentially involved in decision making, combined with reliance on polls, undermines the role of the president as educator and often creates a disconnection between words and actions."[9]

These criticisms, of course, really apply only to major policy speeches. And they ring more true for the Reagan presidency than for the Bush administration. In the Clinton White House, the relationship between speechwriter and president was nothing like the distanced one that Sorensen and the more recent critic condemn.

Consider Clinton's 6,800-word speech in the National Archives Rotunda on July 19, 1995, in which he stated his policy position on the sensitive and much-debated issue of affirmative action. As was briefly described in chapter 2, a duo of senior associates—Christopher Edley, a Harvard law professor and former associate director of the Office of Management and Budget, and White House aide George Stephanopoulos—spent six months conducting a thorough interagency review of affirmative action practices, and developed the controversial policy recommendations.

The two policy designers met again and again with speechwriters Don Baer and Carolyn Curiel and with the president. Stephanopoulos recalled: "He [the president] became more engaged over the course of the review. As I fed him a steady stream of position papers, monographs, and opinion pieces from various sides of the debate, he'd check them off and ask for more. Our core group would meet with him every week or so, and he seemed to enjoy the Socratic dialogues, asking the right questions ('What are the legitimate worries of those who don't get affirmative action?')."[10] Edley describes the final morning before the Archives speech:

> On speeches that he really cares about, he stays up all night and he rewrites furiously. He just fills up the margins of papers. The morning of the event, at about seven, a small group of us were in the Oval Office. He was still working on it. And he was literally dictating—he was reading from scraps of yellow paper, marked up from what he had been up until three in the morning working on. Don [Baer] was there with his cassette recorder, taping it as the president read through—the inserts and so forth. . . . Every once in a while he would stop and say, "Is this OK? Is this right? Does this make sense?" We would talk it through, and we would argue. "We had to change this,"

and "What about this nuance? How about this language?" This, mind you, is two hours before he was supposed to be at the National Archives.[11]

Only for special appearances—for example, before a joint session of Congress or at the United Nations General Assembly—did President Clinton use a formal text, programmed into teleprompters. And even on those occasions (except for State of the Union addresses), recalled speechwriter David Kusnet, 25 percent of the delivery was extemporaneous, and an advance text was almost never given out. Using a teleprompter introduced a new limitation for the speechwriters: no sentence should be longer than what could be displayed within the margins of a teleprompter screen.

Clinton was aided by a technological advance made during the Bush years: electronic teleprompters. Before Bush initiated the use of the electronic version, the machines scrolled down preprinted rolls of paper. But electronic teleprompters use quickly replaceable disks—allowing a president to make changes at the very last minute. One staffer expressed regret at this "improvement": it tempts the president to keep on futzing with the language, even as the limousine rolls into the driveway of the Capitol. Kusnet coined a special adjective to describe President Clinton: "unteleprompterable."

For less crucial addresses, the Clinton speechwriting staff identified the policy issues that they were to write about and discussed them in depth with their senior White House colleagues on the Domestic Policy Council and the National Economic Council. Some of these relationships were especially cordial, dating from collegial experiences years back (such as riding on the same plane in Walter Mondale's 1984 presidential campaign). Bonded by decades-old friendship, "we would sit around the keyboard with all the policy people," speechwriter Kusnet recalled. "We tried to be as inclusive about it as possible. The battles had less to do with policy and more to do with clarity. The policy people, you know, tend to want to plug just about every accomplishment into the speech—when we were trying to cut the speeches back. . . . I didn't feel ostracized; it was a team working together."[12]

The speechwriters also reached out to policy officers in the cabinet departments with whom they had developed an informal personal rapport—"big picture people, who are not special pleaders, who have the president's welfare at heart," as one White House staffer emphasized. But actual drafts of speeches were almost never sought from the line agencies.

The speechwriting and delivery system for these less formal presentations was loose indeed, fitting Clinton's personal style. His writers had a rule:

Never give the president more than five single-spaced pages—and Clinton used those only as a starting point for his own train of thought. "If you gave him a final draft, you would never see it again," Kusnet remembers. "The president would scribble on the margins as a way of making notes for himself, would spot perhaps one line from a drafted page, weave it into his own experience and his own way of expressing himself." Preparing for a speech, he would "make phone calls to friends late at night, read books, talk with Hillary. He would have his own thought processes, entirely separate from and parallel to any 'staffing' processes you could devise," Kusnet adds.[13]

In the Clinton White House, at least, Ted Sorensen's lament—"Alas, the poor speechwriter"—had a different meaning: Could the overworked staff keep up with the policy chiefs and the president, who were engaging in "Socratic dialogue" as the last hours ticked away before delivery time?

President Bush, although more staid and more inclined to keep to written text than Clinton, was often in direct contact with his speechwriters as well. "Too much rhetoric!" he would tell them—meaning, as one remembers, "too highfalutin', too flowery. He liked very plain language."[14] Bush was also apprehensive about giving a speech that included stirring, emotional passages praising the sacrifices made by men and women in battle. He identified so personally with the patriotic poignancy that he feared his voice would break; his speechwriters would have to remind him that he could steel himself to deliver such phrases effectively. Like presidents before him and since, President Bush subjected himself to rehearsals in the White House Family Theater: fifteen staffers would be there to give him on-the-spot critiques and counsel him on his delivery.

Clearly each president has a different style, and the speechwriters—whoever they may be—must adapt to it. Bush, from his long experience in government, was no stranger to the formalities of working with prepared speeches. Clinton, in contrast, as the governor of a small state, had not had any full-time speechwriter on his Little Rock staff: he never used one until he became the Democratic nominee in 1992. His experience in talking extemporaneously carried over to the Washington environment. Apart from the big, formal addresses, one speechwriter estimates that "from 50 to 95 percent of his remarks" were extemporaneous. This was the case, for instance, at a fund-raising dinner speech in California in May of 1999 that ran over 4,800 words.[15]

The Clearance System

The penultimate step in the White House speechwriting process is the clearance system, which is typically managed by the staff secretary. The Clinton White House followed that procedure. After much of the informal, internal discussion had taken place and a nearly complete draft had been composed, at least twenty copies were distributed to other senior officers, including the political affairs director, the counsel, the chief of staff, and the vice president. If the president was scheduled to go on a domestic trip, the White House Office of Political Affairs was expected to advise the speechwriter about the politics of the state where he would be speaking. As to Mr. Gore's views, speechwriter Kusnet comments, "The vice president is not a lawyer but has a disciplined mind, is a very good journalist, is a politician and has written his own book. . . . If he weighed in, you paid him a lot of attention."[16]

The first lady's chief of staff also got a copy—but even before that, if the speech touched on a matter of interest to the first lady, President Clinton would likely have handed her a draft for her own independent critique. "And if something mattered very much to her, you'd try to do it," observed a Clinton staffer. Responsible and affected cabinet members were on the clearance list, too, but comments from them were rarely received with much enthusiasm. Said one officer in State: "At the beginning of this administration, the NSC would at least have a meeting and invite people from State and Defense to talk about a speech—what should be in it, and so forth. None of that happens any more. Now, perhaps at six o'clock the night before the speech, we would get a draft. We are told it has already gone to the president; he likes it. But if the secretary of state really has something she feels strongly about, of course, 'We'll take it into consideration.' So that's another way the system has changed."[17]

The staff secretary imposes tight deadlines, gathers the incoming comments, and puts them into the speechwriter's hands—where judgments are made as to which amendments or corrections might be acceptable. The chief of staff—perhaps the president—will call the shots in the end.

Speeches of Exceptional Political Importance

A presidential speech may announce a major redirection of policy. How to frame such a speech—and whether it should be given at all—can become pivotal issues of political strategy. To hammer out decisions of this import, especially if there is disagreement among his advisers, a president may employ unusually closely held decisionmaking processes. In 1995–96, when the Clinton White House was gearing up for the forthcoming electoral campaign, President Clinton convened in the Residence a series of confidential weekly sessions among his vice president, senior advisers, and a group of political consultants and pollsters. In his book about those two years, political maestro Dick Morris describes not only how campaign strategy was meticulously plotted but also how detailed themes for groundbreaking presidential speeches were laid out.[18] But themes had to be translated into rhetoric. Therefore, after sweating out the heated internal staff conflicts generated by his ideas for themes, the combative Morris—at the urging of the president—took on the role of "speech-designer," fortifying his arguments with results from freshly conducted polls. At first secretly, then in quiet collaboration with the like-minded Don Baer, Morris drafted several presidential speeches whose precedent-making substance mirrored the out-of-the-ordinary process by which they were formulated.[19]

For some speeches of importance, rehearsals were held in the White House Family Theater, with the president using the teleprompter and reading the suggested draft. "[Clinton] would start reading what you had, and he would edit with his mouth, not with his hands. 'That's not me; I can't say that; how does this sound?' . . . As he gave it there would be an entirely different speech taking shape. The rehearsal would make it clear that . . . what was going on wasn't spontaneous; he himself had been thinking about these things. And you would get these fully formed paragraphs out of his head, in response to what you had given him . . . and that would be the nucleus of a new speech."[20]

Speeches by the First Lady

Hillary Rodham Clinton has added high visibility to the role of first lady. In the early period of the Clinton administration she was giving as many as two hundred speeches a year. Her initial support for this effort was a sole, part-time speechwriter, who was soon assigned on a full-time basis exclusively to help her. More than likely, this is the first such position on the staff: another evolutionary step for the modern White House. "I once wrote thirteen speeches in nine days," Mrs. Clinton's speechwriter recalled.

The most important of Mrs. Clinton's speeches were those delivered during her trips overseas, where she turned international attention to human rights issues, and especially to elevating the status of women. "First Lady of the World Stage," one 1993 headline proclaimed.

Mrs. Clinton lived up to that title at the United Nations Fourth World Conference on Women, held in Beijing in early September of 1995. There had been controversy about her even going to China, and debate about how firmly—or even whether—she should criticize the Chinese hosts for their miserable human rights record. Two women's conferences were being held side by side: one of official government delegates and the other of women from nongovernmental organizations. Mrs. Clinton went to China and spoke at both assemblages, but it was the UN Conference speech that was historic.

Her speechwriter put the first drafts together, but only the president and a tight circle of the first lady's associates were privy to them. The clearance was handled enroute to China by the secretary of state herself, an NSC representative, and Assistant Secretary of State Winston Lord, the former U.S. ambassador in Beijing. Chief of Staff Melanne Verveer recalls: "That's when others beyond our small circle read the speech. Was there anything in this draft that was a problem? Then we would finesse it, do whatever was required. But it wasn't widely circulated, to be picked apart and the message diluted. 'She's going to be tough.' 'She's not going to be tough.' 'She's going to be tough!' Nobody knew until we were airborne. It was a closed process, but it was an informed process."[21]

The official *New China News Agency* mentioned Mrs. Clinton's name but did not quote any of her remarks. The *New York Times* called it "her finest hour." The United States Information Agency translated the speech into many languages and distributed it worldwide. Her speechwriter, Lissa Muscatine, observed that "women around the world have copies of that speech. We meet with women in various countries—even the most distant, rural places; they are clutching it."[22]

The first lady gave four speeches in China and one to university students in Ulan Bator, the capital of Mongolia; she was the highest-ranking American to visit that country since it adopted a democratic form of government in 1990.

Even back in Washington, Mrs. Clinton's speeches were not sent through the staff secretary's clearance process—nor were those of the vice president, who had three speechwriters of his own. With the sharply increasing political obligations facing both the first lady and the vice president during their respective campaigns of 2000, their speechwriting resources expanded—although these of course were being paid for by campaign rather than appropriated funds.

On the Speechwriters' Wish Lists

In both the Bush and Clinton White House organizations, the speechwriting unit was tucked under the Office of Communications, an arrangement that frustrated the speechwriters. Said one: "The Clinton campaign had succeeded in large measure because it was a media-conscious campaign. 'Communications' to the campaign staff meant media, press, and so on—not speechwriting. When they got into the White House, they wanted to replicate that model. For them, speechwriting just was not that important in this sort of overall scheme of 'communications.' . . . The speechwriters basically got rolled in terms of offices and staff."[23]

The Bush speechwriting staff had similar gripes: they were relegated to the least desirable offices, given the most outdated computers and—by fiat of Chief of Staff John Sununu—were denied the privilege of eating in the White House Mess.

Recognizing that some presidents (Nixon, Clinton) are what he termed "ideological hybrids"—that is, speaking to one audience with a conservative tone and to a different group with a liberal slant—a Clinton veteran suggested that a president should consider having a stable of speechwriters that would span the same ideological variety that the boss had within himself.

The future always beckons for speechwriters. Several have written books. The *Economist* of February 1994 carried a full-page advertisement: "I can make *you* a more powerful speaker!" Sponsor of the ad, and pictured shaking hands with President Reagan in the Oval Office, was Aram Bakshian Jr., speechwriter for Nixon and Ford and director of that staff for Reagan. It offered—through a "no risk, 30-day trial ('or your money back')"—to teach the subcriber how to give "the perfect speech for every occasion."

CHAPTER ELEVEN

Representing Interests and Building Coalitions: The Office of Public Liaison

Most of the 300 groups (2,000 people) represented at the eleven energy briefings this week were supportive, especially labor, urban groups and trade associations. . . . A task force has been organized and we are working on a detailed outreach program to support the legislative initiatives.

ANN WEXLER

We have people in the White House . . . who aren't there representing the President to the country. They are representing the country to the President. That's not what the White House staff should be.

THEODORE SORENSEN

This book's opening chapter describes an American society of organized disputers: nearly twenty-three thousand national nonprofit advocacy groups contend to represent "the general welfare." They encompass a vast diversity, representing racial and ethnic groups; religious organizations of every denominational stripe; issue-advocacy collectives like the Sierra Club and the American Cetacean Society (whales); and professional and trade associations such as the National Association of Manufacturers, the American Medical Association, and the American Society for Public Administration.

Corporations knock on White House doors, too, but here a line is drawn: while the views of profit-making organizations are often invited and welcome on issues of general public policy, White House doors are closed to any entreaties to intervene in a business firm's dispute with either a line department or a federal regulatory agency.

In this phantasmagoric cacophony of contending voices, issues arise and disappear, coalitions endlessly form and disband. Millions of dollars are amassed and spent, and skilled managers and lobbyists wield letters, e-mails, faxes, testimony, and visits. The policy combat of the nation becomes the warfare of Washington.

The Potential Bargain

This warfare has a dual significance. To the lobbyists, the White House is a target; to the White House, interest-group power is presidential opportunity.

As target: The chief executive is besieged with message-carriers urging him to act or refrain from acting on any of a thousand issues. Some sit on the sidewalk with signs; millions send letters and e-mails; thousands telephone the Comment Line; hundreds ask to be heard in person. All seek a sympathetic reception, and each would like to know that *someone*—if not the president himself, then someone on his staff—will pay attention to their entreaties. Especially expectant are the leaders of America's major nonprofit advocacy groups, who assume that the White House will receive them and give weight to their views.

As opportunity: From where he sits, the president views interest group lobbyists—on issues where he and they agree—as possible extensions of his own salesmanship. They can amplify his influence: first to their memberships—then, through their memberships, to Congress. With skillful staff work, the president can mobilize that extramural power, enlisting organizational leaders to help squeeze out just the few more House or Senate votes he needs to achieve his high-priority objectives.

Here are the makings of a bargain.

The president will include on his personal staff men and women who make it their business to cultivate links to the major interest groups of America. They will be good listeners—but also willing to talk and investigate. They will open doors, guaranteeing advocacy groups a fair hearing: in the White House, in the departments, and on occasion in the Oval Office (unless, as will be illustrated in other chapters, the president insists on secrecy for certain of his initiatives until they are announced).

For their part, the interest groups, even if they are skeptical, will give the president or his representatives the chance to explain their objectives; will attend briefings at the White House; will, on occasion, invite White House staff to their conventions. If they agree with the president, they will join his interests to their own, volunteering to do what he cannot openly request: to put pressure on legislators. For over fifty years, the bargain has been struck: the White House Office of Public Liaison is its embodiment.

There is political cement in the bargain as well. As a campaigner, the president will have asked for, and received, endorsements from specific interest groups or from their leaders. Political action committee funds will have flowed into his treasury. There is no chance that, once inaugurated, he will not have officers on his staff commissioned to be attentive to the concerns of his campaign allies. But how many officers, and how elaborate a structure to do so? One White House veteran has a critical view:

> The public liaison office, the public affairs office: they have people in there who are assigned to very small constituencies. And when that happens, as soon as you assign someone to constituency X, constituency Y begins to demand White House time. What presidents have done, over the decades, is to incur an expectation for attention on the part of all kinds of people in the American public. That is unrealistic and mutually manipulative for both the constituency group and the president. Both want to work the system. . . . It's poor politics, it's gratuitous, it's dysfunctional. . . . I would urge presidents to radically change public and constituent expectations—and the presidential staff.[1]

That view has not found favor in the modern White House. With opportunities for bargaining ever present, the question is not whether there will be an Office of Public Liaison but how it will be organized and used. Will it foster genuine dialogue between policymakers and organization leaders or merely host presentations in the Briefing Room? Will it reach out, to bring into the White House precincts independent—even skeptical or dissenting—viewpoints, or simply market the administration's positions? Does it have the staff resources to do both—or to do either well?

President Bush stated his preference: "I am listening to everyone, not just my friends. That is the way I learn."[2]

Will the Public Liaison Office stimulate, perhaps even encourage, legislative pressure campaigns conducted by others, or will it limit itself to "making the facts available"? From the topmost to the lowest staffer, the members of the liaison group cannot let themselves forget the legal stricture: it is unlawful for any government official to spend appropriated funds to directly influence members of Congress.[3]

Conflicting Loyalties

There are two approaches to setting up a public liaison office: matching staff members to client groups or having staff specialize on issues. The White House typically uses a mixture of both.

A staff oriented to client groups will have assistants labeled—or understood to be handling—the concerns of business, labor, women, African Americans, Hispanics, Jews, Asians, gays and lesbians, senior citizens, veterans, consumers, ethnic organizations, and others. If organized according to issues, a liaison office will be a more flexible unit, with assignments that reflect the president's current legislative priorities.

Will staffers who have interest group assignments be drawn from the groups themselves? Will the Jewish adviser be Jewish, the liaison for African Americans' concerns African American, the link to Hispanic groups a Hispanic? Almost inevitably. In May of 1995, President Clinton addressed the Congressional Asian Pacific American Caucus Institute and, introducing Doris Matsui, of his Office of Public Liaison, complimented her on her appeal even to "non-Asian crowds." "Listen," he exclaimed, "she must be the best politician in the White House."[4]

Instantly, for any such officer, the question of divided loyalty arises. Can the liaison staffer maintain credibility, outside the White House, with the group with which he or she identifies without becoming, on the inside, a mere supplicant to the president? Once any staffer acquires an internal reputation as a special pleader, he or she will be isolated from the president's policy process—which makes even the "outside" role harder to sustain. If, on the other hand, the staffer is seen as objective and dispassionate, will interest groups trust that person to put forward their case clearly in the White House?

If the president takes a position to which certain interest groups are deeply opposed or does not appear to be sympathetic enough to the positions the groups espouse, the liaison staffer to these same groups is likely to feel stress. Some fold under the pressure, leak accounts of internal deliberations, or pass the word to their client groups: "I supported you, but so-and-so didn't go along." A liaison officer during the Bush years felt so attached to the evangelical and fundamentalist Christian community that he considered it his mission to represent their views not to his office superiors, whom he judged to be a "liberal cabal," but directly to the White House chief of staff. That arrangement did not last long.

Presidents Bush and Clinton had public liaison staffs of modest size: twenty-two, including interns (markedly smaller than the Reagan group of over fifty, not counting interns). Both presidents intentionally organized those staffs to minimize the strains of dual loyalty by building diversity into the assignments: individual staff members had to spread their attention over a broad range of public groups. Clinton's Hispanic liaison officer, for example, was also responsible for budget issues; the Jewish member, for environmental and immigration matters; the African American specialist, for veterans' affairs and youth policy issues. In both administrations, it was made unquestionably clear to liaison staffers where their loyalties had to be: they were the agents of the president. A Clinton liaison officer emphasized: "Our client is the nation!"[5]

Public Liaison as Presidential Learning

Quite aside from the business of striking bargains with advocacy groups, the public liaison staff can, if it has the resources, fulfill a further and more substantive function: bringing into the White House nongovernment leaders who have expertise and independent judgment and can help the inquiring chief executive shape his own policy views.

As he was considering whether or not to sign the civil rights bill that Congress passed in July of 1990, President Bush instructed his public liaison director, Bobbie Kilberg, to invite Benjamin Hooks, president of the NAACP, and William Coleman, a prominent African American lawyer, to the Oval Office. A state dinner was kept waiting while the three met for an hour and a half. Their advocacy was not convincing to Bush at that point: he vetoed the bill that year. A year later, having discussed the issue further with business groups whom Kilberg had brought in, and having heard their pleas for closure and clarity rather than continued uncertainty, he signed a revised version into law.

The 1989 revisions to the Clean Air Act were considered a major accomplishment of the Bush administration. Well before the legislation was sent to Congress, the liaison office arranged some three dozen meetings for industry, consumer, and environmental leaders to bring their highly divergent views to the attention of the White House policy staffs. Several of those sessions—called "Roosevelt Room roundtables"—were with the president. These were not photo-ops, nor were they meetings where the president sat passively with the advocates and heard them out. Kilberg recalls: "Half the time they wouldn't even get through their statements before Bush would jump in and say, 'What about this?' and 'What about that?' . . . He just kept going; he knew the stuff inside out, not only from his briefing materials but he remembered the issues and decisions made when the original Clean Air Act was passed. He had opinions, but he had an ability to grow and to refine his views as well. . . . There were two or three issues that the president changed his mind about, after listening to people."[6]

On another occasion, President Bush, overruling the apprehensions of Chief of Staff John Sununu, had his scheduling assistant arrange a private conversation with famed environmental activist Jacques Cousteau; the Public Liaison Office supplied the briefing.

As the crisis with Iraq escalated in August of 1990, President Bush, who had been meeting regularly with American Jewish leaders, asked the Public Liaison Office to find and assemble a comparable group of Arab-Americans with whom he could have a dialogue, to hear another side of the Middle East story. Kilberg reached out to leaders of the Arab-American community, which was not very well organized, and encouraged them to form some kind of leadership council. They did so; and on what happened to be the very morning after the Iraqi invasion of Kuwait, twenty heads of Arab-American organizations met with President Bush.

During the Desert Storm conflict itself, the White House liaison operation arranged four group dialogues with the president: two with Jewish leaders and two with the new Arab-American council. The purpose was not to round up votes or to manufacture publicity but to bring independent, nongovernment viewpoints directly and unfiltered to the president—even at a crisis time.

The "PR" Mode

There is, of course, one more variety of meetings that the Public Liaison Office arranges for the president: those that simply have public relations value. Invitations to newsmaking South Lawn events and Rose Garden bill-signings help keep kinder and gentler the relationships between the White House and outside organizations. President Clinton's 1999 Rose Garden event with the winners of the Women's World Cup Soccer Championship was a more celebratory, if less cerebral, occasion.

All in all, Bobbie Kilberg totaled up, she and her liaison associates arranged 453 events and meetings with the president during her thirty-nine months as public liaison director, plus 156 additional photo-ops—some of which turned into substantive discussions and all of which met important political objectives as well. In addition, Kilberg and her staff assembled sessions—averaging thirteen a week—for outside groups that wanted to meet with senior White House policy officers or with officials at the cabinet or assistant-secretary levels. Readers will realize what "assembled" involves: the time-consuming duties of negotiating with the schedulers, reserving rooms and equipment, preparing fact sheets for the participants and the press, inviting and clearing the guests, and mastering a hundred other details. Kilberg's small staff was pressed to its limits of hours and energy.

After Bush announced in September of 1990 that he would accept a tax increase—a decision made with the foreknowledge of only one or two senior aides and with no consultation whatever with the business community— Kilberg found that her relations with business organizations had become rather frosty. She had to move out of the earlier, collaborative mode and into more of a "selling" posture.

The Public Liaison Office is on the staff secretary's clearance list for drafts of presidential speeches, especially those of interest to the advocacy groups with which the office has supportive connections.

Women's Outreach

Within his Public Liaison Office President Carter created the Office of Women's Affairs and appointed a lawyer—Sarah Weddington—to head it; her responsibility was to keep in touch with national women's organizations concerning presidential activities of importance to women. This office was continued under President Reagan, but President Bush's White House did not maintain a separately identified unit for women's affairs.

In June of 1995, President Clinton recreated this special office (calling it the White House Office for Women's Initiatives and Outreach), provided it with a staff of four, and upgraded the director's title to deputy assistant to the president—thereby giving her a seat at senior staff meetings. The office had the familiar dual purpose: outreach, to keep women's organizations informed (and hopefully supportive) of presidential initiatives; and "inreach," to solicit the views of national women's leaders for injection into White House staff offices as policy proposals were being formulated. As Audrey Haynes, Clinton's former women's outreach director, explained, "We tried to make sure that when the policy offices worked on economic issues—

e.g., when they started to look at pay, minimum wage, social security, and so forth—either myself or someone from our office was at the table to represent the view from the women's community. Once we got into that process, the policymakers could see the value of bringing those suggestions to the table on the front end, instead of the back end."[7] The Women's Outreach Office organized a series of roundtable discussions across the nation—called "At the Table"—between women leaders and administration officials.

One issue of pocketbook concern to women was equal pay: specifically, the extent to which slippage had occurred in the enforcement of the 1963 Equal Pay Act. "We got data from the Labor Department," recalls Haynes, "and we started polling the issue. There had been resistance from the business community."[8] The president later delivered two radio addresses on the subject, and he included the following sentence in his 1999 State of the Union message: "Let's make sure that women and men get equal pay for equal work by strengthening enforcement of the equal pay laws."[9]

To emphasize the White House's special commitment to women's economic issues, in April of 1997 the Women's Outreach Office set up and convened the first Women's Economic Leadership Summit. The president attended, delivered a 4,500-word address, called the participants' attention to the outreach office itself, and introduced its director.[10]

The Women's Outreach Office kept its sights on the statistics for noncareer federal employment: it never stopped reminding the Office of Presidential Personnel of the administration's commitment to nondiscrimination, and it crowed when the figures showed progress—for example, that 34 percent of Senate-confirmed presidential appointments, 41 percent of noncareer Senior Executive Service jobs, and 58 percent of Schedule C positions were held by women.[11]

The women's affairs network is no small universe. The National Council of Women's Organizations, an overall coordinating group with which the Women's Outreach Office worked, has some 120 affiliates; the outreach office itself had perhaps three thousand names in its database. "The ultimate goal," smiled Ms. Haynes, "was not to *have* a women's office; but to have enough of both women and men at the policy tables so that one would always be conscious of the gender side of policy."[12]

Clinton's Public Liaison Initiatives

President Clinton was enthusiastic about reaching out for independent advice on even the most sensitive issues of domestic and foreign policy.

Even before he was inaugurated he convened a public "economic summit" in Little Rock, where a diverse group of economists discussed the budgetary and financial issues that would be lying ahead for him when he took office.

His first great policy battle, during the spring of 1993, was between factions in his own White House and concerned the shape and purpose of the administration's economic program. "Liberal" Democratic staffers faced off against "moderates." In support of the president's own moderate inclinations, the Public Liaison Office reached out to kindred business and financial institutions (Salomon Brothers, for instance), invited them to White House briefings, attended the business groups' own outside meetings, and exchanged detailed information with them. The public liaison staff implied that the president would need every last vote in the House of Representatives (but of course, they themselves could not organize pressure). Caucusing on their own, the business organizations well knew what kind of lobbying had to be undertaken.

One liaison technique used during this period was "Mornings at the White House." Twenty or thirty influential leaders from a state or a single congressional district would come in and be given a private tour of the Residence and a briefing session with the liaison director or the vice president—perhaps even the president—who would make a strong pitch for the administration's economic proposals. Next stop: the North Lawn—where radio, newspaper, and TV reporters from that state or district had been invited to record the participants' supporting statements for broadcast on the local media back home. "The staff work to set up these meetings was impressive," recalled former public liaison deputy director Steve Hilton, "arrangements, scheduling, composing talking points for the administration speakers. . . . It stretched the capabilities of the small public liaison group intensely."[13] The "mornings" were worth every harried minute: the president won his economic package by just one vote.

Foreign trips are liaison opportunities. When Donna Shalala, secretary of Health and Human Services, headed an official delegation to the funeral of South African leader Oliver Tambo, the White House liaison office snagged seats on the plane and arranged for some ten African American leaders—including Maya Angelou, Ernest Green, Jesse Jackson, and Randall Robinson—to join the trip. When the president traveled to Poland, ethnic leaders with Polish and Eastern European ties or interests were reserved seats on *Air Force One*, and special events were arranged for them in Poland. On the president's plane to Russia and the Ukraine, to celebrate the fiftieth anniversary of the ending of World War II, was the commander of the American Legion—along with the American soldier who had been the first to cross the Elbe and shake the hands of Russian troops a half-century earlier.

Seats at the Kennedy Center, invitations to White House musicales, opportunities to witness the president's radio broadcasts: no internal White House resources are overlooked—although the liaison office is always in competition with the political and legislative offices for similar favors for their own constituencies.

During the Kosovo crisis, the president received briefing after briefing from his national security team but asked his public liaison director, Mary Beth Cahill, to go a step further: to invite a group of twelve Serbian-Americans to meet with him. This was a "new dimension to his thinking," Cahill recalls.[14] On a separate occasion a group of Albanian-Americans met with him as well.

Among the many sessions that the public liaison unit set up that did not involve the president was one with the American Muslim Council. On their agenda: hate crimes, the upcoming census, and racial profiling at airports. To discuss the third issue, the liaison director had Secretary of Transportation Rodney Slater come over to the White House for a candid dialogue.

An example of White House liaison energy was seen in President Clinton's visit, in the summer of 1999, to six of America's most troubled and persistent areas of poverty: Appalachia, the Mississippi delta, East St. Louis, a Hispanic area of Phoenix, a run-down part of Anaheim, and the Pine Ridge Sioux Reservation in South Dakota. The purpose of the visit was not to shed crocodile tears in front of the cameras but to encourage profit-minded American businessmen to invest in what Clinton hoped would become "New Markets" here in the United States.

Director Cahill and her associates invited the chief executive officers of several major American companies, including Aetna and BellSouth, to accompany the president—to see for themselves what neither Washington seminars nor think-tank papers could ever portray as clearly and to join in his determination to ignite economic progress in these disadvantaged areas. A five-page fact sheet, highlighting the current and proposed programs that would complement the New Markets initiative, was written up and distributed to the participants. Within a few weeks of the president's return from the New Markets tour, notice had reached the White House that several mayors had already received telephone calls from business firms interested in starting up development in at least one of the areas the president had just visited.

Neither Bobbie Kilberg nor Mary Beth Cahill demanded that their office be the exclusive portal through which outside groups could approach the

White House. Kilberg and Cahill did expect, however, that if their White House colleagues scheduled briefings with private groups, liaison staff would be included and participate. Deputy director Steve Hilton recalled: "There is a tendency across the White House for each office to keep to its little pocket of responsibilities, where on major presidential initiatives the need is for every office in the White House to sacrifice its preoccupation with its own business and help contribute to the achievement of the president's priorities. There has to be teamwork. With slender resources, the liaison office, by itself, found this hard to manage."[15]

The Public Liaison Office is, of course, part of the communications network of the contemporary White House. As chapter 9 recounts, the Office of Communications prepared a daily e-mail of talking points, describing Clinton administration initiatives, that was circulated to some two thousand political appointees in the cabinet departments. The liaison staff sent selected talking points on to its own list of influential business, nonprofit, and religious leaders.

The public liaison director sends the president regular periodic reports on the events that have been arranged, telling him not just which groups came in but what they told the administration and what recommendations they brought. As he did with similar incoming reports from other staff, Clinton would scribble on the margins, sending back comments, guidance, and instructions.

The experience of at least twenty years has shown that the only successful public liaison officers are those with a professional appreciation for the pluralism of American society. The zealot who divides the claimants at the White House gates into rigid categories of "good guys" and "bad guys" will end up frustrated—and will even singe his or her president with the hot atmosphere of animosity.

An extension of the president himself, the Office of Public Liaison is a bargainer in the great American political bazaar. Its wiser members know that they gain some and lose others, are in no group's pocket, make no permanent enemies, but are at home in the turbulent marketplace of national debate. Presidents find such bargaining support indispensable; they will continue to use staff who can open the White House gates—and, while negotiating alliances with some, keep listening to all.

CHAPTER TWELVE

Achievements versus Activities: The Office of Presidential Scheduling

What does a President want to do with his years in office? What is his concept of governing? We made up a four-year schedule, anticipating all the major events of his term. With that we could plan an overarching program of achievements. Without it, every day would simply fill up with activities.

DAVID PARKER

I spend a lot of my time fighting for time on the President's schedule.

I would have to go in and become a lobbyist—an advocate—to get that Union convention on the schedule. . . . Then all of a sudden it's off the schedule, because somebody else came in and pushed harder.

TWO STAFF MEMBERS IN THE CLINTON WHITE HOUSE

The White House staffers in the Office of Presidential Scheduling are much more than mere calendar-keepers. By allocating a president's time, they make possible—or impossible—the accomplishments by which he is judged: they help shape his legacy for history.

There is an inevitable progression for a president: from the goals he holds to the themes he emphasizes to the events in which he participates. If there is no long-range plan against which to measure the cascade of requests, his day will surely fill up, but instead of achievements there will be only activities. "Time is any president's most precious commodity," emphasized a former scheduler for President Clinton: "how he chooses to spend it will determine what people think of him."[1]

"Sixty percent of the president's time tends to be committed to engagements about which he has little choice," observed Reagan's former director of scheduling. "Intelligence briefings, meetings with cabinet members, national security, legislative and staff meetings are preordained. If he did just those things, however, nothing remarkable would come out of his administration. It is the remaining 40 percent of his time which can creatively be used to accomplish the important initiatives and goals of his administration."[2]

Few outside the White House recognize or acknowledge the priority assigned to accomplishments over activities; even some White House staffers, especially at the beginning of an administration, get it backwards. Cabinet secretaries request meetings on nonurgent matters, members of Congress pressure the president to see their constituents, and political and advocacy groups petition to stage Oval Office events or to have the president speak at their meetings. The State Department and the national security adviser urge the president not only to invite foreign chiefs of state to the White House but to allow visiting foreign ministers to call on him as well. The president must also receive new foreign ambassadors when they are presenting their credentials. All in all, requests for the president's time pour in at the rate of perhaps a thousand a week.

The Scheduling Process

How to choose? What is the scheduling procedure in the modern White House?

What first has to be made clear is that no one in the White House except the Scheduling Office is to make scheduling commitments. A new presidential staff may not appreciate how vital is that mandate—or may tolerate (even a new president may tolerate) multiple channels for getting onto the calendar. Unfortunately, this was the case in the early months of the first Clinton term. His first scheduling director recalled: "You would set a schedule and then some other senior adviser at the White House would walk in to the president and say, 'You have to do this!'—and he would agree, and the event would get added to the schedule. What others did not understand, or seem to care about, was that to do this particular event meant canceling another event; or the new event had to be sandwiched into an already overcrowded schedule. After a while, that system was not possible."[3]

Eventually the rule was established and enforced: the Scheduling Office had exclusive control. Only three people—the chief of staff, the national security adviser, and the scheduling director—were routinely accorded morning appointments. "Even President Bush," remembers his scheduler, "would not put anything on his schedule without calling me!"[4]

A second rule is equally strict: all schedule requests must be in writing. Heads of Executive Office and White House units are required to use a schedule proposal form; informal, oral entreaties cannot be handled if the process is to remain orderly. The author recalls that the Nixon schedule proposal form required any staff member who submitted one to list not only the supporting reasons for the appointment but the counterarguments as well.

How to choose, how to evaluate amid the cascade of petitions for the president's time? In the Clinton White House a third rule was employed: schedule proposals were not given serious consideration unless they were "sponsored" by one of the senior White House staff officers. If a cabinet member requested an appointment, the director of Cabinet Affairs was expected to append an endorsement—and a briefing note about whatever the matter was that needed discussion with the president. If a senator or representative asked to see the president, the legislative affairs director was asked to review the request. If a governor or mayor wanted to come in, the intergovernmental affairs assistant had to be a sponsor. If the request came in "cold," it was referred for possible sponsorship to one of the White House staff offices—the national security affairs adviser, the head of the domestic policy council, the director of public liaison. "Somebody had to own it," explained Clinton scheduler Billy Webster. "I was only going to bat for a substantive proposal that somebody else had already done the vetting on, from a policy perspective."[5] Only then did it become a "serious request"—of which there were typically some fifty or sixty a week.

While collecting the sponsored submissions, the scheduling director is also engaged in a parallel enterprise: looking into the future. Nixon schedulers experimented by trying to look ahead four years; in the Clinton White House the forward-planning period was six months, later narrowed to three. Many events can be foreseen: religious and secular holidays, certain summit-level international conferences, the White House Correspondents Dinner, the Gridiron Dinner. "Hundreds of things in hundreds of categories," explains Webster. "You may not do anything on those occasions, but you sure as heck wanted to know if you did something else, you would make somebody mad. . . . You start going down that list: we could put three hundred of those things on the wall in a minute. . . . For instance, the fiftieth anniversary of the end of World War II. There were 115 events around the world. . . . We knew the president was going to do four or five; they were going to carry enormous coverage and emotional weight."[6]

What are the priorities? It is here that schedulers and policymakers put their heads together and ask the most pertinent question: What themes does the president want to emphasize, to showcase, in the upcoming weeks? Is a major legislative initiative about to be proposed on health or education? Is an address to the United Nations General Assembly on the horizon? A summit conference on Middle East peace efforts? A presidential tour of poverty areas in America? "You look over not just the next week, or two weeks, but over the next six months—and have a good sense of what the messages would be during that period of time," advised former chief of staff Leon Panetta.[7]

But President Bush's scheduler, Kathy Super, pointed out: "That's what was so difficult: projecting some sort of strategy theme or issue to drive the White House for a couple of weeks, *and then sticking with it*. It's very hard, because you are bombarded with requests from foreign leaders, and there are international crises, and there are domestic crises, and there are congressional activities going on: you are bashed around by all of that."[8] Added Webster: "The worst thing you could do is to have the president fly up to New York and address the United Nations in the morning, come back in the afternoon and have some health care event in the Rose Garden. The media are looking at only one of these two things—and the other one is dead and gone."[9]

The forum for choosing among competing proposals is, typically, a scheduling committee, which nearly every modern White House has had to organize. Clinton's committee usually met weekly, was chaired by the chief of staff or his deputy, and included most of the directors of the policy offices in the White House, especially if any were "sponsors" who should attend to defend their proposals. Also on the committee were the chiefs of staff of the vice president and the first lady, to ensure close calendar coordination with those two semi-independent offices.

The scheduling director set the committee's agenda, summarized the "sponsored" event requests (along with others that the director, with independent judgment, considered especially worthy), and grouped the requests by date and category: foreign affairs, congressional, and so forth. "Those were probably the most painful meetings we had, in a management sense," recalled President Bush's deputy chief of staff.[10] Kathy Super echoes him: "President Bush told me, 'I want somebody who knows how to say *no* to

people without making them mad.'"[11] Normally only two out of each fifty
to sixty of the serious proposals are approved. (The scheduling committee
is usually not asked to rule on cabinet members' requests for one-on-one
meetings with the president.)

Periodically, especially before a major trip or if there are doubts or controversies, the Clinton scheduling director and a smaller group (often
including the vice president) would meet with the president. After all, it was
his time being divvied up: he had to be the ultimate arbiter. Beginning in
1995, even these outcomes were governed by the overarching political strategy decisions that came out of the "Residence meetings," described in
chapters 10 and 14. At campaign times—in 1992 for Bush, in 1995–96 for
Clinton, calendar decisionmaking was always more frantic: "creative scheduling" for political considerations trumped other priorities.

There are times when a message or a theme has been fixed but a locale
not yet identified: it is then the responsibility of the Scheduling Office to find
one. Networks are activated, cabinet agencies queried, supportive members
of Congress contacted about possibilities in their districts. It is never hard
to generate an invitation for the president, but on occasion the logistics
require last-minute juggling.

Close-In Arrangements

Once the longer-range decisions have been made, the immediately critical
task for the Scheduling Office is to inform the operating elements of the staff
what the calendar will be for the next week and for each specific day—and
what part each White House unit, from *Air Force One* to the Secret Service
to the chief usher, is to play in each event. The calendar-creator on Clinton's
scheduler's computer was activated, and both the weekly and daily schedules were printed and circulated. The vice president's own scheduling staff
held off on its final version for each day until the president's daily calendar
was finished each night. To keep the cabinet departments informed of important decisions about the presidential calendar, the White House scheduling
director joined the deputy cabinet secretary in the weekly "amplification"
conference call (described in chapter 9) that was made among the agencies'
communications directors.

The Clinton administration made a significant change in the allocation
of responsibilities between the Scheduling Office (which reported to the president) and the Social Office (which was primarily in the first lady's territory).
Arranging for and managing events anywhere in the Residence or on the

South Lawn became the responsibility of the Social Office; events in the West Wing or within the Rose Garden were handled by the Scheduling Office. The Social Office, for instance, had to see to it that a presidential event in the Residence was not scheduled on the same day as a state dinner, when the entire Residence was committed for daylong preparations. A picnic under a huge tent on the South Lawn couldn't be scheduled for one o'clock (dismantling the tent alone would take several hours) if the president was departing by helicopter from the same South Lawn at four!

Each day on the schedule was then assigned to one of the "desks" of the Scheduling Office, saddling that "desk" person with the responsibility of ensuring that the major event for that day—and every preparation for it—went meticulously according to plan. The press secretary supplied advice about synchronizing the timing of the event with the filing deadlines that the press had to meet—if any news coverage of the event was going to make the evening broadcasts. "Someone in the White House had to be responsible—and 'own' every event."[12] Every day a scheduling staffer convened a morning meeting with representatives from the Secret Service, the military aides, the pilots, the chief usher's office. Assignments were reconfirmed and signals checked. Late at the end of each day, the next day's schedule was sent to the senior staff.

Flexibility was built into every stage of the process. Last-minute changes may be headaches, but they were tolerated as necessities. The scheduling director had a brief minute with the president each morning to make sure that absolutely everything was in shape. There was always a last-minute walk-through with the presidential aide.

Was the scheduling director a dictator here? "I merely facilitated the flow of information," Webster stressed. "These were not my decisions. If anybody ever thought the scheduler was making policy decisions, I would be dead. That's not what my job was; my job was merely to make sure that people had a voice in that process, and that the process had enough integrity that people would not be motivated to breach it." He added: "People in the White House, in many ways, derive their relative place in the pecking order by how much of the president's time is invested in their priorities. So people became very emotional about a president's schedule."[13]

Giving the President Time to Think

At the beginning of the Clinton administration, after twelve years of Republican control of the White House, the president's schedulers faced a pent-up demand from Democrats thirsty to fraternize with their new leader. Since Mr. Clinton was an energetic president who loved "town hall" policy conversations, his campaign-addicted staff—long on enthusiasm and short on orderliness—allowed his schedule to burst out of control. The president complained; he ended up frazzled at being overbooked. "Before they got the system under control, people were throwing stuff on the schedule, left and right," commented one associate.

After the first one hundred days, the scheduling director made a retroanalysis: How was Clinton actually spending his time? The scheduling staff counted hours, figured out percentages. Found wanting: time to himself, to read, reflect, make phone calls, work on speeches. The president was impressed and pleased to have the facts laid out, made changes in his priorities, and instructed his schedulers to book three or four hours a day for the unobstructed time he needed.

There was slippage: what were supposed to be priorities were invaded; "think time" got nibbled down. A frustrated president complained again, and this time a more comprehensive review was undertaken. With the help of the presidential diarist (a professional archivist who has long been on detail in the Scheduling Office), scheduling director Webster and Deputy Chief of Staff Erskine Bowles combed through the calendars of previous presidents, dug out the records of Clinton's first eighteen months, and added the three upcoming months. Taking a specific sample of two months past and three ahead, they dramatized their findings. They mounted up display boards, then colored in the calendar periods by category: purple for foreign affairs, green for economic discussions, red for politics, blue for domestic issues. The ideal would be, as Webster explained,

> If the president wanted to get his message out, for any given day, or any given week, or any given month, there ought to be a clear investment of time—and where he invests his time is where all the media are going to be directed. There should be one clear message for each day, so one major item or event for each day, and a theme for a week, which would give rise to a theme for a month. The charts were set on easels in the Cabinet Room; the president could view them in a row. They showed not what the president *thought* he was doing, but what was the actual investment of his time. Each day was a big block, and every day was a color. If the color was purple, we might write "speech to the United Nations." If we ended up with a week where Monday was blue and Tuesday was green and Wednesday was purple—if we had a whole bunch of colors—we would know that that week was going to be a screwed-up message week.[14]

In this fashion, looking at the months ahead, Webster and Bowles posted the "required" events—which numbered some thirty occasions—as well as the commitments that the president himself desired to make; then, finally, they could display the "gaps" for accommodating optional opportunities. At this point, for each day, they firmly set aside three and one-half to four hours of undisturbed time for reading, studying papers, and handling telephone calls. Webster concluded: "I think the president was genuinely surprised at how much his own desire to do too many things had blurred his capability to do the things that he really cared about. I do think that we were able to build . . . some discipline into his own thinking processes, so that he would at least think before saying yes to everything."[15]

The charts were used during meetings of the scheduling committee and were also computerized and printed out in page form, in the same color format, for the committee to use. The color coding continued during the remainder of the Clinton presidency; the month-long schedule, called a "block," was entered onto the computer and changed daily to reflect the continuing amendments. Each participant in scheduling committee meetings—and in the scheduling meetings with the president—was given a personal copy of the color printout, while the larger, three-month-projection boards were always available for reference.

At a glance, committee members could recognize that "there's too much blue here—where is the green?" The primary, or "message," event of each day was printed in italics, as a clear reminder of the focus that the president's senior associates brought to the entire schedule decisionmaking process. A volunteer with artistic ability often added tiny sketches to important days in the block: a miniature drawing of the Teton Range in Wyoming signifying the president's vacation there, a birthday cake sketched into the square for August 19, company logos, flags of foreign nations, corncobs for a meeting with farmers, sharks circling in the Martha's Vineyard waves. The president was reported to be particularly appreciative of the artwork.

The weekly schedule and the succinct daily schedule—produced each night and each noon—were circulated by fax or e-mail to all the White House operating units that would have a share of responsibility.

A "Berlin Wall"?

Scheduling is now a strict system. "You have to have a disciplined procedure; you can't function without it!" declared a former scheduling assistant, "or else the poor man would be bombarded. It's not the president's job to say no. Delegation is key; you really have to empower those around him, and have people believe that if the scheduling director is saying this, it is as good as the president."[16] "I would have to say no in nine hundred ninety-nine different ways," said another alumna of the scheduling staff.

There is a political cost: those disappointed are regretful, even angry, and each day occasions many more disappointments than delights. Yet there is no way around the discipline that must be imposed, no way to handle scheduling casually.

In the larger sense, the scheduling director and his or her staff are more than just time regulators: they are, in a tradition going back decades, the pacemakers of the White House heartbeat. Their judgment and skill help make the difference, over the president's years in the White House, between a record of presidential accomplishments and a catalogue of mere activities. In serving the man they serve the office, helping to preserve its dignity and to ensure its proper role.

CHAPTER THIRTEEN

Energizer for Federalism: The Office of Intergovernmental Affairs

Dear Mr. President: . . . On behalf of the nation's elected state and local government leaders, [we] request that you withdraw Executive Order 13083 . . . to provide for meaningful consultations with state and local officials. . . . No state and local government official was consulted in the drafting of E.O. 13083 [which] seriously erodes federalism.

THE BIG SEVEN, JULY 17, 1998

Dear Mr. President: On behalf of the seven national organizations representing state and local officials, we are writing to express our appreciation for consulting extensively with us on a proposed executive order on federalism. . . . The executive order constructively responds to the concerns we raised on the importance of federalism and state and local government authority.

THE BIG SEVEN, AUGUST 3, 1999

The first number to remember is 88,061. That is the size of the U.S. federal system, as detailed in chapter 1: the number of state and local government units and federally recognized Native American tribes and Alaska Native villages. Each of them wields a piece of American political power.[1]

The second number is seven: the "Big Seven." These are the major national organizations that represent governors, cities, counties, mayors, state legislators, and so forth. White House folks can often be found in Big Seven head-quarters offices here in Washington and at their national conferences.[2]

The third number is thirteen: the nine officers and four interns who constitute the White House Office of Intergovernmental Affairs, the forty-five-year-old White House "ombudsplace" for the American federal universe.

The Office of Intergovernmental Affairs

The White House is a welcoming venue for alumni of the federal system: governors such as Sherman Adams, Howard Pyle, Spiro Agnew, Nelson Rockefeller, Jimmy Carter, John Sununu, and Bill Clinton come to mind. President Clinton was chair of the National Governors Association. Under Presidents Johnson and Nixon, the intergovernmental liaison function was vested in the hands of the vice presidents: former mayor Hubert Humphrey and former governor Spiro Agnew, respectively.

It should follow that the Intergovernmental Affairs (IGA) Office would, in every White House, be a capable and strong center of influence, engaged in every presidential policy and action affecting the federal environment. Not always so, as Ray Scheppach, the executive director of the National Governors Association (NGA), observed: "I think its effectiveness depends more on who is there than exactly where it is. I don't think you want it attached to the vice president's office; I think you want it as an adviser to the president. A lot of times in the past it's been a pro forma office, or an extension of the political operation. I think what is important is that it be a substantive office."[3]

What the NGA executive director wants, when he refers to "a substantive office," is for the men and women in the White House intergovernmental affairs unit to be much more than "liaison" officers: they should have a firm knowledge of the specific policy issues being debated around White House tables—and be involved in policy decisions. They must be able to exclaim, "Wait! The governors will go bonzo if we do this!"

Being bridge-builders of that sort between state and local officials on the one hand and White House policy seniors on the other could give rise to feelings of tension on the part of the intergovernmental affairs staff. Do they feel a sense of divided loyalty?

Said Bush intergovernmental affairs officer Lanny Griffith: "Sometimes. My role was to make sure that the views of the governors—the perspective of the governors—were represented at the decisionmaking tables in the White House. I felt that I was serving the president that way. One of my colleagues once accused me of 'going native,' but I think I was able to keep that balance. I was there to be a strong advocate in the decision-making process for the point of view of governors. But I had to go to school in policy."[4]

Adds Clinton's former IGA director, Marcia Hale:

I knew where I belonged: that was to the president. But yes, there is that tension. The governors and mayors and the local elected officials are very important to Bill Clinton. He was one of them. My work with them enabled me to have a keen understanding of where they were coming from—probably more than any other staff officer in the White House. You had to be persistent to make sure that you got the time you needed with all the senior policy folks in the White House, and that the state and local officials' views got represented. If they thought they were getting a fair shake, then their opposition, or their comments afterwards, were mollified, even if they didn't get just what they wanted.[5]

Commenting on the "divided loyalty" dilemma, Scheppach sums up his own answer: "It's both. When those White House intergovernmental affairs officials are in their internal meetings, it is up to them to represent the governors' position. When they call on us, then it is up to them to represent the White House position. But, if *all* they do is represent the president to us, then in my mind it is 100 percent a political office, and that's not helpful to me—i.e., if it's a one-way street all the time, trying to spin me."[6]

Another White House intergovernmental affairs officer sympathizes with Scheppach's emphasis on substantive participation in policy: that's what the IGA staffers there would like to do. "It's a constant struggle to inject ourselves into policy," said this official. "We are almost like a special interest group internally."[7]

How did nine Clinton White House intergovernmental officers stretch themselves over the far-flung federal universe?

Like the members of many other White House units, they were helped by their own network of comrades who handled intergovernmental liaison in the departments and agencies: twenty-seven in all. The White House IGA Office circulated a blue sheet listing their cohorts' names, e-mail addresses, and phone and fax numbers. The White House intergovernmental affairs director called all the departmental IGA units together twice a month to glean information about what problems were being solved—or were festering—in the various corners of the executive branch.

Griffith would use these sessions to remind the departmental representatives that their job was not to be passive and reactive—to wait for a governor or local official to bring in a problem "to be fixed." They were to be "proactive," he emphasized, reaching out to engage governors and local officials in the development of policy initiatives. Senior White House policy officers were often invited to these interagency meetings, to give the departmental representatives a firsthand sense of presidential priorities and of how the executive branch agencies were expected to support them.

A second intergovernmental liaison technique was attendance at the national (sometimes even the regional) conferences of most of the Big Seven and other major organizations. If the National Conference of State Legislatures met in Indianapolis, Clinton's IGA special assistant Bill White would be there—and would take cabinet secretaries Donna Shalala, of Health and Human Services, and Richard Riley, of the Department of Education, with him. When the National Governors Association held its semiannual conference, the president himself would speak. The author, who handled Native American affairs in the Nixon White House, would join the sessions of the National Conference of American Indians and meet with the National Tribal Chairmen's Association.

Conference duties for White House invitees would include formal presentations and informal schmoozing, and at times involved commenting on—and perhaps working to influence—the resolutions that the national bodies were drafting. (While NGA resolutions may carry weight with Congress, the Clinton IGA group gave most of its policy attention to the caucus of Democratic governors, with whom they maintained a more *simpatico* relationship.)

The IGA Office regularly updated a list of all these conclaves, including dates and locations for the coming three years. There were limits, however, to the ability of the small White House staff to cover national and regional conferences. One officer recalled: "I wasn't a liaison to the National Governors Association; I viewed my role as the president's liaison to the governors themselves. I did go to some of those conferences if there was an important issue there, but I wasn't into just attending. You could pretty much make that a full-time job. The trouble is, I wouldn't get anything done."[8]

The Clinton IGA staff put a new twist on the business of attending the Big Seven's national conventions. When staff members went, they didn't go alone; with them went a Clinton innovation, the Federal Agency Showcase. The showcase was a series of information booths, one from each of ten agencies, staffed by the intergovernmental contact person and a senior policy officer from each agency. "I want to bring the federal government to the states," Clinton had said. "Clinton, as governor of Arkansas, remembered his frustration, and the time he had to expend, trying to dig up program information from the federal government, department by department," commented a White House intergovermental affairs assistant.[9] Each booth made plenty of factual material available as handouts; but more important, the policy officers of the agencies were there not to "sell," but to answer questions, field complaints, and enter into candid dialogues with the delegates. The showcase initiative was an innovative example of White House leadership and interdepartmental cooperation.

During the Clinton administration's lengthy negotiations on welfare reform, the National Governors Association formed a governors' task force on welfare: three Democrats and three Republicans. On several occasions the IGA staff arranged for the White House senior staffers who were developing the legislation to meet with the NGA task force and to be quizzed directly on the issues involved in welfare reform—which, of course, were of intense concern to state officials. When the controversial bill came out of Congress, the National Governors Association was among those organizations that recommended that the president sign it.

When legislation that would affect states or cities was pending, the Clinton IGA director would be on the telephone, making conference calls to groups of Democratic governors or Democratic mayors, keeping them apprised of what was important but steering clear of organizing lobbying. Chief of Staff Leon Panetta or principal policy officers like Carol Rasco or Bruce Reed would often be on the line, too, providing immediate and authoritative answers to questions from state or local leaders. These local officials also received copies of selected White House "Talking Points" (described in chapter 9). Thus equipped, the governors and mayors knew perfectly well what to do next: they had their own well-worn channels to members of the House and Senate.

These communications were part of regular business, but they were so constant that personal friendships grew up between the White House IGA staff and the elected officials. If a mayor was in town, "I would take him or her to lunch," Marcia Hale recalled. "It was a good thing, and it's very easy. We didn't have a budget for this, so we had to pay for such lunches ourselves, unless it was a really large group. . . . I tried to make sure that they got invited to White House social events; when they were in town with their kids, we would bring them into the White House and give them tours. That's not political; that's important regardless of what party they belonged to."[10]

The mayor of Indianapolis was a Republican; Hale hired his daughter as a White House intern. "She was there for six weeks—a terrific kid," Hale remembers.

One member of the Intergovernmental Affairs Office had a scheduling responsibility: this meant inviting appropriate elected officials to join the president at White House events or advising them ahead of time when the president planned a domestic trip into their territory. If a governor or mayor asked to telephone the president or the chief of staff, the IGA Office was alerted and sent in a "heads-up" briefing; if a personal visit was scheduled, the IGA director would be present. If a governor or mayor came to Washington, the Clinton IGA Office also notified the vice president: Would he care to have the visitor drop by?

Bipartisanship among Partisans

Of all the domestically oriented offices in the White House, the Intergovernmental Affairs Office is the one that most often has to mute its party ties. The IGA staff, Republican or Democrat as the president may be, must build relationships with state and local officials regardless of party. Governors, mayors, and county officials are elected—and, having been elected, they wield governmental power. It is on that basis that they deserve attention and cooperation from those at the federal level. With respect to natural disasters, nuclear regulatory actions, law enforcement, and many other issues, cooperation must be fostered without regard to party lines. Bush staffer Lanny Griffith recalled: "I've worked doubly hard for Democrats. I always said that it was easier helping out a Democrat governor over a Republican governor because they expected so much less. . . . Then they found out we were just more than eager to help. I remember a governor would come into my office and we'd clear out a place and let him spend a couple of hours working on the phones. . . . The president said it over and over again: 'I don't want this office to be political: I want it to be bipartisan!'"[11]

Clinton's IGA director, Marcia Hale, expressed similar sentiments: "I had to have fairly good relationships across the political spectrum. I think you could call up any number of Republican governors or mayors and they would say they had good cooperation with our office. It didn't mean they always got what they wanted . . . but there were a lot of policy issues where it made sense to cooperate. Also, Bill Clinton knew all of these people. Any one of these guys could get him on the phone."[12]

Griffith emphasized the value to the Bush White House of his being able to build bridges to Democratic officials. When a Bush legislative initiative went to Congress (which was controlled by the Democrats), it would have a better chance of being approved if it could be demonstrated that Democratic governors had been consulted as the policy was being developed.

As a small example of completely nonpartisan functioning, Griffith described how he came to compile an emergency telephone book of governors. A state had suffered a natural disaster, and the president was about to declare it officially, entitling the state to federal disaster assistance. Griffith was at home, putting up wallpaper, when the instruction came: Call the governor immediately and relay this information. How to reach the governor—or the governor's chief of staff—on a Saturday afternoon? After that experience, Griffith wasted no time in assembling a telephone directory for emergencies: it listed every governor's private numbers—at home, on vacation—and the numbers for the chief of staff.

The IGA Office can provide another nonpartisan service to state and local governments: prompt notification about federal decisions concerning major projects or grants. By scrutinizing the weekly Cabinet Report from the White House Office of Cabinet Affairs, the IGA staff could spot a departmental project or initiative that was about to be announced. Perhaps it was good news: a long-sought project had been authorized. (The White House would typically commandeer that kind of announcement for itself.) It may have been bad news: an application had been denied. Whatever the outcome, and regardless of the political affiliation of the governor or mayor, the elected official deserved not to be blindsided or kept in the dark.

There was apparently poor adherence to this policy in the case of the creation of the Escalante/Grand Staircase National Monument in Utah in September of 1996. Egged on by eager environmentalists and by the chair of the Council on Environmental Quality, the Department of the Interior did the planning in secret—allegedly going so far as to deny to the local Democratic congressman that newspaper leaks about the forthcoming proclamation had any basis in fact. Not only the congressman but also the Republican governor of Utah opposed the project, regarding it as a further example of what they considered to be federal aggrandizement in taking control of western lands. However, they succeeded in reaching the president by telephone to voice their objections only at the eleventh hour. The president and the vice president led the ceremony—but in Arizona, rather than in the understandably more hostile Utah—and the congressman lost his seat.

A Bush Intergovernmental Initiative: The Education Summit of September 1989

President Bush, who had declared that he wanted to be known as "the education president," decided to convene the governors of all the fifty-three states and commonwealths in an "education summit" in Charlottesville, Virginia, in the fall of 1989. (The last president to call all the governors together about any issue was Theodore Roosevelt, at the turn of the century.) It was obviously going to be a bipartisan conclave, although the fall date had been set to coincide with Republican Terry Branstad's accession as chair of the NGA.

Funds for the conference came in part from the Department of Education, but the substantive planning and the drafting of the policy papers were all done in the White House, by domestic policy assistant Roger Porter and intergovernmental affairs assistant Lanny Griffith. The small-group and plenary sessions would take place on the campus of the University of Virginia; there would be a dinner at Monticello. The first lady and the entire cabinet were to be at the summit as well.

An executive committee was formed: governors Terry Branstad, Booth Gardner, Carroll Campbell, and Bill Clinton (who was the governors' point man on education). The committee met a half-dozen or more times with Porter and Griffith, at the White House (a point of special pleasure for Governor Clinton). The principal issue of the committee sessions was money: How much and for what purposes? The underlying question was: Would the Bush administration make a commitment to spend significant additional amounts?

The Bush objective was to come out with a set of goals for reform and future progress, but Governor Clinton had to have a financial commitment from the Bush side to convince his fellow Democrats to sign on to the final statement. A distinctly unhelpful press statement from former secretary of education Bill Bennett about "hearing a lot of pap and things that rhyme with pap" threw a monkey wrench into the carefully crafted agreement. However, thanks in part to energetic diplomacy and skillful drafting on Clinton's part—along with a further Bush commitment to increase funds for Head Start—the bipartisanship was rescued—"by a whisker," according to Griffith. Six education goals were developed and then announced in the January 1990 State of the Union message. Governors Branstad, Campbell, Gardner, and Clinton were invited to sit in the first lady's box during that address.

This abbreviated description masks the laborious hours of planning and drafting; the central role played by the White House in managing the summit was indispensable. The two offices—domestic policy and intergovernmental affairs—teamed up to pull the whole thing off successfully.

A Clinton Intergovernmental Initiative: The Executive Order on Federalism

For defining the relationship between the federal government and state and local governments, the Clinton presidency inherited a Reagan legacy: Executive Order 12612 of October 26, 1987.[13] In paragraph after stentorian paragraph, Reagan's order lauded "strict adherence to constitutional principles" and invoked the Tenth Amendment to the Constitution, which reads: "The powers not delegated to the United States by the Constitution, nor prohibited by it to the States, are reserved to the States respectively, or to the people."

The Reagan order told federal agencies to impose limits on the states' policymaking discretion "only where constitutional authority for the [federal] action is clear and certain": that is, "only when authority for the action may be found in a specific provision of the Constitution" and when "the action does not encroach upon authority reserved to the States." Agencies were to "refrain, to the maximum extent possible, from establishing uniform national standards for programs" and were to bend over backward to avoid issuing regulations that preempted state law. The agencies were not even to send to Congress any proposed legislation that would violate the Reagan principles. This order stayed on the books for ten and one-half years.

Meanwhile, the Clinton administration and many members of Congress had become concerned about "unfunded mandates"—federal legislation that required state or local governments to take certain actions without supplying any funds to finance those actions. "Curb unfunded mandates!" became a rallying cry. Nine months after he took office, President Clinton signed Executive Order 12875 "to reduce the imposition of unfunded mandates upon State, local and tribal governments . . . and to establish regular and meaningful consultation . . . on Federal matters that significantly . . . affect their communities."[14] The order, "to the extent permitted by law," forbade federal agencies from promulgating mandates on state, local, or tribal governments without supplying the needed funds—*or* required agencies, before issuing any such mandates, to consult with state or local governments, to inform the director of the Office of Management and Budget (OMB) of the consultation, and to describe the positions taken by both sides. Agencies were asked to liberalize their approvals of requests for waivers of federal regulations and to make prompt decisions on applications for such waivers. The Reagan Executive Order was left standing.

In 1998, somewhat dismayed by the aggressively constricting tone of the Reagan order, Clinton officials in the OMB decided that a different statement of policy on federalism was needed—and drafted a new one. The revised order reaffirmed respect for "strict adherence to constitutional principles" and for granting state and local governments "maximum administrative discretion," but went on to declare that there were "matters of national or multi-state scope that justify Federal action" and proceeded to list nine categories in which overriding federal actions could, and should, be taken. The specific reference to the Tenth Amendment was excised.

Then, mistakes were made.

The revised order was apparently given only the most cursory review by the Justice Department, the White House Office of Intergovernmental Affairs, the White House counsel's office, and at 444 North Capitol Street (the Big Seven headquarters). Distinguished *Washington Post* columnist David Broder wrote that "no state or local government official was consulted in the drafting."[15] Clinton signed the new order while attending a conference in Birmingham, England. It ended by declaring that the 1987 Reagan epistle and Clinton's own October 1993 order were "revoked."[16]

Two weeks later, there was, in Broder's words, a "delayed explosion." There were apparently some in the Big Seven organizations who still cherished Reagan's approach to federalism. Others had substantive objections to Clinton's order but, even more, were outraged by the lack of thorough consultation. After a "stormy meeting" with Clinton's intergovernmental affairs chief, the leaders of the Big Seven wrote the president on July 17, 1998, and requested that the order be withdrawn (see the opening epigraph to this chapter). Clinton thereupon signed a third order suspending his 1998 edict.[17] A revised draft was prepared: it, too, was rejected by the Big Seven.

During the spring and summer of 1999, new minds turned to new language.

Working collaboratively with the OMB and in constant consultation with Big Seven leaders, the Clinton intergovernmental affairs officers prepared still another draft of the federalism order. Reinvoking the Tenth Amendment, the new order offered a softened criterion:

> National action limiting the policymaking discretion of the States shall be taken only where there is constitutional and statutory authority for the action and the national activity is appropriate in light of the presence of a problem of national significance. Where there are significant uncertainties as to whether national action is authorized or appropriate, agencies shall consult with appropriate State and local officials to determine whether federal objectives can be attained by other means.[18]

Limits were placed on preemption, consultation procedures were specified, and the promulgation of unfunded mandates was prohibited unless the issuing agency sent to OMB, along with the text of its proposed regulation, a "federalism summary impact statement" describing the consultation that had been undertaken and the positions of state and local officials. The new order ended by specifying that "the Director of the Office of Management and Budget and the Assistant to the President for Intergovernmental Affairs shall confer with state and local officials to ensure that this Order is being properly and effectively implemented." Translation: a continuing and strengthened—if not increased—responsibility for the energizers in the White House Office of Intergovernmental Affairs. The Big Seven responded on August 3 (see the second epigraph to this chapter), praising the new order and thanking the president for the extensive consultation.[19]

An IGA officer looks back at the past few years: "We should be a little better: more aggressive in asserting ourselves as policies develop. But there are so damned many policies; it's hard to keep track of everything!"[20] The officer is right. There are 1,412 federal domestic assistance programs currently listed in the government's official catalogue.[21]

Hard as it may be, what began with Meyer Kestnbaum in the Eisenhower White House of 1955—that ombudsman-"energizer"-Intergovernmental Affairs Office—continues today, and will unquestionably continue in the White House of tomorrow.

CHAPTER FOURTEEN

Supporting Political Central: The Office of Political Affairs and Independent Political Consultants

When the party of the president wins the White House, the national party organization essentially becomes a political wing of the White House staffed by presidential loyalists and directed by White House political operatives. . . . The establishment of the Office of Political Affairs is an example of the larger trend of centralization and specialization within the White House; in this case the centralization of purely political tasks.

KATHRYN DUNN TENPAS

Many of the duties of the White House . . . could be performed by people outside the White House. . . . Transferring the duties of the political office to the national committee might, at the same time, breathe new life into the party system and increase the president's political outreach.

STEPHEN HESS

When Reagan political affairs director Lyn Nofziger was asked what, in the White House, he considered to be political, he reportedly replied: "Everything." That one-word answer is an accurate summation of the White House environment. Every presidential issue is political, in the broad sense that the president's decisions test the limits of consensus in the country. Politics—in the narrower sense of partisanship—colors each presidential action as well: it may excite—or threaten—the support of the president's party. If an action succeeds, there is political hay to be made; but if even a "nonpartisan" national security initiative crashes, the president's popular standing plunges with it.

Johnson's policies in Vietnam forced him out of the presidential race. The Iran-Contra affair damaged Reagan. Breaking his "no new taxes" pledge cut deeply into Bush's support. But Ford's popularity surged after the *Mayaguez* crisis—and, yes, the picture of tots rolling Easter eggs on the nonpolitical White House lawn under the eyes of a human-sized rabbit leaves a warm, fuzzy feeling in the national psyche.

Policy and politics are inseparable, be they in the Rose Garden or the Persian Gulf. The president is head of his party and a domestic political leader wherever he goes, whether to the Pine Ridge Indian Reservation or the Great Wall of China. Every two years, when congressional elections take place, the White House is drawn deeply into those battles; when the president's reelection is pending, the White House is Political Central.

In recognition of the political "everything," the Bush and Clinton presidencies used two kinds of support teams for the modern White House: the Office of Political Affairs within the formal staff structure, and private sector consultants from outside. The two are different in status. The former are insiders, paid from White House funds. As federal employees, they are subject to federal ethics, conflict-of-interest, and financial disclosure rules and to post-employment restrictions. The latter are outsiders, paid from campaign or national party committee accounts, and may not be required to file disclosure reports.[1]

Both sets of confidants funnel advice to the president and the senior staff. But the political affairs staff, being in the White House, can reach out and pull levers in the cabinet departments; private sector consultants have no directive authority. The Office of Political Affairs staffers will roam the Hill, negotiate on the president's behalf with members of Congress, give speeches to outside groups. The consultants do not have these mandates and concentrate on bringing their counsel directly into the Oval Office.

The consultants have a unique source for much of their advice: polls, which they themselves (and often the president, too) prepare, and which are financed by party or campaign funds.[2] They also place and pay for political advertisements—an action that no White House staffer can undertake with appropriated monies. Both groups have close ties to the press, and some of the consultants—Paul Begala, for instance—have leveraged that access to go public with a much more strident tone than White House staffers would normally use. Unlike the party's national committee, outside consultants do not have to engage in the arduous business of raising funds, nor are they burdened with the administrative responsibility of helping to manage a network of fifty state offices.

In the end and at the top, during the Clinton years, three bands of partisans—the Office of Political Affairs; the outside consultants; and, on occasion, the chairman of the Democratic National Committee (DNC)—collaborated reasonably closely. They conferred with each other, and with the president, in inner-circle "Residence meetings." There they shared poll results, debated their advice to the boss, and set priorities for political spending.

The Office of Political Affairs

While the function of giving political advice in the White House goes back decades, the office was first set up with its own segment of the White House budget in 1980. (President Ford's political staff, however, was funded by the campaign committee.)[3]

In the Bush White House

During the Bush presidency, the Political Affairs Office numbered twelve people; its first head, James Wray, who had been national field director for the Bush campaign, had the title of deputy assistant to the president. Wray was coequal with the director of the Office of Intergovernmental Affairs, and both offices reported to the same deputy chief of staff—"a big mistake," asserted one of the veterans of the intergovernmental relations staff: "That arrangement automatically raises the suspicions of the governors and the other city and county groups that the intergovernmental unit will take on a political cast and that their efforts will be manipulated for partisan objectives."[4]

Wray organized the Bush political office into five regional desks—and hired, as his assistants, people from the 1988 campaign, who were thus close to their fellow campaigners at the Republican National Committee (RNC) headquarters. He arranged to have a politically appointed liaison installed near the top of each cabinet department; once a month, he would gather the liaison officers together in the White House to inform them of the president's priorities at the time—and get an earful of both good and not-so-good news coming the other way. He would read the weekly reports assembled by the Cabinet Affairs Office; if Secretary X was heading to Chicago, Wray would outfit the secretary with political tip-offs about the Windy City.

One of Wray's prime concerns was to link up White House policy officers with party leaders in other parts of the country who might be affected by the initiatives being hatched near the Oval Office. The Clean Air Act revisions, for instance—one of the Bush administration's notable achievements—were going to affect coal-burning industries in the Midwest. Wray hosted a meeting of the domestic policy team and several leaders from that industry—a rather lively session, he recalled. The industrialists did not get a guarantee that the prospective legislative provisions would be watered down, but they did go away with a clearer understanding of what the administration's policy direction was, and why. "It minimized some of the negative impact that could have come out, otherwise, for lack of knowledge," Wray recalled. "They had the feeling that they had their say and that the door was open to them."[5]

The Senate and House congressional campaign committees would ask to come to the Old Executive Office Building for briefings on foreign or domestic policy initiatives; Wray would make the arrangements and call in knowledgeable speakers from the administration. Wray's successor, David Carney, remembers that "in 1990, we scheduled over a thousand events [for congressional candidates] with the cabinet and the president, the vice president, Mrs. Bush and Mrs. Quayle."[6] Along with all the other directors of White House offices, Wray competed for perks that he could pass on to his constituents: invitations to state dinners, guest spaces on *Air Force One*, seats in the presidential boxes at the Kennedy Center.

A president on the road opens up opportunities to cement local political ties. Wray's regional staffers would join the advance teams, where they could influence the stops to be made, the sites to be visited, the people to be invited onto the dais, the extra slots in the greeting line, and the "clicks" made by the local photographer. The Political Affairs Office sent the president periodic reports, especially about progress with fund-raising, but Wray preferred to have more informal talks on *Air Force One* flights—and less on paper.

During the first year of the Bush presidency, the relationship between the White House Office of Political Affairs and RNC headquarters was exceptionally close: Bush had once been chairman of the RNC; he and Lee Atwater—then the RNC chair—were friends from years before. By 1989 the two staffs had forged strong connections through their common experience during the 1988 campaign. Carney explained, "I had a political directors meeting every Thursday with representatives from the Republican National Committee, the appropriate congressional committees, and the Republican Governors' Association; we'd sit down and work out what they needed from the administration."[7] Atwater himself would come over to Vice President Quayle's office every two or three weeks for informal discussions on political strategy.

The party's national committee traditionally supports the president in his capacity as chief of the party: "It subsidizes all White House political expenditures, such as polling . . . political consulting . . . political advertising designed to promote the administration, mid-term campaigning, fundraising events, early campaign trips to New Hampshire or Iowa, the purchase of White House Christmas cards and presidential cuff-links given to generous donors. In addition, the national committee runs a constant fundraising operation to retire the previous campaign debt and to prepare for the forthcoming election campaign."[8]

When Atwater was forced to give up the chairmanship because of illness, William Bennett was named as his successor. White House Chief of Staff John Sununu, however, "moved in to take over Atwater's functions, a blatant move," wrote Mary Matalin, "to 'suck' political power back into the White House from the national committee."[9] Political scientist Kathryn Dunn Tenpas concludes: "The fact of the matter is the national party organization is an entity that lost much of its autonomy to the White House, not to mention a substantial portion of its budget."[10]

In the Clinton White House

President Clinton upgraded the position of director of the Office of Political Affairs to assistant to the president (giving the director a seat at the early-morning senior staff meetings) and redrew the lines of supervision so that political affairs was entirely independent from intergovernmental affairs. For the first two years of the Clinton presidency, however, both the organization and the work of the political affairs unit were quite similar to what they had been under Bush. The staff was divided by region, and a staff member would cover perhaps ten states. If one of the four principals (president, vice president, the first lady, or Mrs. Gore) was traveling to a given region or a state, the regional specialist would supply information on current local political developments.

In collaboration with the public liaison staff, the Political Affairs Office pulled into the White House constituency groups that wanted to add their voices to the White House policy mix—or that were eager to drink in information about presidential initiatives so that they could amplify the message to still others. Senior White House policy staff, top Office of Management and Budget (OMB) officers, and departmental experts were all used as briefers in the Presidential Hall of the Old Executive Office Building.

If events were scheduled with any of the four principals, either in Washington or on trips, the political affairs staff would make sure that party supporters received invitations. With six full-timers, three volunteers, and eight interns, there were never enough aides in the political unit to spend time personally with individual Clinton supporters: political unit staffers had to deal with the constituency groups through their elected leaders.

If a confirmation battle was impending, the political affairs staff would pitch in to help the candidate meet key players. For example, when Clinton nominated a strong union man to chair the National Labor Relations Board, business groups were antagonistic. The White House political operatives arranged for the candidate to meet with the leadership of the Chamber of Commerce and the National Association of Manufacturers. According to former deputy political director Joseph Velasquez, "Even if we knew we were not going to convince them, we thought that it was important that they at least had an opportunity to brief him, and grill him, and discuss their views. They continued to oppose him, but at least some of those people felt better about the White House by the mere fact that they had had an opportunity to speak with him. It was good politics."[11] (The candidate squeaked through the Senate.)

The political affairs unit was represented in the health care "war room" during that all-consuming 1993 initiative, but only for 20 percent of the time: there were too many demands that had to be met in the office. "In the future? If we had more staff, . . ." mused the former deputy director.[12]

A sensitive issue arose in south Florida: rafters from Cuba were trying to reach shore and be admitted as refugees; the president's policy at the time was to intercept them and divert them to the U.S. base at Guantanamo. Incensed, the ethnic Cuban community in south Florida turned its ire against the president. Velasquez flew to Miami and met with Cuban leaders and with the exile community, then flew to Guantanamo and sat down with refugee leaders there. He commented:

A lot of times what you find is that if you have people come in and talk about their problem, if you pay attention to their concerns, accept some of their views, there may be some acceptable ones that you can implement. . . . All of this political stuff is a question of listening to people, respecting people and their views, making them feel they are important and making them feel that their views are important to us. Then they feel that perhaps they are influencing policy. Sometimes people are calmed down on an issue just by the fact that they were able to come in and talk about it.[13]

Finally Velasquez brought a delegation of community leaders up to Washington and escorted them into the Oval Office, where they met with the president and the vice president. "That was the most powerful tool we had," he emphasized. "They felt, 'We have given our views to the highest authority in the land,' and it empowered them."[14]

When African American, Hispanic, and women's Democratic groups would badger the political office to remind the Presidential Personnel Office of one of the president's most publicized objectives—to have his noncareer appointees "look like America"—the message would be passed on with added emphasis.

The Political Affairs Office rarely dealt with individual job seekers, however: there was little staff or time for that. "If we got involved and started to handle that kind of request, that's all we would be doing," Velasquez explained.

The Scheduling Office is an unending battlefield: "Get him to do *my* event, please!" is the cry from every White House office. Staffers will cook up deals with one another: "Hey, look, you help me out this time, and. . . ." There would be a wait while the schedulers did their work; meanwhile, event programs needed to be printed and invitations issued. Sometimes the groups were notified only one day in advance that the president would attend. During Clinton's first two years, fund-raisers were difficult to get approved. "We would come in and say, 'Here's what the party needs over the next six months,'" recalled Velasquez, "and then have a fight with the schedulers. But after 1994 it was Katie-bar-the-door to get on the calendar."[15]

As had been the case under Bush, the Political Affairs Office under Clinton was on the distribution list for the weekly Cabinet Report assembled by the White House cabinet affairs staff. The political affairs group was on the lookout for two kinds of "intelligence": if they read that a cabinet member would be traveling, the regional political staffers would furnish a roundup of political issues in the state being visited so that the cabinet secretary would know what he or she was walking into; if a department was about to announce a grant to a state or local organization, the political office would ask the agency: "Have you notified the congressperson?" (if he or she was a Democrat, that is).

Contributors, of course, are special.

According to Velasquez, "A lot of people give because they like the president. But everybody wants something out of it. In most cases that 'something' is not monetary. People want respect; people want to be able to have a voice within the administration—know that their views are being heard by the president of the United States, or by the vice president. People want to participate in the process; they want some status."[16] One sign of status was routinely allocated to major Clinton donors: two seats on each flight of *Air Force One*.[17]

Coordination between the Political Affairs and the Legislative Affairs Offices always requires attention. The legislative affairs staff need votes on the House or Senate floor; the political affairs group needs votes in the ballot box—and these two objectives are not unrelated. "We had to be careful that we didn't step on each other's toes," observed Velasquez.

The White House Political Affairs Office does not overlook the resources available to it in the cadre of political appointees at the various agencies. Particularly as Clinton's 1996 contest neared, the noncareer contingents, department by department, were brought into the White House for after-hours briefings. (Not that they could be very active: the lawyers ruled that departmental political appointees could not participate in the campaign even on a leave-without-pay basis; they would have to give up their government jobs.) Even the Social Office was leaned on to become part of the political leverage of the White House: during the campaign period, all suggestions for invitations to social events went through the Political Affairs Office first.

Preparing for the 1996 Election

The congressional elections of 1994, the pendency of the 1996 contest, and the dire need for 1996 campaign funds brought big changes in the Clinton political team. There were a new political affairs director, Douglas Sosnik; new DNC co-chairs, Donald Fowler and Senator Christopher Dodd; a new set of outside political consultants, particularly Dick Morris and Mark Penn; and a new deputy White House chief of staff—Harold Ickes, who was put in charge of all the details of the political operation, including fund-raising. How much in charge? An Ickes memorandum addressed to DNC chairman Dodd clarified that point:

> This confirms the meeting that you and I and Doug Sosnik had on 15 April, 1996 at your office during which it was agreed that all matters dealing with the allocation and expenditure of monies involving the Democratic National Committee ("DNC") including, without limi-

tation, the DNC's operating budget, media budget, coordinated campaign budget and any other budget or expenditure, and including expenditures and arrangements in connection with state splits, directed donations and other arrangements whereby monies from fundraising or other events are to be transferred to or otherwise allocated to state parties or other political entities and including any proposed transfer of budgetary items from DNC related budgets to the Democratic National Convention budget, are subject to the *prior* approval of the White House. It was agreed that a small working committee would be established which would include Chairman Fowler (or his representative), Chairman Dodd (or his representative), B. J. Thornberry, Brad Marshall, Marvin Rosen, Doug Sosnik, and others as may be agreed to, to meet at least once weekly, and more often, if necessary, to implement this agreement.[18]

Ickes later assured President Clinton: "I review the materials before giving final 'sign-off' to the DNC. Typically, when your signature is involved . . . I submit the draft document to you for review before I give final 'sign-off' to the DNC. I typically submit DNC direct mail letters to you, even if you are not signing them, prior to giving the DNC the 'go ahead' for such letters."[19]

It is *not* the purpose of this chapter to revisit the catalogue of the activities that Mr. Ickes and others undertook to raise the $113,954,237 that reportedly financed the Clinton 1996 campaign.[20] Readers will remember the news stories detailing the "rapid-response" teams, the 103 White House coffees with the president (some of those invited were shady characters with merely self-serving motivations), the 831 sleepovers in the Lincoln Bedroom, and the hefty campaign donations collected from many of the same coffee-sippers and overnighters.[21] Then there was the famous (or infamous) quotation from Johnny Chung: "I see the White House is like a subway—you have to put in coins to open the gates."[22]

The president, insisting that it was not wrong "for a president to ask his friends and supporters to spend time with him," said, "I don't think that a political party should say, or a president should say, if you want access to us, you have to contribute."[23] He acknowledged that "mistakes were made,"[24] and added, "if I had it to do all over again, we would fix what we have now. We'd have stricter standards about admission to the White House."[25]

A sharply divided Senate Governmental Affairs Committee investigating alleged 1996 campaign finance malpractice produced a 9,575-page report, but the attorney general did not find sufficient justification for calling up an independent counsel investigation of the general fund-raising effort.[26]

It *is* the purpose of this chapter to underscore how centrally the White House is involved in political operations, financial and otherwise.

Independent Political Consultants

Presidents have concluded that the political expertise and intelligence available to them within the White House are not enough: outsiders will be enlisted. The use of outsiders has been spurred, in part, by what is happening in the branch of our government that competes with the presidency: the Congress. It is this "competitive relationship," this race for dominance, "that has provided yet another reason for presidents to seek the advice of political consultants. While members of Congress are increasingly seeking the advice of political consultants on an ongoing basis (e.g., Frank Luntz), presidents seek to match the resources of the 'other branch.' . . . This 'arms race' mentality has no doubt resulted in the proliferation of campaign consultants generally as well as the modern president's desire to seek such advice."[27]

President Bush retained an independent political consultant: Robert M. Teeter, whom he had hired as early as 1980 as his pollster in that year's presidential primary. Teeter, a regular member of the Bush political *apparat*, was one of the first to use the then-novel "dial group" technique (which will be described later in the chapter) to measure Michael Dukakis's vulnerability in the 1988 campaign. Teeter was co-chair of the Bush transition in 1988–89 and was one of the triad who managed the unsuccessful Bush campaign in 1992. One survey, drawing on Federal Election Commission records, states that the RNC spent roughly $1.8 million on political consultants during the Bush administration.[28]

In Clinton's first campaign for the White House there were four outside consultants—Paul Begala, James Carville, Stanley Greenberg, and Mandy Grunwald—who went on to assist him during the first two years of his presidency. One could say that they were de facto White House staff, since they participated so intensely in the internal debates on the budget and domestic economic policy.[29]

In the words of Elizabeth Drew,

> The role of the consultants in the Clinton administration was without precedent. Previous Presidents had pollsters and other outside political advisers, but never before had a group of political consultants played such an integral part in a Presidency. Clinton's consultants were omnipresent, involved in everything from personnel to policymaking to the President's schedule. . . . Their role raised problems of gover-

nance. For one thing, they contributed to the clogging of Clinton's information systems, the size of his meetings, and the policy paralysis that sometimes occurred. . . . Further, the consultants were accountable to no one except the President. They could sashay into the White House, offer some advice, and sashay out again, leaving the hard part to others. They didn't have to carry out their own proposals or live with the consequences. In the eyes of several White House aides, the consultants didn't understand or accept the realities of governing.[30]

As presidential scholar James P. Pfiffner emphasized:

The problem was not that Clinton was getting advice from outside the White House. Presidents often seek the input of those not in the government; and in any case, presidents ought to be able to listen to whomever they choose. The problem was that the campaigners' advice was not being monitored or coordinated with anyone else. The only place where the campaigners' ideas and professional policy analysis came together was in Clinton's head. The outside ideas were not vetted by White House staffers, departmental policy analysts, or OMB budget staffers. Nor was outside advice balanced with the input of White House staffers on the political, policy, congressional, or budget implications. . . . The content of the advice was not a problem, the lack of coordination was.[31]

The original four consultants were replaced by others: Dick Morris, Bill Knapp, Mark Penn, Doug Schoen, and Bob Squier. Morris has written a full description of his own exploits: how he argued for a policy of "triangulation"—taking a "third position" that differed from both the family values, anti-crime, cut taxes, leaner government positions of the Republicans and the boost-federal-spending-to-help-the-disadvantaged philosophy of the Democrats. The third position of the triangle would be based on a motif of "opportunity-responsibility": stealing the most appealing ideas from both of the other camps and mixing them into a unique Clinton package.[32]

Morris relates his experiences with an ideologically divided White House staff, whose rivalries and jealousies, in his telling, forced him to bypass the staff and deal secretively with the president. Working by himself, he would propose speeches, even drafting several. One was composed in such a clandestine manner that, on being handed the draft from the president, speechwriter Don Baer called it the "immaculate conception" speech— since, Morris writes, "as far as he [Baer] could tell, it had come from nowhere."[33] Morris would meet privately with the president and, one on one, design campaign ads and poll questions. "The president became the day-to-day operational director of our TV-ad campaign. He worked over every script, watched each ad, ordered changes in every visual presentation, and decided which ads would run when and where. He was as involved as any of his media consultants were. The ads became, not the slick creations of admen, but the work of the president himself."[34]

Morris assured Clinton: "You'll keep control, total control, the same way you have for seventeen years with me. . . . I'll clear everything with you constantly. . . . You'll be right there every minute."[35] Needless to say, Morris was not popular then (or since) with many of the White House seniors except the one who counted: the president.

One preliminary survey estimates that from 1993 to 1997 the DNC spent "roughly $11 million" on outside political consultants for President Clinton.[36]

Polling as Political Advice to the President

Morris commissioned more than 100 polls. By one accounting they cost about $2.7 million.[37]

First, just what is a poll? Political consultants use several varieties. The most common is a telephone poll. As Morris describes it: "If you got a phone book of the entire United States, from *a* to *z,* and you pulled out every 312,500th name and interviewed that person, the resulting 800 interviews would accurately reflect within a margin of error the opinions of everybody who is listed in the phone book; I've seen it time and time again. The final poll results accurately state the final election results. It's eerie."[38] Morris warns that one has to make allowances for unlisted numbers or people without phones, but notes that these can be factored in.

Then there is the "mall intercept." The consultants rent a storefront at a shopping mall and ask passers-by to come in and view one or more film clips of suggested parts of speeches, proposed TV ads, or rebuttals to same. The viewing is followed by a brief questionnaire to solicit an opinion or an evaluation.

In a third mode, the "dial group," a small roomful of people listen to or view a speech or advertisement while they push graduated buttons to record favorable or unfavorable reactions to certain words or phrases. A computer correlates the degree of approval or disapproval with the words or phrases being tested and graphs out the results.

The polling firm Morris chose, Penn and Schoen, could handle a small test or a nationwide survey of 259 questions. A poll could be completed in days—or, if need be, in hours. When the budget stalemate between president and congress shut the government down in mid-November of 1995, the president insisted that Morris come up with daily polls: "Our interviewers started phoning at seven in the evening and continued until one the next morning, eastern time, to catch West Coast voters before they went to bed. At about four in the morning, I would awaken to the sound of my fax machine as it spat out the results that had been collected only a few hours earlier. . . . When the president was awake, he'd take my call, so he could start his day with a summary of the latest polling information."[39]

An issue arises: Is polling a substitute for leadership? In his book, Morris raises this question himself and gives his own answer: "No," and explains, "Polling shouldn't determine what a political leader does. Much of the time he has to go against what the polls say the people want. But polls can help a leader figure out which arguments will be the most persuasive."[40]

Morris uses a sailing metaphor: two ships of state, two leaders. The leaders know where they want to end up. In his ship of state, which has a motor, the dictator will turn on the motor and sail on without regard to the winds of public opinion. In a democracy (no motor) the leader will use the sails to catch the winds of opinion, will tack one way and then another, but will always be moving toward the goal. Clinton "never used polling to determine what position on an issue he should take. Never."[41]

Sounds definite. But when the question was whether or not to sign the welfare reform bill, Morris tells us that "Mark Penn had designed a polling model that indicated that a welfare veto by itself would transform a fifteen-point win into a three-point loss. . . . I told him flatly that a welfare veto would cost him the election."[42] After a full discussion with his agreeing and dissenting advisers, Clinton signed the bill. He later kept his promise to have the bill amended to take out its most objectionable provisions.

"We sometimes get accused of having an agenda of poll-driven ideas," reflected domestic policy director Bruce Reed: "I think it was, actually, the other way around. We would come up with a host of ideas and we'd use whatever channels we could to convince people around here to do them. It wouldn't hurt if something was popular, but that wasn't where we got the idea in the first place. . . . I think the president had always been interested in the use of public opinion to figure out what are public feelings, not to make the policy decisions."[43]

A former assistant to the chief of staff observed: "If there is sentiment about child care and if we're not going to go with big child care legislation, let's see what we can do as an executive branch, on our own. . . . I can't remember a poll which asked, 'Would you look favorably if the president announced a school-construction proposal?' It would be more of a 'Let's talk about education: what aspects of education concern you most?'"[44]

A different view was expressed by the former aides whom political scientist Charles Jones interviewed for his book, *Passages to the Presidency: From Campaigning to Governing.* Said one: "I think the damn pollsters should be put out to pasture. You don't need to have somebody take a new pulse every two days in transition. You've already won the thing. You ought to be thinking about longer-term stuff." Another commented that too much emphasis on polling "turns leadership on its head."[45]

This debate will not be settled in this chapter, but it must continue, as modern presidents continue to invest in polls and use their results.

High Command at Political Central: Clinton's "Residence Meetings"

The very pluralism of the elements described earlier, and the divisive relationships among some of them, could have added up to trouble amid the stress and frantic pace of the 1996 presidential reelection campaign. This danger was kept under control, however, by an unusual conclave of all the top players: the weekly campaign strategy meetings in the Executive Residence. (The Residence was used because it was not considered a "federal building" within the meaning of the laws that prohibit the use of government property for partisan purposes.)

The meetings began in December of 1994 as intimate sessions among the president, the first lady, and Morris. Deputy Chief of Staff Erskine Bowles, concerned about the secretiveness of the early meetings, had them enlarged. The first lady dropped out and others were added—in particular, the latest group of four outside consultants, Chairman Dodd of the DNC, Deputy Chief of Staff Harold Ickes, and White House political affairs director Douglas Sosnik. Others included cabinet secretaries Ron Brown and Henry Cisneros and Trade Representative Mickey Kantor; from the campaign, the manager and the communications director; from the White House, the chief and former chief of staff, two deputy chiefs of staff, the first lady's chief of staff, the press secretary, the legislative affairs director, the communications director, counselor Stephanopoulos, and the deputy national security adviser (who later withdrew, not wanting to mix politics and national security policy too openly).

Morris's second book was nearly identical to the earlier edition but appended 282 pages of the agendas—some abridged—of the Residence meetings, plus his own comments about them.[46] It was at these meetings that the results of the hundred-odd polls were revealed and analyzed, that legislative and campaign strategies were discussed, speech themes and drafts examined, television advertising laid out, fund-raising efforts appraised, and campaign budgets approved. One agenda went on for more than thirteen pages.

The meetings were held weekly, except when the president was traveling, and were tightly confidential: all attendees except the two deputy chiefs of staff had to hand in their copies of the agenda at the end of the sessions; no minutes or action summaries were made; the poll results were not shared with lesser White House staffers. Morris's comments reflect the divisions among the group; at one point, for example, he notes that Chief of Staff Leon Panetta "squirmed uncomfortably in his seat."[47]

After the election (and Morris's demise as a consultant, following the revelation that he was keeping company with a prostitute), the Residence meetings continued. Membership expanded to include at least two other cabinet members (Secretary of Labor Alexis Herman and Secretary of Agriculture Dan Glickman) and White House policy seniors Bruce Reed and Gene Sperling. The agendas were more focused on general strategy, but doubtless included the election prospects for 2000.

Within any White House, while touching "everything," the Office of Political Affairs and the outside political consultants continue to have their own special focus: winning. They surely keep in mind Mr. Nofziger's nineteen-year-old desideratum: "I will let Mr. Meese and Mr. Baker and Mr. Deaver and all those good guys worry about Reagan being president. They like government, they want to run the government, they can run the government. I'm much more interested in making sure that we go on running it."[48]

CHAPTER FIFTEEN

Control All the Way Down: The Office of Presidential Personnel

Carter asked if I had any questions. "Only one," I responded. "Will I have the ability to pick my own people?" "Yes. Many are presidential appointments, of course, but . . . you can select your own people. I intend to keep my promise of Cabinet government."

JOSEPH CALIFANO

You cannot separate appointments from policy. Appointments *are* policy. . . . Before we appointed a Cabinet officer, we sat him down with President Reagan. Ed Meese would explain: "The White House is going to control the appointment process. We're not going to shove any people down your throat, but the control is going to be right here. All the way down. Do you understand that?" They all agreed to those terms.

E. PENDLETON JAMES

Second to none in importance and priority at the White House is the selection of the men and women whom the president wishes to have serve in policymaking positions in the administration—and serve at his pleasure, without tenure. These jobs, clearly differentiated from the tenured positions in the career civil service, are non-career (sometimes called "patronage") positions—meaning that they are filled on a political basis (in addition to merit considerations).

The Patronage Universe

There are four categories of noncareer positions—and the contemporary White House controls *all* appointments to them.[1] What are the categories, and what are the numbers of positions so controlled?[2]

    1. Full-time positions, almost all established by statute, that are filled by personal presidential appointment

        a. "PAS": Presidential appointees requiring Senate confirma- 1,125
tion (This subcategory includes 185 ambassadors, 94 district
attorneys, 94 U.S. marshals, 15 in international organizations, 4 in the legislative branch.)

        b. "PA": Presidential appointees not requiring Senate confir-   20
mation

        c. Federal judges to be appointed (the typical number of   200
vacancies that need to be filled in a presidential term, out of
a total of 868 federal judges; all require Senate confirmation
and most have lifetime tenure)

    2. Full-time, nonpresidential, noncareer positions (appointments made by agency heads but with the sanction of the White House Office of Presidential Personnel)

        a. Schedule C positions (see sidebar)   1,428

        b. Noncareer positions in the Senior Executive Service   720
(see sidebar)

        Subtotal: Categories 1 and 2   3,493

        Subtotal: Full-time senior-level positions (subtotal of   2,065
categories 1 and 2, less category 2a)

    3. Part-time presidential appointee positions, established in statute (members of advisory boards and commissions)

        a. "PAS": Requiring Senate confirmation   490

        b. "PA": Not requiring Senate confirmation   1,859

        Subtotal: Categories 1, 2, and 3—the patronage universe of 5,842
concern to the Office of Presidential Personnel

    4. White House staff positions

        a. Receiving formal, signed commissions from the president   80
(assistants to the president and deputy assistants to the
president)

        b. Appointed with presidential approval (special assistants   556
and below, typically handled by the White House chief of
staff or by the vice president, for those in his own office; this
subcategory includes the White House Office plus the staffs

of the vice president; the National Security, Domestic Policy, and Economic Policy Councils; the Millennium Council, the Office of National AIDS Policy; and the Residence; it excludes employees with tenure,[3] civilian and military detailees, the Secret Service, the General Services Administration, the National Park Service, Office of Administration support staffs, and unpaid interns and volunteers)[4]

Subtotal: Category 4   636

The total patronage universe: positions that can be filled by   6,478
the White House during a typical presidential term

The White House director of presidential personnel, coming in with a new president, will be responsible, during his boss's four-year term, for making decisions—or recommending presidential actions—on 5,842 jobs. The Office of Presidential Personnel (OPP) does not handle the 636 White House staff positions, which will be decided upon by senior White House officers and the chief of staff (and in some cases, by the president); nor does it have anything to do with the thousands of military and foreign service promotions that are routinely sent up for the chief executive's approval. (One reform study group has recommended that the president no longer have to approve these foreign service and military promotions, except for the highest ranks.)[5]

How does the Presidential Personnel Office control 5,842 appointments? It manages six principal tasks:

—Describing the noncareer positions that need to be filled
—Identifying—and, after election, negotiating—with candidates
—Upon inauguration, opening up the noncareer vacancies
—Selecting and clearing the nominees or appointees
—Providing orientation to new senior political appointees
—Evaluating the performance of senior political appointees.

Describing Positions

What are these 5,842 positions? Especially in the 2,065 full-time and senior-level policy jobs, what do the incumbents do? What skills and experience do they need to discharge their responsibilities effectively? These questions can be answered, and profiles developed, well before the election. Even before the conventions choose their nominees, catalogues exist that describe the most influential positions in the executive branch: the series of five "Prune

Some Facts about Noncareer Positions

—The "PAS" and "PA" positions, some federal judgeships, and the memberships on part-time advisory boards and commissions are created in statute. (Ambassadorships and most judgeships are authorized not in statute but in the Constitution itself.) The number of statutory posts can be increased or decreased only by congressional action. The president personally approves each of these appointments.

—Schedule C positions are established by departments and agencies, but each such post must first be certified by the director of the Office of Personnel Management (OPM) as being "policymaking" or "confidential." Once a Schedule C job is thus authorized, the department or agency head may appoint a person to the post, but only if that person is also approved by the director of the White House Office of Presidential Personnel (OPP).

—The Senior Executive Service (SES) is the corps of professional federal managers just below the level of assistant secretary. By law, only 10 percent of the positions in the SES may be filled on a noncareer basis. A department or agency head may propose a political candidate to be appointed to such a position, but the appointment must be cleared with the director of the OPP. Once White House approval has been signaled, the OPM grants "noncareer appointing authority" to the agency for the placement.

—Both Schedule C and noncareer SES appointees are employees of the agencies in which they work, and their service is at the pleasure of the respective agency heads. The White House OPP tightly controls these appointments, sometimes pushing agencies to hire certain favored political candidates or vetoing an agency's own choices.

Books" published by the Center for Excellence in Government, each one covering a different segment of senior appointive positions.

The five now cover some 250 key positions and include five- to eight-page descriptions of each and a list of the previous incumbents. Thus, preconvention, a serious presidential contender of either party already has a resource to begin thinking privately about what may later be a crushingly acute area of decisions. By each fall, the Office of Personnel Management publishes in the *Federal Register* a complete list of all the Schedule C positions that it has authorized in the executive branch; this is a second resource for preelection research.

In its September 1996 report, the Twentieth Century Fund Task Force on the Presidential Appointment Process recommended the following:

> Major party candidates should begin to devote some attention [to presidential appointments] before the election, perhaps at the time they secure their party's nomination. Candidates should appoint a staff to plan, in confidence, the personnel aspects of a transition with the full support of the nominee and his or her political and policy advisers. The staff could collect information on the full scope of the president's appointment obligations, gather or create job descriptions for key positions in the administration, master the technical details of the appointment process, become acquainted with officials in the agencies like the Office of Government Ethics that play a key role in the appointment process, and begin to develop a personnel strategy. . . . A good deal of the preparatory work can and should be done before the election so that the staffing process can proceed expeditiously immediately after the winner is determined.[6]

Specifically to finance this kind of preelection personnel planning, Paul Light, the director of governmental studies at the Brookings Institution, has recommended that Congress provide each of the two major national parties a grant of up to $250,000.[7]

Every four years, the Senate Governmental Affairs Committee and the House Government Reform and Oversight Committee take turns publishing the *Policy and Supporting Positions* catalogue, colloquially known as the "Plum Book," but this comes on the scene rather late—that is, just at election time, when the winner is already being deluged by tens of thousands of petitions. The Plum Book lists titles, salaries, and the current incumbents, but contains no information about the nature or requirements of the positions listed. Both the Prune and Plum Books share a disadvantage: they list positions as of a date in the recent past, and are thus silent about whether a new department head has, as some statutes permit, shuffled the agency's authorized assistant secretaries or other subordinates into different functions and titles. As a consequence, some hungry Plum Book readers may send in applications for jobs that have been reorganized out of existence.

After the election, the president-elect and the transition personnel staff, regardless of party, can count on the cooperation of the outgoing White House OPP to share its factual data on noncareer executive branch positions. The Presidential Transition Act specifies that "it is the intent of the

Congress that all officers of the Government so conduct the affairs of government for which they exercise responsibility and authority as . . . to promote orderly transitions in the office of President."[8] Of all the offices in the White House, the outgoing Presidential Personnel Office, pursuant to that congressional intention, has traditionally been especially forthcoming in extending help to its successors.

It would be greatly to the advantage of a president-elect to emulate Presidents Reagan and Bush by designating the director of the OPP at the earliest possible moment. To have a change from one OPP director to another, midway through the transition, as Presidents Carter and Clinton allowed, exponentially compounds the inherent chaos of that period.

Identifying Candidates

The task of identifying candidates can also be started well before the election, as the Reagan experience demonstrated: he had his future White House OPP director quietly set up in a private office as soon as the convention was over. Key positions were highlighted and acceptable names assembled. Currently, the five Prune Books are at hand to help with this assignment. But preelection planning can raise hackles. A former aide recalled what happened in the Carter pretransition period: "The people that are out on the campaign have been there sometimes for two or three years, with no pay, no sleep, eating terrible food. The last thing they really want to be told is that there is a group of pros sitting back in some comfortable office in Washington . . . basically planning who's going to get the spoils of the victory."[9]

The transition period itself is a superpressurized eighty days. The Presidential Transition Act authorizes office space, salaries, supplies, expenses, and travel for the newly elected president and vice president and their supporting staffs: the 1993 transition personnel staff had 250 helpers at work, digging out from under some 100,000 resumes.

Potential candidates come from many sources: the president- and vice president–elect will have immediate prospects of their own; others emerge from among the campaign staff, major contributors, Congress, lobbyists, and interest groups. The first lady will get many supplicant letters for jobs and refer them to the personnel folks.

It is critical that the president-elect designate his senior White House staff very early on—even before he makes cabinet appointments. The reason? In the months to come, policy development and coordination will be centralized in the White House staff. That staff and the director-designate of the

Office of Management and Budget (OMB) should be in position, to advise the president-elect on which cabinet candidates will most effectively fit into this sensitive matrix.

The OPP director does not handle White House recruitment, and cabinet selection will be closely in the president-elect's hands, so a priority task for the personnel director is to identify the several hundred candidates qualified to be nominated as undersecretaries and assistant secretaries in the departments and agencies. Some newly elected presidents put together transition teams to move into the departments even before their respective secretaries have been appointed. But this technique, which looks like good preparation, then produces extra problems, as one experienced aide recalled:

> They scatter out to the agencies. They are putting together briefing books. They are becoming more self-important by the day because they are the president's . . . [emissaries]. They get deferred to when they go to the agencies. And all of a sudden the real person is appointed. That person doesn't necessarily want these folks. . . . They're perfectly happy to say good-bye to them. They have said "Thank you for the briefing books. See ya." Then they get pressure put on them to bring some [of the transition team] to the deal and negotiation goes back and forth. Others pretty much adopt the team as their team so they become the new staff at these agencies. But it's always a tense and confusing process. . . . It often causes the first tension between the White House and the cabinet appointee, because these people who were there first by definition will have good campaign contacts.[10]

Immediately after the election of 1988, President-elect Bush instituted a "silent committee" chaired by his son, George W. The task of this group of veteran Bush loyalists, later known as the Scrub Team, was to look over the campaign roster and identify those people whose exceptionally effective efforts marked them as meriting special attention for appointment in the new administration. The committee did not try to specify placements, just to tag those who truly deserved a patronage reward: they came up with some fifty names.

A second, parallel project was also organized under Scott Bush, the president-elect's nephew, to sift out especially capable young campaigners to be referred, after the inauguration, by the White House to the agencies for possible placement in Schedule C positions. A subsequent presidential personnel director, however, expressed reservations about placing large numbers of young political activists into Schedule C posts. Rather than inject them directly into line positions, it would be better, she said, to choose a small number of them as members of advisory boards and commissions, to train them for "serious leadership roles" a decade or so in the future.[11]

The Clinton personnel operation in 1993 had a silent committee of its own, headed up by campaign aide Michael Whouley: it had the same objective for the Clinton workers and fund-raisers that George W.'s group had had for the Bush loyalists four years earlier. The finance committee of the Democratic National Committee (DNC), for example, sent Whouley a list of some sixty "must consider" individuals, even specifying which executive branch positions or ambassadorships the respective donors would prefer. When the lists were made public four and one-half years later, the DNC simply pointed out that "there is nothing unusual about trying to get jobs for people who have been supportive of the party and the president, whether it be someone who donates money or donates time."[12]

The transition employment officials were aided by the extensive personal contacts Messrs. Clinton and Gore had had from their experiences at Yale, Oxford, the National Governors Association, and the Senate. It wasn't long before Clinton's Presidential Personnel Office had 160,000 resumes optically scanned into its Resumix computer system.

Opening Up Vacancies

When a president leaves office, the greater part of the 5,842 patronage positions catalogued at the beginning of this chapter theoretically become available for the new administration to fill.[13] The two hundred prospective judicial vacancies will open up gradually over the president's four years; new appointments at the several regulatory commissions can be made only as the incumbents' fixed terms expire (or at their death or resignation). Will all the others automatically become vacant? The answer is no—not without some special efforts.

If an election brings a switch in party, the changeover will of course be widespread, but not necessarily total even among those who are dismissible. The new president would be foolish to sweep out of the White House the skilled veteran professionals who, although they serve at his pleasure, keep the place running: telephone operators, Residence staff, assigned military technicians.[14] Nor would he immediately demand the resignations of the 70 percent of his ambassadors who are career foreign service officers. Members of advisory committees might be allowed to continue—with a change of the chairperson. Some Schedule C and noncareer SES employees may be asked to stay on to provide the continuity that an agency head deems essential; others may linger in their posts until the new department head takes a firm hand and requests their departure.

The White House personnel office, pressured by thousands of thirsty job seekers, will use a magnifying glass to reinspect the noncareer landscape, and put the squeeze on the agencies to expedite the changeover. But even as it does so, the new White House will temper diligence with sensitivity. Clinton OPP director Bob Nash recalled instances in which Republican hangers-on were given extensions—when there were just "a few more months until retirement age" or when "the wife has just been diagnosed with cancer."

When the new president is of the same party as the departing one (as in the cases of Kennedy to Johnson, Nixon to Ford, Reagan to Bush) there is more ambiguity and much more tension. Many veterans of the outgoing administration are still imbued with party (if not personal) loyalty, enjoy their work, represent valuable political as well as policy experience, and have settled into Washington—with friendships, mortgages, and children in college. They really don't relish being replaced. Bush personnel director Chase Untermeyer ruefully remarked:

> The one thing I would clearly do differently was not assume that cabinet secretaries were going to manage the firing of the Reagan Schedule Cs and the hiring of the Bush Schedule Cs in a kind and gentle way. I just assumed they would, and I assumed wrong. . . . Secretary [—], . . . who was appointed by Reagan and retained by Bush . . . was basically waiting for the day when he could kick them all out. . . . This happened in lots of the departments. . . . The truest believers of Ronald Reagan . . . were abused. They were not treated in a dignified and polite and politically sensitive way. . . . That one area was dreadfully handled.[15]

There is a third kind of transition when a president wins a second term. In the administrations preceding Nixon's, it was the tradition that all presidential appointees (other than those serving statutory terms) were to submit pro forma letters of resignation to the reelected president. White House Executive Clerk William J. Hopkins would, if needed, telephone diplomatic reminders to the innocently ignorant cabinet officers. He would then give the president the bundle of signed letters, most of which the chief executive would pitch into the waste basket. Until Nixon's reelection.

Immediately following the 1972 election, Nixon chief of staff Bob Haldeman issued a presidential directive to all noncareer appointees who were not serving fixed terms and to all lower-level Schedule C employees: submit a letter of resignation. The same mandate went to Nixon's White House staff officers but with an invitation to accompany the pro forma letter with a second communication stating the staffer's actual personal preference. Nixon accepted a significant number of the departmental resignations, much to the dismay of those who had loyally served his administration, only to find that they had lost their jobs. (Nixon later wrote that this was "a mistake" because of its "chilling effect on the morale of people who had worked so hard during the election.")[16] Neither Reagan nor Clinton repeated Nixon's action; it may be that the long-standing tradition in which a reelected president requests resignations across the board has come to an end.

During the course of an administration, vacancies of course open up for other reasons: deaths, resignations, the expiration of terms. In the spring of 1998, the Clinton OPP notified the noncareer ambassadors (except those who were newly appointed) that it was the Department of State's policy to rotate all ambassadors after approximately three years of service and that their tours of duty would therefore end around June 30.

The resignation of a Schedule C incumbent does not create a vacancy: the "disencumbered" position evaporates. The agency head must submit a new justification for reinstituting the job, and only if the OPM director approves the request can the noncareer placement follow.

Selecting and Clearing New Political Appointees

Typically, on the morning after inauguration, over one hundred of the transition personnel staff are, jurisdictionally if not physically, moved into the White House environment: the extra hands are temporary, but essential to continuing the frantic work begun at transition headquarters. Now, however, their responsibilities are different: what was then the job of recruitment is now the task of selection. The *new* White House Office of Presidential Personnel is in operation. Several old rules are reactivated.

First, no other person or office in the White House is to make personnel *commitment*s. The presidential personnel specialists will often turn to the domestic policy, economic policy, or national security offices in the White House for advice about the selection of candidates—asking those offices to "sponsor" promising candidates, in effect. The political and legislative liaison staffs will funnel in streams of additional resumes from their own respective constituencies. But when it comes to decisionmaking, there can be only one point from which the final recommendation goes to the president. Nash emphasized: "When I came here I made that rule. I said, 'Listen, we don't serve the president very well if we have three people in the White House who will call an agency head and say, 'The White House wants X or Y.' Now, does that happen occasionally? Yes. Do I get mad? Yes. Do I jerk people up? Yes. Because it doesn't serve the president."[17] (Readers will recognize this exclusivity rule as one that emanates from the counsel and the legislative and national security bailiwicks as well.)

Second, the cabinet heads are informed that the White House will govern the selection of their political subordinates "all the way down." Tempting though it may be for a new cabinet secretary to boast that "the president has given me a free hand to pick my departmental associates," that is almost never the case. There will be discussion and negotiation, but in the end, each appointment will be a White House call. Even for the Schedule C and non-career SES appointments—which are not presidential but are made by the cabinet officers themselves—the OPP insists on signing off on every selection. Exclaimed one Reagan White House personnel officer: "We wanted the receptionist who answered the secretary's telephone 'to have a Reagan tone to her voice.'" Did the Bush administration demand the same sign-off? Bush personnel office director Constance Horner emphasized: "Absolutely every single one. I was quite fierce about this, because I saw it as a process of building future leadership. So it mattered to me what the quality of the appointee was, and it mattered to me what their decisional level was, and what their loyalty was, and their intellectual capability."[18]

Another Bush personnel office director had a run-in with an uncooperative cabinet secretary: "He was flabbergasted. He said, 'Do you mean to tell me that just because some people worked in the Bush campaign that I have to hire them at my department?' And the answer was, 'Had it not been for these people, and a lot of other people, George Bush would not have been elected, and *you* would not be the secretary of this department. That's the only way it can be!'"[19]

On rare occasions a cabinet officer will personally appeal a personnel office decision to the president, and will win. Commented Untermeyer: "If a cabinet secretary is willing to wage the battle to that level, the president is typically going to concede the fight. That's the reason why it is important to set up the rules in advance, and have a president who is willing to follow the rules as much as anybody else in the system."[20]

As the first chapter epigraph indicates, President Carter did allow his cabinet officers to make the decisions about their own—even presidentially appointed—subordinates. In a November 1992 column directed at president-elect Clinton, Carter's former chief of staff, Hamilton Jordan, warned: "Don't give the government away. We gave Cabinet officers too much latitude in selecting their key appointees, which resulted in a government staffed by people who did not share or understand our different dream."[21]

The Clinton staff did not make the Carter mistake; it, too, followed the rule the Bush White House had adopted. As Nash diplomatically explained,

> The president needs to be happy and the secretary needs to be happy. This is a delicate area. . . . I have never *made* a secretary do anything by saying, "I don't care what you think; this is who you're going to take." I have never done that because it doesn't work. . . . Now, I do get very perturbed if a secretary goes off on his or her own and attempts to select somebody and then says, "Oh, I have already decided: this is the person who is going to be my deputy assistant secretary." I get perturbed about that . . . just as they would have a problem if I said, "I don't care what you think." . . . I want the president to be happy, and I represent the president. I want them to be happy, because they are running the departments. It gets gray sometimes.[22]

The selection process is a consultative one. The OPP staff—which in other than postinaugural periods may typically have twenty-seven members, augmented by perhaps ten interns—is usually organized into subunits, each of which is assigned to a cluster of agencies; this specialization brings extra expertise in substantive areas. Like other White House units, the Office of Presidential Personnel has a counterpart: an official in each department and agency who is assigned to handle noncareer placements.

In addition to negotiating with the affected cabinet secretary, the OPP will ask other White House colleagues for advice on personnel. The national security adviser, for example, is usually asked for an opinion on ambassadorial nominations. Bush counsel Boyden Gray was an expert in (and had strong views about) regulatory issues, so Constance Horner sought his views on appointments in this area. For the same reason, Bob Nash regularly asked Vice President Gore for his assessment of candidates who would take office in agencies with environmental missions. If the first lady has a personal interest in a particular post (as Mrs. Clinton did in the position of chair for the National Endowment for the Arts), the PPO will learn of it and enlist her help. Senior political staff in the Office of Management and Budget may be invited to comment on appointees who would carry fiscal responsibilities: OMB officers can sum up for the White House the pending budgetary issues with which the novitiate will have to struggle.

Political checks will be made: the legislative liaison staff does soundings on the Hill. The OPP director often conducts personal interviews inquiring about what are called the "new sins": drug and alcohol abuse, womanizing, failure to pay the "nanny tax." Finally, the most penetrating question (as phrased by a veteran executive recruiter) will be asked: "Are there ANY skeletons in your closet? I want to know. And if you DON'T reveal them now, and leave me to make a judgment call not knowing about them, finding some way to handle them, I will STILL find out about them, and then you are out, REALLY OUT."[23]

With these consultations completed, a memorandum is prepared for the president: only a single name is put forward, although the president is informed of the others who were considered. The memorandum goes through the chief of staff; in the Bush administration the phrasing was, "The Chief of Staff and I recommend . . ." Controversies may erupt even at that level: the chief of staff or even the president may suggest, "Why don't we look at more names?"

Only after the president signals his decision do the other clearances begin; these are both numerous and, in truth, quite burdensome for both the candidate and the government. *Ten* forms must be executed by the candidate, including (1) a White House Personal Data Statement, (2) a waiver permitting the review of past tax returns, (3) a lengthy questionnaire so that the FBI can initiate its time-consuming full-field investigation, and (4) a financial disclosure statement for the Office of Government Ethics so that it can identify possible conflicts of interest. The candidate will be taken aback upon discovering the time involved in completing these forms—and upon finding that the required level of detail is so great that he or she may need the help of both an accountant and lawyer.

The results of all these investigations are examined not by the OPP but by the White House counsel. If the financial disclosure check reveals possible conflicts of interest, the candidate will be required to sit down with the ethics officer of the employing department and negotiate divestitures, the establishment of blind trusts, the sale of assets, or any other measures necessary to ensure that the candidate is "clean" of possible incompatibilities. If an unacceptable negative arises from any of these investigations, the counsel and the presidential personnel director will derail the entire selection. Until all these checks are complete, the public remains under the impression that the post is vacant; the personnel office may still be importuned by competing candidates and their supporters for a job vacancy that, really, isn't there any more.

The president's signature on the nomination papers, their dispatch to the Senate, and the press announcement are the last three steps in the White House decisionmaking process—an ordeal of sorts that may have created months of nail-biting uncertainty for the candidate and his or her family.

Next looms another probative transit: the Senate confirmation process. Does the White House play a role there? The White House counsel may gingerly share the FBI report with the chair and ranking minority member of the responsible Senate committee, but unless the nominee is destined for the cabinet or the Supreme Court, neither the White House Office of Presidential Personnel nor the president's legislative liaison group has the staff or the time to shepherd an individual one of those hundreds of nominations through the Senate meat-grinder. Following Senate confirmation, the president will sign the official commission—to hang grandly on the new appointee's office wall.

Providing Orientation for New Senior Political Appointees

Having arrived from Peoria or Pocatello, the president's newly appointed senior-level men and women feel a tinge of apprehension amid their exuberance. What are they getting into? What is a "continuing resolution?" Will "Circular A-95" affect them? How can they fire "foot-dragging bureaucrats"? Will they ever see the president who hired them?

Assistant secretaries remain on the job an average of only twenty-two months. If their on-the-job training can be shortened, their effectiveness for the president increases. In the words of a memorandum by several fellows of the National Academy of Public Administration,

> An incoming presidential administration brings in roughly 3,000 new political appointees after taking office. Many of them are extremely able people with impressive backgrounds. Typically they come to the nation's capital both mission-minded and in a hurry to make changes and to pursue new policy initiatives.
>
> But few have any realization of what awaits them in Washington. Their new environment is very different from what they have seen in their prior careers in business or private professional life. Little in their experience has equipped newcomers to comprehend the complexity of government, the power of myriad special interest groups, and the level of increasingly intense scrutiny to which they will be subjected in both their public and private lives. The contemporary public policy and operational processes in government present to newcomers limitless chances for missteps and embarrassment.

Many incoming appointees also have been immersed only weeks before in campaigns which have been exceedingly negative about Washington, its people and its processes. They arrive, therefore, loath to listen to advice from either Washington career "bureaucrats" or former political appointees whom they either distrust as representing the other party, or believe have become captured by those entrenched denizens "inside the beltway."

Burdened by these perceptions, these new political executives, however capable and well-intentioned, are in danger of stumbling during the first crucial months of an administration—causing grief to themselves and to the president who called them here, thereby injuring the chief executive's hard-won political capital.[24]

Out of such concerns came, in October of 1975, an added responsibility for the White House staff: President Ford's personnel office began an orientation program for senior political executives who were new to Washington. Groups of some thirty-six appointees were invited to the White House on three separate occasions. In the Family Theater, from Friday morning until midafternoon on Saturday, they went to presidential appointee school.

Their "professors" included the White House chief of staff, the principal domestic policy assistant, the OMB director, and the chairman of the Civil Service Commission. The House minority leader told them "How the Congressional Leadership Looks at the Policy Executive," the president's counsel reminded them about standards of conduct, the press secretary described "Dealing with the Press." Each "student" was given a thick notebook with descriptions of the White House and Executive Office units with which he or she would have to work. At 6 P.M. on Friday, the group joined President Ford in a reception in the Jacqueline Kennedy Garden. Later, within their respective departments, agency-specific briefings completed the appointees' preliminary education.

The Carter White House gave little support to this program, and it faded away temporarily. The Reagan staff not only resumed the practice but also contracted with Harvard's John F. Kennedy School of Government to lead seminars based on case studies; larger conferences and briefings were hosted as well. President Bush's personnel directors dropped the (expensive) Harvard sessions but regularly held daylong orientation conferences in the Old Executive Office Building. The Clinton White House had a three-tiered program: all-day sessions in the Old Executive Office Building for one hundred or more new Schedule C appointees; similar seminars for one hundred or more men and women of the SES (which were combined meetings of both career and noncareer officers); and larger conferences for Senate-confirmed appointees, which were managed under contract by the Center for Excellence in Government.

It is hoped that future presidents will continue programs of this type. The House has passed and the Senate is expected to approve an amendment to the Presidential Transition Act that would specifically authorize transition briefings and workshops for newly designated subcabinet officers and White House appointees.

Evaluating Political Appointees

Except for commission members and department and agency heads themselves, executive branch political appointees report to—and are presumably evaluated by—their cabinet superiors. But if they are presidential appointees, their performance reflects, for good or ill, on the person who appointed them: the president. Recognizing this fact, the OPP will, informally, hoist a sensitive anemometer, attuned to cabinet winds.

Bush personnel director Chase Untermeyer made periodic personal visits to cabinet secretaries' offices to discuss how the PAS subordinates were performing, "just to keep the dialogue going." On rare occasions a resignation was arranged. His successor, Constance Horner, emphasized: "The OPP staff . . . depending on the interest and energy level of the staffers, rode tight herd on what was going on in the departments and agencies. And I was acutely aware of cases where failure was occurring anywhere in the [noncareer] SES level and up. I was especially aware of failure occurring at the agency head level and, in a couple of cases, made people move."[25]

The Clinton staff was equally informal and equally sensitive. Said Nash: "I got a call from an office that said, 'This person is not performing.' I knew about it before; I talked to the person once before. Now, the next call is going to be, 'You've got about thirty days to look for something else.' . . . No formal system. . . . We don't go through the system and say, 'Let's figure out . . . let's grade them all.' Don't do it."[26]

An Exceptional Process: Judicial Selection and Department of Justice Appointments

It is the White House counsel, not the Office of Presidential Personnel, that handles the selection of federal judges, of which there are two kinds: Article 3 judges, who serve for life; and Article 1 judges, who specialize in particular areas, such as customs, patents, taxes, and military law and who serve for specific terms, such as fifteen years.

The first step in filling a district judicial vacancy in a given state is an invitation from the White House to that state's senators to propose a name. A single name is asked for (it used to be three), which may be the cause for considerable delay if the first candidate doesn't pan out. Attorneys in the Office of the Assistant Attorney General for Legislative Affairs, within the Department of Justice, typically screen potential nominees; additional interviews are conducted by the White House counsel. More and more of that workload, however, is moving from the Department of Justice to the White House. For appellate court candidates, the review has been "centered in the more politically sensitive White House staff, with much less involvement by Justice Department attorneys."[27]

Each candidate fills out three lengthy questionnaires: one for the Department of Justice (and the White House); one for the American Bar Association's Standing Committee on the Federal Judiciary, which then weighs in with its own recommendations; and one for the Senate Judiciary Committee. There is considerable overlap in the information that the three require.

A distinguished commission of former attorneys general, senators, American Bar Association judges, and White House counsels, reporting in 1996, expressed concern about Justice Department and White House staff personally interviewing judicial candidates:

> Not only do we question the need for interviews but we believe they may be offensive to some candidates. Moreover, the public, and especially the bar, may see the effort as one to inquire into and perhaps even to attempt to influence the candidate in his or her judicial views. We are satisfied that this is not the intention of those in the Department involved in the process, but the perception may nonetheless exist. The participating personnel are either involved in the political process or perceived to be, and can hence be seen as interested in more than simply professional competence. Further, the persons conducting the interviews are relatively young and inexperienced in litigation as compared with the candidates. Questions not intended to probe personal beliefs may be perceived otherwise and that, coupled with the relative inexperience of the interviewer, may offend some candidates.[28]

The commission specifically recommended that "the White House and the Justice Department should review their current procedures with a view to simplifying the process. In particular, consideration should be given to reducing the breadth and extent of questions posed to judicial candidates, to duplicative inquiries, and to whether personal interviews are really needed."[29]

Former White House counsel Lloyd Cutler believes that the vetting process of the American Bar Association could be relied upon for lower-court appointments.

The White House counsel and staff study the analyses and views of the Department of Justice. They also review the completed questionnaires; examine any opinions, briefs, or other legal publications of the potential nominee; and assess the personal interviews that have been conducted with the candidate. A White House judicial selection committee then convenes, chaired by the counsel and made up of other concerned White House colleagues, such as the directors of the Legislative Affairs and Presidential Personnel Offices. A coordinated recommendation is presented to the president through the chief of staff. In six and one-half years, President Clinton sent 392 judicial nominations to the Senate.

In September of 1999, the Task Force on Federal Judicial Selection (created by the bipartisan Citizens for Independent Courts, an independent, nongovernmental organization) issued a report noting that in the Clinton administration, for district and circuit courts, the average number of days between the "nomination opportunity" (that is, the occurrence of a vacancy) and the president's nomination of a replacement was 315. The task force recommended, therefore, that

> the President and other executive branch officials should make it a high priority to choose nominees for federal judgeships in a more expeditious manner . . . [with a goal of making] nominations within 180 days of vacancies. . . . The President and other involved executive branch officials should routinely engage in advance planning for possible vacancies on the federal bench. Such advance planning should include developing lists of available, qualified candidates for judgeships, while coordinating early in the process with concerned senators.[30]

Implementing these recommendations, especially the second one, would mean significant additional responsibilities for the staff of the White House counsel.[31]

When a presidential appointment, such as that of assistant attorney general, is to be made in the Department of Justice, the White House counsel participates in the vetting procedure and presumably advises the presidential personnel director and the president if the candidate has written law review articles or done other legal scholarship that the president should read to gain a sense of the nominee's policy outlook. This chain of staff work obviously broke down in June of 1993, leaving the president out on a limb. He sent up the nomination of Ms. Lani Guinier as assistant attorney general for civil rights without having been warned about some of Ms. Guinier's writings—which, he later had to admit, were "inappropriate . . . anti-democratic, very difficult to defend."[32] The embarrassing incident, hurtful to everybody involved, simply illustrates what is at stake in the business of doing White House staff work, and the price that is paid for slipups. Readers will recall Bob Haldeman's ambitious dictum for White House staff performance: "Zero defects!"

Proposals for Reform

In recent years, at least four commissions or task forces—most of them composed of former government executives—have examined the White House's patronage system and spoken up to recommend changes. They are the National Commission on the Public Service (the "Volcker Commission," 1989); the Twentieth Century Fund's Task Force on the Presidential Appointment Process (authors of the *Obstacle Course* report, 1996); the President's Commission on the Federal Appointment Process (1990); and the Presidential Appointee Project of the National Academy of Public Administration (1985). So distinguished is the collective experience of their members in the very system that they criticize that the proposals of these committees warrant attention here, alongside the views of the three most recent directors of the White House Office of Presidential Personnel: Chase Untermeyer, Constance Horner, and Bob Nash.

One recommendation is supported by all four study groups: cut back the number of political positions—by 33 percent, say the first two.[33]

The two Bush OPP directors concur with the idea of cutting back the total patronage universe but would wield the knife primarily in the lower- to midlevel Schedule C contingent: the "confidential assistants" and "special assistants," perhaps also some deputy assistant secretaries. "They don't pull their weight," explained Ms. Horner. "They are a distraction to the serious political leadership, they generally are of insufficient quality, they damage the relations between the very senior civil servants and the senior government executives, by getting in between them." Added Untermeyer, "Schedule Cs are not getting much patronage for the party anyway; cutting them would mostly be a big blow to Johnny and Jane who are the son and daughter of the big banker back home in the congressional district." Untermeyer would concur in some trimming of PAS (and also noncareer SES) positions but points out that these are matters of statute and would require "restraint on the part of Congress" to desist from creating more of the PAS posts.[34]

Clinton personnel director Bob Nash did not concur with the proposal to reduce the total patronage universe; he would, instead, reconstitute it by moving a goodly number of the PAS positions—"those that don't have massive responsibilities" for budget or policy—out of the Senate-confirmed contingent and into the noncareer SES and Schedule C categories. "There are too many Senate-confirmed positions," he added, noting that they take thirty or forty-five days for confirmation.

As part of his downsizing of the federal government, Clinton himself took aim at the size of the Schedule C contingent: he and the OPM director cut some three hundred positions from the total that OPM had authorized at the beginning of his administration; his objective was to stay under a ceiling of 1,500.

In August of 1995, Senate Bill 125 passed by unanimous consent; the bill would, in effect, have abolished all Schedule C and noncareer SES positions and cut the PAS contingent by 570. A prominent conservative argued that, if it passed in the House as well, the president should veto it:

> Republicans are forgetting that Bill Clinton will not be in the White House forever. Someday, one of their own will be there, and he will need all the help he can get to put his imprint on the government. Otherwise, he'll be like a conductor trying to lead Beethoven's Fifth Symphony as the orchestra plays punk rock. . . . The federal government needs balance between political appointees accountable to the president and career employees who ensure administrative continuity and institutional memory. Republicans shouldn't let their opposition to the Clinton administration blind them to the importance of maintaining this balance.[35]

The measure was dropped in conference with the House.

Other reform recommendations endorsed by at least three of the commissions include the following:

—Immediately after their respective conventions, both presidential nominees should initiate a planning process for recruiting noncareer appointees.

—The federal government itself should draw up lists, job descriptions, and qualification statements for presidentially appointed jobs. (There was a divergence as to which office should do this: the OMB, the OPP, or the White House executive clerk.)

—The Office of Presidential Personnel should expand its staff to provide guidance, counseling, and support to nominees (and their families) to help them through the confirmation maze.

—The array of forms that nominees must fill out, for the White House and for the Senate, should be streamlined or consolidated.[36]

"Personnel is policy," a White House patronage aide once wrote. Several thousand times in his term, a president—or his staff, with his authority—choose the twain together. The "tone" of presidential policy may be expected in the voice of the receptionist, in the pen of a Supreme Court Justice, and in the work of all the noncareer men and women in between. Without that leverage, a president—and, through him, the electorate—enjoy less than their full constitutional powers.

CHAPTER SIXTEEN

Manager of Apparently Effortless Success: The Advance Office

Advancing is an art! It is the exhausting, detailed planning that makes each presidential trip and event appear to be an *effortless* success. An incredible diversity of activities . . . is involved. . . . The advance person is manager, integrating and coordinating. . . . The lead advance is the head of a highly professional and dedicated team of White House experts. The advance group must accomplish these things in an anonymous fashion—giving gladly the credit for a successful visit to the local people or event sponsors.

WHITE HOUSE ADVANCE MANUAL

Railings had been erected at the edge of the stage, but, unknown to those on the dais, they were only for decoration. Senator Dole, just before his speech, reached over the railing to shake hands with a supporter, and it gave way. Dole tumbled three feet into a swarm of photographers, slightly injuring his left eye.

FROM NEWS REPORTS, CHICO, CALIF., SEPTEMBER 18, 1996

Presidents never stay home. From Shawnee Mission High School to the emperor's palace, from the Kentucky State Fair to the Kremlin, the president of the United States is visitor in chief, representing now his government, now his party, now all the people of the nation. As chief of state, he has words of encouragement for the National Association of Student Councils; as chief partisan, he addresses a Senate candidate's closing rally; as national spokesman, he stands on the cliff above Normandy Beach; and as chief diplomat, he spends weary hours at the

Wye Retreat Center, extracting tenuous Middle East peace agreements from skeptical antagonists. The lines between his roles are of course never quite that distinct: in each place he travels, the president is all these "chiefs" at once.

His national and political roles are public and he wants them to be so: cameras and the press are invited to witness every handshake, film each ceremony, record all the ringing words. A presidential trip is often substantive, but it is also always theater: each city an act, every stop a scene. As the Secret Service recognizes, however, in any balcony can lurk a John Wilkes Booth, at any window a Lee Harvey Oswald; a Sara Jane Moore or a John Hinckley may emerge from any crowd. One other presidential role is quintessential but usually more concealed: as commander in chief, the American president must always—no matter where he is in the world—be able to reach his national security command centers.

A presidential trip, therefore, is not a casual sojourn: it is a massive expedition, its every mile planned ahead, its every minute preprogrammed. The surge of cheering thousands must stop just short of a moving cocoon of security; curtained behind each VIP receiving line is the military aide with the "doomsday briefcase." Except for the military aide with the "satchel," all of the first lady's travel presents similar requirements for minute care and advance attention.

These massive expeditions are the responsibility of the White House Advance Office. How large a job is this? In seven years in office, President Clinton made some 2,500 appearances in over 800 foreign or domestic cities or destinations, plus some 450 appearances at public events in the Washington area.[1] The pace of the work in the Advance Office was nothing short of breathtaking.

While each chief executive's travel style is different, trip preparations are similar; the art of "advancing" is common to presidency after presidency, although new technological gadgetry has made the whole trip-preparation process swifter and more efficient.

Within any White House staff, trip planning calls for intricate choreography among more than a dozen separate offices: cabinet affairs, communications, domestic policy, intergovernmental, legislative, medical, military, national security (if the trip is overseas), scheduling, political, public liaison, press, Secret Service, social, speechwriting, transportation, the vice president's office, and the first lady's staff. The Advance Office is the orchestrator of this cluster and the manager of all the forthcoming on-scene arrangements.[2]

How does the Advance Office organize a presidential trip?

Advancing Domestic Trips

A domestic presidential visit can get its start from any one of the hundreds of invitations that pour into the White House, but more likely it originates from within, as a homegrown idea. What policy themes is the president emphasizing? To which areas of American life does he wish to draw attention? Educational excellence, industrial competitiveness, athletic prowess, racial harmony, minority achievement, environmental improvement . . . ? At campaign time, of course, electoral issues are foremost: What voters are targeted, which senators need help?

Like the daily schedule (discussed in chapter 12), a trip is not a casual event but a calculated piece of a larger theme—and, as such, is designed to convey a message. A presidential trip, in other words, is an instrument of persuasion.

Forward planning for domestic presidential trips may be done from four to eight weeks in advance but is more likely compressed into an even shorter lead time. As soon as the desired message is framed and agreed to, through discussions within the White House, the Advance Office reviews the choices for domestic travel: Where in the country can the presidential theme best be dramatized? Which groups, which sponsors, which cities or towns? What already-scheduled local event could the president join, transforming it into an illustration of his own policy initiative? Local and state calendars are scanned, the *Farmer's Almanac* is studied. Invitations are searched, private suggestions reviewed. Long lists are discussed with the Scheduling Office and vetted into short lists; tentative alternatives are identified. If the president is campaigning, all the processes mentioned here are melded together: the president may do twelve to eighteen events in a week.

For domestic trips, in previous years, "site surveys" would be undertaken perhaps six weeks ahead of time, and "pre-advance" teams would be sent out weeks beforehand. Money then became tighter and staffs smaller. The Bush Advance Office staff totaled eighteen; the Clinton White House had only twelve, four of whom were interns. Communications have speeded up as well. "Reactivity time"—that is, the period needed to respond to changes in circumstances—has dwindled, with the consequence that lead time for decisions may be greatly shortened, alterations more easily tolerated, last-minute revisions accepted. All arrangements can be more flexible; some can be consummated with only hours to spare. The final "go" decision, therefore, has sometimes been made as little as two weeks before the event—or less, as Clinton Advance Office director Paige Reffe described:

> I was walking into an afternoon meeting in the deputy chief of staff's office that I thought was supposed to be about the first family's vacation . . . and the deputy turns to me and says, "By the way, we are thinking of the president going to New York at nine o'clock to meet with the TWA Flight 800 families." I said, "Nine o'clock when?" And she said, "Nine o'clock tomorrow morning," about eighteen hours from now. I said, "I didn't bring my top hat, I didn't bring my cane, and I don't have any rabbits to pull out today. . . . Let's stop *thinking* about this; there is a 5:30 P.M. flight to Kennedy; I can get people on that flight. I can actually get something set up if the decision is made in the next hour." In the end, sometimes those things are easier than normal events, because there isn't time for people to start picking them apart and making changes.[3]

Floods, disasters, hurricane damage, funerals: a presidential presence is often required. But then the advance office looks less like a long-range-planning unit and more like a firehouse.

The White House counsel makes a key determination: Is any part of the trip for a clearly political purpose? Is the president going to be partisan in speech and act, or will he be entirely "presidential"? In scrupulous detail, all the proposed meetings, site events, rallies, and addresses are divided into rigid categories so that mathematically precise formulas can be used to allocate expenses between the political sponsors and the government: "21.7 percent of the trip is political, 78.3 percent is official," explains one illustrative memorandum. The counsel and the political affairs director sign off on the allocation. If the White House asks any federal political appointees to serve as volunteers on the advance team (which it often does), they must take annual leave if they work on any part of the trip that is political—and any expenses they incur must be paid for by the host political group or by party national headquarters.

Funding is a sensitive issue. There is a four-way division: (1) Assuming the trip is nonpolitical, the White House budget itself supports only the travel expenses of the advance teams and the presidential party (and its VIP guests), including the staff of the White House Press Office. (2) For any trip, political or not, the government covers those costs that relate to the president's security. In this category are the costs incurred by the White House Military Office (financed by the Department of Defense); this office covers the expenses of its medical personnel, military aides, and the White House Communications Agency (WHCA), which supplies lights and amplification equipment as well as its own ample communications gear. Also in this category are the costs incurred by the Secret Service (actually part of the Treasury Department), which has its own budget for travel and equipment (including the presidential limousine and other special cars). The Military Office's *Air Force One* will be supplied, but its costs must be reimbursed if the trip is political. (3) Members of the White House press corps pay for their own travel expenses (via reimbursement to the White House Travel Office). (4) All local "event" expenses must be borne by host groups: for example, the costs of renting a hall, constructing risers for the press, furnishing the stage backdrops, providing banners and hand-held signs, printing and sending out flyers, printing tickets, arranging for advertising, and providing motorcade vehicles for nonfederal dignitaries. A letter spelling out these financial obligations is sent to the host, who must send back a signed formal agreement.

The government's actual total cost for a domestic presidential trip is almost impossible to pin down, but it is high. No host group, political or otherwise, could afford all the charges, including those relating to security. Therefore, no matter what reimbursement is obtained, there is a significant publicly financed subsidy for any presidential expedition. It is simply the cost of having a president who travels.

Within the White House, an Advance Office "staff lead" is named who will head up all the advance work. In addition, a trip coordinator is designated—a stay-on-home-base "ringmaster" to whom the advance team's queries are directed and on whose desk all plans and all logistical details are centralized. "She is the lifeline for the advance people," explained Bush advance director John Keller. "Whenever the advance people call back to the office, that's the one they talk to."[4]

Once the two lead people are designated, internal assignments are specified. It is a broad "ring": the Intergovernmental Affairs and Political Affairs Offices will recommend governors, mayors, or local officials to be asked to sit on the dais; the legislative affairs staff will identify the senators and representatives who would be affronted if they were not invited to accompany the president. If the trip is political, the political affairs director will compose a detailed list of themes that will gain a warm local reception, and of issues to avoid. The event will usually be designated as "open press"—but if not, the Press Office will organize a pool of the White House press corps, and the media relations unit will prepare credentials for the local press.

Speechwriters are at work, the medical staff makes its preparations, the Secret Service will ask its local field agents to supplement its regular presidential protective detail. WHCA will box up a mobile satellite sending and receiving station along with the president's armored "Blue Goose" podium. The Air Force will make sure that the local airport can handle the "footprint" of the huge 747 *Air Force One* and will stash two presidential limousines, the necessary Secret Service vehicles, and WHCA's "Roadrunner" communications van into a C-141 transport. If it is called for, the Marine Corps will add in HMX-1, one of the presidential helicopters.

The White House advance team itself is assembled. Headed by the staff lead, the team includes representatives from many of the offices just mentioned. Unless the occasion is unusually complicated, current practice is for the advance team for a domestic trip to leave the White House only six days before the president is scheduled to arrive (seven for a RON—"remain overnight"—visit). In what is likely to be a rather frantic final five days, the advance team must complete an unbelievably complicated checklist: one such list was twenty-six pages long and included 485 items.

The team visits the airport, draws (and faxes to Washington) rough site diagrams—showing where planes, helicopters, and cars will park—and reviews the planned arrival ceremonies. Who will the greeters be? (Each hand-shaker must be approved in Washington.) Are the toe strips in place to show the greeters where to stand? Where is the rope line? The team is admonished: "Inconvenience as few commercial airline passengers as possible." Not even a wheeled set of stairs needs to be commandeered; *Air Force One* has its own mobile stairs.

The motorcade is organized with minute precision. The advance team is reminded that "all the substantive success in the world can be overshadowed if those involved cannot get where they need to be."[5] The motorcade may be the standard minimum of twenty-four vehicles or it may be a hundred cars long. Each car is labeled and spotted on the diagram; every driver must be approved by the Secret Service. The last two cars, which are called "stragglers," will pick up staff members who may have missed the departure; the stragglers can also be used as alternates in case of breakdowns. Motorcades used to be important for generating crowds of sidewalk spectators—but no longer. Primarily for security reasons, the line of cars speeds by: the onlookers not only don't see the president, they can't even figure out which limo he is in.

Each event site must be examined in detail: What will be the backdrop, the "storyboard"—that is, the picture that television will capture? "Distill the message into a brief and catchy phrase," advises the detail-conscious Advance Manual, but "you *do not* want shiny white letters on shiny yellow vinyl." This is not some "pizza-parlor's grand opening." Walking routes are plotted: for the president, the guests, the press, the staff, and the public (more diagrams). There must be a presidential "holding room" where he meets sponsors and guests. What will be the program? What kind of audience is expected—students? senior citizens? friendly? skeptical? How long will it take for them to go through the magnetometers? If hotel overnights are planned, floor plans are needed.

No team is without its conflicts. The press advance staffers want to have an airport arrival at high noon, big crowds, remarks, greetings, bands, balloons ascending, people pressing against the ropes. The Secret Service looks through different eyes. "If they had their way," commented one advance veteran, "they would have the president arrive after dark, in an out-of-the-way corner of the airport, put him into a Sherman tank, lead him to a bank, and have him spend the night in a vault." He added: "They would say, 'You cannot choose that route,' and we would counter, 'No, he *will* drive that avenue, you go ahead and protect him.'"[6] Since the assassination attempt on Reagan, the Secret Service wins more of these battles.

There are conflicts with the local hosts as well: Who will sit on the dais? Will spaces be saved for the local as well as the national press? One sponsoring group for a fund-raiser had sold every seat on the floor of a gymnasium: the advance team had to insist that the tables and seats be squeezed together to make room for the camera platforms. There must be two sets of such risers: one facing the speaker and one at an angle in the rear, for over-the-shoulder "cutaway" shots of the president together with the audience he is addressing. With luck, the risers can be borrowed; the advance team is instructed: "Don't go cutting down virgin forest to build press risers for one-time-only use."[7]

The White House advance person, the instructions make clear, is a diplomat-in-temporary-residence, "the mover and the shaker, the stroker and the cajoler, the smoother of ruffled feathers and the soother of hard feelings. The staff lead is the captain of a great team."[8] But the captain is forewarned: shun all media interviews. "*Never* be a spokesman or go on the record with the press. . . . You are invisible to the camera. Your work is done just outside the four corners of the picture frame. You do not eat up an inch of the screen that is the canvas that you and your colleagues have designed to be a 'picture of the day.' You and your advance team colleagues are not the story, the *president's visit* is. . . . And don't snack on the buffet food which the working press has paid for. . . . But get the job done."[9]

A former advance chief slyly recalls:

> To be a successful advance person . . . you have to have that minor crooked side to you, and you have to be willing to do whatever you have to do. That doesn't necessarily mean breaking the law, but it means that you can't be shy and you have to be assertive. If I tell you to go find a podium, I know you're going to come back and you're going to find a podium. You may have just happened to have gotten it from that event three doors down, and they're wondering where their podium is right now, but the fallout had there not been a podium would be a hell of a lot bigger than somebody asking where the podium came from![10]

The advance team may include nongovernmental companions: technical experts from the news networks, news photographers, and representatives from the White House Correspondents Association. Satellite time must be reserved, transmitting "dishes" placed, camera angles planned. What will be the dramatic scenes? Where will the sun be?

The advance team's instructions leave no doubt as to the purpose of a presidential trip: "The President has a point to make and that's the message. The message of a trip . . . is the *mission* of a trip . . . The public events of a trip are the expression of the message. It is central to advance work and deserves a lot of time and energy. Every event or site must capture or reinforce the reason the President is there. . . . The trip's message has already been through a wringer of careful deliberation at the White House."[11]

The government team and the news planning team represent institutions that are different and often at odds. In this mini-universe, however, they have a common purpose: to get the fullest stories and the best pictures to the most people the fastest. "All of them know that, visually and technically, there are right and wrong ways to do things," explained one former participant, "and this is true whoever is president; it's a professional business." Such symbiosis disturbed newsman Martin Schram, however. He quoted a colleague: "In a funny way, the . . . advance men and I have the same thing at heart—we want the piece to look as good as it possibly can. . . . That's their job and that's my job. . . . I'm looking for the best pictures, but I can't help it if the audiences that show up, or that are grouped together by the . . . [White House] look so good. . . . I can't help it if it looks like a commercial."[12] Schram then adds, "That is what White House video experts . . . are counting on. Offering television's professionals pictures they could not refuse was at the core of the . . . officials' efforts to shape and even control the content of the network newscasts."[13]

A Clinton advance officer described this duality from another angle:

The most frustrating part of my job: . . . the advance team will make sure that [the press] are supplied with very nice visuals, with a great venue for the speech, and then you will see the most unbelievable choice of pictures that the producer or editor or newspaper . . . will actually decide to run. . . . We put all that blood, sweat, and tears into creating this beautiful visual backdrop and instead they will wind up with pictures of the president talking with some aide backstage. . . . The picture that we actually got out of all this hard work was completely disconnected from the story we were trying to achieve. So I think that coziness may not be as prevalent as it used to be . . . not with the people who are deciding what goes on the evening news or the front page. . . . It is also a function of volume: President Clinton travels exponentially more than President Reagan; editors probably tire of running the pictures that we "give" them.[14]

There are still other items on the final checklist: "Effect of the motorcade on normal commuting patterns," "Lighting: 320 foot-candles on the speaker and 200 foot-candles on the crowd," "Overtime cost estimate," "Other appropriate music—can the band play it?" "Empty seats filled or draped," "List of gifts accepted for the President," "Bad weather alternative."[15]

The advance team has a daily "countdown" meeting, where the team members make sure that they are all on the same page. "Never miss it!" warns the manual. There is also a daily conference call to home base, with the trip coordinator and all the affected White House offices. "Date-time stamp and file every piece of paper," the team is instructed, and "Keep Everybody Informed."[16]

If the trip is political and a big rally is scheduled, the advance team will include another specialist, a "crowd-builder," who comes with the attitude that this "is a historic occasion, a great party, the biggest thing to ever happen to this town. If Joe Public misses it, Joe Public will regret it for the rest of his/her life. So, Joe Public better pack up the kids and bring Grandma and Grandpa or they will have missed one of the biggest days in their town's history!"[17]

The local hosts must do the actual work, mobilizing hundreds of enthusiastic volunteers. A vast menu of techniques is systematically used, but all are on the advance team's checklist: not a single step is left to chance. For illustration:

—Event sites should be "expandable" or "collapsible," so that new seats can be added or empty chairs removed.

—Ten times as many handbills should be printed as there are places to be filled: enough for every shopping-center grocery bag, for door handles in parking lots, to tape to mirrors in public rest rooms, even to lay (right side up) on busy sidewalks. One last idea is suggested: "Stand on top of the highest building in town and throw the handbills into the wind." Leaflets must list the event as beginning at least one half hour before it will actually start: a president on the platform with a crowd still at the gates is chaos.

—*Air Force One* should be mentioned in leaflets for an airport rally; some folks will come just to see the plane. News stories about the history of presidential aircraft should be used to spark the interest of the crowd (but mention of their cost should be avoided).

—Bands, cheerleaders, pom-pom girls, and drill teams are to be mobilized (but the Secret Service has to check every make-believe rifle).

—Banner-painting parties are suggested, with supplies of butcher paper and tempera paint; a "hand-held sign committee" should be organized.

—Three thousand balloons are recommended, with balloon rises preferred over balloon drops. The truly experienced may try to do both simultaneously in the same auditorium: helium in the ones to go up, air in the ones to come down. The hall manager must be consulted first, however: the risen balloons will cling to the ceiling for two days afterwards.[18]

No matter how rah-rah some aspects of a trip may be, White House advance staffers are forever conscious that it is the president of the United States who is there. They strive for a "colorful and mediagenic setting"— but never at the expense of the dignity of the person or the office. Their instructions state: "The President must never be allowed into a potentially awkward or embarrassing situation, and the advance person is sometimes the only one who can keep that from happening. . . . For example, an oversized cowboy hat, a live farm animal, an Indian headdress, or a Shriner's 'Fez' could produce a decidedly un-presidential photograph. Common sense must be used to make sure that the dignity of the office of the President is never compromised by the well-intentioned generosity of local partisans."[19]

And no thank you to sound trucks, bands on flatbed trailers, elephants, clowns, and parachutists.

Like crowd-raising, press-advancing is a special skill of the advance team. At a major event site, a press area must be set apart. Camera platforms and radio tables must be of the required size and height, and press-only magnetometers must be installed. Each event site must be equipped with a half-dozen long-distance telephones, and each desk needs an electric outlet for plugging in a laptop. Four nearby rooms are reserved (at their cost) for the three television networks to edit their tapes. A filing center is set up with tables and chairs for a hundred people; the press secretary and his staff need a large adjoining office area with six tables to hold their equipment. "We duplicate the White House Press Office on the scene of a presidential visit," one expert explained. "The White House press staff can do their work just as if they were at 1600 Pennsylvania Avenue."[20]

The advance team stays on site, completing its prodigious checklist, until the very moment the president is to arrive.

Back at the White House, the formal press announcement is made, with the local sponsors tipped off ahead of time and the necessary representatives, senators, governors, and mayors likewise alerted just before the White House release. The speechwriters have prepared their drafts, idea notes, or complete remarks ahead of time for arrivals, departures, and each stop in between (but word processors and copiers are aboard *Air Force One* if last-minute changes are ordered). The earlier sketches of airports, motorcade arrival and departure points, corridors, rooms, and walkways are transformed into minute diagrams, with arrows drawn in showing each presidential footstep.

When its own thousand details are done, the White House Press Office compiles a "Press Schedule Bible," which is given out to the national press representatives.

On the morning before the day of departure, the Advance Office holds a final trip briefing for the chief of staff; it will be the chief of staff who gives the final imprimatur for the *Air Force One* manifest. The advance team staff lead composes the president's and first lady's personal schedule sheets. Even when airborne, *Air Force One's* communications desk buzzes with last-minute advice from the advance team waiting at the arrival site.

As the presidential party approaches the runway, what goes through an advance person's mind? One veteran remembers: "There are a hundred bad variables when you look at a situation and go down your list. What you try to do is to reduce those down to zero. You never get them to zero, but if you get them down to six or five or four when the event occurs, then the odds are with you, and if they do go wrong they are at least in the manageable range."[21]

The Advance Manual emphasizes: Pictures of the president standing behind the podium are dull stuff, and could just as well be snapped in the Rose Garden. Plan to have the cameras catch the president doing something unique and special, of exciting human-interest quality:

The high point . . . is "The Moment," the one snippet of action that visually tells the story of why the trip was undertaken in the first place. Media organizations need this moment to encapsulate the event. It will be rare that a newspaper will carry the complete transcript and equally rare that a local affiliate will broadcast the event "live" on television. . . . So we strive to create a moment: that ten-second slice of uplifting video . . . or that full-color, top-of-the-fold newspaper photo. . . . As the cliche goes, a picture is worth a thousand words. . . . "The Moment" is what you make of it. Don't let a visit go by without creating one.[22]

Advancing International Trips

If the domestic arrangements seem lengthy and elaborate, they are modest when compared to the preparations for a presidential trip abroad. An overseas journey that involves multiple stops is truly a massive enterprise.

Advance teams for a foreign trip must also contend with two institutions that are unique to the scene outside of the United States: the sovereign host government and the American embassy. In the few countries that an American president has never visited (very few), neither of those establishments may comprehend the magnitude of a presidential visit. In addition to the U.S. officials involved, an important world conference will be covered by four hundred more men and women from the American press alone.

It is more than mere staff and press numbers that give some foreign governments pause, especially those that are just emerging from or are still within an authoritarian system. An American president or first lady who, Clinton-style, meets with local nongovernmental leaders, who addresses huge student gatherings (President Clinton gave an open-air speech to a crowd of half a million in Ghana), who conducts wide-open press conferences, who delights in call-in radio shows, is a stunning—possibly even worrisome—anomaly: so much so that the advance teams in such countries may have some very special apprehensions to overcome, and must therefore be extraordinarily sensitive diplomats.

The first advance contingent for a major presidential trip abroad is the "site survey": a group of some twelve White House and Department of State representatives that typically arrives three months ahead of time. "They get the lay of the land," explained Clinton advance director Dan

Clinton's April 1998 Visit to Africa:
A Few Facts and Figures

In March and April of 1998, when President Clinton made a twelve-day trip to six countries in Africa, *fifteen hundred* officials from *fourteen* federal agencies were needed to accompany or support the president (and the sixteen invited members of Congress) on that journey:

—904 from the Department of Defense (some 600 of whom were troops from the four armed services, which supplied medical support and aircraft maintenance—for example, erecting a dome shelter for helicopters; the others were largely from the WHCA or were members of the Air Force, Marine Corps, and Army air crews).

—205 from Executive Office units (mostly members of the White House staff).

—103 from the U.S. Information Agency (USIA), who supported the U.S. press representatives by organizing press briefings and arranging for lodging, transportation, telecommunications, and interpreters.

—44 from the Department of State.

—16 members of Congress.

—30 more from the Departments of Agriculture, Commerce, Labor, Transportation, and Treasury (trade relations were discussed) and from the Agency for International Development. (The Immigration and Naturalization Service and the Customs Service each sent one official to "facilitate reentry into the United States by stamping passports and collecting import duties.")[1]

The expenses of those agencies, as reported to the General Accounting Office (not including salaries and benefits) totaled $42,805,992.[2]

The Department of Defense (DoD) share of that total was $37.7 million. DoD flew 98 airlift missions "to move vehicles and other

Rosenthal, "where we are going, maybe eliminate some ideas that have been proposed for the president's schedule, come up with ideas for some other stops—get an overall sense of how the trip might flow."[23]

The site survey group meets with the U.S. ambassador. Hopefully they find one who has had previous experience with a presidential, vice presidential, or secretary of state visit and is willing to play the role of policy adviser but not that of the trip's general manager. The advance group and the embassy diplomats compare expectations, and explain to the host gov-

equipment," plus 110 aerial refueling missions to transport thirteen Army and Marine Corps helicopters, and established "at least four maintenance support teams on Cape Verde and Ascension Islands and at two locations in South Africa . . . and two temporary medical evacuation units in Ghana, Uganda and South Africa."[3] DoD fixed-wing planes put in 3,508 flying hours; helicopters, 148 hours.

The Department of State's costs totaled $3,665,155, which included the travel expenses of the White House advance teams and the expenses of the sixteen members of Congress.

USIA bore costs of $986,606 after the reimbursements from the U.S. press organizations.

Presidential travel abroad does not come cheap, but in these years it seems to come more and more frequently. There are more, and larger, advance teams; the Department of State incurs increasingly burdensome expenses. So does the Department of Defense: more military backup planes are used. No foreign nation provides reimbursements, of course. This is simply a tiny piece of the price that America pays for being a major actor in the life of the world.

---

1. The General Accounting Office (GAO) conducted a special investigation of three presidential trips and published the results: *Costs and Accounting for the President's 1998 Trips to Africa, Chile, and China* (GAO/NSIAD-99-164, September 21, 1999). The reported total of accompanying or supporting officials for the Africa trip was 1,302—to which the author would add a personal estimate of some 200 Secret Service personnel (the Secret Service does not make the actual number public). The GAO findings for the other two presidential trips were as follows: Chile, 592 officials participating at a cost of $10,540,226; China, 510 officials at a cost of $18,830,092. Neither figure includes Secret Service expenses.
2. Ibid.
3. Ibid.

---

ernment the exceptional White House interest in access to the media—in communicating the president's message both to his home and to a world audience.

Still not comprehending the magnitude of the task of moving the president from one place to another, the embassy officers or the host foreign minister may suggest seven or eight events for each day's schedule: the advance officers must explain that a three-event day is nearer the true maximum. A rough itinerary of visits and events is finally agreed to. The site survey team returns to Washington, briefs the chief of staff and the president, gets needed decisions.

A pre-advance team is then assembled and arrives overseas four to six weeks before the president. This is a much larger group of perhaps forty. It includes experts—the "leads" who will head up their specialized, respective units during the visit itself. If the first lady is to accompany the president, an officer from her staff will come.

If the visit is one during which the president will entertain his hosts at a formal state dinner at the American embassy, someone from the president's household staff will be on the pre-advance team. Up to 150 place settings of White House china, silver, and matching serving pieces—packed in transportable cases—will have to be flown in. Navy chefs and stewards from the White House Mess will bring the food and oversee the cooking.

The pre-advance team also includes press professionals: a producer (representing the networks in a pool arrangement—one for each country in which the president will stop), accompanied by lighting and sound advisers. These representatives will handle advance preparations for the press pool: Where will be the press room, the editing room, the satellite uplinks? Some individual network shows, such as *Nightline*, may send their own producers independently. White House advancers and network people make an informal agreement: the press will keep mum about the visit until the White House announces it.

A host government may wish to limit the number of media representatives: crowd-raising and prime-time television production for the benefit of U.S. audiences may not be high on the prime minister's own agenda. Foreign governments do not always understand the American president's role as commander in chief, and they may be perturbed by American insistence that the president use only his own limousine and aircraft. (The principal reason for this requirement is the vehicles' built-in communications facilities, which the American president must always have at hand for national security needs. A U.S. military transport plane will, if several countries are being visited, bring three or four spare limousines, many extra mechanics, and even a *Marine One* and other helicopters from home—all similarly equipped with the necessary communications gear.)

"You have to rely on the embassy people to tell you how far you can push or how far you need to retreat to get things done," said a former advance staffer. "But you work off a different checklist," he added. "Generally your objective is to have the host government as happy as possible, and you come away with more than your minimums."[24] The reason for the "different checklist" is that the advance teams tend to have a short-term perspective: the success of that one presidential visit. Embassy officers, however, remember that they must preserve an amicable relationship with the host government into the years ahead.

The full advance team—still larger, and this time including the operating personnel who will stay on during the presidential visit—arrives a week or ten days before the chief executive. The checklist is somewhat the same as for the domestic trips, except that every detail is complicated by the fact of being in a foreign nation, with its own rules and customs. One aspect of advancing has changed: the sheer fact of distance between a foreign city and Washington does not pose the obstacles it once did in terms of communication—sending questions to and getting prompt decisions from home base. The fax machine that took eight minutes a page (four hours to transmit a thirty-page survey report) has been replaced by laptop computers that can send text instantly to the trip coordinator's monitor in Washington. The long-distance phone call that passed through many local switchboards now reaches the cellular phone of an advance staffer—instantly, in a secure mode, and on any street in the world—when a White House aide taps a five-digit number on the WHCA instrument at his desk. The camera loaded with film that needed to be developed chemically has been replaced by a digital video machine—that, in effect, lets the White House trip coordinator in Washington look over the advance person's shoulder in Rabat at alternative views of the palace steps. Remarked a former White House aide: "You could manipulate the image so you could see what it would be like if the president actually walked out onto the scene."

From the perspective of an advance team staffer, "this 'advantage' cuts both ways," observed Dan Rosenthal. "Now they sometimes feel they are being micromanaged. Those who have done advance work for years sort of feel, 'I have done this for so long that I think I know what I am doing, and don't need such supervision.'"[25] Nonetheless, the overall result is that fewer staff can get much more done in much less time. And time is sometimes extremely short. Within eight hours of the news that Prime Minister Rabin had been shot, Clinton advanceman Paige Reffe had his team on the way to Israel, to begin preparing for the arrival of the four plane-loads of congressional and other dignitaries who would come to the funeral.

When the president and his party of fifty-odd finally arrive at a conclave of chiefs of state, the combined number of U.S. support staff and American press together is literally enormous: at the Malta conference between Bush and Gorbachev, seven hundred attended; at their Helsinki meeting, eight hundred.

The Summer 1998 Visit to China

Clinton's multistage trip to China in the summer of 1998 is an apt illustration of an especially unusual and sensitive undertaking. For that quintessentially important trip, the Advance Office had four months' notice. They had time to gather and read a five-inch-thick ring binder of articles and background studies. They asked themselves:

> What would be the places that would communicate to the American people the richness of the Chinese culture . . . and would communicate to the Chinese people our president's, and our nation's, respect and appreciation for China's rich culture and history . . . while at the same time reflecting the modern realities—which are quite different from people's preconceptions? We started in Xian, the ancient capital; then went to Beijing, the current capital and the scene of more recent history; Shanghai, the symbol of the new China of today, with a very imposing, ultramodern skyline; and then Hong Kong, the symbol of what China could become in the future.[26]

After meetings with the president (and with input from the first lady, who had ambitious schedule ideas of her own), the twelve-member site survey team went to China in April, and were joined by senior embassy staff and Chinese foreign ministry officials. In the "strongly wanted" category was the kind of rural village where most of the millions of Chinese people actually live: a village with both collective and private enterprises, and elected village leaders. The site team visited several and found that most of them were geographically infeasible.

Staffs of the U.S. consulates were asked to do what was euphemistically referred to as "primary research": in other words, legwork. The consulate staffers took a boat and climbed up into every hamlet between Guilin and Yangshuo, eventually visiting more than a dozen villages. They talked to village elders, met families, toured homes and schools. The villagers were incredulous: "You? Here? From America?" The Beijing officials were nervous: Why these lower- and middle-class places? Surely these Americans would want to see shiny new buildings. What were their real motives? Chinese officials tried to steer the team to particular communities, but the advance group was very firm: the president would only visit a village that *his* own agents had selected. Even the embassy knew that in comparison with requests made on any other visit in the past, this one was "pushing the envelope." As staff lead Dan Rosenthal and trip coordinator Aviva Steinberg explained, "That was part of what we were trying to achieve on the site survey: to stake out some things, and to make it clear, at the very early stage, what our requirements were, rather than have these issues become problems in the last couple of weeks."[27]

Two villages were tentatively selected: Xiahe, to be visited on the second day; and Yucun, a hamlet on the edge of the famed Li River, which would be the next-to-the-last stop. There was no road to Yucun: access for the presidential entourage would be via the river only. But plans for the village visits would not be made final until the last minute: this "programmed uncertainty" would obviate the need for security sweeps and the use of metal detectors.

Returning to Washington, the site survey group had only two weeks before the pre-advance team of three dozen departed. This second team, now including representatives from the White House press corps, visited all the planned stops, got personally acquainted with the local and village officials, and explained how important it was to the president to have conversations directly with ordinary Chinese citizens. There were misunderstandings. In Xian and Yangshuo, the local police, thinking that their security responsibilities were primary, had been intimidating local shopkeepers, admonishing them to "keep their distance" from the president. In some villages, local officials had moved people out of their homes so that the Americans could more easily inspect them, and these leaders tended to dominate the conversations that the advance people were trying to initiate. At Xiahe, where the president, Mrs. Clinton, and Chelsea were to engage in a roundtable with a question-and-answer dialogue, the local leaders, like politicians everywhere, wanted to manipulate the meetings so that their own supporters would be the ones to meet with the president. The members of the pre-advance team had to iron out all these potential rough spots—and in so doing, had to exercise exceptional sensitivity and diplomacy. Rosenthal remembers:

> This concept to them was very foreign: a president sitting down with average citizens that were not handpicked by the government. . . . We really had to walk through the process with them, reassure them, explain it to them ad nauseam. . . . We made the point very clearly to the Chinese that it was in their own interest not to try and stage everything. . . . The number one thing we laid out . . . was that the presi-

dent and the first lady not only had to *seem* to have been allowed to interact with the Chinese people, but they actually had to *be* allowed to interact. . . . Their attempts to manipulate . . . would be noticed . . . and would be a negative as opposed to a positive. We reiterated that many, many times. In the end I think it sank in to an extent that really exceeded our expectations.[28]

Finally, twelve days ahead of time, the seven actual advance teams—one for each of the presidential stops—fanned out to their respective destinations. Each team would build up to nearly one hundred people before the president's arrival. A senior-level committee of five—Rosenthal, the deputy director of the Secret Service, the deputy chief of mission at the embassy, the Chinese major general in charge of security, and the Chinese director of protocol—did a mini-tour of all the stops.

Despite weeks of preparation, the China visit was nonetheless an example of the appearance of the unexpected. On June 27, the third day of the trip, the program was to begin with a formal arrival ceremony in Beijing's Tienanmen Square and to include a joint press conference between President Clinton and Chinese president Jiang Zemin. The two leaders met first behind closed doors. As that meeting continued beyond its allotted time, advanceman Paige Reffe became increasingly nervous about the shrinking number of minutes that President Clinton would have to prepare for a broadcast to the U.S. (where a few East Coast midnight viewers might be watching). "Oh, we forgot to tell you," Reffe's Chinese counterpart mentioned, "the joint press conference will also be live on Chinese television." A startled Reffe crept into the summit session and passed this news to an equally surprised president. Here would be a two-president press conference broadcast live to *a quarter of a billion* Chinese people. The advance team *could* believe their eyes: they turned on local television to confirm that the joint broadcast was really happening.

On the fifth day an indoor address was scheduled—with extemporaneous Q and A—at the library of Beijing University. Would these, too, be covered live by Chinese radio and television? The Chinese government representatives assented at the last minute: a twist of the knob on the Beijing TV showed that the session was indeed being broadcast. Rosenthal observed: "To have the president of the United States be heard and seen by a television audience of two hundred and fifty million Chinese people—*unedited*—that was a completely foreign concept. It was a struggle to achieve. . . . In the end the Chinese came around to understand the point we were making to them: 'If you want this visit to be successful in terms of how China is going to be perceived around the world, you need to do something new and different to show people China is changing.' I think in the end they understood that."[29]

The indoor address was followed by an outdoor speech to thousands of cheering Beijing University students—held, to the surprise of the embassy, and despite a governmental post–Tienanmen Square ban on planned student gatherings of any kind—on the very campus that had produced the leaders of the Tienanmen protest ten years before. Rosenthal used understatement: "That was a sort of a high-energy event."

Throughout the visit truly unusual things took place—events so unprecedented that even the seasoned advance experts were astonished to actually see them happen. In addition to the joint, televised press conference between the two presidents, there were a roundtable and open exchange with academic, press, and community leaders in Shanghai; a visit with young people at Shanghai's Internet Café; and a presidential call-in show on Shanghai radio—heard by thirty million listeners. The president gave an address to business leaders in Shanghai, then had an interview with China Central Television and delivered a speech to Shanghai's building and construction community. In Guilin he participated in a lengthy and candid roundtable on environmental issues, then gave a speech to the people of the city. The visit ended with a reception in Hong Kong, with remarks from Hong Kong's chief executive. Rosenthal looks back: "Without hesitation I can say that we far exceeded what we thought could be achieved when we went there on that site survey. I had a list of about six or eight things that were a priority and I would say we got, basically, all of them. When I went there I thought that if we got three of them we would be very successful."[30]

During one of the flights that the "committee of five" took from event site to event site, a tense moment arose. The three Americans had taught their two Chinese counterparts to play Hearts. The Chinese major general tried to "shoot the moon" but was defeated by one card, played by the deputy director of the Secret Service. Rosenthal caught his breath: "Was our whole visit going to go down the tubes?" It did not. "There was this personal trust that we had built up by virtue of this trip we had made together. We had a comfort level which allowed us to speak very candidly and frankly without offending the other person. This allowed things to happen that probably would not have happened otherwise. . . . That was a valuable lesson . . . something that really counts if this sort of trip ever arises again."[31]

The December 1998 Visit to Gaza

In the tortured half-century of Israeli-Palestinian clashes and negotiations, no American president had ever gone to Gaza, a major Palestinian population center. At the end of 1998, Clinton decided to make a trip to Jerusalem and Tel Aviv and visit Gaza as well; his visit would include a speech to Palestinian leaders. This plan presented the advance officers with some uniquely sensitive issues.

It was long-standing U.S. policy that the United States would not take any action to recognize, *or appear to recognize*, a Palestinian state until "final status" negotiations between the Palestinians and the Israelis had resulted in an agreement to create one. The Palestinians would have dearly welcomed any U.S. "tilt" toward such recognition—but that would have angered the Israelis.

The president was already evidencing a shift in U.S. policy by even going to Gaza. Now, how was he to show up in Gaza; arrive at its airport; meet with Mr. Arafat; and, in the city's landmark Shawa Cultural Center, speak to Palestinian leaders—many of whom had been considered terrorists only a few years before—without appearing to "tilt"?

The Wye accords of October 1998 had reached a tortuous compromise between the Israelis and the Palestinians concerning the requirement in the original Oslo agreement that the Palestine National Council was to annul all the rhetoric in the Palestinian National Charter that called for the destruction of Israel. The Palestinians claimed to have done just that, shortly after the Oslo agreement was signed, but the Israelis, under Netanyahu, were not persuaded. At Wye, it was agreed that "elements" of the Palestinian National Council would meet, along with other Palestinian "political entities" to "reaffirm" the changes in the charter. The Israelis wanted the Gaza meeting to resemble as far as possible a formal session of the Palestinian National Council. The Palestinians definitely did not want to create such an appearance.

The Palestinians did, however, aim to seize this opportunity to dramatize the existence of a Palestinian governmental entity; the Israelis balked at the possibility of any such advertisement. There would be a battle of appearances—and the advance team found itself having to operate in this diplomatic and political minefield.

How to make this first presidential visit to Gaza stately but not "state"? Should *Air Force One* land ceremoniously at Gaza? No, use helicopters. Should anthems be played? Should flags fly? No, on both counts. Critical question: What would be the backdrop in front of which the president would speak—and what would thus be displayed on television to the world? Any writing on it? Bunting? Drapes in the Palestinian national colors? A sign saying "Palestinian National Council"—or even the word *Palestine*?

The advance team found itself mired in endless, three-way negotiations that finally resulted in the approval of simply the words *Gaza, December 14, 1998* (in English and Arabic), on a plain-colored fiberboard background (a sign that read "Meeting of the Palestinian National Council and the Palestinian Legislative Council and Other Palestinian Entities" was posted up—but out of TV range.) The negotiations had been so prolonged that there was no time to find the right material for the backdrop locally: the fiberboard sections were constructed in Washington and flown in on one of the Air Force C-5As (along with enough automobiles to make up the ninety-car motorcade). How would the cameras be placed? Where would the dais be? How close to the edge of the crowd? The arrangements were changed ten times.

As is doubtless typical in every such momentous event, despite months of organized preparation, the final hours before the presidential arrival were in part chaotic. Cell phones didn't work in Gaza. American English had to be translated into Palestinian Arabic, and vice versa. And security issues tended to dominate all other decisionmaking. The media representatives wanted, above all, a dramatic "cutaway," over-the-shoulder, TV shot of Arafat, with Clinton next to him, acknowledging the changes in the charter.

The dramatic moment arrived: the audience not only raised exuberant hands but jumped to its feet in enthusiasm. But the U.S. Secret Service had ruled that the "cutaway" camera would block an emergency exit route—so the "momentous" picture couldn't be taken. The Clinton speech, however, did set exactly the right tone for the occasion, and the visit was considered a genuine success for American diplomacy. (Even Mr. Netanyahu later conceded that the Palestinians had met their Oslo and Wye obligations regarding the charter.)

The overarching and continuing question was the one that all advance teams face on every visit they prepare for, anywhere in the world: What was to be the message? Often, as in the Gaza visit, the line between policy and logistics is blurred to the point of nonexistence. On that occasion, *how* the visit was orchestrated and executed was as important as—or more important than—*what* official statements were made by the U.S. spokesperson.

The Advance Staff's Credo

"You look at each and every situation you become involved in, and try to figure out what are all the worst things that could happen in that situation, and then develop your own little mental plan as to how you would deal with each one of those problems, before you were faced with it, so that, before an event ever took place, you could try and resolve them all."[32] The words are those of a professional, and the Advance Office is a professional place. Devoted as each staffer is, to Nixon or Reagan or Bush or Clinton, in a larger sense there lies in every one a dedication to a goal beyond mere partisanship—a commitment to excellence. Take away the political names and labels: the commitment endures.

The very words of the Nixon Advance Manual, while Republican in origin, speak to a profession that is both within and beyond politics: "This is the advance-person's reward: the challenge of the task, and the knowledge that only a few—but a very unique few—will give credit where due. Those who look for public praise and gratitude should look elsewhere for their challenges. The true advance-person settles—indeed thrives—on a quiet kind of satisfaction, and a private kind of pride."[33]

CHAPTER SEVENTEEN

First-Magnitude Czars: Special Assistants for Special Purposes

If . . . an official is appointed with the charge to be a czar, the government organism almost always rejects him. Like thrombogenic materials introduced into the human body, czars cause clots in the administrative organism. I avoided the appellation like the plague.

JAMES R. KILLIAN JR.

This position has never existed before, but circumstances now require us to look for unprecedented remedies to an unprecedented problem. . . . By now appointing an AIDS Policy Coordinator, we will ensure that one person in the White House oversees and unifies governmentwide AIDS efforts.

WILLIAM JEFFERSON CLINTON

The preceding fourteen chapters have been fourteen photographs of the principal, continuing functions of the White House staff. Their origins can be traced back for decades; they will be there in the future.

No president is confined by the organization charts of the past, however. A president's priorities change—as do his views of the nation's priorities— and may well expand in new directions. The White House, as the support center for furthering those priorities, will be flexible and will adapt to those changes. Its organizational structure will jump beyond the "continuing" arrangements. If a president wants to begin important new initiatives, to dramatize the extent of his personal commitment, to respond quickly to today's crisis or tomorrow's threat, he will be pressed to create new organizational forms to support his efforts. How can a president do this? To alter his executive branch would take months (and may never happen), but he has an appealing and facile alternative: in the flexible organizational environment of the White House, he can create a new presidential assistant—and do it in an hour.

While the White House is the first target for crisis-criers, the president does have some flexibility in determining its structure and organization. Thus, when an overwhelming problem lands in the president's lap or a new initiative is aborning, he can bring in a White House assistant—perhaps a "czar" or "czarina"—to add the new, needed focus and energy to deal with it.

Neither legislation nor confirmation need be wrestled through Congress. Little money is involved. And a suite can always be found in the Old Executive Office Building or along Jackson Place, across the street. Political momentum can be regained, and the apprehensions of a large interest group—or perhaps those of the general public—can be assuaged. Of course, the czar or czarina may really be needed; it is even possible that he or she can match the rhetoric of the opening press release with the substance of some closing accomplishments.

Never mind that the new White House assistant may be a pain to the cabinet and will appear to the cabinet secretaries to fuzz up their direct lines to the president. And don't mention that the problem the czar is poised to tackle may not be curable by means of administrative fixes anyway. The title of assistant to the president conveys a sense of action; he or she will be publicized as the superperson who will "knock heads," "cut red tape," "ensure coordinated effort."

The president can collect some praises for his initiative; indeed, the very fact of the czar's appointment will help rebut the political attack that the beleaguered chief executive is "doing nothing" about the problem at hand. So frequently have recent presidents resorted to this tactic that proposing the creation of such offices (Eisenhower had ten of them) has become a regular Washington caper—and not just on the part of presidents. Especially after a presidential election, citizens' study commissions, advisory task forces, or bills dropped into the congressional hopper will solemnly invoke the "indubitable need" for an added White House potentate.

As seen in the previous chapters, the White House staff has a center of continuing offices, but the staff is—and always will be—the mirror of the president's priorities; as these surge and expand, the staff will change to reflect the new urgencies. Flaring out from that center, therefore, will be a corona of ephemeral luminaries. Here are six examples from the Clinton presidency.

AIDS Policy Coordinator

It was in 1990 that the National Commission on AIDS recommended that someone with authority and responsibility "institute a 'cabinet-level process to articulate the federal component of an HIV plan' and promote 'interagency as well as state and local participation and coordination.'"[1] In the fall of 1993, the zestfully activist AIDS advocacy group, ACT-UP, was more specific: such a position "requires the immediate attention [of] and direct access to the president, with special powers to coordinate, across all government agencies, the federal government's response to AIDS."[2]

Candidate Clinton made the creation of an AIDS czar a campaign pledge, stating that "we need to put one person in charge of the battle against AIDS, to cut across all the agencies that deal with it." As president he started recruiting—but for what? There was no statute, no executive order, no definition of mission other than those campaign words and the remarks he made in swearing in the first "czarina," Kristine Gebbie, in June of 1993 (the second epigraph to this chapter), to which he added: "She has my full support in coordinating policy among all the executive branch departments."[3]

A pause is needed at this point to compare the vacuum yawning beneath the AIDS policy coordinator with both the statute and the executive order that undergird the position of the director of the Office of National Drug Control Policy. Colloquially known as the "Drug Czar," the director (an officer of the Executive Office of the President rather than the White House staff),[4] is vested, by law, with a lengthy catalogue of responsibilities, specifically including the authority to "review the annual budgets . . . for the Federal departments and agencies engaged in drug enforcement and make recommendations to the President respecting such budgets before they are submitted to the Congress, and . . . evaluate the performance and results achieved by Federal drug enforcement and the prospective performance and results that might be achieved by programs and activities in addition to or in lieu of those currently being administered."[5]

President Clinton followed up that statute by issuing, in November 1993, an equally explicit and authority-studded executive order that cemented and supplemented the 1988 law. In contrast, the AIDS policy coordinator has no charter—other than the president's informal words—to stand on.

After thirteen months of being "the official who must deal with sex, drugs, death and money," as the *New York Times* put it, Gebbie resigned "by mutual agreement." The head of one of the principal AIDS advocacy groups commented that she "suffered from a lack of clarity, a lack of specificity and a lack of mission. Unless they fix that this time around, they're going to have the same problem all over again."[6] Ms. Gebbie's parting advice was, "Get more clarity, right from the beginning."[7]

Ms. Patricia Fleming, who was called over from the Department of Health and Human Services to be an interim coordinator and was later made AIDS policy coordinator, served for three and one-half years, during which time she succeeded in securing significant increases in funding for AIDS research, treatment, and prevention. A third policy coordinator, Eric Goosby, held the position for a few months; the current incumbent, Sandy Thurman, was sworn in on April 7 of 1997, with the president and the vice president joining in the induction ceremony.

There is still no statute and no executive order, and Ms. Thurman was not awarded the magical title of assistant to the president, which her friends told her she should have insisted upon. What she did have was (1) an impressive background of four years' front-line experience with AID Atlanta, that city's largest AIDS service organization, and (2) political depth. A fourth-generation Georgia political activist, this czarina was completely at home in a political environment—emphasizing, in her own words:

> I grew up in politics. I've been in public health, but I've also done politics. The White House is a political machine. Certainly we do policy there, but if you don't understand how to move the policy inside a political system, it is very hard to be heard and very hard to be effective. . . . I grew up . . . watching how you can use your relationships . . . to get things done that mattered. . . . While I preferred to do the work on the front lines [of social service], having done that, I understand that if policies don't reflect the needs of those on the front lines— if there is a gap in between—then nothing really happens. I sort of seized on that experience to move into this arena—the policy arena— to get some work done.[8]

To further those relationships, Ms. Thurman attended senior White House staff meetings and had White House Mess privileges (indicia of inner-circle status).

Thurman's staff numbered ten, including several interns, and was assisted by occasional detailees from the Department of Health and Human Services, depending on the priority of various issues at the time (such as vaccine research and the special problems facing minorities). The office budget was approximately $1 million. While Thurman had access to the president and used it whenever necessary, her primary contact in the White House was

Bruce Reed, assistant to the president for domestic policy. Her deputy attended his staff meetings, and Thurman herself saw him often. She also chaired an interagency task force on AIDS, which met quarterly, and had monthly luncheons with the undersecretary of Health and Human Services (more relationships).

Some of her relationships could be painful. A presidentially established AIDS advisory council of thirty grass-roots organizers, advocates, and service providers met with her every three months—and often scolded both her and the president, claiming that progress was too slow and arguing, for instance, that a "vaccine coordinator" should have been added to her staff.

Ms. Thurman was unusual among White House staff members in that the problems she was tackling led her to be engaged in both of the world's hemispheres. "In just two decades," she explained, "AIDS has surpassed malaria and tuberculosis to become the number one infectious disease killer in the world."[9] In 1999 the president gave her an international assignment: to head up a governmental team to Africa, where AIDS is an overwhelming problem. Her delegation included three members of the Congressional Black Caucus, four congressional staff members, three representatives from private organizations, a United Nations official, and two filmmakers—plus officers from the Department of State and from the Agency for International Development.

Upon returning, Ms. Thurman, with the collaboration of the group, prepared the twenty-seven-page *Report on the Presidential Mission*. Published under the White House imprimatur, the report emphasized the need to increase total annual spending on AIDS from $165 million (the 1998 figure for all of Africa) to $600 million in sub-Saharan Africa alone. The report also included an eleven-point international action plan to combat AIDS in Africa.[10] President Clinton more than once picked up the phone and expressed his concern to Thurman about the enormity of the AIDS problem in developing nations.

While not a commander with any fiscal authority, Thurman did use her persuasive powers to leverage budgets, informally allying herself with the Office of Management and Budget at one end of Pennsylvania Avenue and with Senate and House Appropriations Committee folks at the other.

Thurman also touched bases throughout the government: with the wife of the vice president, who joined her in the annual AIDS walk; with the first lady, who shared her concerns about women's health; with the director of the National Institutes of Health and his associates; and with the National Security Council staff for international briefings. She was strong on outreach: she formed connections to the Hispanic Caucus and to the gay and lesbian community; she addressed the National Conference of Mayors and the Congressional Black Caucus; she joined the 1998 Washington AIDS Ride, a group of hundreds who biked the 350 miles from Raleigh, North Carolina, to Washington, D.C. Thurman reflected: "We spend a great deal of our time taking in that information and trying to craft policies out of here that make sense—to serve all of those different constituencies. So much of that depends on our input directly from those groups. We will bring them in, take them over to the White House, invite some other folks from the White House senior staff—so they can ask questions themselves."[11]

In 1999 she savored a budget and program victory when she attended the laying of the cornerstone of the Dale and Betty Bumpers Vaccine Research Center at the National Institutes of Health. In fiscal year 1998, she saw an increase of $200 million for vaccine research.

Then there was the battle she lost. As a means of reducing AIDS incidence in an extremely hard-to-reach population, should the federal government pay to supply clean needles to drug addicts? Ms. Thurman herself, the constituency groups she worked with, and the secretary of Health and Human Services supported the proposal. General McCaffrey, the director of the Office of National Drug Control Policy, was strongly opposed—as were some in Congress and several of the president's political advisers. "I was advocating from a public health perspective and they were advocating from a political perspective," Ms. Thurman commented. However contentious, it was an open process: Thurman's arguments, along with those of all the others, were laid before the president; he made the call. "I was greatly disappointed with that decision," she remarked later.

> I would like to have seen the federal government provide funding. But on the other hand, I realize that this was a very hot political issue; what the president and his advisers didn't want to do was to politicize the issue any more than it was already. I think it was sort of a 50 percent win for us in that we were able to say that science does indeed work, and that we could give the local communities across the country, which have needle exchange programs, the opportunity to use the imprimatur of the federal government's own scientific research to say: yes, these programs do work. The dialogue will continue.[12]

Thinking of the future, the AIDS policy coordinator looked at the White House wistfully. Having the title of assistant to the president would surely be helpful—to be "elevated and institutionalized in the White House," she commented.[13]

To have her position be in statute? The advantage would be that who-ever held the job could formally testify before Congress, perhaps receive appropriations directly. But then the post would be subject to more detailed congressional scrutiny and review. "I am not sure which is better," Thur-man concluded.

Special Envoy to the Americas

In Miami in 1994, President Clinton convened the Summit of the Ameri-cas, an extraordinary conclave of the presidents of all thirty-four democratically governed nations of the Western hemisphere. A second sum-mit was convened in 1998, with the same distinguished participants. The outcome of these events was an agreed-upon agenda of twenty-six initia-tives: improvements and reforms in the areas of education, health, and human rights, among others. The centerpiece of this agenda was an impor-tant diplomatic and economic goal: the creation, by 2005, of a "free trade area of the Americas." A treaty would be drawn up, negotiated, signed—and, the participants hoped, ratified.

This was an imposing assignment for each of the individual countries (it had taken fifteen European nations thirty-four years to achieve such an arrangement), and it was also a challenging task for the U.S. government machinery.

Many agencies were involved: Agriculture, Commerce, State, Treasury, and the Office of the U.S. Trade Representative, to name a partial list. How to coordinate the effort? How to underscore to those diverse agencies the president's personal interest?

President Clinton used a well-established technique: he created a new position in the White House to superintend this enterprise. He appointed his former chief of staff to the position and later named Kenneth MacKay, a former congressman and a former governor of Florida, to the post—which by then was titled special envoy to the Americas. MacKay's office had a staff of eight.

Clinton's first objective in establishing the post of special envoy was to raise the profile of nations north and south, within this hemisphere, in the consciousness of his own country—which had long been preoccupied with the transatlantic East and the transpacific West. A second purpose was to communicate to those thirty-three other democracies (some of them new) that the United States was going to be a genuine partner with them in a path-breaking cooperative enterprise. It was because this enterprise would require energy both within and across the cabinet departments that it needed a point of leadership within the White House itself. The special envoy to the Americas and his staff would "ride herd" on what was going to be, step by arduous step—interagency, interbranch, international—a difficult undertaking.

"Transparency" was going to be an objective: sweeping away the miasma, and burden, of internal corruption that plagued some of these new democracies. The rule of law would have to be nurtured. In the U.S. executive branch, the participating departments and agencies would need to be encouraged to collaborate not only with one another but also with their counterpart agencies in the other nations of the hemisphere—a novel assignment.

The special envoy would not be a negotiator: that was an operational task that belonged to the U.S. trade representative. An international working group was established to start framing the specific issues that the future treaty would have to address. The U.S. member of the working group was the trade representative, but the special envoy was closely watching the progress. Various interagency task forces were created (to deal with the rebellious situation in Colombia, for example); the special envoy had a seat at all these interdepartmental tables.

The special envoy's responsibility was not to take over, second-guess, or duplicate the work of the individual cabinet agencies or of the National Security Council's senior director for inter-American affairs. It was MacKay's job, however, to keep the free-trade treaty and all the other initiatives on schedule and to evaluate the collective effort. If necessary, the special envoy would be able to present the president with a completely independent view of how his goals were being met and when and where the president might have to do some prodding himself. MacKay met with the president on occasion and gave him a weekly report, which came back covered with presidential scribbles and suggestions for extra action or effort.

Like the national security advisor, the special envoy and his team were apparently successful in discharging their responsibilities with sensitivity and diplomacy, which helped alleviate the traditional suspicions and animosities that have often marred the relationship between White House assistants and cabinet officials.

Assistant to the President for Environmental Initiatives

If one were to hunt for a presidential concern that touches nearly every cabinet department, environmental issues—especially in the area of climate change—would be Exhibit A. Affairs foreign and domestic, economic and scientific, budgetary and industrial, health and demographic, tax and energy, legal and political, private sector and governmental: all are squeezed under this rubric. No surprise that that architectonic institution, the White House, is in charge. No surprise that a czar—albeit a quiet and modest one—was appointed to head up a small office that would help the president bring order to that policy universe.

The unit was first called the Office for Climate Change, later the Office of Environmental Initiatives. What the first assistant, Todd Stern, had going for him was service on the staff of the Senate Judiciary Committee and experience at the heart of the White House: initially as deputy staff secretary and then as staff secretary, from the beginning of the Clinton presidency. Stern was given the climate change assignment in July of 1997, in time to participate in the intricate triangle of policy preparation—among the Council on Environmental Quality, the National Economic Council, and the National Security Council—for three major events: the 1997 White House Conference on Climate Change—at which the president gave a 2,000-word speech and answered questions from expert panelists—and the major international conclaves in Kyoto and Buenos Aires.[14] Mr. Stern was later succeeded by Roger Ballentine, a senior officer from the legislative affairs staff.

The job had five elements: domestic policy, diplomatic issues, congressional actions, outreach to interest groups, and communications. Stern, and then his successor, supervised an interagency staff team that worked at Jackson Place, within the White House complex. When, three days a week, Stern assembled the entire support group, some fifteen officers were around the table. So intricate were the interdepartmental relationships that there were two interagency policy groups: one focusing on domestic issues and a second covering the diplomatic front. The White House assistant chaired them both.

Squads of agency specialists met on specific issues, sharing expertise and developing policy questions for referral upward. Problems requiring high-level attention were discussed at sessions with the deputy secretaries, then with the cabinet principals if needed. Issues that demanded presidential resolution were argued out in six- or seven-page memorandums drafted by an inner-core White House group of senior representatives from the several policy councils: the Council on Environmental Quality, the Domestic Policy Council, the National Economic Council, and the National Security Council. (If readers comment that this looks like a council of councils, they would be right!)

It was these White House–prepared papers that went into the Oval Office. The Clinton decisionmaking style favored the study of policy option papers; face-to-face cabinet-level meetings with the chief executive were rare.

The results of these deliberations invariably involved budgetary—and hence congressional—action. As 1999 approached, the several climate change initiatives—a $4 billion package of specific programs—were wrapped into the president's fiscal year 2000 budget. It was the climate change assistant who met with reporters for an advance press briefing, and it was the climate change assistant who traveled to the Hill to present the package informally to a group of congressional staffers.

It is not the purpose of this chapter to detail the sweeping catalogue of Clinton proposals in that budget, but a few examples will illustrate their scope and variety—and will evidence the depth and complexity of the inter-departmental staff work that the White House team had to shape and supervise:

—Clean Air Partnership Fund: $200 million in grants to state and local governments for projects to reduce the level of both greenhouse gases and pollutants.

—Climate Change Technology Initiative: a package of tax incentives and investments ($3.6 billion over five years) to increase energy efficiency and spur the broader use of renewable energy. For example, the initiative included tax credits for the purchase of selected energy-efficient products for homes and other buildings; for the purchase of energy-efficient cars; for the installation of rooftop solar systems; and for the production of energy from wind and biomass.

—Global Change Research Program: $1.8 billion for scientific research to improve our understanding of the human and natural forces that influence global warming and to assess the likely consequences of global warming.

—$1.4 billion for fiscal year 2000 (a 34 percent increase over the previous year) to research, develop, and deploy clean technologies for the four major carbon-emitting sectors of the economy: buildings, electricity, industry, and transportation. Included here: a doubling of funds for research on "a next generation of vehicles."

—$399 million (an increase of $50 million) for the Department of Agriculture to research how carbon is absorbed by agricultural soils and forests and how improved farming practices can help store carbon.

—$191 million (a $25 million increase) to deliver energy conservation services to low-income Americans.

—$122 million for research and development in next-generation technologies for coal combustion.

The climate change staff team put together a fifteen-page fact sheet giving the details of these proposals: the first step in a comprehensive White

House effort to explain and defend the president's initiatives to the press, to the public, to interest groups, and to Congress.[15] The importance of the fiscal year 2000 budget package reached far beyond its domestic scope: it was essential as diplomatic leverage, to demonstrate to foreign nations that the United States was serious about doing its share of what must become a worldwide effort.

In April 1999, the president transmitted to Congress a message that, in his words, summarized the "domestic and international programs and activities related to climate change and [contained] data on both spending and performance goals."[16] This message was yet another product of the assistant's interagency cooperators. In June of that year the president signed a 6,800-word executive order instructing the agencies of the executive branch on how they were to bring the federal government itself into compliance with the presidential objectives of saving energy and reducing greenhouse gases and pollutants.[17]

The assistant for climate change was not a czar in the public perception, but he exemplified the central thesis of this work: public policies of this magnitude, duration, and complexity require nothing less than central management and direction—by the White House staff.

Assistant to the President for the Year 2000 Conversion

A third area of public policy concern—also totally disrespectful of agency jurisdictional boundaries—was the challenge that the federal government faced in attempting to ensure that the computer systems of modern society would continue to function when the year 2000 (Y2K) arrived. This concern encompassed the federal government's own systems as well as those of the states, local governments, Indian tribal governments, key areas of American industry (banking, public health, telecommunications, transportation, and electric power generation, for example), and other nations and industries important to us throughout the world.

There was no way that any one department or agency could handle both the initiative-taking and the coordinating responsibilities: Y2K was a White House task. Recognizing this inescapable fact, the president signed Executive Order 13073 on February 4, 1998, creating the Year 2000 Conversion Council: a team composed of a representative from each executive department and agency.[18] The president specified that the council would be chaired by an assistant to the president; in the spring of 1998, Clinton asked John Koskinen, former deputy for management at the Office of Management and

Budget (OMB), to accept the post. At least quarterly, Koskinen and the OMB director jointly gave the president a report on the council's activities.

To facilitate cooperation in mastering Y2K problems among companies that were normally in competition with one another, Congress passed a statute that created an exemption in the antitrust laws for such information sharing.[19]

For the first one and one-half years of its existence the council concentrated on reaching out to governments and businesses at home and abroad, urging them to pay attention to the Y2K issue: Were their computers potentially subject to Y2K glitches, and were they taking the necessary steps to address such problems? The council organized a senior advisers group, made up of the chief executive officers of major organizations; sponsored the creation of twenty-five "sector working groups" of industrial experts; and conducted local "Y2K community conversations" across the country. Within the federal government itself, the council identified as points of possible Y2K assistance twenty-five emergency operations centers, some of which were within institutions (such as the Federal Emergency Management Agency and the various departments of the national security community) that had long been in the business of rapid communication and coordination.

In July of 1999 Mr. Koskinen informed a special Senate oversight committee that the council was shifting its emphasis to "event management"— that is, to an effort to keep on top of what would actually be happening in the nation and the world when the clocks struck midnight on December 31, 1999.[20] The president had established, and a former Army lieutenant general would be directing, an information coordination center in downtown Washington. The center would report directly to Koskinen and the council; initially it had a staff of thirty to forty detailees, which would increase to perhaps two hundred as the New Year's holiday approached.

Within the federal government, Koskinen and the council had identified forty "high-impact" programs; the center would be prepared to answer inquiries from states about the "systems operations status" of these programs (for example, the Global Positioning System, the national airspace system, the National Weather Service, the National Crime Information Center, navigable waterways, and the U.S. Postal Service).

Status information—from industry information centers within the nation and from abroad, via the Department of State—was to flow into the coordination center. The center itself was not to be a command bunker or a decisionmaking body; but, through two standing working groups—one domestic and one international—it was to immediately inform the responsible departments of breaking problems. Special lookouts were also posted to detect cyber-incidents or other "unauthorized intrusions."[21]

By the time this book is printed, this effort will have become history. It is cited here simply to demonstrate how a modern White House meets an ultramodern problem of management and public administration: that is, by strengthening its own resources.

Office of the President's Initiative for One America

In a statement on June 14, 1997, President Clinton announced: "Today, I ask the American people to join me in a great national effort to perfect the promise of America for this new time as we seek to build our more perfect union. . . . That is the unfinished work of our time, to lift the burden of race and redeem the promise of America."[22]

By Executive Order 13050 of June 13, 1997, the president established a seven-member federal advisory board on race to advise him "on matters involving race and racial reconciliation." Chaired by distinguished historian John Hope Franklin, the board held fourteen meetings and forums and presented a report to the president in September of 1998. Among the board's recommendations was the establishment of a continuing body—the "President's Council for One America"—to "ensure that the work that lies ahead will be coordinated, focused and productive." The council's task would be to "support opportunities for sustained dialogue at all levels, continue to identify leadership being demonstrated in local communities, expand research to include the experiences and analyses of increasingly diverse populations, and continue to educate the public about the facts and myths surrounding racial disparities and the value of our racial diversity."[23]

Clinton accepted this recommendation and established the White House Office of the President's Initiative for One America in the spring of 1999. The staff of five was headed by an assistant to the president, Ben Johnson, who reported directly to Mr. Clinton. Its task was to encourage the formation and strengthening of private local and professional organizations in every corner of America that would be working, each in its own way, to "improve the lives of individuals affected by past and present discrimination and/or eliminate racial prejudice and discrimination from societal institutions such as workplaces, schools and retail institutions."[24]

Within each cabinet department, an officer was appointed to serve as a contact person for this White House enterprise. Johnson met with these officers regularly to assess the continuing contribution that each federal agency, with its far-flung staff, could make to the president's initiative.

The director also met with racial and ethnic advocacy groups to keep them informed and to seek their support. Without organizing any lobbying himself, Johnson was able to acquaint advocacy group leaders with the progress of the Hate Crimes Bill and related presidential legislative priorities—for example, the proposed funding increases for civil rights enforcement included in the president's budget.[25]

Here are two examples of the office's work:

—On July 20, 1999, at a White House dinner that was addressed by the president and the deputy attorney general, the leaders of several different bar associations established an organization entitled Lawyers for One America. The mission of this new group was to work with minority bar associations, with corporate leaders, and with law schools to widen opportunities for minority lawyers and law students.

—The Office of the President's Initiative for One America sponsored the publication of a 194-page list of 124 local organizations, all over America, that were "working effectively to facilitate constructive dialogues and to establish opportunities to bridge racial and ethnic divides." To facilitate intergroup cooperation and the exchange of information and experience, each entry included the name and telephone number of the organization's director. A "promising practice assessment worksheet"—which these and other similar groups could use to guide their work—was included in an appendix.

The Office of the President's Initiative for One America was not a policy analysis unit; it focused instead on outreach, on action, and on mobilizing private efforts at the local level throughout the nation. Director Johnson prepared a weekly report for the president—receiving in return presidential comments and further guidance for the work of this relatively new White House staff enterprise.

Senior Adviser to the White House Chief of Staff for Native American Affairs

The office of senior adviser to the chief of staff for Native American affairs was established in February of 1999 as both an outreach and a policy advisory unit focusing on the concerns of the 558 federally recognized tribes of American Indians and Alaska Natives. The elevation of this special advisory office—which had previously been a subordinate unit in the Office of Intergovernmental Affairs—reflected President Clinton's personal interest in the issues and problems facing Native Americans. The origin of the office dates back to the Nixon administration, when the president's special counsel—Leonard Garment—and the author spent five years dedicating special attention to this area of public policy.

The concerns of Native Americans touch many of the cabinet departments: Interior, where the Bureau of Indian Affairs (BIA) is located; Commerce, which supports economic development on reservations; Defense, which sometimes has surplus lands available for donation to tribes; Health and Human Services, home to the Indian Health Service; Housing and Urban Development, which assists with housing for Native Americans; Justice, which has established a special Office of Tribal Justice; the Small Business Administration, which subsidizes minority businesses; and the Office of Management and Budget—to mention only a few.

As was the practice in the Nixon era, the Clinton administration maintained an "Indian desk" in each of the relevant departments and agencies. As a mechanism for interdepartmental policy coordination, President Clinton established the White House Interagency Working Group on Indians and Alaska Natives, whose members were the senior adviser for Native American affairs and representatives from the responsible departments and agencies. The group, which met quarterly at the Department of the Interior, was chaired by the secretary of the interior. The White House adviser was in constant communication with the outside advocacy groups in this field, especially the National Congress of American Indians, which has its headquarters in Washington.

Among the principal issues affecting Native Americans are the following:

—The reluctance of Congress to support the president's appropriations requests for Indian health, education, and law enforcement, and for aid to tribal colleges

—The question of whether receipts from gambling enterprises on reservation lands should be taken into consideration in allocating federal monies to tribes

—The decades-old chaos in the BIA's records (which provide the documentation for extraction royalty payments to tribes and to individual American Indians)

—The allocation of radio spectrum space to permit the accelerated introduction of information technology into isolated rural areas, such as Indian reservations. Such allocations would require an arrangement to be worked out between the Department of Defense and the Federal Communications Commission.

These and similar issues, arising in other venues, are and will continue to be on the typical menu of concerns for any White House person or office with responsibility for Native American Affairs.

The Clinton White House sponsored conferences on Native American economic development and arranged to have a comprehensive sourcebook prepared that lists the federal assistance programs that tribes can call upon.

Many of these American Indian issues—water rights, fishing rights, land disputes, and allegations of state and local encroachments on Native American sacred sites—end up in litigation in federal courts. The White House adviser was aware of this, but the White House counsel was opposed—perhaps for "turf" as well as substantive reasons—to giving the adviser the opportunity to review proposed Department of Justice briefs, even in cases of consequence to policy. (This is not a new conflict between the White House and the Department of Justice; see chapter 4.)

Did the White House adviser for Native American affairs feel a sense of divided loyalty between the Native American advocates, who emphasized injustices so deserving of rectification after so many years, and the government, which could often provide only limited redress? "My loyalty is clearly to the president," said Adviser Lynn Cutler, "but I certainly feel sad sometimes that we simply cannot meet all their requests and meet all their needs."[26]

Other "Czar" Proposals

Creating White House czarships is an idea with continuing appeal; groups of many political flavors argue for establishing special White House (or Executive Office) units to elevate and dramatize their respective agendas. Some examples:

—In the aftermath of Hurricane Andrew, which devastated parts of Florida and Louisiana in August of 1992, Congress became concerned that the federal government's domestic emergency management system was significantly weaker than its national security decisionmaking and operations systems. At congressional request, a panel assembled by the National Academy of Public Administration conducted a study and found that "no counterpart exists [to the National Security Council] on the domestic side." The panel recommended that the government establish a "Domestic Crisis Monitoring Unit" in the White House. The unit would be under the direction of an assistant to the president and would include a small staff of detailees working out of the White House Situation Room.[27] Senator Barbara Mikulski introduced a bill to create such a unit under the direction of the vice president.[28] No such formal unit was created, but the Federal Emergency Management Agency and the White House later made an arrangement under which the deputy director of the White House Office of Cabinet Affairs would step in to handle government-wide coordination during natural disasters.

—Between Mr. Clinton's election and inauguration in 1992–93, several distinguished voices (including Senators Sam Nunn and Richard Lugar, diplomats Max Kampelman and Madeleine Albright, and columnist Hobart Rowen) issued strong public statements calling for a "single, high-level coordinator" to manage U.S. relations with the economically troubled Russia and the newly emerging states of central Asia. The president paid attention; but rather than appoint a grand new White House potentate, he laid this responsibility on the shoulders of his old friend and close associate Strobe Talbott, the deputy secretary of state.

—In a report aimed at the incoming Clinton administration, the Progressive Policy Institute proposed, in January of 1993, that the new president create a "Federalism Czar," to "work out a 'new federal compact' with the states, and to eliminate more than one hundred of the federal government's 'categorical grant' programs."[29] This didn't happen; but see chapter 13.

—At the end of President Clinton's first year, during which the first lady took the lead on the administration's heath care reform proposal, there were news stories that another "health care czar" was about to be appointed; the names of New York political veteran Harold Ickes and of former Ohio governor Richard Celeste were floated. Didn't happen. The first lady stayed in charge of the health care initiative until it collapsed in September of 1994. Mr. Ickes was later appointed deputy chief of staff.[30]

—According to an April 1994 news story, Assistant Secretary of the Interior Leslie Turner had proposed transforming her Office of Territorial and International Affairs into a "new mechanism that would allow the five territories (i.e., Virgin Islands, American Samoa, Guam, Northern Marianas, Palau) to deal directly with the White House." The story concluded with a tongue-in-cheek paragraph: "Nobody in Washington believes one Cabinet department can orchestrate the activities of others. . . . Somebody's got to be the boss. That's why the territories are likely to find direct White House 'coordination' of their concerns a more attractive option. If you need a friend in high places, why not the best?"[31]

—In January of 1995, the Citizens Committee on Civil Rights called for the president to appoint a White House official who would be, in the words of a news account at that time, "specifically responsible for civil rights policy."[32] The president chose a three-element alternative course to demonstrate his concern about racism in America: creating the Advisory Board on Race, undertaking the affirmative action review (see chapter 2), and instituting the Office of the President's Initiative for One America, an outreach rather than a policy office.

—The Office of Consumer Affairs, a part of the White House at least as far back as Richard Nixon, was killed off by Congress at the end of 1995.

—During the summer of 1997, the president brought in Jason Berman, an experienced business executive, to head the interagency effort to persuade Congress to pass the "fast track" trade legislation, which would provide for "up or down, no amendments" congressional votes on trade agreements that the administration had negotiated. Despite the best of efforts, the enterprise failed: it had started too late, and the Democrats in the House were divided. Berman's own conclusion was that bringing an outsider into the White House—under those conditions, for such a high-powered but short-term effort—was not a tactic that should be repeated.

—In the fall of 1997, President Clinton created the position of White House senior adviser for women's health, but the designated person resigned before she could assume the post, and the position was dissolved.

These recommendations will not be the last proposals for "czarships"; new ones (and some of the same ones) will arise in the future. A few will appear tempting; almost all will have political muscle behind them. In each case, the president will have to do the calculus: balancing the disadvantages of administrative disruption and muddiness in accountability and lines of jurisdiction against the benefit of being seen as courageously "out front" and "taking the initiative" on an issue about which the public is genuinely concerned. The czar idea will occasionally win out in that calculus—and new first-magnitude luminaries will, here and there, continue to appear in the White House constellation.[33]

CHAPTER EIGHTEEN

First Special Counselor: The President's Spouse

The role of the First Lady must be tailored to the individual First Lady involved. . . . She can be an activist on policy, but she should not be out plowing her own furrow. . . . I found it best to ask the First Lady to undertake certain missions, not give her ongoing assignments.

FORMER PRESIDENT GEORGE BUSH

The First Lady has influence and resources. You see the problems that come to the president's desk and see how far short governmental programs fail in meeting the needs of the people. It made me want to do what I could while I was there and had that platform.

ROSALYNN CARTER

[Mrs. Clinton] was not only America's first career professional First Lady; she had also been given authority never previously granted a President's wife to shape policy. She had not been elected or confirmed to any position. Controversy over her role was inevitable.

DAVID BRODER AND HAYNES JOHNSON

One of the opportunities I have is to bring public attention to what is working in America and around the world and to be a catalyst for the constructive exchange of ideas and creative solutions.

HILLARY RODHAM CLINTON

B esides being a wife, the first lady is a senior counselor for the president—perhaps his closest and most trusted. The Constitution gives her no duties, and she is neither an elected nor an appointed and confirmed officer of the government. She has a foot in officialdom, however—as evidenced by the following statement from the U.S. Court of Appeals: "We see no reason why a President could not use his or her spouse to carry out a task that the President might delegate to one of his White House aides. It is reasonable, therefore, to construe [Section 105(e) of Public Law 95-570] as treating the presidential spouse as a *de facto* officer or employee."[1]

Like other high-ranking White House assistants, the first lady can speak for the president with a special credibility. The past four decades have shown that the president's spouse has the broadest turf of any White House counselor. If she wishes and the president agrees, the first lady can not only be the supervisor of the Residence and the manager of the events and social obligations of the first family, but she can also, in the iconoclastic tradition of Eleanor Roosevelt, do things such as crisscross the nation, journey to the most out-of-the-way places on earth, give press conferences, speak at the United Nations, discuss matters of state with national and foreign leaders, meet and talk with ordinary folk of modest or little means, write a book, address political rallies, write newspaper columns, attend cabinet meetings, have weekly business lunches with the president, convene White House assemblages, host television specials, and testify before congressional committees.

In *First Ladies: The Saga of the Presidents' Wives and Their Power,* Carl Sferrazza Anthony has comprehensively described how American first ladies, from 1789 to 1990, have interpreted their roles and fulfilled those interpretations.[2] The purpose of this chapter, therefore, is to begin with the Clinton presidency in 1993, and to focus on the unusually active role of Hillary Rodham Clinton and on the staff work that supported her activities.[3]

How did Mrs. Clinton, as first lady, assist the president?

Her activities differed in degree, not kind, from those of her predecessors—but the degree is striking. In her first seven years as first lady, Mrs. Clinton made, on her own, some nine hundred appearances in three hundred cities or other destinations in America and abroad, and participated in over five hundred public events in and around Washington. She testified before five congressional committees. The subsections that follow describe some of the initiatives that she undertook. The first—the health care reform enterprise at the beginning of the Clinton presidency—will be examined at some length, and the others will be summarized.

On the Domestic Front

Several presidential spouses (Mrs. Roosevelt, Mrs. Carter, Mrs. Reagan) have taken a hand in policy issues being handled by the president and the White

House, but none have been as specifically and deeply engaged as Hillary Rodham Clinton was in the health care initiative of 1993–94. She was qualified: she was a lawyer, had for two years led a task force on rural health in Arkansas, was on the board of the Arkansas Children's Hospital, and was chair of the board of the Children's Defense Fund. In their recent book detailing the White House's handling of the health reforms enterprise of 1993–94, distinguished journalists David Broder and Haynes Johnson describe the principal reasons that Mrs. Clinton was chosen for the health care task:

> Where he was dilatory, open-hearted and diffuse, she was disciplined, tough-minded, focused. Because of her work on the Arkansas education reform, the President told us "I knew that she could manage a long, complex, highly contentious process [involving] something people care a lot about." From his first, losing campaign for Congress in 1974, and especially when he plotted his comeback from the bitter 1980 loss after his first term as governor, Clinton had acknowledged that Hillary was probably better than he in managing big and difficult enterprises. Bill Clinton knew how to charm people; Hillary Rodham Clinton knew how to get things done. . . . [She] remained a strong voice in campaign strategy meetings and obviously a powerful influence on his thinking. . . . That kind of toughness would be needed in the upcoming fight, and especially in guiding the new task force toward the goal Clinton announced of submitting legislation to Congress "within one hundred days of our taking office."[4]

To launch the health care initiative, Mrs. Clinton chaired a cabinet-level task force and, aided by senior White House officer Ira Magaziner, organized and ran a working group (actually a series of working groups) made up of more than 630 advisers, including congressional staffers and experts from inside and outside the government.[5] The development and drafting of the entire health care plan was put into Hillary's and Magaziner's hands. As White House colleague George Stephanopoulos described it, "Health care was her baby, a sweeping program that would save lives and prove to the world that a first lady could be a fully public presidential partner. Working with Magaziner, she had established a wholly owned subsidiary within the White House, with its own staff, its own schedule, and its own war room, called the Intensive Care Unit. . . . But inside the White House she must have felt like a single mother raising a problem child in a hostile neighborhood."[6]

Why was this? Because on a simultaneous, parallel track in the spring and summer of 1993, the president was goading the rest of the White House to focus on what was really his highest priority: to get Congress to pass his budget and economic plan. One of the greatest fears of White House staffers was that leaks might come from Hillary's group that tobacco taxes or other expensive proposals were being considered—which would have raised congressional hackles and diminished the voting margin for the president's program (which, in the end, passed by one vote). As their project progressed toward the decisionmaking phase, therefore, Hillary and Magaziner were told to lower a curtain of secrecy over the enterprise. She and he also suffered from some intellectual hubris and a sense of independence—which had its roots in the long-standing lacuna between "East Wing" (first lady) and "West Wing" (presidential) sides of the White House. The result of the secrecy was that even such experienced cabinet officers as Lloyd Bentsen, of Treasury, and Donna Shalala, of Health and Human Services, were shut out from some meetings and from the distribution of some papers.

It was not 100 days, but 212 days after inauguration—on September 22, 1993—that the president introduced the health plan in a speech to a joint session of Congress. Six days later, over a three-day period, the first lady appeared before five congressional committees, three in the House and two in the Senate. (Only two other first ladies had ever done so, and their appearances were on much narrower issues.)[7] Johnson and Broder describe Mrs. Clinton's manner: "She was cool and poised as she sat alone, without notes, expressing herself clearly and convincingly, hour after hour, easily fielding all questions. . . . It was a bravura performance. . . . As Tamar Lewin wrote in the *New York Times,* virtually overnight Hillary became 'feminism's first mainstream icon: a powerful, smart woman with mass-market appeal.'"[8]

But there was criticism of the role she played. Within executive branch councils, her very presence inhibited open give and take. Johnson and Broder quote one cabinet officer as observing, "You make your point once to the President's wife, and if it is not accepted, you don't press it."[9] Another said, "The person who's in charge shouldn't sleep with the President, because if you sleep with the President, nobody is going to tell you the truth."[10]

Having the first lady be the principal manager of a policy development team, furthermore, meant that the president's flexibility to judge, qualify, or amend the product of that team was narrowed—if not eliminated. "He could profess flexibility as much as he wished," Johnson and Broder observe, "but he could not remove his fingerprints from the detailed design that his personally chosen and high-visibility agents had created."[11]

On the Hill, as Johnson and Broder recount, the first lady won bipartisan compliments. Ways and Means Committee Chair Dan Rostenkowski pronounced that "no longer was it the question of whether America *would* have health reform, but what type of health reform we *should* have." "We will pass a law next year," Republican senator Jack Danforth predicted confidently. "Most members of Congress, in that male-dominated bastion of political power, were almost obsequious—many women thought patronizing—in their praise."[12] Deep-seated congressional opposition, however, was concealed behind those encomiums. Republican Jim McDermott, "noting the deference paid the first lady by congressional colleagues who he knew believed her to be wrong, remembered thinking 'It shows you the way politics really is, that no one's going to tell the president's wife, Ma'am, you don't have any clothes on. Nobody's going to say that.'"[13]

It was sixty more days—November 20, 1993—before an actual bill (1,342 pages long) was finally sent to Congress; the heavy congressional action would be deferred until mid-1994. During the intervening months, the first lady and her colleagues spent countless hours in meetings and negotiations, and in speeches to key professional groups. The opposition to the health plan was skillfully and massively orchestrated, and on at least one occasion the first lady lashed out publicly with biting criticism of the insurance and pharmaceutical industries.

In July the first lady had flown to Portland and Seattle to give the send-off to a cross-country bus caravan designed to whip up enthusiasm for the pending legislation. She was greeted by protesters and hecklers. Cursing that the first lady was intending to "ban guns, extend abortion rights, protect gays and socialize medicine," hundreds of angry men surrounded her limousine, unconcealed hatred on their faces; some, the Secret Service found, were carrying concealed weapons.[14]

By August of 1994 the opposition had gathered such force, and the factions in Congress were so splintered, that no bill was ever reported out of any House or Senate committee; in September the entire effort finally failed. Johnson and Broder conclude: "The decision to create the special White House task force headed by Hillary Rodham Clinton and Ira Magaziner was a major mistake. . . . The First Lady was an eloquent, tireless, and, for the most part, effective advocate for the cause. But the consequences of the President's decision to entrust the task to them were overwhelmingly negative. Having Hillary at the head of the task force inhibited the political debate within the administration."[15]

Stephanopoulos came to the same conclusion: "In a way, her leadership was more than the political system could bear. It's difficult to escape the conclusion that having Hillary run health care was a mistake."[16]

Whether a future president will—or should—call upon the first spouse to develop and coordinate a major policy initiative will depend first on the personalities and capabilities of each of them. But, as evidenced by the Clinton experience, that decision ought also to be influenced by a sober calculation of the advantages and the disadvantages. The issue of health care reform is still on the nation's agenda, but Hillary did not retain the policy lead in that area, and it is unlikely that any future first lady will be put in charge of an undertaking of such enormity.

Her experience with health care, however, did not deter Mrs. Clinton from pitching in and helping the president on other national issues. There were several areas in which Mrs. Clinton had recognized and valuable experience, to which she felt profound personal commitment, and to which she could offer intense personal energy.

What goes on in the earliest months of a child's growth? What do scientists know about the patterns of brain development in the very young, and how can this research—most of which is government funded—be directed to help parents and caregivers? In April 1997, the first lady joined the president in convening the White House Conference on Early Childhood Development and Learning. The conference brought together scientists, physicians, sociologists, and other professionals, encouraging them to reach across the boundary lines of their specialties and focus on actions that they could take in common. Through hundreds of satellite downlinks across the country, many other Americans were able to enter into the White House discussions. As Hillary's chief of staff commented: "The benefit of this, in terms of follow-up, is that people in various fields who should have been working together more closely, often were not. They were not necessarily working at cross-purposes, but they too often did not realize their common cause and the benefits of working more cooperatively."[17]

Knowing the importance of early encouragement in helping children learn to read, the first lady convened a group of "interested parties" in the winter of 1997, then lent her public support to Reach Out and Read (ROR), a nine-year-old program that had begun at the Boston Medical Center. Through this program, pediatricians were encouraged to prescribe books as well as medicines to their young patients. The idea caught on: in connection with the early childhood development conference just described, the first lady launched the Prescription for Reading Partnership. The number of participating pediatric hospitals and community health centers climbed to at least 425, over a million books were donated, and private foundations and professional medical societies joined hands in what became a nationwide early literacy program.

Anxious to increase the number of children moving out of foster care and into permanent homes, Mrs. Clinton lent her support to—and was central to the eventual passage of—the 1997 Adoption and Safe Families Act, which provides tax credits to families who adopt a child. In December of that year, the president—crediting his wife, "whose efforts have made today possible"—issued a directive to several of his cabinet officers to work to double by 2002 the number of children placed out of foster care.[18] Nine months later the first lady presided at the White House ceremony in which the president signed the Adoption and Safe Families Act and added "a special word of thanks . . . to the First Lady, who has been passionately committed to this issue for at least 25 years."[19]

In October of 1997 the first lady convened the White House Conference on Child Care—a gathering that included the vice president and Mrs. Gore; Robert Rubin, secretary of Treasury; Donna Shalala, secretary of Health and Human Services; and Richard Riley, secretary of Education. During the conference, the president announced several legislative and executive initiatives that the administration was undertaking.[20] On January 1, 1998, in a press event, the president announced a package of proposed child care legislation, commenting: "And . . . I thank my wife, who has been talking to me about all these things for more than 25 years now and is sitting there thinking that I have finally got around to doing what she has been telling me to do. [Laughter] I was thinking it would be nice to have something new to talk about for the next 25 years."[21]

In the fall of 1996, Mrs. Clinton inaugurated a personal initiative to aid economic and social development in the nation's capital, hosting a White House meeting of major foundations and urging them to support programs started by a group of local congregations called the Washington Interfaith Network.[22] In December, accompanied by Housing and Urban Development Secretary Henry Cisneros, she unveiled a $5.8 million grant to the Development Corporation of Columbia Heights, a new community bank whose mission was help small businesses get started in inner-city neighborhoods. At a press conference on that occasion, she "pledged to help the struggling District of Columbia overcome its many difficulties"; according to "administration sources," Mrs. Clinton had "privately . . . strongly urged the president to do more to help the . . . city."[23]

In February 1997 the first lady accompanied the president to a District elementary school, where they both read the story of the Tortoise and the Hare to a class of first graders. The president announced the District of Columbia College Reading Tutor Initiative, whereby seven District-area colleges had agreed to place seven hundred college students as reading tutors in District public schools. The president added "a special word of appreciation to . . . the First Lady who has been telling me for a long time that we had to do more and that we could do more" to help make "America's capital . . . a world capital, second to none."[24]

Visiting another elementary school in the District's Shaw neighborhood, Mrs. Clinton learned about its partnership arrangement with a local law firm—one of six such arrangements: lawyers and staff from the firm were rendering pro bono legal assistance, mentoring the students, taking them on field trips, and donating supplies and used computers. Not long afterward the first lady addressed the local bar association and endorsed the partnership idea. In late February of 1997, writing personally to dozens of other local law firms, the first lady asked each of them to "strengthen any existing partnerships you may have with a public school" or to "form one."[25] At least six large firms made serious commitments—doubling the original number of partnerships.

On January 29, 1998, it was Mrs. Clinton who made the White House announcement of a $120 million increase in federal funding for the District. Both she and her staff had worked with the Office of Management and Budget to nail down both the concepts and the details of that budget package. Mrs. Clinton was the keynote speaker at two meetings of the Washington business community convened to encourage greater philanthropic involvement in the nation's capital. She also gave her support to a national music museum for downtown Washington.

Among other domestic initiatives, the first lady met with Desert Storm veterans; forced a cabinet-level reexamination of the causes of Gulf War Syndrome, which led to the establishment of an independent presidential commission; held a discussion about race in a Boston sports arena filled with 11,000 teenagers; and spoke at the 1998 convention of La Raza, the nation's largest Hispanic advocacy group.

Mrs. Clinton also played a key role in the creation of the White House Millennium Council, an interagency body, supported by a director and staff, whose purpose was to encourage an array of local and nationwide activities "in a national and educational celebration of our culture, democracy, and citizenry." The council undertook initiatives such as the following:

—Giving recognition to "Millennium Communities" for taking the lead in celebrating the millennium through "community-enhancing . . . celebration events and programs"

—Sponsoring "Millennium Evenings at the White House," a "series of lectures and cultural showcases, hosted by President and Mrs. Clinton, that highlight creativity and inventiveness through our ideas, arts and scientific discoveries"

—Helping "Saving America's Treasures," a partnership "to preserve our . . . important historic sites, documents, art and monuments"

—Sponsoring "My History Is America's History," a project to "encourage families to collect, document, and preserve their family histories, and to tie these stories to the broader patterns of American history"

—Recognizing "2000 Millennium Trails" projects, which encourage communities to build new trails and to enhance those already existing.[26]

International Activities

It was in the international arena that First Lady Hillary Rodham Clinton made what may have been her most illuminating contribution to her husband's presidency. In the first six and one-half years of Mr. Clinton's time in office, she took forty overseas trips—twenty-one on her own—and visited eighty-three countries.

Whether addressing hundreds of social workers in Copenhagen or thousands of leaders at a United Nations conference in Beijing; whether sitting with some of the world's most marginalized and impoverished human beings—in India or Bangladesh, in dusty villages in Senegal, yurts in Mongolia, or South Africa's Soweto (she was the highest-ranking American ever to have gone there)—Mrs. Clinton tried to light beacons of hope and change, focusing on her core message: in every corner of the earth, human rights, women's empowerment, and children's health are the indispensable keys to civil society—and, in turn, to democratic nationhood.

In Ahmedabad, India, in March 1995, Mrs. Clinton (and daughter Chelsea) sat down under a cloth-roofed arbor and talked for more than two hours with a group of several hundred women—Harijans, who are at the bottom of the Indian economy: rag pickers, street vendors, farm laborers. Some of them had walked for two days to meet with her. But, organizing 200,000 others like themselves, they had created their own co-op bank for microcredit loans and their own "union": the Self-Employed Women's Association. "I was afraid of all men," one of the women spoke up and told the first lady," of my father-in-law who used to beat me, of the policemen who used to beat me. Now I am not afraid of anybody!" The session ended with the whole group singing "We Shall Overcome" in the Gujarati language.

On that same trip, Mrs. Clinton visited Pakistan, Nepal, Bangladesh, and Sri Lanka; in each of these countries, she continued to follow her practice of meeting with women and men in grass-roots settings. Upon her return, she prepared a formal, seven-page "Memorandum for the President," with copies addressed to the secretary and deputy secretary of State, the national security adviser and his deputy, and the administrator of the Agency for International Development. She stated her findings and recommendations and included the following language:

> I recognize that discussion of such problems as education and health care for girls and women is viewed by some as "soft," labelled dismissively as a women's issue belonging, at best, on the edge of serious debate about all the problems we confront [in] the 21st century. I want to argue strongly, however, that the questions surrounding social development, especially of women, as discussed at the recent social summit in Copenhagen, are at the center of our political and economic challenges. Government, businesses and citizens must recognize and act upon that truth for the betterment of nations and our global family.[27]

Six months later, Mrs. Clinton delivered her most notable speech abroad, to the United Nations Fourth World Conference on Women, held in Beijing in September of 1995. Her address ended with the following words:

> Let us heed the call so that we can create a world in which every woman is treated with respect and dignity, every boy and girl is loved and cared for equally, and every family has the hope of a strong and stable future. That is the work before you, that is the work before all of us, who have a vision of the world we want to see for our children and our grandchildren. The time is now. We must move beyond rhetoric, we must move beyond recognition of problems, to working together, to have the common efforts to build that common ground we hope to see.[28]

Following another trip she made to central Asia, where she visited the newly independent states of the former Soviet Union, the first lady—armed with slides from the trip—convened a debriefing session in the Department of State auditorium. Her chief of staff described the occasion:

> We invited the diplomatic corps from the countries she visited, as well as representatives of nongovernmental organizations and government officials, and others working in development, human rights, and international affairs. The first lady provided an overview of her trip and what she had hoped to accomplish. She used the slides to illustrate the positive difference that programs advancing microcredit, girls' edu-

cation, health care improvements, and civil society development are making. She wanted her audience to understand why these investments are critical, to validate the work of those involved, and for others engaged in foreign policy to see these things perhaps with her eyes.[29]

On their joint visit to Africa in 1998, the first lady and the president, with the president of Uganda, visited a Ugandan village. In President Clinton's words, "We were walking along this little rocky pathway into this village, to see all these village women who now had their own businesses. [The Ugandan president] looked at me and he said: 'That's some wife you have got there. Until you [plural] showed up, I didn't know we had these programs in our country.'"[30]

After returning from inspecting the damage that Hurricane Mitch had caused in Central America, Mrs. Clinton held another briefing, inviting representatives from the nongovernmental relief assistance community. She again sent the president a memorandum with her observations and recommendations. She was instrumental in assembling the supplemental budget request that the president sent to Congress to help rebuild the infrastructure in those hard-hit countries.

Typically, a Hillary Clinton overseas trip would become a continuing enterprise: the U.S. ambassadors in the countries she visited began extra efforts to follow up on her initiatives and to maintain contact through the doors that she had opened. Cables came back to her office: "You will want to know that this has been happening!" Follow-on enterprises were started: a partnership between a U.S. hospital and a women's wellness clinic in Uzbekistan, for example. When a St. Louis hospital began a partnership with a health care facility in Riga, Latvia, the first lady of Latvia came to the East Room of the White House for a ceremonial ribbon cutting. After a forty-five-minute conversation with Mrs. Yeltsin, Mrs. Clinton took the lead in scrounging enough surplus equipment from U.S. military bases in Europe to equip two children's dental clinics in Moscow.

These expeditions of Mrs. Clinton's were rewarding for the National Security Council (NSC), State Department, and AID officers who accompanied her. Chief of Staff Melanne Verveer recalled: "To a person, they had a high regard for the impressive manner in which Mrs. Clinton demonstrated diplomatic skills and expertly integrated women and development into our overall foreign policy concerns. Some officials admitted they had overlooked the critical importance of these issues. Mrs. Clinton forcefully articulated democratic values and the importance of investments in civil society, women's progress, and social development. It was often a transforming experience to travel with her."[31]

Staff for the First Lady

Readers can easily imagine the workload that cascaded onto the shoulders of the first lady's staff as they strove to support the sheer amount and variety of her activities. Such an active presidential spouse requires help—as surely as the president did when adviser Louis Brownlow diagnosed the chief executive's needs in 1936.[32]

Can the first lady tap the president's staff for extra duty? Only to a limited extent. NSC experts could supply briefing material for her international trips and would accompany her on the plane; the Domestic Policy Council assigned one or two assistants from its own staff to help Mrs. Clinton with the health care and other domestic policy initiatives.

Fortunately, the law provides that the first lady may have assistants of her own. The same 1978 statute that authorizes staff for the president contains the following language: "Assistance and services authorized . . . to the President are authorized to be provided to the spouse of the President *in connection with assistance provided by such spouse to the President* [emphasis added] in the discharge of the President's duties and responsibilities."[33]

Mrs. Clinton's personal staff numbered twenty, plus another fifteen interns and fifteen volunteers. Her Millennium Council, located in the Jackson Place row, across the street from the White House, had a paid staff of three, supplemented by fourteen agency detailees and eight interns and volunteers. The White House Social Office, which was under Mrs. Clinton's purview, had five paid staffers, perhaps eight interns, and a sizable and indispensable cohort of volunteers. Each event in which the first lady participated required almost as much preparatory effort as was required for the president. And each of her trips was advanced, but all her advance people were volunteers.

Mrs. Clinton was the first presidential spouse to have a full-time speechwriter; eventually her staff included two writers. Even then, since Mrs. Clinton's speechwriters were too busy to join the advance teams, the word processor on her plane got constant duty—"at the price of some sleep deprivation," wryly observed one. Coordination on the outbound aircraft was simple: on her African trip, officers from the Department of State and the NSC senior director for Africa were aboard. The speechwriter could lean over and ask, "Mr. Senior Director, should we say this, or that?"

Whatever consultation was needed with the departments or agencies concerning the first lady's speeches or other policy ideas was handled through Domestic Policy Council staffers assigned to her. She and the president introduced so many domestic policy initiatives jointly that her staff and his staff had no choice but to work arm in arm. Neel Lattimore, her former deputy press secretary, commented: "The best thing here was the huge crossover between her staff and his staff. Our office was greatly respected for being organized, being careful with details, and being good at what we did. We earned the respect of both the president and Mrs. Clinton. In the first four years there was practically no turnover; I think that speaks volumes about the first lady and those who worked for her. There was tremendous dedication."[34]

The first lady's chief of staff also held the title of assistant to the president and attended the White House senior staff meetings. Her scheduler met with the president's appointments secretary; at times, the four schedulers for the two first families would all sit down together. Explained her chief of staff: "The weekly cabinet reports, the intergovernmental reports, the political reports: there is no way we didn't have a sense of what was going on. This office is totally integrated into the overall operations of the White House."[35]

An example of that integration occurred when Leon Panetta took office as White House chief of staff. He would meet weekly with the first lady in her office, filling her in on activities and issues that would concern both of their offices. As the three-way relationship between the president, the first lady, and the chief of staff matured and grew, the need for these special sessions tapered off.

Although the first lady did not pay avid attention to press stories about her activities, Lattimore pulled wire-service items from his computer and dropped them off at her office, and interns on her staff combed the news clips for "mentions"—that is, for the appearance of Mrs. Clinton's name in any press or magazine story. If a piece was unfavorable to her because of inaccuracies, her press office would send factual rebuttal material to the offending author.

Mrs. Clinton had small but strategically located office space on the second floor of the West Wing, more spacious staff quarters in the Old Executive Office Building (which she often visited), and offices for the social secretary and her staff in the East Wing (their traditional location).

"There was a very unusual, close-knit chemistry in our staff," remembered her former speechwriter. "We really worked well together. Mrs. Clinton did not tolerate a lot of egomaniacal behavior. When you worked for her, you really felt that you were not in it for her, but for something way beyond her."[36]

The Social Office

Including the Social Office in the chapter about the president's spouse might seem to imply that (1) the social secretary works exclusively for the first lady and (2) almost all Social Office duties are connected with White House entertaining. With respect to the Clinton administration, both implications are inaccurate.

In two important respects, the Clinton White House changed the Social Office into something quite different from what it had been in the past. First, the White House social secretary had an additional title: deputy assistant to the president. "You don't just work for the first lady," explained former social secretary Ann Stock. "While it [the Social Office] falls under the aegis of her office, you do three-quarters of your work for the office of the president. You do some public liaison, handle some intergovernmental affairs matters, and deal with the press. Basically the reason you are there is to support the office of the president. And the people in the West Wing have come to realize the impact of what the Social Office can do for them, politically."[37]

The deputy assistant title carried another responsibility: the social secretary attended the morning senior staff meetings—an effective way to diminish what used to be endemic "East Wing–West Wing" tensions.

Second, the Clinton White House charged the Social Office with major new responsibilities. In addition to carrying out its traditional assignment—general management of the entertaining functions of the first family—the Social Office became the point of logistics management for all presidential and first lady events held in the White House or on its grounds (other than in the Oval Office itself). The Social Office therefore had to create a kind of ad hoc committee for each event: the offices represented would typically include those of the vice president, the chief of staff, and the first lady; plus communications, intergovernmental affairs, legislative affairs, military, political affairs, public liaison, scheduling, the chief usher, the Secret Service—and, if the event involved foreign participants, staff from the NSC. The social secretary had to be a mini–chief of staff, asking, as Stock remembered: "What's the purpose of this event? What's the message? Who's going to be there? What outside groups should be represented? Who speaks? How do we go about the politics? How will it play in the papers? The whole group, not just the Social Office, would meet and go through all of that. I was helpful, frankly, because I had spent four years as Vice President Mondale's press assistant."[38]

No one in the Clinton White House, including Stock herself, forgot for a moment that such occasions were not just presidential events: they were political statements. Making them successful called for a very new and different breed of social secretary. Arguably, even the name "Social Office" was a misnomer.

With a first family headed by two very active people, the Executive Residence was used morning, noon, and night. On five days each week, the public tours (and the cleanup afterward) consumed the hours from 7:45 A.M. to 2 P.M. How soon must a South Lawn picnic end to permit a presidential helicopter pickup from the same greensward? Can a Red Room reception in the Residence be arranged on the afternoon before a state dinner? Scheduling meetings were indispensable. One rigid principle governed: nobody used the Residence for an event except the first family (not even the vice president, unless he was a last-minute substitute for the president).

Managing the traditional social functions was, of course, a continuing part of the Social Office's responsibility. There were, on average, five hundred occasions each year; during the fall, winter, and spring, major White House social events often took place more than once a day.

A state dinner is a classic production. If it is held in the State Dining Room, only 130 guests can be accommodated. President and Mrs. Clinton switched many of their state dinners to the East Room, which can squeeze in 240. When necessary, even larger assemblages could be accommodated. At a 1998 awards dinner, 470 guests sat down for dinner under a large tent on the South Lawn. On another occasion, a single dinner was served under an enormous temporary cover: 137 tables seating 1,370 people. Musicales were held under specially constructed tents (heated in winter) in the Rose Garden, or on the roof of the colonnade that separates the Residence from the West Wing.

For an upcoming state dinner, the Social Office is the heat sink for the incandescent pressures that burn in from the State Department, the rest of the cabinet, and the legislative, political, and public liaison offices—all arguing that the guest list should make room for one more of their favored clients. ("If X is not there, he may lose face.") The list and the seating chart go to the president and the first lady for their personal approval. The Clintons were often intrigued by questions of who would be or should be seated next to whom, and they engaged in some horse trading. Ann Stock further recalled: "I used to think about the president's time at a state dinner. There are eight outside guests at his table. Eight people for an hour and a half: in one way of looking at it, that's twelve hours of presidential time. You don't want to waste that time. If there is business to be done—political, international, financial—you would never waste twelve hours of the president's time. You would never waste a minute!"[39] "A good list," said Social Secretary Capricia Marshall, "is where the visiting Head of State says 'Thank you for introducing me to these people.'"[40]

The Social Office keeps track of acceptances and regrets (via computer), and puts forward—for the approval of the president and the first lady—suggestions for menus, programs, entertainment, and artists who will perform. (President Clinton would sometimes ask: "Can they play this piece?") It arranges for performers' hotel rooms and sends cars to meet them at the airport. The office instructs the chefs and has the invitations, programs, and menus printed. The admission cards are coded to prevent counterfeiting or gate crashing (one young man tried it and was caught). The musical selections, flower arrangements, wines, and guests' attire are specified in advance.

Which china will be used? Only the Johnson and Reagan china have enough place settings for a formal dinner in the State Dining Room; only the Reagan china has 220 place settings. The White House buys china (with the help of the White House Historical Association) to fill out some of the beautiful older patterns, but some can no longer be obtained. On occasion, even if the patterns are different, sets from former presidencies are mixed with the more recent ones, and often the Social Office must arrange to combine sets with those from Blair House (the presidential guest house, across Pennsylvania Avenue).

Social aides—single young men and women officers from the five military services—are chosen to assist at formal functions in the Residence: thirty-five at a state dinner, three or four at a reception. Being a social aide was like being a "potted plant," Truman's White House assistant Clark Clifford once remarked, but that may have been an unfair jibe. The aides announce the guests as they are about to enter the receiving line and are expected to have studied the history of the White House—and perhaps to be fluent in a foreign language. They volunteer their time, and they pay for their own formal uniforms. The social secretary briefs them on their assignments.

Gifts to visiting heads of state are purchased (by the Department of State), toasts are written (by the NSC staff), and reporters and photographers are invited. Those who will participate in the receiving line are selected; mikes, lights, and pianos are supplied. Even a portable stage may have to be assembled (there is one that matches the East Room's decor). The social secretary's last duty before the doors open is to compose a "scenario" memo for the president and first lady.

Noticing that long queues were piling up at the receiving line, Stock introduced an innovation: the guests were given tickets that specified what time they were to start through the line—an arrangement that allowed visitors to enjoy the party more and permitted the president to spend more time with each guest.

Staff of the Social Secretary

The size of the social secretary's staff under Clinton did not keep up with the expansion of its responsibilities. During Ann Stock's four and one-half years, she managed two thousand breakfasts, dinners, receptions, and picnics attended by half a million people. In a typical Clinton year, 100,000 to 125,000 people were guests at White House official and social events; that figure does not include the 1,500,000 people annually who walk through the rooms of the Residence on tours. Assuming that the 125,000 were all couples, 60,000 invitations were issued, checked, and confirmed. Who did this prodigious task?

To survive unimaginable pressures, the five paid staffers in the Social Office relied on eight interns and a dozen volunteers—who handled at least 50 percent of the work. One volunteer, for instance, dealt with the seven hundred letters that typically come in each year from local musical groups that want to be invited to play at White House events. The groups would enclose cassettes or compact disks, and the volunteer—who had an excellent musical ear—would listen to each, rate it, and store the file for possible future use.[41] Such relatively unknown groups are not used at state dinners, but during one Christmas holiday period, eighty of them were invited to perform.

The Graphics and Calligraphy Office

The fine art of calligraphy is alive and well at the White House. The envelope for each formal invitation is hand inscribed by the Graphics and Calligraphy Office, which officially reports to the chief usher but is in fact allied most closely with the Social Office. Countless gift and acknowledgement cards are created in the Graphics and Calligraphy Office and then engraved from the original handwork. The graphics staff make the final diagrams for presidential trip arrivals and may create "Happy Birthday" or "Welcome Home" posters, but it stays clear of political duties.

The presidential seal is a familiar motif, but only the White House can sanction its use: such approvals come from the Graphics and Calligraphy Office. If a private donor, for instance, wishes to engrave or inscribe the seal on a gift to the president, that is permissible. But commercial use of the seal is forbidden, since the seal implies presidential endorsement. The office, supported by the White House counsel, is strict in its guardianship.

Presidential Spouses of the Future

Is Hillary Rodham Clinton the new "model" of a first lady? Did she set an example that her successors should emulate? Her chief of staff warned:

> This is a derivative position—a position without a job description. It is totally dependent on presidential prerogative and the experiences and interests of the person who is brought into this position. Mrs. Clinton spent more than twenty years of her adult life working on issues relating to children at a policy level; she had a capacity to do these kinds of things. What she has done has enhanced this administration's work. But the next person—and the first lady would be the first one to say this—shouldn't have to be like her. She has to be herself. Maybe she—someday he—will be as good or better in these various roles. But she shouldn't have to do it the same way.[42]

As of this writing, Mrs. Clinton has been pursuing her campaign to represent New York in the U.S. Senate. This has considerably altered her role as first lady during her husband's final year in office—a fact that she herself recognized: "I will still be in Washington from time to time. I have to be. There are many things that I will still have to attend to. But I will be living in Westchester and I'll be traveling around the state campaigning."[43]

A New York state Democratic leader bluntly challenged her: She should "give up her day job."[44]

Should she? Let this chapter end with a basic, long-range question: Should any presidential spouse sidestep the optional opportunity of playing a role in administration policymaking or the not-so-optional responsibility of supervising the Residence and managing White House social life in favor of concentrating on a career of her—or his—own?

A well-respected woman columnist opined:

> Hillary Rodham Clinton has abdicated the role of first lady. . . . But she may find she has tested the tolerance of the American public one

time too many. The role of first lady is not a constitutional office, but it has always been a very important part of the institutional glue that holds this country together. . . . First ladies are an integral part of the presidency, wielding power behind the scenes and helping to shape the public perception of their husband's administration. . . . Will voters accept yet one more precedent-shattering move by the Clintons? . . . From Martha Washington to Hillary R., first ladies have been woven into the tapestry of American history. When crisis has overtaken a president, they've risen to the occasion. They are ballast in the ship of state. Mrs. Clinton is turning her back on that and on the very great honor the American people bestowed upon her when they made her husband president.[45]

Readers are challenged to reflect on this question. How future first families answer it will have consequences not only for the presidential spouse but for White House staff arrangements as well.

CHAPTER NINETEEN

Second Special Counselor: The Vice President

> The chief embarrassment in discussing his office is, that in explaining how little there is to be said about it one has evidently said all there is to say.
>
> WOODROW WILSON

> Whenever possible, the vice president should serve as general adviser to the president on the full range of presidential issues and concerns. . . . The president [should] assign the vice president other responsibilities that do not conflict with the role of general adviser.
>
> TWENTIETH CENTURY FUND TASK FORCE ON THE VICE PRESIDENCY

Within the White House environment, the president's second and highly valued special counselor can be—and since 1977 has been—the vice president. Only in the last four presidencies has the vice president been welcomed into such a principal advisory role and been afforded the aides, the facilities, and the access to support it. The Office of the Vice President is thus a significant new center of participation in White House decisionmaking.

The vice president's role, of course, has much firmer constitutional underpinnings than that of the first lady. It is not the Constitution, however, that has assured the vice president's place in the decisionmaking process of the White House: it is the personal trust and respect between president and vice president that are the binding elements. In the words of the Twentieth Century Fund Task Force on the Vice Presidency, "Each president and vice president [should] define their working relationship, taking into account their temperaments, experiences, and strengths as well as their views of executive leadership."[1]

That they have done, but the years since 1953 have by now constructed a precedent of expectations—a growing precedent. A statute has facilitated the growth. Under the heading "Assistance and Services for the Vice President," a 1978 law authorizes paid staff, including temporary experts and consultants, "in order to enable the Vice President to provide assistance to the President in connection with the performance of functions specially assigned to the Vice President by the President in the discharge of executive duties and responsibilities."[2]

Costs for that assistance (including residence expenses) were $2.5 million in fiscal year 1988; the requested appropriations for fiscal year 2001 were $3.9 million. In addition to his residence, the vice president has four offices in the nation's capital: in the West Wing of the White House, in the Old Executive Office Building, and in the Dirksen Senate Office Building (on Capitol Hill); he also has a small ceremonial office off the floor of the Senate.

As it does for the president as well, the 1978 statute limits the number of vice presidential staff who can be hired at or above the GS-18 pay level and authorizes the use of detailees. Volunteers also serve in the vice president's office, especially in connection with advance work and in his correspondence unit.

How have the two most recent presidents employed their vice presidents?

Vice President Dan Quayle

President Bush was no novice when it came to using vice presidents: he had been one for eight years. Reflecting on his twelve years of White House experience, he ranked two elements as the most important in the relationship between the president and vice president: trust, "the sacred commodity"—which, Mr. Bush warns, "can be squandered too easily"; and "the reality of ready access—the ability to walk into the Oval Office at any time—unannounced," which, he also warns, "should not be over-used."[3] Having the vice president situated in the West Wing, with the vice presidential staff in the Old Executive Office Building, Mr. Bush observed, facilitates that access and helps to ensure that the president's own staff will be "less apt to try to undermine the V.P."

What were Vice President Quayle's assignments? Former chief of staff William Kristol remembers the advice Quayle received from two former vice presidents, George Bush and Walter Mondale: "Don't take on fixed responsibilities as vice president. You just get blamed if things go wrong, and you don't get credit if they go right. You have these cabinet officials; you can't go pushing them around too much; they get annoyed. Your best bet is to be an all-purpose V.P., an all-purpose helper and troubleshooter for the president."[4]

In domestic affairs, Mr. Quayle did inherit one responsibility from Mr. Bush: heading the appellate function in the process of Executive Office review of departmental regulatory actions. Vice President Bush had chaired the Presidential Task Force on Regulatory Relief, which had been created "by informal presidential direction" immediately after President Reagan's inauguration in 1981. On March 31, 1989, President Bush created a successor organization, the Council on Competitiveness.[5] Like its predecessor, the council reviewed disputes between the Office of Management and Budget's Office of Information and Regulatory Affairs and the departments and agencies, most notably the Environmental Protection Agency, concerning the economic burdens that new agency regulations would allegedly impose on the business community. President Bush wanted Quayle's council to settle these controversies; a few (relating to wetlands and to microscopic particulates in the air) nonetheless had to be taken across West Executive Avenue for presidential resolution.

By statute, Vice President Quayle was chair of the Space Council, which met some thirty times during his years in office. As head of that council, Quayle was reportedly instrumental in bringing about a change in the leadership of the National Aeronautics and Space Administration (NASA). Quayle also pushed NASA to be more aggressive in developing the space station, which he saw as valuable to both America's military program and to its world reputation. He urged Congress to give the space station the necessary appropriations support, and helped to work out cooperative space relationships with Russia and Japan.

A former senator, Mr. Quayle kept up his friendships on the Hill; as president of the Senate, he was welcome to attend the weekly lunches of the Republican Caucus. While some of these meetings were "real bitch-sessions," according to one observer, Quayle returned from them with valuable political intelligence for the White House; he realized similar benefits through his frequent informal contacts with Lee Atwater, chairman of the Republican National Committee, and through the links he maintained with conservative Republicans. On the road, Quayle was an effective speechmaker and fundraiser for the party. The vice president was among those to whom the White House staff secretary sent drafts of presidential speeches for comment; he also received copies of the weekly Cabinet Reports and the weekly legislative affairs summary. Finally, Vice President Quayle had a regular Tuesday lunch with the president. There were no minutes, no records of action, and no use of those occasions to litigate bureaucratic fights or appeal earlier decisions.

Vice President Quayle visited forty-two countries: meeting with heads of state, explaining and defending U.S. positions, and supplementing negotiations on trade agreements. Staffers from the National Security Council or the State Department would accompany him on those trips, but Quayle always cabled a personal report to the president.

In late November 1989, while the president and his entourage were aboard *Air Force One* enroute to a summit conference with Russian president Gorbachev, Vice President Quayle was called to the Situation Room. A coup attempt was raging in Manila against Philippine president (and U.S. friend) Corazon Aquino; rebellious members of the Philippine Air Force were threatening to bomb the presidential palace. What action should the United States take? Quayle presided over a late-night NSC meeting held via video-conference: the Sit Room was linked with the Pentagon and with those national security leaders who could be reached in Washington. The deliberations resulted in a recommendation that modern U.S. fighter-bomber aircraft fly over the antiquated Philippine planes on the ground—to intimidate them from taking off and to attack them if they tried.

Quayle telephoned the recommendation to the president on *Air Force One*, secured his approval, and had the orders relayed to U.S. forces. His memoir recounts: "Because I had been well briefed on the Philippines and knew Aquino, I was prepared for the crisis. I was the one asking the questions, seeking the options, and pushing for a consensus. I can remember [Undersecretary of State] Larry Eagleburger saying afterward that if I hadn't been there, we might not have stopped the coup in the Philippines. It was a great hour in the relations between our two countries, and a great moment for me personally. We saved democracy without firing a shot."[6]

As a member of the National Security Council, the vice president was one of the inner-circle "Big Eight" who in 1991 managed the policies and operations of the Desert Storm encounter. He argued for the option of seeking congressional authorization to sanction that engagement and joined in the successful effort to persuade Congress to pass it. He also argued, later, that our forces should have gone farther into Iraq—leading president Bush to note, in his private diary, "It doesn't help Quayle with me, and it doesn't help him at all."[7] From that comment it can be deduced that the vice president was a member of, but not a dominant participant in, the Bush team of national security heavyweights: James Baker, Dick Cheney, Robert Gates, Colin Powell, Brent Scowcroft, John Sununu, and the president himself.

Counting volunteers, interns, and White House Fellows, Vice President Quayle had a total staff of nearly one hundred. His staffers were invited to the meetings of their White House counterparts until Bush's decision to increase taxes, when vice presidential Chief of Staff William Kristol's opposition strained the erstwhile close relationship that he had had with White House Chief of Staff John Sununu.

Summing up his own experience, former president Bush has one further word for vice presidents: "The big thing the V.P. must do is to recognize that he is not the President, must work as closely as possible with the various Cabinet officers in an unthreatening way and not try to grab special assignments and have them on-going."[8]

Vice President Albert Gore Jr.

The Clinton-Gore relationship was unusual: the duo were not older and younger, not experienced and inexperienced, not ticket-balancers from different parts of the country, not ideologically somewhat apart; neither was imperiously protective of his own position, and the president genuinely wanted to see his vice president follow him into the top job. Theirs was a combination that opened the way for a strikingly expanded public policy role for the vice president.

To illustrate the number and diversity of the assignments that Vice President Gore was handed, there follow brief excerpts from presidential statements or news stories that identify thirty of them (undoubtedly there have been more):

—"I will give our vice president, Al Gore, responsibility and authority to coordinate the administration's vision for technology, and lead all government agencies, including research groups, in aligning with that vision."[9]

—"Today I am . . . announcing the formation of a national performance review. . . . Working under the direction of the Vice President . . . we'll conduct an intensive national review of every single Government agency and service . . . in a search not only for ways to cut wasteful spending but also for ways to improve services to our citizens and to make our Government work better."[10]

—"The Presidents [Clinton and Yeltsin] agreed to establish a United States–Russian Commission on Technological Cooperation in the fields of energy and space. They intend to designate Prime Minister Chernomyrdin and Vice President Gore to head this commission."[11]

—"Several weeks ago I asked the Vice President to work with our Departments and Agencies to examine what more might be done about the problems along our borders. I was especially concerned about the growing problems of alien smuggling and international terrorists hiding behind immigrant status, as well as the continuing flow of illegal immigrants across American borders. . . . The Vice President presented me with a report. . . . I have reviewed that report and approved it."[12]

—"I . . . hereby establish the President's Community Enterprise Board . . . to advise and assist me in coordinating across agencies the various Federal programs available (or potentially available) to distressed communities and in developing further policies relating to the successful implementation of our community empowerment efforts. The Vice President has agreed to chair this Board."[13]

—"The Vice President is the principal adviser to the President on, and shall coordinate the development and presentation of recommendations concerning, regulatory policy, planning, and review. . . . Early in each year's planning cycle, the Vice President shall convene a meeting of the Advisers and the heads of agencies to seek a common understanding of priorities and to coordinate regulatory efforts to be accomplished in the coming year."[14]

—"No matter how well Al Gore does tonight against Ross Perot on CNN, the Clinton administration still faces a dangerous stretch run to the wire on NAFTA [North American Free Trade Agreement]. . . The choice of Gore for this debate was not the hastily made, last-minute gamble. . . . It is part of a broader White House strategy to have Gore become a spokesman on foreign policy. . . . Gore's maiden effort will be a challenging one."[15]

—"Vice President Gore, using Mexico as his platform, urged Latin American nations today to take advantage of new trends toward regional economic cooperation as a way to strengthen their democratic values."[16]

—"Gore met briefly with Ukrainian President Leonid Kravchuk. . . . The meeting was meant to speed a deal between Russia and the Ukraine involving financial compensation for the elimination of highly enriched uranium and nuclear warheads deployed on Ukrainian territory by the former Soviet Union."[17]

—"Vice President Gore is scheduled to outline today the Clinton administration's support for sweeping deregulation of the telephone and cable industries that would permit greater competition between them and would let regional phone companies offer long-distance service. Gore, in a speech at the National Press Club, is likely to focus attention on the need for new federal laws to govern the fast-changing telecommunications businesses."[18]

—"'Al Gore is going to play quite vigorously in foreign policy,' said a senior U.S. policymaker. . . . Gore certainly showed no lack of . . . stamina on the busy, seven-day trip to five countries in Europe and Central Asia . . . meeting with Kazakhstan President Nursultan Nazarbayev. . . . [This was followed later by] a 'town hall' meeting in Bishkek [Kyrgyzstan]."[19]

—"The White House, stepping up its efforts to reach a post-NAFTA reconciliation with organized labor, will send Vice President Gore to Florida next week to talk with top leaders of the AFL-CIO about favors the Clinton administration might do for them. . . . The last time a vice president met with the union leaders at their mid-winter meeting in Bal Harbour, Fla., was 1982, when George Bush made the trip as a peace gesture by the Reagan administration."[20]

—"The Act [the Violent Crime Control and Law Enforcement Act of 1994] creates the Ounce of Prevention Council . . . to . . . oversee and coordinate the various crime prevention programs governed by that Act. . . . The Vice President shall serve as the Chair of the Council and shall appoint a staff to support the work of the Council."[21]

—Vice President Gore attended the United Nations Population Conference in Cairo, fashioning a compromise with the Vatican concerning population stabilization.[22]

—"I direct all executive departments and agencies to review every program, policy and initiative . . . that pertains to families to ensure . . . that they seek to engage and meaningfully include fathers. . . . The information gained from this review will be combined with information gathered through the Vice President's 'Father to Father' initiative . . . to determine the directions of those programs for the future."[23]

—"Vice President Gore vowed at a meeting of Western Hemisphere defense ministers today that Colombia drug cartels 'will be defeated' by joint efforts of governments in the region. . . . He spoke to defense ministers and other officials of the United States, Canada and 32 Latin American and Caribbean nations, gathered for their first-ever meeting to tighten security ties and promote civilian leadership of armed forces in the Western Hemisphere."[24]

—"I have proposed to set aside Government contracts for businesses that lay down roots in poor communities, to locate there and hire people there. I think we ought to have contracts that can bring money and opportunities to poor neighborhoods every day. . . . I have asked the Vice President to examine this challenge and to take it on, as he has so many others, and to come up with what I have to do to get this done."[25]

—"With U.S. aid to South Africa likely to decrease over the next several years, Vice President Gore and South African Deputy President Thabo Mbeki signed several agreements today. . . . The accords were formalized at the first meeting of the U.S.–South African Binational Commission."[26]

—"Federal authorities, saying the U.S. Olympics in Atlanta this summer could become a prime target for terrorists, for the first time at such a gathering, are taking precautions against the use of unconventional weaponry such as poison gas, germ weapons or even a nuclear device. . . . A task force under Vice President Gore has been devoting considerable effort to preparing for what officials say until recently was a virtually unthinkable event in this country."[27]

—"There is established the White House Commission on Aviation Safety . . . [which] shall advise the President on matters involving aviation safety and security, including air traffic control. . . . The Vice President shall serve as the Chair of the Commission."[28]

—"There is established the Advisory Commission on Consumer Protection and Quality in the Health Care Industry. . . . The Secretary of Health and Human Services and the Secretary of Labor shall serve as Co-Chairs . . . . The Co-Chairs shall report through the Vice President to the President."[29]

—"Today I have approved and released a report—'A Framework For Global Electronic Commerce'—outlining the principles that will guide my Administration's actions as we move forward into the new electronic age of commerce. . . . I am asking the Vice President to lead an interagency group coordinating the U.S. Government's electronic commerce strategy. Further, I am directing that executive department and agency heads report back to the Vice President and me through this interagency group every six months on their progress."[30]

—"Kuwait's potential purchase of 72 Chinese-made self-propelled howitzers instead of competing and, by most accounts, superior American, British and South African versions, has raised eyebrows among U.S. defense contractors and prompted a personal appeal to Kuwaiti leaders from Vice President Gore."[31]

—"Let me say in closing, I want to thank the Vice President, especially, who cares so passionately about [protecting youth from tobacco]. . . . I've asked him to take the lead in building broad bipartisan support around the country for our plan."[32]

—"Recognizing the growing economic and commercial ties between the two nations, the two Presidents [Clinton and Nazarbayev] expressed their strong support for the 'Action Program on Economic Partnership,' signed in Washington, November 18, 1997, by President Nazarbayev and Vice President Gore, in their capacity as co-chairmen of the U.S.–Kazakhstan Joint Commission."[33]

—"The Vice President's team at the National Partnership for Reinventing Government . . . is ready to assist [departments and agencies] in developing a waiver process based upon lessons learned and best practices from agencies that have experience with waivers. . . . [Departments and agencies] should report to the Vice President on actions taken to implement this memorandum by July 1, 1998."[34]

—"Gore arrived here [Cairo] early this morning after an extraordinary, two-hour unscheduled meeting with Israeli Prime Minister Binyamin Netanyahu that ended at about 4 a.m. with an emotional embrace on the tarmac of Ben-Gurion airport. Gore sought that meeting after talks with Palestinian leader Yasser Arafat. . . . [In] Saudi Arabia, . . . Gore spent six hours in private talks with Crown Prince Abdullah."[35]

—"For too long, we have seen some criminals go free because the methods used to gather evidence were not up-to-date. But when police can report from their squad cars, rather than fill out paperwork, they spend more time on the beat. . . . The Vice President has put together a task force to help more communities take maximum advantage of available technology."[36]

—"Dozens of vice presidents and high-powered delegations from 89 countries have come from around the world this week to attend a conference on corruption sponsored by Vice President Gore."[37]

How did Vice President Gore handle such a voluminous and disparate pile of assignments?

There were two "secrets" to Gore's successful organization of effort: first, the extraordinarily close relationships that linked the vice president's and the White House staffs; second, the technique of "virtual departments," which Gore used to gather together experts from the responsible agencies.

"Those close relationships started in the 1992 campaign," recalled Gore's domestic policy chief, Greg Simon. "We traveled so much together. We were integrated in the campaign. . . . So when we got into the White House, it was no big embarrassment for the presidential staff to give way to the vice presidential staff; they had been up to four in the morning, in the campaign together."[38]

Crossovers were frequent between the two groups. The vice president's counsel moved over to become the counsel to the president. Gore's legislative affairs director became Clinton's cabinet secretary. The president's deputy press secretary became Gore's communications director—who said, "I think I knew every public affairs person in the cabinet."[39] If people did not physically switch over, the doors to meetings were always open on both sides of West Executive Avenue. "The vice president's chief of staff, Ron Klain, is in any White House meeting he wants to be in," said one White House veteran. Gore's domestic policy director participated in the White House domestic policy and national economic policy sessions. Papers on policy issues were shared back and forth. "I can't imagine life in the White House without Al Gore and his staff," commented another Clinton alumna, "I don't think we had a single working group set up that . . . didn't have somebody from his office on it." Added Clinton domestic policy chief Bruce Reed: "The president is more comfortable with his vice president than any president I have ever seen. There is almost no tension between them so it is real easy for the rest of us to get along. I used to work for the vice president; his chief of staff, Ron Klain, is godfather to my daughter."[40]

There were some substantial tensions, however, not only within the White House staff but between some of them and Vice President Gore, if Dick Morris is to be believed. In *Behind the Oval Office: Getting Reelected against All Odds,* Morris recounts one meeting between Clinton, Gore, and himself in which Morris had complained about being undercut by Clinton staffers. Morris then adds: "Gore spoke up for me and talked of his own frustrations in dealing with the staff on issues dear to him like reinventing government and protecting the environment."[41]

When Gore took on a major project that required the skills and expertise of staff from a number of departments and agencies, Simon would reach out, convene the agency heads, and identify and assemble the officers in those agencies—political and career alike—who knew the most about the issue. From then on these experts would meet under the chairmanship of a senior Gore staffer. The agency experts would not be hired; they would not be detailed; they would not be physically moved into vice presidential space. As they worked together, on behalf of their respective agencies, on vice presidential projects, they constituted a set of what could be termed "virtual departments"—Greg Simon's term for the mode in which he and Gore mobilized executive branch staff to work together to handle some of the vice president's assignments. Simon remembers:

We would set up meetings; they would come; they were our team. They would work closely with me or with somebody else on the vice president's staff; periodically the vice president would meet with them. He would deputize me and say, "Greg is my guy." Everybody knew that *he* was the *president's* guy. So all of these people would want to know, "What can I do to help the vice president on this issue?" I think the fact that Gore reported to the president on these issues energized people throughout the departments, because they knew their advice was going to the president through the vice president. When I went to a department, I got a ready response because they knew their product was going to the vice president but then would not just lie there but would be given to the president.[42]

"The Gore staff," emphasized Simon, "was never treated as a subordinate adjunct to the office of the president. They were treated as part of the office of the president."[43]

An unusual form of the "virtual departments" mode was the vice president's interagency task force for the National Partnership for Reinventing Government. Based in a set of offices near the White House complex (the Department of Defense paid the rent) and working on behalf of their respective agencies, the sixty or so men and women of the task force pushed, prodded, negotiated with, and monitored the executive branch departments and agencies, to move them toward the president's and vice president's objective: a government that "works better, costs less and gets results Americans care about." Beginning in 1993, approximately 1,200 government officers— working three- to six-month stints—were rotated through this unusual staff unit. The director of the staff reported to the vice president and had his office in the vice president's area of the Old Executive Office Building.[44]

In the voluminous material documenting Vice President Gore's activities, one memorandum is unique in demonstrating the vice president's assumption of a very firm leadership role in a major interagency enterprise. In a "Memorandum for Heads of Departments and Agencies," dated October 18, 1997, Mr. Gore used the directive-style wording only presidents ordinarily employ. Under the heading "Subject: Clean Water Initiatives," Mr. Gore issued, in four single-spaced pages, direct instructions to cabinet officers. Some examples (italics added):

—"*I am therefore requesting* that the Secretary of Agriculture and the Administrator of the Environmental Protection Agency . . . develop a comprehensive action plan."

—"EPA and the Department of Commerce *will identify* steps."

—"NOAA [National Oceanic and Atmospheric Administration] *will develop* an action-oriented strategy to comprehensively address coastal non-point source pollution."

—"The Action Plan *will be submitted to me within one hundred twenty* . . . days."[45]

This is presidential language—somewhat unusual, coming from a vice president.

Vice President Gore visited many foreign countries—and, like the president, spoke with foreign leaders by telephone. Was there a risk that vice presidential forays into international affairs might have mucked up sensitive diplomatic relationships or negotiations? Not if the briefing was done carefully—and Mr. Gore's sizable national security affairs staff made sure that was the case. A vice presidential *demarche* strengthened the secretary of state's arguments. "It gives Secretary of State Albright an even more direct imprimatur that she is doing the president's bidding," commented one Gore veteran. "As a Cabinet official you like it when the White House is treading the same ground you are treading."[46]

As additional evidence of the degree to which Gore was within the Clinton inner circle, he attended the Residence meetings on political strategy that were started with Dick Morris in the preelection period of 1995–96. Observing Gore at these meetings, Morris came to a judgment about the vice president: "As I saw the byplay between Clinton and Gore, I began to understand how important the vice president was to the president. Gore is the single person in the world whose advice the president most values. He sees Gore as a junior president—not at the top yet, but good enough to serve when his time comes. When he wants a clear-eyed assessment, he turns to Gore, as he does when he wants something really important handled really well."[47]

Outranking all other meetings in importance, however, were the weekly Thursday luncheons between the president and the vice president. Simon remembered that Gore would comment: "I'm meeting with the president tomorrow; give me a memo." "If the vice president liked it," Simon recalled, "he would put it in the book, take it with him, and then send it back to us, marked up. You couldn't ask for better communications! We never asked, 'What did you say? What did he say?' It was just, 'What's the decision?'"[48]

Summing up, Simon looked ahead: "You really do need a vice president who is a partner—who synergistically increases the business of decision-making, rather than being somebody who is just window dressing or in training. I don't ever remember being in the room when the president was asked to decide anything major without his stopping the meeting and asking the vice president what his opinion was, before he made a decision. The vice president can no longer be just a president-in-waiting."[49]

Like that of first lady Hillary Clinton, whose role has been transmuted into that of a senatorial campaigner, Vice President Gore's role has, as of this writing, also been transformed—into that of a presidential candidate. As a campaign colleague of his put it, "He has been an exceptional vice president in part because he is an incredibly adept team player. But now the country is willing and eager for him to come forward and show his own flag."[50] In Gore's own words, "Running for president of this country is far more important than being the best vice president I can possibly be."[51]

CHAPTER TWENTY

Third Special Counselor: The Vice President's Spouse

> Assistance and services authorized pursuant to this section to the Vice President are authorized to be provided to the spouse of the Vice President in connection with assistance provided by such spouse to the Vice President in the discharge of the Vice President's executive duties and responsibilities.
>
> PUBLIC LAW 95-570, SEC. 106(C)

> I'm nothing. I'm *zip*. I'm not a government employee. I can't even get a government rate from airlines. I'm a volunteer in the Office of the Vice President. There is no job description, no pay, no career path and limited opportunities for promotion. The way I see it, the post is an opportunity to further the causes I believe in.
>
> TIPPER GORE

O ver the years, the flow of mail and other communications to the spouses of the vice presidents has steadily increased, bringing a mounting series of requests for appearances, endorsements, interventions, and other similar actions. The spouses themselves have more and more openly evidenced their interest in the concerns that are on the minds of the American public and in the federal programs that attempt to respond to those concerns. As the vice presidents' own duties grew, the spouses saw opportunities to join their husbands in assisting the president—especially after 1961, when the principal vice presidential office was moved to the White House neighborhood.

In 1978, Public Law 95-570 came into effect, authorizing federally funded staff assistance not only for the first lady and the vice president but for the vice president's spouse as well. The vice presidential spouses have taken advantage of that statute. Joan Mondale had a staff of four assistants—one who used space at the vice presidential residence and three who worked in the Old Executive Office Building. By Barbara Bush's time, a staff of six was needed, including a chief of staff; they were likewise located in the Old Executive Office Building, close to Mr. Bush's suite.

As described in chapter 19, the vice presidential role has continued to expand, and the spouse's opportunities for public service have grown in parallel.

Marilyn Quayle

For the first two years of her husband's tenure, Mrs. Quayle worked out of an office at the vice presidential residence; when she had occasion to visit her staff's suite at the Old Executive Office Building, she shared space with her chief of staff. In 1990 a further significant evolution occurred in the position of the vice presidential spouse in American government: Marilyn Quayle was given her own office in the White House complex.

Mrs. Quayle had a staff of six, plus a summer intern and volunteers; one of the volunteers handled gifts, and others came in on an ad hoc basis to help with individual events. Her chief of staff had a second title—special assistant to the vice president—symbolizing the fact that her staff and her husband's staff were a single team. Mrs. Quayle's chief of staff attended the twice-weekly vice presidential staff meetings and kept in close touch with first lady Barbara Bush's chief of staff, who had been her predecessor.

Before her husband entered political life, Mrs. Quayle had been a lawyer in the office of the Indiana state attorney general. After Mr. Quayle's elevation to the vice presidency, Mrs. Quayle, according to newspaper accounts, seriously thought about joining a Washington law firm, but two factors made such a move impractical: the financial disclosure rules, which would have required her to list all her clients, and the logistical difficulties of being under round-the-clock Secret Service protection. There were job offers from some federal agencies, which she also declined.[1]

A few vice president's wives have had young children while their husbands were in office; Mrs. Quayle had three. Attending her children's events and being present at their activities were among the highest priorities on her calendar.

The recently acquired vice presidential residence had several drawbacks: it was not well adapted to the needs of three young children; it needed an addition for office space; and it was not accessible to visitors who used wheelchairs. To raise funds to undertake the necessary renovations, Mrs. Quayle engaged the interest of friends who helped her form a private organization, the Vice President's Residence Foundation. The group raised $215,000 in donations; Congress later added extra construction funds to complete the necessary renovations.

After her mother's death from breast cancer, Mrs. Quayle took up the cause of early detection and prompt treatment of that disease. She actively supported the work of the Susan G. Komen Foundation for the Advancement of Breast Cancer Research, which is located in Dallas, and delivered an address at one of its awards luncheons. With her whole family, she participated in the National Race for the Cure, a five-kilometer walk-run event to raise funds for breast cancer research, detection, and education. Seven thousand people joined in that first race in Washington, in 1990; Mrs. Quayle's staff helped organize teams from several federal departments.

Mrs. Quayle's concern with breast-cancer awareness led her to keep in touch with, and be briefed by, research leaders at the National Cancer Institute. On May 16, 1990, she testified before the House Subcommittee on Health and Long-Term Care, which was considering legislation that would authorize grants to states to improve their facilities for breast-cancer detection. (One of the women on Mrs. Quayle's staff specialized in this area of public policy.) The bill passed—authorizing, for fiscal year 1991, $50 million in grants to be released through the Centers for Disease Control and Prevention.[2]

When the president was about to sign the bill, Mrs. Quayle's chief of staff drafted a schedule proposal for a signing ceremony. The president and his staff saw an opportunity to highlight the importance of this issue to the administration. Working together, the president's and vice president's staffs organized the ceremony, which was attended by the first lady, the Quayles, Health and Human Services Secretary Louis Sullivan, members of Congress representing both parties, and key members of the health care community.

As a child, Mrs. Quayle had watched her parents, both of whom were physicians, help victims who were injured when a skating rink collapsed. The issue of disaster assistance stuck in her mind, coming to the fore when she was a vice presidential spouse. She recalled: "My friends and I were discussing how I could best proceed, not wanting to make any mistakes, because everything always ends up on the front page. . . . We started to talk about foreign travel, and I wanted to do more than just visit museums. . . . A friend said there was a role I could play in the area of disaster mitigation. . . . The more information I got the more I realized that there was a need to focus people's attention on this."[3]

Mrs. Quayle got in touch with the Federal Emergency Management Agency (FEMA) and personally participated in—and received certification from—one of FEMA's field-training programs. When Hurricane Hugo struck South Carolina in the fall of 1989, Mrs. Quayle went on duty, staffing a desk in Charleston and working directly with hurricane victims seeking federal assistance. Some months later, after an earthquake in San Francisco, she traveled to the West Coast; her itinerary included a visit with the mayor of San Francisco, whose ruffled feathers required smoothing (the mayor was upset because the vice president had not come by personally during an earlier visit to survey the devastation).[4]

Mrs. Quayle's interest in and experience with disaster relief led her to associate herself in a voluntary capacity with the Office of Foreign Disaster Assistance of the Agency for International Development (AID). Later, she agreed to chair AID's Advisory Committee on Foreign Disaster Assistance; in that capacity, she accompanied the director of that office, Andrew Natsios, to witness AID foreign disaster relief operations in Mexico and Bangladesh.

When a severe drought struck southern Africa, an AID group—including Natsios and Mrs. Quayle—traveled to the region. Noting the danger that the drought presented to the stability of several nations in the area, the group recommended a prompt increase in the level of food aid. When questions were raised about how much food should be made available from the Department of Agriculture's reserves, Mrs. Quayle, in her capacity as chairperson of the advisory committee, telephoned the secretary of agriculture to underscore the urgency of the request. The informal channel of Quayle-to-Quayle-to-lunch-with-Bush was apparently used—and the hesitations of one or two reluctant underlings were extirpated in a hurry.[5]

In her official capacity, Mrs. Quayle led a U.S. delegation to a United Nations conference on disaster assistance in Geneva, Switzerland; she delivered several speeches to the attendees. Later, while her husband was visiting government leaders in several Latin American countries, she met with officials from local relief agencies and talked with them about disaster assistance planning. "She could do my job," commented Natsios.[6]

Recognizing the importance of legal education, Mrs. Quayle joined an attorneys' mentoring program to encourage young people of high school age to stay in school and to help them learn about the legal profession. She continued her own legal training during her husband's tenure as vice president, studying for and taking the Indiana test to maintain her legal credentials in that state.

One of her sisters is deaf, and Mrs. Quayle also supported programs to aid Americans with hearing impairments and other disabilities; she was active in the Deafness Research Foundation in New York and in the Alexander Graham Bell Association in the District of Columbia.

In addition to all her other activities, Mrs. Quayle, collaborating with another sister, Nancy Northcott, made time to write a novel: *Embrace the Serpent,* published in 1992.[7]

Mrs. Quayle's chief of staff, Denise Balzano, reflected on the evolution of the role of the vice president's spouse:

> I think it is important that that role be a natural outgrowth of that person's interests, skills, and experience. It much depends on the person herself and what that relationship is with the first family. A person who was less secure than George Bush might have found Marilyn's involvement intrusive. But he was very secure about it—enjoyed it and supported it. On the other hand, there might be a vice president's wife who would be shyer, more retiring, less interested in a public role or a public policy role. It would depend on the individual, and on the administration itself.[8]

Tipper Gore

Mrs. Gore was the fourth of the exceptionally energetic foursome at the top of the executive branch in the years 1993–2000. She was "zip" in the Constitution perhaps, but a dynamo in the precincts of the White House. Like Marilyn Quayle, she was university educated, with a graduate degree (in psychology). Like her predecessor she was a political teammate of her husband as he went from the House to the Senate to the vice presidency. Like her predecessor also, Mrs. Gore was an active stay-at-home mother, giving priority attention to her family. And like her predecessor, she drew from her personal life experience a strong motivation to use whatever resources she had to make a difference in specific areas of public policy.

For Mrs. Gore the area of greatest concern was mental health. To help overcome the stigma associated with treatment for mental health problems, she publicly admitted having received professional help to cope with depression after her youngest son was nearly killed in an auto accident; she also revealed that her mother had suffered from serious depression. For her work in this area, President Clinton gave Mrs. Gore the title of adviser to the president on mental health.

But by no means were either her interests or her energies limited to this one area—as is evident from the following brief descriptions of her activities as vice presidential spouse.

At the beginning of the Clinton administration, when the first lady organized specialized working groups to put together a comprehensive health care plan, she asked Mrs. Gore to shepherd the work of a thirty-member subgroup on mental health and substance abuse. Tipper Gore and her associates reached out to the several disparate and heretofore fragmented professional organizations and interest groups in those areas and persuaded them to set aside their differences and to agree on some core proposals that eventually became part of the president's 1993 health care package. In May of 1993, before the Senate Special Committee on Aging, Mrs. Gore testified on mental health issues as they related to older Americans.

While the president's comprehensive health care proposal did not make it through Congress, part of the mental health package did, in the form of appropriations legislation. At a Rose Garden signing ceremony on September 26, 1996, the president pointed out that the new act "requires insurance companies to set the same annual and lifetime coverage limits for mental illness that now apply to physical illness. No more double standards; it's time that law and insurance policies caught up with science." He then added: "I want to thank Tipper Gore for her passionate, persistent, unrelenting advocacy of this position to the President among others. When I walked up here—you know, there's always a marked contrast when you see someone happy and someone sad. I know no one in whom the contrast is more marked. I would do anything to see Tipper Gore as happy as she is today. . . . She has fought for all of you who believe in this position."[9]

In May of 1993 the president sent new instructions to the Interagency Committee on the Homeless: come up with a plan "for breaking the cycle of existing homelessness and for preventing future homelessness."[10] Mrs. Gore served with this interagency group and helped develop its recommendations; when the one-hundred-page plan was published the following May 17, she participated in the public ceremony accompanying its release.[11]

Mrs. Gore was a long-standing advocate of empowering parents to choose the kind of television programming that they felt was suitable for their children and for incorporating the V-chip into newly manufactured television sets. Her efforts, along with those of many others, paid off: on February 8, 1996, the president signed the Telecommunications Act of 1996, which imposed the V-chip requirement on TV manufacturers. In his remarks the next day, the president praised the vice president and Mrs. Gore for their contributions to this initiative.[12]

In July of 1996, Mrs. Gore and her staff, collaborating with her husband and his assistants, played a significant role in organizing the White House Conference on Children's Television. Industry leaders and network executives came from all across the nation. Geraldine Laybourne, the president of Disney/ABC Cable Network, and Fred Rogers, the host of "Mr. Rogers' Neighborhood," were among those attending. The president and Mrs. Clinton opened the conference; the Gores then introduced several conference participants, and each chaired a panel discussion.[13] "Greg Simon and I were responsible for the briefing materials as well as for preparing the four principals for the conference," recalled Mrs. Gore's former chief of staff, Skila Harris.[14]

Since 1992 the Gores had convened and co-moderated the annual Family Conference in Nashville, Tennessee. The Children, Youth, and Families Consortium of the University of Minnesota and the Child and Family Policy Center of Vanderbilt University have cosponsored the conferences. Each year the conference focuses on a different area of public policy related to families. Eleven hundred experts, leaders, and researchers from federal, state, and local institutions and universities attend, and the sessions are relayed by satellite to perhaps two hundred other sites. Mrs. Gore plays an all-year-round role in preparations for each conference, co-chairs many of the sessions, and is usually the solo chair of at least one of the plenary assemblies. In his State of the Union message of February 4, 1997, the president included these sentences: "The Vice President and Mrs. Gore will host their annual family conference this June on what we can do to make sure that parents are an active part of their children's learning all the way through school. . . . I thank you, Mr. Vice President, and thank you especially, Tipper, for what you do."[15]

Mrs. Gore joined the Take the Lead against Lead drive, and in April of 1998 launched the Campaign for a Lead-Safe America as national spokeswoman.[16]

In early 1998 President Clinton sent Mrs. Gore to represent the administration at the 1998 Winter Olympics in Nagano, Japan.[17]

When Hurricane Mitch struck Central America in November of 1998, President Clinton sent Tipper Gore to head an American delegation to survey the damage in Honduras and Nicaragua.[18] She immediately organized briefings for herself and her associates by the Geological Survey and the National Oceanic and Atmospheric Administration. The eleven-member delegation included the AID administrator, officers from AID and the Department of State, six members of Congress, and supporting staff—some forty-two people in all. The delegation pitched in; shoveled muck (while TV cameras watched); helped take care of children; unloaded supplies of baby food, water, and diapers; and slept out one night in tents.

By telephone, Mrs. Gore gave an on-scene interim assessment to the president;[19] on her return, she prepared a four-page report to the president that included specific recommendations for alleviating the current catastrophe and improving preparedness for such emergencies in the future. The White House put the report on its Web site. The president then invited her to join him in delivering a joint radio address to the nation, during which he announced some of the emergency measures that he was taking as a result of her recommendations.[20]

Tipper Gore took the lead in planning and arranging for the White House Conference on Mental Health, held in early June of 1999. All four of the nation's two first couples attended, as did several members of Congress. The president spoke at length, announcing several actions that the administration was taking to help ensure better access to mental health services.[21]

Among her other activities, Mrs. Gore of course accompanied her husband on many of his domestic and international trips; she and the former Russian premier's wife, Mrs. Chernomyrdin, for example, became good friends. Accompanied by John Shalikashvili, chairman of the joint chiefs of staff, she flew to Zaire in 1994 to visit Rwandan refugee camps. She hosted the Clinton administration's first luncheon for cabinet wives, which became an ongoing activity. She identified cabinet and congressional spouses who shared her concern about mental health issues and organized them into the Congressional and Cabinet Spouses Working Group on Mental Health.

Since her days shooting pictures for the *Nashville Tennessean* in the 1970s, Mrs. Gore has been an expert photographer. She published two books of her work: *Picture This* and *The Way Home: Ending Homelessness in America*.[22] Introducing the latter, in November of 1999, she told of a low-visibility trip that she had taken to Miami: "I visited homeless shelters. If someone asked me who I was, I told them the truth. . . . You can talk about statistics, but I thought it would be important to use photography to communicate the problem to the American people at large."[23] She was an avid participant in sports and served as the chairperson of the National Youth Fitness Campaign of the President's Council on Physical Fitness and Sports. And of course she received enormous amounts of mail.

How did she do all this?

In 1999 as many as thirteen members of the vice president's staff had assignments that included supporting Mrs. Gore, but they all had dual responsibilities to the vice president as well as to her. They were aided by a rotating contingent of volunteers (numbering between thirty and fifty) and by some eight interns each semester. Mrs. Gore shared with the vice president the statutory authority to hire experts and consultants.[24] Her chief of staff was also a special assistant to the vice president and attended White House senior staff meetings along with the vice president's chief of staff. The communications, scheduling, and press assistants in all four top offices kept in constant contact.

The once-common tension between presidential and vice presidential staffs was nearly absent in the Clinton White House; many members of the two groups had become very well acquainted when they worked side by side in the 1992 campaign. The former chiefs of staff to the first lady and to Mrs. Gore, for example, had been close friends for fifteen years.

If this inventory of Tipper Gore's activities listed all the hundreds of speeches, events, and media appearances in which she participated, it would be considerably longer. In fact, each of the foregoing inventories—the vice president's, the first lady's, Mrs. Quayle's, and Mrs. Gore's—is equally incomplete. But the case is made. Whether quietly and behind the scenes, or out front in the public spotlight, the spouse of the vice president has in recent years become a principal player in the policy environment of the White House.

"I think that the American people—it's almost like a demand—believe that you have four working principals," commented Mrs. Gore's chief of staff. "I just see that; I feel it. Now you may get a spouse of the vice president who really may not like so much public exposure and does not want to be out there. That is for each and every spouse to decide. But I have to tell you: if this White House was not as it is, and if the president and the vice president did not have the partnership they do—which translates completely throughout this whole complex—we would have a very, very difficult time functioning here."[25]

In closing, let the president describe the quadriad:

Let me say, you can't imagine—you know, Al and Tipper and Hillary and I, we've done a lot of campaigning together. We did in '92; we did in '96; we do a few events together now, even though our lives are considerably busier, and often with conflicting schedules. But I think that one of the real secrets of whatever success that we've had for the American people has been that we have really tried to be a team; we've tried to be friends; we've tried to be family; and we've tried to be frank with each other. And each person has made a unique contribution. . . . It seems to me, that's the way people ought to live, but it turns out it's a fairly effective way to do business.[26]

CHAPTER TWENTY-ONE

The President's Centripetal Offices

As the White House staff becomes internally differentiated, it also grows bigger. But this spawns an additional problem. Because there are more staff with narrower concerns, managing their activities becomes more crucial, and more difficult. In response, every president since Nixon has routinely delegated internal management functions to senior aides, thus creating additional hierarchy within the White House. But this layering of positions removes the president from direct oversight of staff activities. Consequently, he is less able to ensure that they are working in his interest.

Roosevelt seemed reluctant to delegate coordinating authority to any individual or committee short of himself. Perhaps he recognized that the only way a subordinate could truly coordinate the cabinet on his behalf was if FDR delegated inherently presidential powers to that person. But that FDR refused to do.

MATTHEW DICKINSON

The speech comes in late. Now, what's the chief of staff's job? The chief of staff has to heave his body in the middle and try to figure out a way for the . . . speech to reach the substantive people. . . . But what happens when you do that? That's throwing sand in the gears and it gets grindy, and pretty soon out come news stories that Cheney is having a fight with the speechwriter. He couldn't care less about the speechwriter. All he wants is for the ultimate product to accomplish what the president intended. It isn't personal . . . and yet that's where the rubber hits the ground. And if there's no rubber on the tire, it's steel and that's sparks.

DONALD RUMSFELD

The previous chapters in part 2 of this volume described the eighteen policy offices of the modern White House. The place is like a racing car, its cylinders primed with political high-octane.

The president climbs into the driver's seat and turns the inaugural ignition. Will the engine hum or sputter? Will those cylinders fire haphazardly or in well-tuned order?

The White House power pack hums only if there are "distributors" in the system: signaling and control centers to ensure that the heated machinery will move in synchronization and at the president's pace. There are five such centralizing points in the contemporary White House: the president's personal office (now called Oval Office Operations), the Cabinet Affairs office, the staff secretary, the assistant to the president for management and administration, and the chief of staff.

Why are they indispensable?

As the preceding chapters reveal, today's White House staff is a super-charged engine made up of superbly capable but quite diverse presidential instruments. The eighteen policy domains are specialized, and necessarily so—from the national security affairs office (which has nineteen subordinate policy units), to the legislative affairs group, the speechwriters, and the advance teams. The foregoing chapters have provided a glimpse of the immense panoply of demanding assignments that reverberate in each of these eighteen jurisdictions. What terms to insist upon in the trade negotiations with China? How to design a presidential trip to southern Africa? How to persuade more senators to support the New Markets initiative? What is the most effective speech the president can give at the National Governors Conference?

Addressing each such issue is not like trying to crack a single nut; it's more like yanking loose a many-rooted vine whose tendrils entwine the departments, advocacy groups, Congress, the courts, and other nations. Each week, the White House is engulfed by these and hundreds of other similar responsibilities; the following week brings hundreds more. The exigencies of substance as well as time crush in upon those who are laboring to do this work: deadlines are everywhere closing in. Yet, in the White House, nothing is acceptable but the very highest quality output; the president's—the nation's—reputation is on the line.

As readers have noted, each of these eighteen offices is territorial, asserting exclusive jurisdiction over its responsibilities. No one but the Office of Presidential Scheduling makes presidential calendar commitments; no one but the Office of Presidential Personnel makes promises about appointments; no one in the White House is to bargain on the Hill without the imprimatur of the Office of Legislative Affairs. Such jurisdictional separations are indispensable; contradictory commitments emanating from different parts of the

presidential staff produce administrative chaos within the White House—
and political damage to the chief executive himself.

The staff is more than boxes surrounded by rules. It is a nest of brainy,
aggressive, and intellectually extroverted people. The eighteen chiefs and
their several hundred assistants are men and women of varying ages and professions, both military and civilian, from every corner of America, and of
different races and religions. Of especial significance: they have been brought
into the White House from different factions of the president's party: liberal,
conservative, and moderate. They share the president's joy at being in office—
but, as Bob Woodward's *The Agenda* aptly illustrated, they are likely to harbor
very different visions of which policies the president should pursue.

Controversies about ideas, policies, and priorities erupt in every corner
of the White House. As long as these debates remain internal, the president
benefits. In option papers, drafts of speeches, and cloistered meetings, the
clash of viewpoints illuminates his choices. But the more heated the dissension, the greater the temptation for a protagonist to evade the debate—to
run privately to the president with a distorted presentation and extract a
premature commitment. Left to himself, and unprotected, a president may
tolerate or even encourage such forays.

And the more unfriendly the dissension, the more likely it is to break out
in public: the protagonists leak their one-sided accounts to favorite colum-
nists or reporters. Such is the end stage of White House debates.

To complicate matters further, a few individuals may be hatching political ambitions of their own. But political ambitions or not, all White House
staffers have electric egos: and the higher the rank, the higher the voltage.

The White House staffers' sense of self-importance is nurtured by the
perquisites of office: handling important matters in close proximity to the
world's most important public figure; access to radio-equipped limousines,
the White House Mess, ubiquitous communnications gadgetry, *Air Force
One*, Camp David—and honed to a sharp edge by the realities of sacrifice.
Seventy-hour weeks are the norm; Saturdays are given up, and often Sundays as well. Pagers and cell phones mean that no staffer ever really leaves
the office; a special White House telephone rings at any wee hour in senior
staff members' homes. Staffers' private lives are disrupted by presidential
travel. Even the off-duty activities of White House staff are subject to media
scrutiny; their spouses and children are put under stress. A few receive
threats to their lives. White House staff, accordingly, are men and women
who are warm in their common loyalties, but tense from the pressures of
unending demands. It is a molten environment.

The specialization and jurisdiction-mindedness of these eighteen offices make for an atmosphere of "centrifugality" in the modern White House; each unit is almost desperately preoccupied with staying on top of the inundation of duties—with serving the boss in its own expert way. But across the whole White House is a demand that overrides any and all individual preoccupations: the necessity for coordination. The eighteen units of the White House staff must be as precisely interlinked and sequenced as the pistons in an engine.

The introduction to part 1 emphasized how functionally obsolete are the boundaries demarcating the operating departments and agencies of the executive branch—how their historical separateness has melted in the hot reality of economic, social, and national security issues that today jump across all the old jurisdictional fences. It is the same within the White House itself.

Successfully launching a presidential policy initiative, effectively staging a presidential event, planning and conducting a meeting of world leaders, or delivering a major address to the nation—all require the collective contributions of *many, if not all,* of those eighteen White House fiefdoms. Regardless of their jurisdictional jealousies, they must reach out to one another across their specialized turfs, lay out and follow a common course of action, spare no detail in exchanging information, and make their respective contributions to the presidential objective with minutely calculated, supportive timing. Will this happen automatically? Emphatically not. In the modern White House there must be a few tough, strong offices exerting centripetal force: pulling the pieces together, planning—and then enforcing—the indispensable coordination of the whole institution. The presidency cannot function without them. The five are described here.

Oval Office Operations and the Presidential Aide

The title of director of Oval Office Operations was new with Clinton; the function is decades old. It is centered in the tiny enclave just outside the "back door" to the president's office. The Clinton director has been with the president—first as a campaigner, then as an office manager—for twenty-four years. She supervised the president's personal secretary, one other aide, the (separately located) office of presidential correspondence, and the presidential aide. Her two most demanding responsibilities were (1) keeping a meticulous finger on all the presidential papers going into or coming out of the Oval Office and (2) watching exactly who was—and who was not—going through that back door.[1]

Most of the papers would have come up from the staff secretary, but also among them were letters (using the president's private zip code) from Arkansas friends and others—all of whom she knew well—that were delivered to her directly. Incoming phone calls to the president went through the director and her staff. As for that doorway, even those with walk-in privileges (the vice president, the first lady, and the chief of staff) checked with her before barging in on the boss.

She attended the morning senior staff meetings, which alerted her about any changes in the order for the day. Of course, the "final" schedule for the day had been put together the night before, but changes were always being requested to handle unanticipated events; the director of Oval Office operations supervised any such alterations. If "this bill needs to be signed by three o'clock," she would know it—and if necessary, have the photographer primed. A *Washington Post* story summed up her skills: "[Her] job is basically to orchestrate the minute-by-minute progress of the presidency. At her desk outside the Oval Office, she prepares Clinton's daily schedule, enforces it, decides who gets in to see him and when they must get out. . . . [Her] most frequent expression is 'No,' but she says it with empathy."[2]

The presidential aide (there were three in succession—all men—during the Clinton presidency) really had to be single. Not by any edict, but because no young person holding that office would have time for anything else. The aide was "the loyal shadow," glued to the president's side between scheduled events. The aide clutched the big, military-looking binder that contained two principal sets of papers: the daily schedules of the president, the vice president, and the first lady; and a copy of the president's daily briefing book. The briefing book was, in turn, divided into sections: one for each event of the day, with the relevant briefing papers and background information.

The presidential aide would read through the entire briefing book each morning. He made no pretense of being a policy officer but was nonetheless the last quality checkpoint for the briefing materials. "If they did not seem adequate, it was my responsibility to catch that," explained one. "Based on my own knowledge of the president, he is going to ask about this and this—and then I would request the staff secretary to get supplementary information to answer those questions."[3] Before each event actually started, the presidential aide would summon the event coordinator and do a walk-through of the event. Of what possible pitfalls should they be aware? What last-minute changes were being made?

The binder had plenty of blank pages. The president might have been walking to his limousine: "Say, remind me about so-and-so," or "Whatever happened to such-and-such?" or "Where did I put that?" or "Can you see if you can track down Mr. . . . ?" It was jotted down—and taken care of.

The aide would read draft speeches with extra care. One remembered: "Over time, you develop a sense of what the president likes and doesn't like. If there are new speechwriters who come in, you might have positive suggestions for them, such as, 'I think he's not going to like the way you said this.' There is nothing more vindicating than to see him turn around and complain about exactly what you had in mind!"[4]

If the president's remarks included a greeting to a VIP who was presumably in the audience, the aide would make absolutely certain that the dignitary was in fact present. Conversely, if there was a no-show, the laudatory language would be scratched, with seconds to spare. "We would look for typos in those drafts, too," an aide added.[5]

Every president is a very human being—usually gracious but occasionally letting go with his temper. Commented one aide: "You are a sponge. Being the closest, sometimes when things don't go exactly as they should, you bear the brunt of the reaction. Nine times out of ten, it's not directed at us, but we happen to be the closest to him. His temper's not that bad; when it surfaces, it's short-lived."[6]

For the unexpected, the vexatious, the sudden bursts of presidential temper, "I was part of the ventilator," said a former Nixon presidential aide. "There are always two people in that Oval Office," he said, "the president, and the human being who happens to be the president of the United States. I had little to do with the first, but concentrated on the second. There was such trust, that when he and I were together, the president was alone."[7]

On the road, with the director of Oval Office Operations back at the White House, the duties of the presidential aide expanded: he would help the switchboard place presidential phone calls and keep the minute-by-minute phone log that listed the names of people with whom the president had talked. "You kind of serve as the piece of the president's brain that he shouldn't have to use, so he can think about policy, or whatever," one aide recalled.[8]

Then there was "working the rope line": shaking hands down the long stretch of exuberant spectators. The presidential aide would be inches behind the boss:

> President Clinton jokes that his autograph will probably be the least valuable of any president's, because he never will refuse to sign anything. I try to limit it beforehand, but he will turn around and take

something and sign it, or hand it to me. I have to come up with some way to keep the things in order and get them back to the appropriate people—and then *not* get left behind by the motorcade. What I do is walk behind the president as he works a rope line; as he is given something, I would take it and have the person put his or her name on it. At the end of the rope line we would go to a sheltered area and have the president sign them, and then I would run back and give them back to the people.[9]

People in a crowd would hand the president gifts to keep. The Gift Office supplied the presidential aide with a pocketful of gift forms, and on the spot the aide would get the name and address of the donor. Back home, the Gift Office would acknowledge each one. Inevitably, on the plane home, the president would ask: "Where is that such-and-such thing I got?" An example was a little giraffe, made from Lego blocks, given to the president when he visited a child care center in Woodstock, Kansas. Noting its ingenuity, the presidential aide had kept it nearby. His hunch was right: the president asked for it, and displayed it on his own desk in the Oval Office.

The presidential aide was not a note taker in Oval Office meetings; other staff officers handled that duty. Nor did he carry "the football" (the satchel with the coded wartime commands); that is a military responsibility.

A presidential trip would have its unglamorous aspects: at a big hotel reception, the president would never get to see the front door. One aide remembered wryly:

The president has said that he has seen more service hallways and kitchens in hotels and buildings than any other person has ever seen. The Secret Service is always bringing him in the back way—the secure way. The smell of fresh paint is overwhelming. Sherwin Williams owes us a great deal, because these hotels always want their service hallways to look good—and instead of coming in the grand entrances, the president of the United States is being shoved through by the garbage dumps and through the kitchens. The service elevators we take are freshly painted, and the holding rooms are usually freshly painted, and the storage rooms and the back corridors. You have to be careful where you lean up against![10]

"It's a fantastic experience," recalled one aide, "but your life is not your own. You have to design your daily schedule around what the president's is. You can never plan your weekends, because you don't know whether you

will be there or not. . . . Things always come up—disasters, what-have-you—
where the president has to travel at the last minute. It makes it tough to keep
up with people, girlfriends. But it's been the most interesting job I will ever
have."[11] "I'm nobody," added former aide Steven Goodin, "and I got to follow the most powerful man on the planet around."[12]

Cabinet Affairs

President Eisenhower created the office of cabinet secretary to support the
mode in which he used the full cabinet itself: that is, convening—and personally chairing—weekly meetings to discuss policy issues.[13] No president
since Ike has used the cabinet in this fashion; as the cabinet has grown in
number, its usefulness as a policy advisory group has diminished. The office
of Cabinet Affairs, though, has continued, with new and different functions,
as a central part of the coordinating machinery of the contemporary White
House.

Under President Bush, the cabinet met infrequently—usually quarterly—
and Cabinet Affairs of course made the meeting arrangements. The sessions
were principally for team-building purposes rather than for detailed discussions of policy papers. Following the Reagan practice, President Bush
employed two cabinet-level councils (domestic and economic) as the locus
of policy coordination. (Reagan at one time had seven such councils.)

In both the Reagan and Bush White Houses, the staffs for these councils—the executive secretaries and their assistants—were placed in the office
of Cabinet Affairs. Under this arrangement, the head of cabinet affairs managed the interagency preparatory process for the domestic and economic
policy issues that were handled in those councils. (But when trade issues
were up for discussion, national security adviser Brent Scowcroft would be
invited to the meetings of the Economic Policy Council, and Secretary of the
Cabinet Edith Holiday would participate in summit briefings.)

The executive secretaries consulted with the chairs of their respective councils, developed the agendas, helped the agency representatives work through
their policy differences, identified issues on which there was serious interagency disagreement, called the meetings (in the White House), and drafted
the decision memoranda, which set forth alternative options for the president's action. The secretary of the cabinet went to the meetings of both policy
councils, along with the chief of staff; the president himself attended when
needed. Holiday and domestic policy assistant Roger Porter always ensured
that there were "no surprises": meaning, first, that the president was fully

aware of any differences among cabinet officers; and second, that the coun-
cil-meeting presentations were made in an "honest broker" fashion—so that
the president never made a decision with incomplete information.

But Bush's office of Cabinet Affairs was more than a policy staff and executive secretariat. "We were the eyes and ears for the cabinet within the White
House," explained Holiday. If a member of the cabinet wanted an appointment with the president, the head of cabinet affairs would find out what
topic the cabinet secretary wanted to discuss, and prepare a briefing memorandum for the chief executive. Unless the meeting was of an unusually
personal nature, Holiday would join the session; if a decision memo was
needed afterwards, she would write it for the president's initials. As appropriate, she would attend the meetings of the White House scheduling
committee to support cabinet requests. If an event was scheduled with a cabinet member and the president, she or one of her assistants would help plan
the event to ensure that both the cabinet secretary and the president would
make a success of it.

Ever aware that in some presidencies, estrangement between the cabinet
and the chief executive was a fact of life, Ms. Holiday and her deputy, Steve
Danzansky, devoted much of their time to creating an environment of friendship and good relations. Several times a year she would arrange luncheons
with the president: Bush, Chief of Staff John Sununu, herself, and two or
three cabinet officers who had common policy interests. They were unstructured, "let your hair down" sessions, she remembered: "Sometimes the
cabinet has a hard time getting the pulse of a president. They read his
speeches, they hear from White House staffers what he is thinking about,
but unless you are sitting there, and hear him say, 'I'm so mad at Senator X
for what he did to me on this,' you don't understand; you don't get the pulse
of what he is trying to do. He would often use this as an opportunity to let
them get a directional bearing."[14]

Danzansky added to these initiatives his own informal sessions, convening a weekly breakfast with the deputy secretaries of the departments that
were members of the Economic Policy Council. The value here, as he put
it, was that "by the time things got to the Economic Policy Council, the cabinet secretaries were sitting around the table, and if they had differences they
were usually pretty large—and the president would have a big decision to
make. To keep the coordination going and to find out what was trouble-
some and what might bite us in the back of the heel, I thought it was
important to keep in touch with all of them."[15] In a further step to minimize agency estrangement, Danzansky hosted a weekly White House

What Is "the Cabinet"?

The cabinet, as a collectivity, is established neither in the Constitution nor by statute but is solely a creation of custom and tradition, going back to the first president. Its traditional core membership, besides the president, consists of the (now fourteen) secretaries of the departments.

Recent presidents have brought others into cabinet membership: Eisenhower added the vice president, the U.S. ambassador to the United Nations, the director of the Office of Management and Budget, and the director of the (then) Office of Defense Mobilization. (To confer national visibility on civil defense, Ike also had the civil defense director sit with the cabinet.)

Clinton has conferred cabinet membership on ten others: the director of the Central Intelligence Agency, the chair of the Council of Economic Advisers, the administrator of the Environmental Protection Agency, the director of the Federal Emergency Management Agency, the administrator of the General Services Administration, the director of the Office of National Drug Control Policy, the director of the Office of Personnel Management, the administrator of the Small Business Administration, the administrator of the Social Security Administration, and the U.S. Trade Representative. Members of the formal cabinet under Clinton thus numbered twenty-six, plus the president and Mr. Gore.

A point presidents should remember when they consider conferring cabinet membership on top-level executive branch jobholders in agen-

breakfast with department and agency deputies in the environmental field, including Environmental Protection Agency Administrator William Reilly (who on other occasions often found himself on the losing end of arguments with White House Chief of Staff Sununu).

A Clinton addition to the responsibilities of the office of Cabinet Affairs was the occasional preparation of written "talking points," which the office distributed to cabinet secretaries, equipping each of them to support presidential initiatives (such as those described in a State of the Union address or other major speech).

Thanks to the Situation Room, described in chapter 3, presidents may read instantly the latest from Islamabad or Chad, but what about Chicago? What problems are vexing the secretary of the interior? What is the secretary of commerce going to say in that upcoming speech in San Francisco?

cies other than the core fourteen: the privilege tends to become attached
to the job. When successors take over they are reminded, "In this job you
have cabinet status!"

Presidents can further augment cabinet membership by conferring
cabinet status on any other officials they please, such as senior officers
in the White House—as Ike did with his chief of staff and his deputy chief
of staff and as Clinton did with his domestic policy chief, his national
economic policy director, and his national security adviser. Near the end
of his second term, Ike invited the chairman of the Republican National
Committee to join the cabinet meetings. In effect, the "cabinet" is composed of whomever the president invites regularly to attend cabinet
meetings. It is a loose arrangement!

Does the cabinet meet in the Cabinet Room? Only if the president convenes the meeting; if the president is not in the chair at the outset (even
if he drops by later), the cabinet meets in the (smaller, windowless) Roosevelt Room. Who attends cabinet meetings besides members (and the
cabinet secretary)? White House senior staff sit around the edge of the
room; in the Clinton White House, all staff members with the rank of
assistant to the president were invited as guests, to witness and listen.

Since there are only twenty chairs at the cabinet table (fewer in the
Roosevelt Room), but there were twenty-eight members of the Clinton
cabinet and at least twenty-five staffers with assistant-to-the-president
rank, readers will be pardoned if they surmise that the (understandably
rare) Clinton cabinet sessions were perhaps standing room only.

Is there a "Domestic Affairs Situation Room" where a computer blinks early
warnings?

There is not, but there is a near substitute: the weekly Cabinet Report
prepared by the office of Cabinet Affairs. This had its origins under President Eisenhower, who initiated a daily, cabinet-level reporting system called
Staff Notes, with the departmental contributions selected and edited by the
office of the staff secretary. Under Kennedy, this summary became a weekly
digest prepared by the secretary of the cabinet.[16] Every succeeding president
has followed Ike's example—and has built on it.

In the Clinton administration, the reporting process began with each
departmental executive secretary collecting material that had been written
up by the bureaus and offices of that department. From this initial dragnet,
each executive secretary would select items of presidential interest to send

to the White House: activities and accomplishments of note, problems on the horizon, the cabinet secretary's travel and speaking schedules for the previous week and for the week to come. Each department's contribution totaled perhaps fifteen pages. "Anything that might be going on, controversial or not," explained cabinet affairs head Thurgood Marshall Jr.[17] "Even if it's something that reveals a problem we have!" observed a departmental executive secretary—reflecting his recognition of the universal temptation to lard the output with good news.[18] Bush's deputy director of cabinet affairs commented: "If it didn't appear there, and there was a surprise, the department heard about it. 'Why wasn't this in the Cabinet Report?' 'What do you mean you are testifying about X, Y, or Z?' 'When did *you* know about this?'"[19]

Clinton's first secretary to the cabinet, Christine Varney, adopted the same disciplinary tone: "If you don't surprise us, we won't micromanage you!"[20]

"But we do it anyway," was the wry comment from one of Clinton's senior White House policy directors.

The Clinton system required that submissions arrive in the Cabinet Affairs office on Wednesday evenings, and many arrived not on paper but by e-mail. The nine-person cabinet affairs staff would pore over the stack of incoming raw material, scrutinize the messages on the monitors, pick out the items that the president should see, edit them, and print out a succinct twelve pages. (Will the Cabinet Report someday take the form of paperless words on a presidential laptop?)

On Friday the Cabinet Report went to the Oval Office, to the vice president, and to all other senior assistants to the president, including the first lady's chief of staff. Occasionally one of those recipients would spot an upcoming departmental announcement of good news: a program initiated, a major grant awarded, a success story for the feds. There would be no hesitation about stealing it—and transforming it into a White House announcement.

Was the Cabinet Report a "brag sheet," as one White House senior officer characterized it? "It depends on the cabinet members," observed a former White House chief of staff. "Some were more honest and direct than others. Others, I think, just put it through their bullshit operation."[21] In recent years, the reports have tended to feature less substance and more of the secretaries' schedules and travel plans.

Commented Steve Silverman, Clinton's deputy cabinet secretary: "Some of the reports were better than others, as you can imagine. When people realized that the president was reading them, that perked them up. I think they were also useful tools *within* the agencies, because they gave leverage to the chief of staff in, say, the Commerce Department: he would order the subordinate units in the department, 'You get this to me by Tuesday, because this is going to the White House tomorrow!' I think we get mostly a good product."[22]

During a CNN interview in 1995, President Clinton was asked, "What is your favorite thing about being president?" His response: "On Sunday nights I love being home, in the Residence, reading the weekly reports from my cabinet agencies."

Typically the president did more than read the reports: he filled the margins with presidential scribbling (it took a seasoned expert to decipher Clinton's handwriting). "Why don't we do more of this?" "If Secretary X is going to do that event, we or the vice president should be part of it." "If Secretary Y is going to be in Chicago, be sure he meets with this outfit." "Stop this in its tracks!"

The Cabinet Affairs office would promptly relay the instructions to the appropriate department (and would send a copy of every scribbled request to the chief of staff's office as well). Nixon chief of staff Bob Haldeman used to mask the president's hand with memos that began, "It has been requested. . . . " The recipients damn well knew where that came from.

The weekly incoming submissions from the departments and agencies were not only screened for nuggets for the regular digest to the president but were also used as the basis for special reports: on race relations, on drug control efforts, on the drought in California, and so forth. The president often suggested to the Cabinet Affairs office subjects that he would like to hear more about. The cabinet affairs staff would translate the suggestions into specific assignments to the appropriate departments and follow up to ensure responsive replies.

The Cabinet Reports were only half the story. The Clinton White House inaugurated an even more immediate to-and-fro information system: cabinet conference calls. At 8:30 every morning, the deputy cabinet secretary held a conference call with the chiefs of staff of twenty-six departments and agencies. No complicated operator assistance was needed: each participant dialed a special number and was in on the "meeting." Explained Silverman:

> The conference calls are for the purpose of keeping the departments apprised of what is going on with the president at the White House that day; they also report in to us. Mondays through Thursdays are no more than ten minutes. Fridays are twenty to thirty-five: what we do then is the week ahead. We go around to every agency and ask,

'What have you got coming up?' It is helpful for the agencies to hear what they each are doing, because there is a lot of overlap or coordination that can go on. . . . One will say that his boss is going to a school and another might say, 'My boss has been to that school; it's a great place.'[23]

The conference calls were expected to be as candid as—or even more candid than—the written cabinet reports. Varney observed: "The potential issues that could be problems are really our job to solve; they should not go to the president in most instances. To the extent that an agency could solve the problem on its own, that's fine, but to the extent they couldn't, I always said to them: 'You need me on the front end; you do not want me coming in at the twelfth hour! If you think there is an issue coming up, you need to let me know.'"[24]

In 1995 Varney added a further elaboration to this White House–cabinet coordination system: an e-mail summary of the daily conference calls. The summary was distributed to the departmental chiefs of staff so that they could, in turn, make copies for their deputies, their press secretaries, their communications directors, and their scheduling offices.

Another Varney innovation was a breakfast with the departmental chiefs of staff, held every two weeks in the White House Mess by the deputy cabinet secretary. Here was an opportunity for the senior practitioners of top-level staff work in the entire cabinet to sit around a single table, exchanging information and comparing notes on both the policy and the process issues that they had in common.

An additional Clinton administration practice was a weekly conference call, hosted by the White House deputy cabinet secretary, with some of the senior departmental political appointees who were located in the field. Departments and agencies such as Education and Labor, the Environmental Protection Agency, Health and Human Services, Housing and Urban Development, the Federal Emergency Management Agency, the General Services Administration, and the Small Business Administration had over 150 political assistants in various positions in ten federal regions. Some were former mayors or local political leaders; all had good grass-roots connections. Each week two or three of them in each region would join the White House conference call; the deputy cabinet secretary would use this informal system to fill them in on events and priorities in the White House and would receive, in turn, candid and on-the-spot assessments of what issues were really on the minds of state and local officials and the heads of regional federal agencies. Once a year the cabinet secretary convened the whole group in Washington; the gathering included a meeting with the president.

Like so many offices in the White House, cabinet affairs operated with the help of designated contacts in each of the departments—usually the chiefs of staff. The entire group of departmental contacts often met with cabinet affairs staff at the White House, to look ahead to problems and questions that were bubbling beyond the more immediate horizon of the weekly reports.

President Bush never wanted White House staff at any level to make it difficult for cabinet members to reach him: he wanted open channels between the cabinet and the chief executive. Early on he instituted a private letter box that allowed department or agency heads to communicate with him unimpeded by any White House staff review—even that of Chief of Staff Sununu, who had gained a reputation for insisting on participating substantively in almost any matter that came forward. The staff secretary could examine this correspondence, but only if the transmitting envelope was unsealed. The president himself was savvy enough—from long years of experience in government—not to allow the system to be misused.

Bush veterans speak of the contrapuntal sources of policy strength in the Bush presidency: strength in the cabinet from players like James Baker, Nicholas Brady, Richard Cheney, Richard Thornburgh, and James Watkins; strength in the White House personified by John Sununu, Richard Darman, and Brent Scowcroft. The Bush Cabinet Affairs office existed between these massifs of power, aiding the president in his determination to create—and benefit from—a balance of forces.

As described in chapter 2, the Clinton cabinet was often convened with the White House chief of staff in the chair. He or other White House senior staffers would use these sessions to brief cabinet members on important White House initiatives, thus preparing them to speak knowledgeably in explaining and supporting current presidential policy objectives. Clinton sometimes dropped in on these meetings to add his own personal perspective and emphasis.

As of this writing, there are still three principal policy councils: the Domestic Policy Council, the National Economic Council, and the National Security Council (NSC). The members of these councils are all cabinet heads, but the center of policy development strength is now in the White House policy staffs—in the directors of those three dominions. Each of the three has its own chief of staff and supporting assistants. In a change from the Bush years, the first two are no longer located within Cabinet Affairs but, similarly to the NSC, now have their own respective precincts.

The Clinton Cabinet Affairs office was charged with ensuring coordination among the three policy councils. The deputy director of cabinet affairs convened weekly meetings that included the staff directors of all three councils plus representatives from the chief of staff; the vice president; the Council on Environmental Quality; and the Office of Science, Technology, and Space Policy. What were the issues upcoming on each council's agenda? What future White House events were being scheduled that would affect their work? What forthcoming departmental events would have an impact on their activities? Was the work of one council going to be duplicating that of one or both of the other two? Were the departments being tasked to perform work for the White House in an uncoordinated or confusing fashion? Which were the priority assignments? If one of the three councils had a matter under consideration, had it left out of its deliberations any agency that should have been included? (An example: the NSC at one point had been discussing the Haitian refugee issue but neglected to involve the Department of Transportation, whose Coast Guard was on the operational front lines.)

When policy matters arose that did not fit clearly into the bailiwicks of any of the three councils, the Clinton Cabinet Affairs office took on the responsibility for coordination. An example was domestic emergency management. Because emergency operations could come up swiftly and require rapid and comprehensive interagency coordination, the Federal Emergency Management Agency needed—and then got, in the Cabinet Affairs office—a contact person in the White House.

The Clinton Cabinet Affairs office sponsored at least one subcabinet retreat—held in the Department of State—where deputy secretaries and senior political appointees from the several departments and agencies met, got to know each other, and compared notes on common interests.

Looking back—and thinking forward to presidencies of the future—several Clinton White House leaders observed that they would like to see some rejuvenation of the old-style cabinet meetings—with the boss. Commented one:

> I found that these people needed to be touched and seen and heard—by him. He is an incredible communicator. I think it would be good for him to talk to his own people. He does it ad hoc; he sees them all the time at events, but I would suggest to him that they have a meeting, at the very least, once a quarter—something fairly regular. They can get inspired by it. What happens, you see, is, they turn around and when they go to Detroit the next day they can say, "I was just with

the president." It's a little awkward when they are not getting to say that. It is nice when they can tell people, "The president asked me yesterday to make sure you understand this is important for our economy, for our country." I would do a little bit more of that.[25]

The Staff Secretary

The office of staff secretary, proposed in 1949 by the first Hoover Commission, was established by President Eisenhower in 1953 and has been a quintessential part of the White House coordination system since 1969. Apart from personal intervention by the chief of staff, the staff secretary is the last substantive control point before papers reach the Oval Office. Outside of a few highly sensitive national security items, there are no exceptions now—no private mailbox for the cabinet to use as a back channel to the president.[26] Every substantive piece of paper—letters for signature, papers for decision or information—goes through this screen.

The first question raised about any decision recommendation is the elemental one: Have all affected White House offices been consulted? To fail this initial test from the staff secretary means that the internal White House preparatory work has been inadequate—and must be redone.

But what about the involvement of the departments and agencies? Former Clinton staff secretary Todd Stern makes a highly significant observation about the workings of today's White House:

> The great majority of what gets to go to the president is internally generated. Obviously, much of the policy work of the administration is initiated and developed in the cabinet agencies, but where a policy question involves the White House, it is typically coordinated by one of the four policy councils: the National Security Council, the National Economic Council, the Domestic Policy Council, or by the Council on Environmental Quality. It is these councils that are responsible for seeking the views and clearances from the agencies on decisional matters, and it is the councils which typically prepare the memoranda which actually go to the president. We do not get a large number of memoranda directly from the cabinet officers to the president.[27]

In the Clinton administration, the staff secretary was much more than a screen. Each paper that passed the initial test then moved to the next stage: it got a covering memorandum. The paper might have been a lengthy document or a one-pager—no matter: the staff secretary put a summary chit on top. "Attached is a memorandum from X. It says A and B, C and D. The issue being focused on is E, and there are two views: this person thinks F, this person thinks G." The whole package was of course attached; the president could decide that the top chit told him what he needed to know, or he could study not only the original memorandum but the in-depth attachments and the separate views of the dissenters. President Clinton, a fast reader, might delve into the whole package, but if he was already familiar with the issue, he saved inordinately valuable time by relying on the staff secretary's brief cover. The staff secretary never failed to call the president's attention to a paper that contained a controversy: the cover memo zeroed in on what the issue was that required decision.

The staff secretary was not merely an administrative but a substantive officer; all four who served in that post during the Clinton administration were lawyers. If the issue coming forward had generated disagreement and was being hashed out in the chief of staff's office, the staff secretary would often be there, drinking in the debate. Stern explained: "One couldn't write the kind of memo, reflecting people's views, that ought to be written for the president if you didn't hear the conversation."[28]

Did the staff secretary ever decline to send a memorandum forward? Stern responded: "Yes, but it doesn't happen very often. If something was not decisional, we were less concerned about it. If it was decisional, and if it was off base or exorbitantly wrong, yes, we would send it back. You use your judgment; time is often short. If something was a little rough around the edges, we could fix it with our cover memo. We would give the president a cover memo that was totally sharp, clear, focused. Generally the work product was pretty good."[29]

Did the staff secretary express a personal judgment about the content of a document? "It was very important," Stern emphasized, "that we be viewed as honest brokers—that we didn't slant things one way or another, else we would not have retained the confidence of the people who had written those papers!"[30]

The staff secretary took care not to squeeze the president into narrow, yes or no choices; besides the "approve" and "disapprove" alternatives there was always the "let's discuss further" option—which President Clinton often elected.

For informational memorandums, the early practice was to handle each one separately; later, in the interests of efficiency, the staff secretary would bundle a group of them together, put a short memo on top with a paragraph summarizing each item, and save the package for the president's weekend reading.

At the end of each day, a highly important final package went to the president from the staff secretary's office: the next day's briefing book. It opened with the president's schedule and had a separate section for the briefing papers that accompanied each event on the calendar: the substantive background, the logistics of what was to take place. There was an event coordinator—a staff person responsible for each event—and part of the coordinator's responsibility was to ensure that the briefing papers were in the staff secretary's hands by four o'clock the previous afternoon. The presidential aide, the vice president, the chief of staff, and several other White House senior officers received copies of the presidential briefing book.

One more function has traditionally been assigned to the staff secretary: running the speech-clearance operation. The staff secretary's office photocopied every draft speech and sent a copy to each interested White House policy unit—with a cover sheet stating the deadline for comments. In the Bush administration, reportedly, the staff secretary acted as a referee, helping to ensure that the incoming comments were reflected in the revised text. The Clinton staff secretary eschewed a mediating role: the comments went directly to the speechwriter.

To cover their relentlessly demanding duties, the staff secretary's office assistants worked staggered hours: a first shift from 7 A.M. to 4 P.M. and a second from 4 P.M. to 1 A.M. The first Clinton staff secretary took—and kept—several staff assistants from the Bush White House; they were an irreplaceable resource of professional skill.

The staff secretary supervises two very large White House support organizations—the Correspondence Office and the Office of Records Management—as well as the smaller office of the executive clerk. These three entities are described in part 3 of this book.

The Assistant to the President for Management and Administration

President Reagan initiated the position of assistant to the president for management and administration within the ganglia of centripetal White House offices; President Bush elevated it in rank and made it directly accountable to the chief executive. Mr. Bush then made this officer responsible for the largest unit in the modern White House, the Military Office (discussed in part 3). He also gave his assistant for management and administration supervisory authority over the Office of Administration (OA)—the unit in the Executive Office of the President that President Carter had created by executive order in 1977 to consolidate Executive Office administrative functions.[31]

The third segment of the management and administration office is the White House Operations section, which encompasses the Conference Center, the Intern Program, the Photography Office, the Travel Office, and the Visitors Office—all described in part 3.

The assistant for management and administration is the control point in the White House for budget, staff, space, and privileges. Can so-and-so have a bigger office? Is special assistant X going to get White House Mess privileges? Does deputy Y really need twenty of those minipagers? May this cabinet secretary use one of the White House–controlled military aircraft? As one former assistant put it to the requesting cabinet officer, "That's ridiculous; there's a commercial flight to London which leaves about every hour. . . . Have a nice trip!"[32] The management and administration berth is not for popularity seekers.

The Budget of the White House

Is there a "White House budget?" The answer is both no and yes.

As for the *no*, readers may be astounded to learn that with all the improvements in federal accounting and financial reporting practices that have come about in recent years, there is still no government-wide reporting system that requires each agency to identify—much less aggregates—the specific sums of federal dollars that support the presidency. Whether or not there is a chief financial officer within the Executive Office of the President (there isn't yet) is not even the point: there is no single account number or line item—common throughout the federal agencies—that would say, for example, "This is how much the Navy spends to support the presidency." When the General Accounting Office undertook to determine the costs of three foreign trips that the president took in 1998, it found the task extremely difficult—and observed that "the executive branch does not have a single system to account for the cost of presidential travel overseas."[33] Nor, strangely, has Congress ever mandated that such a system be put in place. So, no; there is no "White House budget"—no single amount, in one place, in any federal document.

But of course the answer is also *yes*: those expenditures exist, and if they were all discoverable, they could be totaled. The White House budget would be the specific outlays, including personnel costs, of (1) all the 125 units that constitute the modern White House (see the list of White House units at the end of the introduction to part 2), regardless of which department actually finances them (Defense, for example, finances the Military Office; Treasury, the Secret Service; Interior, the White House Liaison Office of the National Park Service) plus (2) the outlays of other federal agencies (for example of the FBI, for its personnel security investigations) that are not identified in the following list but that also directly contribute to and support the White House. The trick is to dig out these figures from multiple sources, some of which are allegedly cloaked for security reasons, and some of which are quite inexplicably concealed. Apparently no person or institution has put all these costs together; in the following list, the author has had to rely on personal estimates—which are, of course, only approximations.

The units that can be deemed immediate and identifiable parts of the White House are the first six items in the list; the figures are from the president's fiscal year 2001 budget as submitted to Congress in February 2000. The Office of Management and Administration controls these six segments; any internal requests for increases would come from the affected office but would then have to be negotiated with the assistant for management and administration—and then with the chief of staff.

Since assistants to the president do not testify before congressional committees, it is the director of the Office of Administration who annually defends these budget elements before the House Appropriations Subcommittee on Treasury, Postal Service, and General Government, and before its Senate counterpart. The appropriations hearings are usually businesslike, if not friendly—but not always. On occasion, appropriations subcommittee members will grumble over the fact that senior White House assistants don't come in person to submit to budget questioning. The assistant for management and administration will attempt to defang that resentment by personally going up on the Hill and talking informally with the subcommittee chair and the ranking minority member.

During the 1997 contretemps about overnight entertaining of political contributors, the assistant for management and administration brought along Gary Walters, the chief usher, to trace out for the subcommittee his meticulous billing procedures: "the eggs in this soufflé were billed to the State Department because it was for an international dinner, but the eggs in *this* soufflé. . . . "[34]

The next eight items in the list represent the cost of staff time and services that are contributed directly to the White House by non–White House departments and agencies.[35] (See the descriptions in part 3.) These contributions are based on arrangements that date back many years. While the terms of this support are negotiated regularly with the White House (primarily with the Office of Management and Administration), the contributing agencies themselves—not White House representatives—present and defend their respective budget numbers before various appropriations subcommittees. There is no place (except here!) where these figures are brought together. As noted earlier, these are the author's own estimates.

The following, the author believes, is the White House budget for fiscal year 2001:

1. The President and the White House Office $53,288,000
2. Office of Policy Development   4,032,000
3. Office of the Vice President (including maintenance,   4,027,000
repair, and restoration of his official residence)
4. National Security Council (including the value of   22,689,080
an estimated 130 detailees in addition to the staff
total of 60 specified in the fiscal year 2001 budget)[36]
5. Executive Residence (including maintenance,
repair, and restoration)   16,410,000
6. 50 percent of the Office of Administration[37]   21,868,500
7. Department of Defense: White House Military[38]   320,000,000
Office (eleven elements—the director's immediate
office, the Military Aides to the President, the White
House Communications Agency, the White House
Medical Unit, the White House Staff Mess, Camp
David, Air Force One, Marine One, the White House
Transportation Agency, Presidential Contingency
Programs, and the Ceremonies Coordinator)
8. Department of the Treasury: Washington-based   230,000,000
presidential and vice presidential protective functions
of the Secret Service (including the Protective
Research, Technical Security, and Uniformed Divisions
and part of the James J. Rowley Training Center)[39]
9. Department of the Interior: National Park Service   23,109,000
White House Liaison Office
10. General Services Administration: White House   9,450,000
Service Delivery Team (maintenance for the buildings
in the White House complex other than the Residence)[40]
11. U.S. Postal Service: White House Branch[41]   1,000,000
12. President's Commission on White House   753,000
Fellowships[42]

13. Department of State (costs of state dinners at   20,000,000
the White House, official gifts to foreign chiefs of
state, and travel expenses for White House advance
teams and other staff on international presidential
trips)[43]

14. National Archives and Records Administration: 700,000
Professional archival support

15. Estimated (unreimbursed) salary costs for the   3,214,000
eighty-eight detailees from the various agencies to
the White House, the Vice President's office, and
the Office of Policy Development[44]

Rounded total[45] $730,500,000

The Size of the White House Staff

The size of the White House staff is another principal area of White House management and organization that is fraught with ambiguity and controversy.

Presidents are filled with angst when talk turns to the numbers of the White House staff. There is somehow a sense that the word *staff* connotes a huge outfit, "interposing" itself between the president and the cabinet and subtracting from his own responsibility. The politically safe maxim is: keep it small—and out of sight. In his 1992 campaign, Clinton made what he calculated to be a politically helpful promise: he would cut his White House staff by 25 percent (he also proposed that Congress do likewise). Using some definitional sleight of hand (he counted the Council of Economic Advisers; the Council on Environmental Quality; the Office of Administration; the Office of National Drug Control Policy; and the Office of Science, Technology, and Space Policy as within what he meant by "White House" in his 1992 campaign pledge), he came up with a 25 percent reduction in February of 1993. The wisdom, and consequences, of this move will be discussed in the final portion of this volume. In subsequent years the president relented, permitting the staff to "re-grow" to come closer to meeting his needs. It was his Office of Management and Administration that was saddled with the unattractive task of enforcing the original edict, and it is this office that continues to control overall staff size. (And Congress paid no attention to Clinton's suggestion.)

The employment of a White House staff is authorized by Public Law 95-570, a 1978 statute that deftly balances the president's need for staff assistance with Congress's concern for limits on the number of personnel at the White House.[46] The law provides that in the White House Office, the president may hire twenty-five assistants whose salaries are up to level II of the federal Executive Schedule and twenty-five whose salaries are up to level III. Six more of the latter category are authorized in the domestic policy staff. Also in the White House Office, fifty people may be hired whose salaries are up to the General Schedule (GS) 18 level. Eighteen more may be hired at this level in the domestic policy staff and three in the Executive Residence. These positions add up to a limit of 127 senior staff members whose salaries are at or above the GS-18 level.

The statute then goes on to authorize the president to hire and fix the pay of "such number of other employees as he may determine to be appropriate" in the White House Office, the domestic policy staff, and the Residence, at up to the GS-16 level. The hiring of temporary experts and consultants is also authorized. A further section (see chapter 18) allows the spouse of the president to use some of the aforementioned staff services. A separate additional section authorizes the vice president (and spouse) to employ staff in the vice president's office: eleven at the GS-18 level or higher. The vice president's office also has the same open-ended provision that the White House has for additional staff up to the GS-16 level. The 1947 statute that created the National Security Council—exemplifying the latitude afforded the executive in those years—authorizes the council "to appoint and fix the compensation of such personnel as may be necessary to perform such duties as may be prescribed by the Council in connection with the performance of its functions."[47]

As a former OMA head emphasized, White House organization cannot be based on a "stovepipe" model, in which each unit functions with vertical independence. If the president needs some positions for his Initiative for One America, if the first lady wants to set up a Millennium Council, if the domestic policy staff needs another hand to deal with the issue of tobacco lawsuits, the head of management and administration has the flexibility to shuffle positions and move slots to accommodate changing priorities. Since short-term detailees, interns, White House Fellows, and volunteers are not counted in OMA's White House ceilings, appointments and assignments that use these categories of employees can be rather readily accommodated, but staffers on the White House's own payroll are subject to the described statutory limits and to additional internal management controls.[48]

A word about detailees at the White House: these are employees of departments and agencies whom the 1978 statute permits the White House to borrow. Detailees may be either career or noncareer employees, but their term of service at the White House is entirely at the president's pleasure. The same statute requires the White House to reimburse the home agency of any detailee who works more than 180 days in any one fiscal year.[49] A separate, more recent statute imposes some special limits: no agency may establish a Schedule C ("confidential or policy-determining") position unless it certifies to the Office of Personnel Management that the position "was not created solely or primarily in order to detail the employee to the White House."[50]

Congress requires two reports from the president about White House employment: First, section 113 of Public Law 95-570 requires the president to send an annual public report to Congress that lists, for the previous fiscal year, the number of employees who worked for the White House Office, the vice president, the Office of Administration, and the Office of Policy Development, and the total compensation paid them. He must also report the number of experts and consultants in those offices and the number of detailees who worked there more than thirty days.[51] Second, a separate statute requires the White House to submit an annual report giving the names, titles, and salaries of employees and detailees.[52] The White House contends that since names and exact salaries are divulged, the report constitutes "private and personal data on employees within the White House Office," and therefore transmits it to Congress marked "For Official Use Only." To protect national security, the president is permitted to exclude some names from this second report (for example, those on the staff who have intelligence duties).

How big is the White House staff now? Within the context of this volume, a better question is: How big is the White House staff community? The phrase *White House staff* connotes rings upon imposing rings of senior policy advisers; the phrase *White House staff community* simply refers to the cohorts of men and women who serve all the immediate needs of the modern presidency, from crafting a major address to oiling up his helicopter. They are, one and all, White House.

Here, as this book goes to press, are the parts of the White House staff community:[53]

1. The president and the White House Office (including the Office of the First Lady and the six "special purposes" offices described in chapter 17)   462

2. Office of Policy Development (that is, the Domestic Policy Council, the Economic Policy Council, and the Office of National AIDS Policy)   62

3. Office of the Vice President (including the staff of the spouse of the vice president and the sixty-member "reinventing government"   144

team; excluding the vice president's campaign staff)

4. National Security Council	190
5. Executive Residence (including the curator)	96
6. 50 percent of the Office of Administration[54]	101
7. Military Office (including its eleven constituent units, each of which is made up principally of Department of Defense personnel who directly support the president)	2,200
8. Secret Service (Washington-based presidential and vice-presidential protective units, including the Protective Research, Technical Security, and Uniformed Divisions and part of the James J. Rowley Training Center)[55]	1,200
9. White House Liaison Office of the National Park Service	100
10. White House Service Delivery Team (part of the General Services Administration)[56]	133
11. U.S. Postal Service White House Branch	21
12. President's Commission on White House Fellowships	6
13. White House interns (as of the fall semester, 1999)	200
14. Volunteers at the White House (total available pool)	1,000
Total White House staff community	5,915

The Chief of Staff

It seemed as if two traditions were in the making: Republican presidents, following the Eisenhower model, emplaced chiefs of staff in their White Houses; Democratic presidents, aghast at the Nixon experience, shunned the idea. The second "tradition" came to a halt with Clinton. As presidential scholar James Pfiffner succinctly put it: "A chief of staff is essential in the modern White House."[57]

This chapter has described four of the elements of centripetal force that help tie together all the policy offices of the contemporary White House. The fifth, the chief of staff, is the nexus of those centripetal players: the first four support the chief's function. Beyond the chief of staff, there is only the president to try to knit his administration into a coherent set of institutions—and the president has vastly graver, and "undelegatable," responsibilities. The chief of staff is *system manager*: boss of none, but overseer of everything.

Does a new president understand this?

One former aide believes that a new chief executive often has a misconception:

[Presidents] always treat chiefs of staff incorrectly. They . . . think of chiefs of staff as nothing more than foremen, hired hands basically. Whereas chiefs of staff and everybody else think of [them] as exalted kinds of rulers with great power. So I think presidents need to think more about staff functions—how the White House operates, how it's going to operate, and the kind of people they choose to be around them. They don't seem to have that sense of history about them. It's like staff history is below them.[58]

Thirty-eight years of experience—nineteen White House chiefs of staff—have, in this author's view, demonstrated a number of principles for effectiveness in fulfilling that central responsibility.

A chief of staff needs to be familiar with the unique pressures and pitfalls of public life in Washington. This means recognizing—and being comfortable with the existence of—the contravening authorities and forces from the vigorously competing centers of power in the nation and in the nation's capital: the cabinet departments, Congress, the courts, the press, the lobbyists, professional societies, interest groups, and the international community. The more successful chiefs of staff have had some thorough experience in one or more of those institutions. Former chief of staff Leon Panetta emphasized: "You really need to have somebody in that position who has some experience in Washington. It's just absolutely essential. The president can have somebody close to him, but it better be somebody who has some experience with what Washington is about, because that person has to make sure that the president isn't making any obvious mistakes."[59]

The chief of staff needs to have firm, four-way support: not only from the president but from the first lady, the vice president, and the vice president's spouse as well. Nagging doubts or lack of confidence on the part of any of these four will eat away at the chief of staff's stature and authority. The wise chief will stay in especially close communication with the vice president and the two spouses. But communication is one thing; responsibility is another. In the end, the chief of staff has only one boss.

The chief of staff should be someone who is not only close to the president but also very familiar with those who operated the campaign. Most of the campaigners will have their hearts set on positions in Washington, hopefully on the White House staff. The incoming chief of staff must be able to distinguish effectiveness in campaigning from effectiveness in the business of governing—and give preference to those who share the president's political ideology rather than to factional advocates who are not necessarily on the same "policy wavelength" as the president.

The chief of staff has comprehensive control over the activities of the White House staff. Comments Panetta:

> I had some military background—which was probably of even greater value than any kind of management background you have when you take a position like that. The role of a chief of staff is more like a battlefield commander: you've got a mission to accomplish, and you have to, sometimes, fight your way through a lot of incoming fire to make sure that the mission is done, but you need to have everybody knowing exactly what he or she has to do, in order to accomplish the mission. . . . It was very important to establish that the chief of staff had control.[60]

But what does "control" mean? One Clinton staff chief allegedly tried to keep most of the policy balls bouncing on his own desk: he acted as the budget director, the legislative liaison head, the economic and domestic policy principal—and was the major White House spokesman. He handled all those functions superbly, it was acknowledged, but how long can such concentration be sustained? Another Clinton chief of staff preferred delegation: each senior presidential staffer was given goals, objectives, and guidelines—and then held firmly accountable for achieving them. "You have to empower people!" he said.[61]

Former president George Bush would advise a president: "Get someone [with whom] you are totally comfortable. He/She must be a strong manager. Must be able to inspire confidence and loyalty in the rest of the staff. Must have had enough experience in some phase of life to walk in the White House door with a certain respect level already in place."[62]

None of the policy centers of the White House—including the National Security Council apparat and the offices of the first lady and the vice president—can be allowed to work independently of the rest of the institution. In the Clinton White House, the national security adviser and the vice president's and the first lady's chiefs of staff all attended the chief of staff's senior staff meetings. The chief of staff attended the NSC principals' (cabinet-level) meetings and the intelligence briefings with the president. If even the most sensitive national security issue is being presented to the president, the national security adviser and the chief of staff jointly go into the Oval Office.

Chief of Staff John Podesta described his relationship with national security adviser Samuel (Sandy) Berger: "The one person I do not view, from a policy perspective, as reporting 'through me' is Sandy. I think it works better that way. I am not only comfortable with that; I think that is the better model. As long as we get along. He runs almost every big decision by me; I don't feel left out by him. He can keep a deeper sense of what is going on in his world; I keep a deeper sense of what is going on in my world—and we are pretty well integrated."[63]

All presentations to the president are subject to the chief of staff's review. Issues—particularly those involving differences of opinion—are first vetted around the chief's table. The chief must ask: Is this an open process? Are the right people here? Have we asked the right questions? Are all the key options included? Has the "underbrush" been cleared out and the issues reduced to their core substance? Can consensus be reached on the lesser, "compromisable" differences?

The chief of staff controls the president's schedule. And the look-ahead period is not days but weeks—often, in fact, months. As for the schedule on a given day, the chief of staff's goal is to keep the focus on *the* principal event, ensuring that activities that would compete with news of that principal happening are downplayed or pushed aside. On policy issues awaiting discussion with the president, the chief of staff determines priorities: Which matters require attention and in what order?

The chief of staff controls the president's doorway. Who is invited to meetings and who is not? There may be some hurt feelings, but temporarily bruised egos are a small price to pay for conserving the president's absolutely invaluable time.

Review, by the chief of staff's office, of all papers that come out of the president's office is as important as scrutiny of those that come in. The president's scribbles and marginal comments are likely to be as important as the check marks in the decision box.

The chief will set up a special system for controlling the White House responses to congressional mail that contains important policy questions. Are budgetary issues being raised that require advice from the Office of Management and Budget? Constitutional ones? Is litigation possible? (The counsel must be consulted.) Who will draft the response? Have all the necessary clearances been obtained? Who will sign the outgoing letter?

The chief of staff may wish to have two or three deputy chiefs of staff. One perhaps will specialize in national security issues, another in management and operations matters, a third in domestic or economic questions. The various White House policy units may be divvied up to report on their work to the appropriate deputy *first*—before the chief of staff and the president get involved. Can such sequencing of reporting procedures be put in place without attenuating the relationships between the chief of staff and the principal White House assistants? The three most recent Clinton chiefs of staff all used this system with apparent success.

The chief of staff cannot avoid dealing with Congress. In fact, he may spend a great deal of time negotiating on the Hill on the president's behalf. The chief will likely have to take calls from governors and meet with the leaders of advocacy groups. As the chief does so, however, he always keeps the appropriate White House colleagues—legislative, intergovernmental, public liaison—closely informed and involved. The effective chief sets a firm practice: other staff members are not to be "disempowered." (Such wide-ranging extramural responsibilities are yet another reason that the contemporary White House chief of staff has deputies: to help create time for the chief to handle such external duties and not shirk his own responsibilities to the president.)

Perhaps the chief of staff's most sensitive judgment call is deciding where to draw the line: when to take an issue to the president and when to settle it before it gets that far. Podesta reflects:

> I think I have a regulator that says to me, even if the president is likely to be with the consensus of his advisers, I will still have to take it into the Oval Office. There is a level of importance which, even if there is consensus, requires that the decision be signed off by the president. I think Berger would probably agree with that, from the national security viewpoint. He takes care of a lot of issues over in his office. But there is a certain level of decision which you can't just inform the president about; you really have to have his input. He may say, "I don't have a strong view; you decide." Which he will often do, if everybody is on the same page. "We'll just decide it here."[64]

Podesta's predecessor, Erskine Bowles, expressed similar sentiments:

> I made a lot of budget decisions that some people would probably have taken, on balance, right in to the president. But the president made it clear to me that he wanted me to do things like that, and the reason is: everyone has individual strengths and weaknesses. I don't have the vision; I can't dream like Bill Clinton. I can't see the things he can see. . . . But I am a doer; I can get things done. I am a negotiator; I can take tough positions and say no. The president would never say, "Erskine, you go out and make this final decision and just bring

me the answer." At the same time, I didn't seek permission every time I did something. We would decide in advance what the ground rules were, what he wanted done and what I thought was practical. We would decide together: "This is what we have to have; it's going to be really tough." My job then was to "go to it." If he didn't like what I had negotiated, I expected him to let me know, which he would, quite clearly. At the same time, whether the results were positive or negative, good or bad, the president had to know it all.[65]

Readers will instantly appreciate what a thin line this is—and will recognize how easily an egotistical chief of staff could be tempted to get into the habit of walling off staff or cabinet pleaders with the dictum "Take it from me: the president has decided!" when in fact the chief, rather than the president, was the decisionmaker.

In the decisionmaking process, the chief of staff is always an honest broker. But only an honest broker? By no means. Presidents expect their chiefs of staff to hold, and to express, their own independent judgments about any issue in the Oval Office neighborhood. They must do so, however, without using their stature and their proximity to give their own arguments an "edge" over competing contentions from other staffers or cabinet disputants.

The chief of staff must be possessed of the exceptional sensitivity to recognize a presidential command that is given in unthinking anger, frustration, or exhaustion—and to lay it aside. Scholar Fred Greenstein quotes Eisenhower: "I told my staff . . . once in a while you people have just got to be my safety-valve. So I'll get you in here and I will let go, but this is for you and your knowledge and your knowledge only. Now I've seen these people going out, and I've gotten a little extreme, a little white, but pretty soon one of them comes in and laughs and says, 'Well, you were in good form this morning, Mr. President.'"[66]

Former presidential assistants Bob Haldeman and Joseph Califano both describe similar experiences. When Nixon issued an intemperate instruction on one occasion, Haldeman remembered: "I said nothing more, then stepped out of the office and placed the order immediately on my mental 'no action ever' shelf."[67] President Johnson had the same habit, and Califano used the same response. Califano commented: "After three years of serving on his White House staff, he would have expected me to have some sense of how to measure his true meaning when he spoke in anger."[68] (It is the author's belief that in May of 1993, when faced with what appeared to be a directive from on high to fire the staff of the White House Travel

Office, OMA director David Watkins should have emulated the Haldeman practice.)

The chief of staff or one of the deputy chiefs of staff goes on each presidential journey as principal manager of the overall odyssey, since a presidential trip, particularly one overseas, presents a very special challenge for White House preparers and coordinators.

For nearly half a century it has been the chief of staff's responsibility to convene White House staff meetings. Harry S. Truman was the last president to do so personally. Under President Clinton, Chief of Staff Podesta inaugurated what he called strategic management team meetings, a daily morning gathering of the legislative, domestic, economic policy, and national security heads with the deputy chiefs of staff, the director and deputy director of the OMB, the secretary and deputy secretary of Treasury, and a few other senior staff. One could almost have called the group the "White House Executive Committee."

Because of the chief of staff's stature and proximity to the president, invitations for media appearances—speeches, Sunday television talk shows—pour in. True, the chief is one of those in the White House best positioned to speak for the president—but any chief, even today, remembers Louis Brownlow's long-ago admonition to President Roosevelt: White House staff officers must have a "passion for anonymity." The need to explain or defend a president's actions may be almost overwhelming on some occasions, and a chief may be a spectacularly lucid and persuasive spokesperson. *Each chief of staff and each president will come to their own agreement on how public the chief's persona should be.* The author's personal preference is to give greater weight to Brownlow's advice.

The chief of staff must continually build bridges to the cabinet. While it is the fundamental thesis of this book that policy development and coordination are becoming more and more centralized in the White House staff, there is a risk in this development. Some cabinet secretaries, especially those with narrower and more specialized policy and operational responsibilities— and thus less contact with the White House—may tend to feel isolated, perhaps even alienated. *Locked in the Cabinet,* the memoir of former secretary of labor Robert Reich, evidences this sentiment:

> The Secretary of Transportation phones to ask me how I discover what's going on at the White House. I have no clear answer. . . . The decision-making "loop" depends on physical proximity to B—who's whispering into his ear most regularly, whose office is closest to the Oval, who's sitting or standing next to him when a key issue arises. . . . One of

the best techniques is to linger in the corridors of the West Wing after a meeting, picking up gossip. Another good place is the executive parking lot between the West Wing and the Old Executive Office Building, where dozens of White House staffers tromp every few minutes. In this administration you're either in the loop or you're out of the loop, but more likely you don't know where the loop is, or you don't even know there *is* a loop.[69]

The chief of staff's antennae must be attuned to pick up such alienation—early.

Concerned that the 1998–99 scandal investigations and impeachment proceedings had led cabinet members to have "gotten kind of distant," Podesta began a series of breakfasts at the White House for small groups of cabinet secretaries. "Seven or eight at a time," he said, "just to kick things around, listen to them, let them tell me what was going on."[70] A former assistant to Chief of Staff Bowles emphasized:

> One of the challenges for our office was to act as a nexus, and to remember to keep everyone in the fold, and aware of what was going on in different parts of the White House. It is so big and there are so many different things taking place. There is a certain level of paranoia when you reach certain levels of power in government—in which everybody wants to know what everybody else is doing. The family—the organization—in my mind works better when people understand what's taking place. For the chief of staff to collect information is important, but so is it for the chief of staff to share information.[71]

The chief of staff, finally, runs one more risk: that of becoming insensitive to the perquisites and privileges that necessarily accompany his status. The use of limousines and planes, proximity to the president, the toleration of what may be the chief's personal rudeness, the alacritous attention of subordinates—have gone to the heads of some. Over the years of their incumbency, having had to say no to so many supplicants (including members of Congress) will have added up to a paucity of close friends and a host of enemies. If the chief of staff—a Sherman Adams, a Donald Regan, a John Sununu—makes a stupid, even if unintentional slip, there may be only one friend left: and if he, the president, is embarrassed by the error, there is only the sad and sometimes precipitous exit. Would that the electronics wizards could invent a pocket-size "egometer" that would measure a chief of staff's ego, calculate his insensitivity index—and beep a warning!

The chief of staff is system manager, but around the cabinet and in the White House the system he is trying to manage throbs with centrifugal thrust. While the White House is a unifying counterforce to the pluralist cabinet, within the White House staff itself eighteen miniworlds spin in separate orbits. The four central staff offices described in this chapter, and the chief of staff, are the centripetal force for the lot of them.

PART THREE

The Professional
White House

CHAPTER TWENTY-TWO

Serving the Presidency: The Professional Staffs of the Modern White House

During his forty years in the White House, under seven Presidents, [he] has written a record of skilled and devoted service unique in the annals of the Presidency. Not only has he borne heavy responsibilities with great efficiency and uncommon good sense, but each new President in turn has learned to rely on him as a fount of wisdom, a reservoir of experience and a rock of loyalty. Guiding each new administration through its initial steps, standing as a staunch friend to all, he has been, in the best sense, a selfless partisan of the Presidency, and of the Nation that these seven Presidents have been able to serve better because of the help that he gave.

MEDAL OF FREEDOM CITATION PRESENTED BY PRESIDENT NIXON
TO EXECUTIVE CLERK WILLIAM J. HOPKINS

As a new president inches down Pennsylvania Avenue in the inaugural parade, the music and cheering proclaim an exuberant message: the changing of the guard. Unless the occasion is a second-term inauguration, the presidential and vice presidential families and their staffs celebrate the coming fresh start, the break with the past. The "empty" White House, the nation assumes, awaits the surge of new beginnings. The reality, fortunately, is not as stark.

Throughout the modern White House are teams of men and women who serve the continuing office of the chief executive: loyal to whoever is the incumbent and proud of their unique place in American public administration. These are the men and women of the professional White House, the support staffs for the contemporary presidency. Some of their heads or members will change with a new administration, but for almost all of them the morning after inauguration will be one more—albeit breathtaking—day in years of White House service.

The support teams are large, unknown, unsung—and indispensable. No book about the White House staff is complete without a look at who they are and what they do.

The Office of the Executive Clerk: The Oldest Operating Unit in the White House

Every office in the White House handles presidential papers, but one category of papers is so special that it is under the exclusive care of a staff that handles nothing else: these are the original copies of the documents that, signed by the president, represent his official public actions. Included among these documents are public laws, vetoes, executive orders, nominations, proclamations, commissions, pardons, treaties, reports and messages to Congress, and public directives to executive branch departments and agencies. For all such presidential papers, the executive clerk is just about the last stop before presidential signature.

The office itself began in 1865, and the executive clerk and his small staff work in a room that is packed with history. In a corner of their suite hangs a picture of Maurice C. Latta, who joined the White House staff when McKinley was president and served in or at the head of the clerk's office for fifty years. Latta's predecessor, Rudolph Forster, served for forty-six years; and Latta's successor, William J. Hopkins, for forty. The incumbent, G. Timothy Saunders, is already a twenty-year veteran. In the clerk's card file of presidential appointees, the opening entry is dated 1911. While the clerk's computer terminals blink with the urgency of the present, the surrounding shelves are crammed with the precedents of the past.

The executive clerk's office doesn't just "handle" the cascade of presidential documents: it researches them. Each nomination, for instance, is checked against the law that authorizes the appointment; the paper the president will sign is carefully compared with the precise requirements of the statute. In the clerk's office are twenty loose-leaf volumes specifying the legal authority for each of the close to four thousand nominations or appointments the president can make. William Hopkins began the compilation in 1952; today every page of every new law Congress passes is scrutinized for changes that may have to be made in the loose-leaf collection. As of August 1999, President Clinton had sent 3,108 civilian nominations to the Senate.

Frequently there are communications to Congress that the president signs but does not present in person—messages and treaties, for example. Drawing on a tradition of considerable antiquity, the executive clerk puts each such message into an envelope, pastes it shut with a melted glob of special red wax, and—with a brass die—imprints the presidential seal: the unique imprimatur of the envelope's origin. Each message is hand delivered to both houses by one of the staff of the executive clerk's office, acting as "the secretary to the president." (Historical vignette: when delivering the sealed messages to the House and Senate, Forster and Latta wore formal attire—coat and tails—and rode up to Capitol Hill on bicycles.)

A veto message will be similarly delivered, to the house in which the bill originated. The aides who undertake such deliveries are the only White House staff officers permitted on the floor of either body. The aide must stand in the back of the chamber until recognized by the chair; the aide then comes forward, formally bows, and addresses the presiding officer: "Mr. Speaker, I am directed by the President of the United States to deliver a message in writing." "The aides," the executive clerk recalls, "have on occasion been literally hissed and booed—usually good-naturedly—off the floor of either house" when delivering an unpopular veto.[1]

Enrolled bills coming from Congress are no longer inscribed on parchment but on paper that is specially designed for durability; they are deemed "presented to the president" (the Constitution's language, article 1, section 7) when they reach the executive clerk's doorway. The clerk keeps rigid watch over the ten-day clock that then begins to run; at the end of a congressional session, there may be two hundred bills waiting in the White House at one time. (Once one arrived without any room at the bottom for the president's signature; it was sent back for re-inscribing.) The clerk's office is the president's "pocket" for pocket vetoes (bills left unsigned—and thereby disapproved—by the president after Congress has adjourned).

As of July 1999, President Clinton had sent 1,164 presidential messages to Congress, twenty-five of them vetoes. (As of this writing, Clinton had not given a pocket veto to any bill during his presidency.) If, while Congress is in session, a veto is not received within ten days, an enrolled bill becomes law; on several occasions, veto messages have been rushed to the Capitol with less than twenty minutes to spare.

The president is directed by dozens and dozens of separate statutes to send reports to Congress, some of them annually. Over the years the cumulative total has come to be in the hundreds. As they research the newly enacted statutes, the staff in the executive clerk's office identify any new requirements for reports and determine which executive agencies are responsible for their preparation; they are especially watchful about expiring deadlines. When a report reaches the executive clerk's office on its way to Congress, it is first checked against the requirements in the applicable statute; the executive clerk's office then works with the staff secretary to arrange for an internal White House review. Once signed by the president, the report is delivered in the aforementioned fashion to Congress. Knowing, as they do, the exact status of each bill awaiting signature, the executive clerk and his staff field telephone queries from agencies and the public. A taped message recites to callers exactly which bills have been signed by the president on that day and which are on their way to the White House. On one day at the end of a congressional session, 2,400 calls were answered.

The executive clerk's office continues to be the modern end of a 135-year White House tradition: its computer records, notebooks, library, and card files are, fortunately, not cleaned out the night before inaugural, but are passed from one administration to the next.

The White House Military Office

Few in the public know—and few even in the White House realize—the extent to which the president is given hour-to-hour service by men and women of the U.S. military. Since the president is commander in chief, military support for the presidential office is everywhere in the White House establishment; indeed, the military group is the largest part of the White House staff family. It is also quiet, professional, and—except on a few occasions—almost out of sight.

The White House Military Office reports to the assistant to the president for management and administration. The director of the Military Office is a deputy assistant to the president; he is aided, in turn, by an active-duty military chief of staff. Beginning with Carter, every president has determined that the Military Office be headed by a civilian, but previous military experience is considered essential. Under President Bush it was a retired lieutenant general; under Clinton, a retired colonel with thirty years of military service.

Twenty-two hundred military men and women serve the White House daily; large numbers of others support the president and his staff on a less frequent basis. In keeping with the concept of the presidency as a civilian office, uniforms are rarely worn during daytime hours. Understating the presence of military staff is especially important when the president travels abroad; some host nations resent any visible evidence of U.S. armed forces.

Unlike that of the Roosevelt and early Truman years, the military staff today is not involved in defense policy matters; as described in chapter 3, these are the exclusive province of the national security adviser. The Military Office does, however, review the four hundred to seven hundred letters a week that their commander in chief receives from men and women in the armed forces; Military Office staff help to untangle hardship cases and ensure that the petitioners and their families are treated fairly.

The White House Military Office has eleven elements under its command, including the director's office. Although all of them function behind the scenes, each deserves a description in any book that aims to give a complete picture of the contemporary White House staff.

The Military Aides

The most visible military personnel are the five military aides: one from each service, including the Coast Guard. Career officers at the level of lieutenant colonel, the five are selected by the director of the White House Military Office—but it is the president who signs their annual performance evaluations. The aides' White House assignments are, of course, at the president's pleasure.

Each advance team includes a military aide; one is always on duty with the president. It is a military aide who constantly has the "presidential emergency satchel" in hand. Colloquially known as "the football"—because it is passed around—the satchel carries authentication codes and presidential emergency declarations. The aide who carries the satchel has been trained in emergency drills and facilities and is competent not only to open the bag but also to explain to a chief executive exactly what each of its contents is and does. (The vice president's military aide carries one, too.) One military aide, when asked by a group of young people what was in the satchel, humorously explained, "Well, let's see—there is the red button for thermonuclear war and the green button for 'more coffee' . . . or is it the other way around?" Writing in his diary, President Bush once asked, "Does Mil Aide need to carry that black case now every little place I go? . . . With the cold war over, I did not think it was necessary for [it] to go everywhere with me. However, Brent [Scowcroft] disagreed."[2]

Some military aides in the past have succumbed to the temptation to elevate parochial service viewpoints into the environment of the White House. Harry Truman's military aide, General Harry Vaughan, so vexed Army Chief of Staff Dwight Eisenhower with intercessions that Eisenhower "had to go right to the President to get who was running the Army straightened out."[3] When Ike became president, he was determined not to have flag-rank officers as military aides; that tradition continues.

The White House Communications Agency

The largest and a necessarily very secretive part of the White House military support team, the White House Communications Agency (WHCA), is an elite organization whose mission is to "to duplicate the White House telecommunications environment anywhere the president happens to be."[4]

While taking all its assignments from the director of the White House Military Office, who is responsible to the assistant to the president for management and administration, the White House Communications Agency is technically a "Department of Defense field activity." WHCA does not have contracting authority or disburse funds; for such administrative support (including auditing, budgeting, personnel management, acquisition planning, and legal counsel), it relies on the Pentagon's Defense Information Systems Agency.

WHCA is made up of fourteen elements: its director's office, seven staff units, and six operational sections. Within the White House, WHCA operates the signal board that connects the president with all of the nation's military and diplomatic communications nets. Each senior White House staff member has a telephone at home that is hooked directly into the White House signal board. WHCA also operates the secure voice board, a parallel facility that has worldwide capability as well. Secure voice is of special importance because, in addition to the espionage threat, there are radio amateurs whose personal hobby is to monitor presidential radio nets and notify news media of what they hear.

WHCA's radio console, which has the call sign CROWN, is the switch for radio traffic among, for example, the staff cars in Washington. WHCA runs the National Security Council's classified computer center; supplies communications equipment (including hand-held secure radios) for the Secret Service (on a nonreimbursable basis); and operates the White House paging system, which can reach staff members anywhere in town.

WHCA's 111-person audiovisual unit provides all the audiovisual equipment for the president's public appearances: mikes, lights, public address systems, flags, the presidential seal, teleprompters, and even the armored lectern. Within the White House itself, this unit (known as "White House TV") makes audio and video recordings of all presidential events for the National Archives; these can be broadcast over the White House's internal television system.

Every advance team has a WHCA member, and if the president is going to be somewhere other than 1600 Pennsylvania Avenue, WHCA will deploy multiextension switchboards, automated satellite-relay base stations, two-way radios, and pagers; even if the president flies in a Chinese or Soviet airplane (as Nixon did), portable and secure communications equipment ties him to the White House. As soon as *Air Force One* parks, a landline is plugged in and the blue "bat phone" connected at the foot of the ramp. A signal-board extension is concealed at every wreath-laying; WHCA even had a telephone at the Great Wall of China. The presidential limousine has four fender jacks for loudspeakers, should the chief executive want to stop and make remarks enroute.

When President Carter took a three-day raft trip down Idaho's Salmon River, in 1978, portable satellite links had not yet been developed. To keep in touch with the president, WHCA had to install and staff base stations on seven riverside mountaintops. The crews went in by helicopter, camped out, and leapfrogged from early sites to later ones. Since Secretary of State Cyrus Vance was preparing for the Camp David summit meetings at the time, four or five calls each day were exchanged between Washington's Foggy Bottom and the river-bottom White House in the Idaho wilderness.

A decade and a half later, when first lady Hillary Rodham Clinton rode on an elephant in Chitwan National Park in Nepal—a spot equally devoid of ground communications infrastructure—the INMARSAT satellite was hovering in space and WHCA's portable uplink was operating: Hillary could phone husband Bill in Washington to describe the tiger she may have been looking at.

Where once WHCA had to lug an entire switchboard on a presidential trip, now one can be pre-positioned in any nearby metropolitan area, instantly establishing secure, remote links between the chief executive and the White House. Less and less is there the need to lease expensive circuits or deploy squads of communications officers. For trips in developing countries that have little or no communications infrastructure, WHCA boasts two recently acquired Air Transportable Integrated Communications System (ATICS) vans. These are custom semitrailers, each with an on-board generator powering both satellite and radio communications. Because the ATICs vans are capable of self-loading onto aircraft and can also function independently as motor vehicles, they have further reduced the requirements for planes and personnel. The vans are especially suited for trips that are scheduled at the last minute, when there is little or no time to send out WHCA teams to rig up complicated systems in advance.

In fact, for presidential trips of five hundred miles or less from Washington, WHCA is switching from planes to ground vehicles to move all its gear. There are now encryption cards that can be slipped into slots on ordinary telephones to provide secure communications—by radio or satellite—wherever a telephone signal can go. Such technological improvements will enable WHCA to reduce its personnel and equipment costs even further. Other improvements likely in the future: secure wireless conference video (for example, extending to *Air Force One*) and secure e-mail by radio.

WHCA's budget has gone down from $90 million in fiscal year 1991 to approximately $60 million in fiscal year 2000. In addition, the White House—rather than WHCA—is now paying for some stenographic and other services that did not belong in WHCA's budget in the first place. In fiscal year 1996, WHCA employed 1,017 men and women; it is still authorized for 954, but because of the efficiencies just described, is operating with 100 fewer. A price is paid, however: the typical WHCA communications staffer spends 130 days a year traveling; each trip lasts from five to twenty-one days, and each "trip" day is between fourteen and twenty hours long—with no time off.

WHCA's director assembles management boards (drawn from the organization's own employees) whose task it is to analyze how well the agency is meeting its "customers'" needs, and to draw up plans that look ahead from six to ten years into the future. In 1996 WHCA went through a formal audit, the first in its fifty-five years of existence. The director was proud to tell the congressional oversight committee that every one of WHCA's 45,624 items of equipment could be accounted for.[5]

The White House Medical Unit

The president's personal physician and a group of twenty military colleagues from the armed services (five doctors plus physicians' assistants, nurses, and paramedics) are assigned to duty at the White House; the principal medical suite is in the Residence and a second is in the Old Executive Office Building. A dental suite is also available for a dentist who makes periodic visits.

The Medical Unit's principal patients are the two first families, including the children; staff members are permitted to use the unit's help in emergencies; even a White House tourist who is experiencing chest pains may be assisted.

In Washington, the physicians' first objective is to ensure that the president gets specialized care when needed (usually at one of Washington's military hospitals) rather than to provide it themselves in the limited White

House facilities. On trips, the medical staff provides support not only for the first family but also for those who are traveling with the president—for Secret Service personnel, for example, and even for the press. The president's personal physician (currently a Navy captain, an expert in internal medicine) always flies with the president; during public appearances, she takes care not to be anywhere in the president's immediate vicinity—to avoid even the remote chance of an assassin's bullet hitting her.

A medical staffer is on each advance team and visits nearby hospitals at every planned presidential stop, determining which hospital would be used in an emergency and which would be a backup; finding a backup facility is particularly important if a summit conference involving a number of chiefs of state is being scheduled. The hospital will likely be asked if a supply of the president's blood type is available, and the president's physician may even dispatch extra medical personnel to that hospital to be on hand if needed. A temporary White House telephone may be installed in the hospital that has the best emergency facilities, but the hospital will be warned against advertising itself as "the president's hospital."

The Medical Unit is in close touch with the Secret Service and runs weekly drills to be prepared for various contingencies. Medical supplies always include breathing equipment and antidotes for biological and chemical agents. The president has an annual physical and arranges for the results to be released publicly.

A presidential illness is not only a medical problem but also instantly injects the president's physician into a tangle of internal strains within the White House. There is likely to be a gritty three-way tension among the physician, the press secretary, and the first lady, as the three struggle to balance the public's need for straightforward information with the protection of the first family's privacy. "We should not be yakkers," commented a former White House doctor. "The public should know if the president is or is not able to go back to work, but they don't have to know his blood count or his urine's specific gravity."[6]

If a presidential illness is serious—with general anesthesia in prospect—the most elemental question arises: Should the president, pursuant to the Twenty-Fifth Amendment, temporarily transfer his powers to the vice president? (See chapter 6, "Presidential Disability.") In counseling the president, the physician, the president's spouse, the counsel, the chief of staff, and the vice president may all be swayed by different professional viewpoints or personal inclinations. How will the nation's interests be safeguarded from the potential dangers lurking in their individual biases?

One observer has proposed that the physician to the president be confirmed by the Senate—to ensure that Congress would have a source of direct information concerning the president's health. In 1981 a pair of physicians suggested that a "President's Official Physicians Panel be established, appointed by a special committee of Congress or a committee of high judicial officers."[7] This proposal was echoed by *New York Times* columnist (and former White House staff member) William Safire, who recommended, in 1987, that "the next President should ask a panel of doctors appointed by all three branches of government to check him out once a year, the results to be made public. In his case, the doctor-patient relationship might suffer; the patient-voter relationship would improve."[8] Strongly opposing views were put forward in 1988 by a distinguished commission co-chaired by a former attorney general and a former senator; the commission argued that "the president's physician must remain a person of the president's own choice. . . . [He] or she should not be subject to confirmation by the Senate or to approval by any other body, medical or otherwise."[9]

And where should the line be drawn between safeguarding the president's personal privacy and informing the nation? Said the aforementioned commission: The president's physician "should abide by the views of the American Medical Association Council on Medical Ethics regarding doctor-patient confidentiality and those instances when it can be abridged in the national or community interest."[10] The AMA language reportedly is that a physician is "freed from the strictures of confidentiality in the presence of 'overriding social considerations' and where there is the 'need to protect the welfare of the individual or the public interest.'"[11]

The physician's necessary involvement in issues of such import is but another illustration of the borderless swamp, in the White House, in which both professional skills and political issues are inextricably submerged.

Finally, a group of former and current military physicians assigned to the White House (including President Clinton's physician, Dr. E. Connie Mariano) asserted that "the office of Senior Physician in the White House should be an entity separate from the White House Military Office."[12]

The White House Staff Mess

Managed by the Navy, the White House Staff Mess consists of three adjacent dining rooms in the lower level of the West Wing that seat forty-five, twenty-eight, and eighteen, respectively, in paneled decorum, for each of two noonday shifts. Some two hundred staffers and the cabinet are eligible. Dinners are now served as well—a reflection of the lengthening White House workday. Private luncheons in their own offices are available from the mess for West Wing senior staff, and carryout trays are provided to harried aides on the run. At the entrance to the mess, hanging noiselessly under glass, is a hallowed symbol: the 1790 mess gong from the USS *Constitution*.

Presidential valets serve lunches in the Oval Office and occasionally serve breakfast or other meals in the Cabinet Room. The White House Mess is entirely separate from the first family's kitchen and dining facilities in the Residence. The mess and valets—a staff of fifty—are supervised by the presidential food service coordinator. Those who eat in the mess pay for their food, but the salaries of the Navy service personnel are borne by the Navy. When the president travels, mess assistants prepare some of the first family's meals, and when the chief executive hosts a dinner during a state visit abroad, mess personnel oversee the food preparation.

Camp David

Once called Shangri-La, but renamed by President Eisenhower after his grandson, Camp David is a favorite presidential retreat. Eighteen hundred feet up in the Catoctin Mountains, the 221-acre camp is a hideaway rest and recreation spot, ten degrees cooler than the valley below. A 1996 count showed that eleven presidents had gone there 781 times. Roosevelt, who visited on twenty-two occasions, "slept in a plain iron bed in a room with a clothes locker and a shabby rug. A bathroom door in the president's lodge never did close properly. Most of the staff stayed in unheated cabins and washed in cold water in metal troughs outside."[13] Margaret Truman wrote, "Deep in the woods, *Shangri-La* was damp and cold most of the time. I thought it was a terrible place and went there as little as possible."[14] Her dad visited it only ten times.

Today, after a half-century of careful refurbishment and development, there are some forty-nine buildings on the site, including seven fireplace-equipped guest cottages. The presidential lodge, Aspen, has four bedrooms, a heated pool, and a glorious view over the distant Maryland countryside. During President Reagan's years, $1.2 million in private funds were used to build a bell tower and a 130-seat octagonal chapel. The Bush administration added family quarters for Camp David's resident staff and new communications and guard quarters. The camp has a driving range, but only a five-tee chipping green and no nearby restaurants—perhaps a bit of a disincentive to the gregarious Clintons.

In 1992, former President Reagan's advice to president-elect Clinton was, "It's about the only place you can really walk freely and be alone virtually unencumbered. It will help you keep your peace of mind."[15] Camp David is used for much more than R and R, however. Presidents have also chosen to hold cabinet meetings and host gatherings of international leaders there, so a conference center has been added to the original facilities. President Clinton held a cabinet retreat there ten days after his first inauguration. (The cabinet members wore name tags and made a long list of "what we want to accomplish over the next four years.")[16]

The camp is managed by the Navy, at a cost of about $3 million a year; when the president is on the scene, security (a Marine Corps responsibility) and other staff number close to four hundred.

Air Force One *and the 89th Military Airlift Wing*

In 1990, just in time for the Bush presidency, two new Boeing 747-200Bs were outfitted (at a cost of $250 million each) as presidential aircraft, each carrying up to ninety-seven (passengers and crew combined). The planes are cared for at Andrews Air Force Base by a group of 160 Air Force personnel. Each plane (either of which is called *Air Force One,* but only when the president is aboard) is in effect a flying White House. Each has a presidential suite (complete, for the first time, with VIP shower); a private presidential office; a staff conference room that seats eight; separate space that can be converted into a complete trauma center with a foldout operating table; and an office area fully equipped with computer, fax, and copiers (so that a speech can not only be composed but also edited and reproduced in flight). There are a guest area, a Secret Service section, a fourteen-seat rear compartment for the press, and seven bathrooms. An entertainment menu has eighteen movies available; three digital clocks show the time in Washington, at the plane's current location, and at its destination. The passengers have access to eighty-seven telephones (some white, others beige for classified conversations), sixteen video monitors, and eleven videocassette recorders. The entire upper deck is given over to state-of-the-art communications gear. There is no "escape pod," but the plane has sophisticated antijamming and antimissile gear, a tactical collision-avoidance system, wind-shear detection capabilities, wiring that is protected against the electromagnetic effects of a nuclear blast—and aerial refueling capacity, should that be needed beyond the plane's initial range of 9,600 miles. Complete with gum-and-candy basket and boxes of M&Ms, *Air Force One* flies at six hundred miles an hour—and costs at least $35,000 an hour to operate.

A new, 140,000-square-foot hangar—110 feet high and 500 yards across—was built at Andrews to accommodate the presidential planes. The

Presidential Aircraft

The Boeing 747-200B is only the latest in a line of presidential aircraft. Its predecessor, SAM (Special Air Mission) 27000, a Boeing 707, began duty August 4, 1972. It was first used by President Nixon in February of 1973 and continued until recently in a backup role, carrying the vice president, the secretaries of State and Defense, and congressional delegations. Before SAM 27000 there was SAM 26000, also a Boeing 707, which entered service in October 1962 and flew 13,000 hours—including backup service as late as 1998, when it was retired to Wright-Patterson Air Force Base, in Ohio.

The very first presidential jet plane was *Queenie* (number 58-6970), which served for thirty-seven years beginning in May of 1959. On its inaugural presidential flight, *Queenie* carried President Eisenhower to West Germany to meet with Chancellor Adenauer. *Queenie* was retired in June of 1996 to the Boeing Museum of Flight, in Seattle. *Queenie's* predecessor was a Lockheed Constellation, *Columbine II*, Ike's favorite from 1953 to 1959. It was the first plane to which the Air Force gave the designation *Air Force One*. In 1989, after twenty years in a junkyard, *Columbine II* was rescued, restored, and refitted. *Columbine I*, also a Constellation, is on display in the Pima Air Museum, in Tucson.

President Truman's DC-6 plane, "Sam Fox" ("Special Flight") 6505, was called the *Independence;* Roosevelt's "Sam Fox 7451" (made by Douglas in 1944) was named the *Sacred Cow.* His very first—a borrowed Pan American airliner—was used to transport him to the Casablanca conference with Prime Minister Winston Churchill in 1943.[1]

1. See J. F. Ter Horst and Col. Ralph Albertazzie, *The Flying White House: The Story of Air Force One* (New York: Coward, McCann and Geoghegan), chapter 2.

planes have more landing wheels than their predecessors, so their "footprint" is lighter, enabling them to land at smaller airports; each also has its own extendable staircase.

Each of the huge blue and silver planes is symbol as well as transportation; as the advance teams report, crowds come to presidential arrivals as eager to see *Air Force One* as to see the chief executive himself.

The 89th Military Airlift Wing, also based at Andrews, has a stable of SAM (Special Air Mission) aircraft that are available—but only with White House approval—for use by the vice president, members of the cabinet, and official congressional delegations. The Air Force recently purchased four new Boeing 757-200 aircraft for this purpose, replacing the older, fuel-gobbling C-137s that dated from the 1960s. A smaller aircraft is also available for the president's use on short domestic flights.

Marine Helicopter Squadron One (HMX-1)

Marine Helicopter Squadron One, with a crew of two hundred, primarily uses nine Sikorsky Black Hawk and Boeing helicopters. The president's *Marine One*, a Sikorsky VH-3D Sea King, has its home base for maintenance and repair at the Marine Corps Base at Quantico, Virginia, but it operates from the Anacostia Naval Air Station, only minutes downriver from the White House; the Bush administration built a new hangar there for the presidential aircraft.

Marine One, with special communications gear and an interior modified for comfort and sound suppression, can carry fourteen passengers and their luggage. Its presidential helipad is the South Lawn of the White House: three bright disks are placed on the grass where the wheels must land, and a portable control tower is trundled into position when the big "white top" bird is approaching.

Because the Sea King won't fit into a transport aircraft unless its rotors are removed (which then requires that it be reassembled and flight-tested before use), an "executive" version of the Black Hawk has been developed for trips abroad. This ten-passenger VH60N is smaller than the Sea King and transportable for overseas use, saving on both staff time and money. An extra-large 'copter was tested a few years ago, but the blast from its blades blew limbs down from treasured White House trees, and the experiment was not repeated.

The White House Transportation Agency

Fifty military chauffeurs, on rotating duty, drive cars for White House staff members on official business. (The former privilege of home-to-office transportation is now rarely, if ever, provided.) The radio-equipped cars put every staffer within reach of every other one. When trips begin or end, the

Transportation Agency staff are the baggage coordinators for the first family, guests, and staff, helping to ensure the security of the cargo and luggage on *Air Force One* and the accompanying support planes.

Presidential Contingency Programs

The fifty-five-person Presidential Contingency Programs unit reviews and keeps current the various options a president has for evacuation and security in emergency situations. It was Eisenhower who took this planning the most seriously: he would annually move his whole cabinet to relocation centers and convene the cabinet members to discuss hypothetical postattack recovery actions. "After a nuclear exchange it would be the blind leading the blind," he used to remind them. "If you just knew where your desk was, you would at least be ahead of chaos."[17]

The Ceremonies Coordinator

If White House events require the presence of military units such as honor guards, bands, the Herald Trumpets, or other musical ensembles, the ceremonies coordinator serves as the link between the Military Office and the Military District of Washington in making the necessary arrangements.

Asked what he would tell a future president, a Military Office senior staffer reflected: "To have a feel for this place—to understand what our roles and functions are. A lot of people, especially those new to this place, don't know all of our Military Office components, how we interact with the president's staff to make things happen. We need to have a constant dialogue between the White House civilian staff and the military. The president's personal staff is working to support him; we are working to support him. We must have a rapport—and that is what we have done in the Clinton administration."[18]

The Secret Service

The Secret Service regards itself as the premier law enforcement agency in America, and it has the premier task: protecting the nation's executive branch political leadership.

Who Is Protected?

The law authorizes Secret Service protection for the president and vice president and for the president-elect and the vice-president-elect—and prohibits them from declining this protection. Others who are eligible for protection (and who may decline it) include the immediate families of the two top officers; former presidents, their spouses, and their children under the age of sixteen (for ten years after leaving the White House); and visiting foreign heads of state. Almost all of those eligible have accepted protection.

Also eligible for protection (if the president directs) are "other distinguished foreign visitors to the United States" and U.S. envoys being sent on special missions abroad.[19] Members of the White House staff who have received threats on their life may also be given coverage, at the discretion of the president. Major candidates for president may be granted Secret Service protection if the coverage is approved by a committee of five (the majority and minority leaders of both the Senate and the House plus a fifth member chosen by the other four).

Some mutual benefit accrues when a Secret Service protective detail guards a candidate during a presidential campaign: the candidate comes to learn why and how the service does its work and how professional the agents are. If that candidate becomes president, the mutual trust and understanding—indispensable between protector and protectee—are that much further advanced.

Protecting world leaders when they are in the United States can be a considerable challenge for the Secret Service. During the fiftieth anniversary of the United Nations, in 1996, more than 150 foreign heads of state gathered in New York City; during the NATO summit, in 1999, more than 60 heads of government were in Washington simultaneously. The Foreign Missions section of the Secret Service's Uniformed Division protects the Washington embassies of foreign nations.

The 5,100-person Secret Service has 2,200 agents in Washington and in 126 field offices, including fourteen foreign cities such as Moscow, Hong Kong, and Bangkok. Its Uniformed Division consists of 1,100 officers at the White House and on the embassy patrols; 1,800 professional and support staff also serve. The director of the Secret Service is appointed by the secretary of the Treasury but historically has always come from within the ranks of the service itself.

Guarding the White House

Within the White House complex, several hundred officers from the Uniformed Division are on duty (in shifts) at the outer perimeter; others are in the middle perimeter, within the buildings. On the inner protective perimeter are the agents in civilian clothes: perhaps two hundred on the White

House detail, and a second group with the vice president. The Secret Service's presidential protective command post is immediately under the Oval Office; throughout the White House establishment, electronic locator boxes tell agents or others exactly where the principal protectees are every minute of the day or night. The members of the protective details are all professionals: there was neither a "Bush" nor a "Clinton" detail; the agents' assignments vary from three to five years and therefore often overlap a four-year presidential term.

The largest unit of the Secret Service in Washington is its Technical Security Division, which provides the physical security for the White House, the residence of the vice president, Camp David, and the homes of former presidents. This division built the hydraulic gates at the vehicular entrances to the White House, emplaced bollards (the massive concrete posts) on the sidewalks around the White House, and installed the video and alarm systems located just inside the perimeter of the White House and the vice presidential residence. On the division's staff are experts in the detection of listening devices, weapons, and radioactive or other materials that could endanger those being protected. "Red teams" practice penetration to make "vulnerability assessments." Packages are X-rayed, and bomb squads are on call.

Several hundred weapons are detected every year at the White House gates, almost all of them carried by people who have state permits to do so. Unless they are among the very few who have District of Columbia permits, however, pistol packers are taken to local police headquarters for the embarrassment of arraignment (although the D.C. felony charge is usually reduced to a misdemeanor).

People who are mentally ill walk in off the street demanding to see the president, and about 250 each year are taken to the District of Columbia's St. Elizabeth's Hospital for observation. There have been so many of these cases that the District had to sue the federal government to get reimbursed for the expense of handling them.

The Secret Service has made a recent addition to its patrols of the White House perimeter: bicycles. In black combat gear and silver helmets, radio-equipped officers use twenty-four-gear mountain bikes to cruise President's Park and keep on the lookout for suspicious lurkers.

Long before the drunken and cocaine-addicted pilot flew his small plane into the south wall of the White House in September 1994, airspace over all of downtown Washington, as well as over the vice president's residence, had been prohibited to all aircraft flying below 18,000 feet. But there have been frequent unintentional violations: thirteen in fiscal year 1996, twenty-seven in FY 1997, and twenty in FY 1998. In January of 1999, when a private plane, pushed by high winds, unintentionally entered the restricted airspace over the White House, the Secret Service launched a red flare—"to warn the pilot and assist him," explained spokesman James Mackin.[20] The service reportedly has a "radar repeater" which, connected to several local Federal Aviation Administration (FAA) installations, picks up images of intruding planes so quickly that the service notifies FAA controllers before even the controllers themselves have noticed the violation.[21] A 1983 *Time* magazine story indicated that fixed-base ground-to-air missiles had been installed in the White House area; shoulder-fired Red Eye antiaircraft weapons are also reportedly stored for use.[22]

Screening Visitors

Entrance to the White House complex—that is, to the White House, the New Executive Office Building, and the Old Executive Office Building—is available only to (1) pass-holders, such as White House staff; (2) couriers and delivery personnel who are on an "access list," who have identification, and for whom permission to enter is confirmed by a phone call from the appropriate office in the White House; (3) ticket holders on tours; (4) invitees to social occasions (with preclearance and identification); and (5) guests entering at the request of pass-holders.

For the fifth category, the Secret Service has used the Worker and Visitor Entrance System (WAVES) since 1984. First, the WAVES Center obtains the names of the pass-holder making the request and of the person to be visited. Next, the center requests the name, date of birth, and social security number of the prospective guest. The center then conducts a "national agency check" of the guest through the National Crime Information Center; the check reveals any criminal history or outstanding warrants. A "hit" is communicated to the Secret Service's presidential, vice presidential, or White House protective division (depending on who is to be visited), and a Secret Service supervisor determines whether the visitor can be admitted with a pass-holder escort or a Uniformed Division escort—or not admitted at all. The service looks only at potential security risk, not at the individual's "suitability" or "appropriateness." An *XX* is put beside the name of anyone who is given conditional entrance or denied entrance.

At the end of each month, WAVE records (in keeping with the Privacy Act, minus the *XX* notations) are transferred to the White House archives; lists can easily be compiled of how many times a given individual has come into the White House and whom he or she has visited. As of May 1997, there were 6,500 pass-holders, and an additional 6,800 workers, members of the press, or others had been permitted access.[23] In a typical recent year some 1.5 million tourists; over 216,000 official visitors; more than 18,000 guests; and 88,000 couriers, delivery people, and messengers were admitted to the White House complex.

Gamma-radiation detectors have been installed to supplement the regular magnetometers that screen White House visitors.

Identifying Threats

The Secret Service's Protective Research Division has devoted a great deal of effort to attempting to determine whether people who are a threat to a protectee can be identified in advance. Is there a "profile" of a would-be assassin? From 1992 to 1997, in conjunction with the Bureau of Prisons and the National Institute of Justice, the service undertook the Exceptional Case Study Project, which investigated the "thinking and behavior of . . . 83 persons known to have attacked or approached to attack a prominent public official" in the United States during the years 1949–96.[24]

What did they find? The researchers discredited three myths: (1) that there is "a" profile, (2) that assailants are mentally ill, and (3) that attackers threaten their targets directly in advance. They did find, however, that two-thirds of the attackers "did tell family members, friends, colleagues and associates about their thoughts and plans, or they wrote down their ideas in journals or diaries."[25]

These findings clearly pose an extremely complicated challenge to those who are protectors. If the government had total intelligence about everyone's private comments and writings, then it might know who is dangerous. But that is not the kind of government the nation would ever want. "There's no hard and fast way yet to make those predictions," explained one agent. "Intuition still plays a major role."[26] But profiling research continues; the Secret Service enlists the assistance of psychiatrists and other members of the mental health community, artificial intelligence computers, and the FBI. "At one time," commented a former Secret Service official, "the mental health experts said that our agents' gut reaction is as good as their Ph.D.'s: their street experience works just as well."[27]

At any time and almost any place in the world where there is a bombing or an assassination attempt, the Secret Service will try to collect data, make comparisons, learn new lessons. Even Hollywood is not overlooked as a source. If a screenwriter dreams up a bizarre attack technique (for example, the plastic gun in the film *In the Line of Fire*) the Secret Service will reproduce it in its own testing lab. "We are constantly second-guessing ourselves," said a former official.[28] Assassination attempts on foreign leaders abroad are included in the Secret Service's study agenda.

The service's Protective Research Division maintains a list of several thousand Americans who are potential threats. Some four hundred of them are on a "watch list" of individuals who are known to be dangerous; field-office agents will periodically check to see where they are and what they are doing. The agents may visit the person's relatives and ask, "How's Joe these days?" The families are often aware of the potential danger and genuinely cooperative.

Some angry or mentally ill people write threatening letters to the president (a felony). The Secret Service has a unique computerized system for matching handwriting—the largest database of its kind. As is the case with a fingerprint collection, samples from unknown sources can be compared with known samples on file.

Providing Protection during Trips

A presidential trip requires extra mobilization of the Secret Service's resources. When any protectee travels, the usual protective detail is augmented by agents from the service's field offices. "Our mission is to duplicate the White House protective environment," declared one agent.[29] And how frequently does this requirement arise? The service measures a trip in "stops"—that is, when the limousine comes to a halt or when the airplane lands and the protectee gets out of it for an event, however brief. As was noted in chapter 16, during his first seven years in office, President Clinton made some 2,500 appearances in over 800 cities here and abroad plus some 450 appearances at public events in the Washington area; the first lady visited 83 countries. Vice President Gore and his wife have been almost equally on the move.

If the trip is domestic, the Protective Research Division's entire collection of several thousand names—especially those on the watch list—will be combed in relation to each area the president will visit. The division will then compile a "trip file" of perhaps one hundred names and ask state and local police to help account for all those on the list. Some who are in the trip file who have threatened the president outright may already have been prosecuted and jailed. If detention is not possible and a presidential trip is imminent, the agents may begin temporary surveillance: "We will sit on them for a day," one agent explained. Another remembered, "I have been sued sixty times for invasion of privacy or false arrest, and won every time." Just before the trip starts, a photo album is made up of individuals who are judged truly dangerous but who have not been located; agents try to memorize the pictures.

Some years ago, the treatment of two groups of citizens who are not dangerous—members of the professional press and orderly demonstrators—raised controversy. A 1985 White House Correspondents Association report accused the Secret Service of letting itself be used by White House staff to keep the press away from the president—not for security reasons but to protect the president from questions. This practice, wrote White House reporter Lou Cannon, "keeps the Secret Service preoccupied with the busy work of distancing the news media and saving the President from annoying questions. This inevitably diverts the Secret Service from its real job."[30] An arrangement has since been agreed upon in which the host committee or the White House press secretary decides where the press is to stand; the Secret Service stays out of that decision entirely.

In an arrival crowd, hostile demonstrators are anathema to public-relations-conscious White House aides; there have been instances in which the staff have tried to use the Secret Service to move demonstrators out of the way—again, "for security reasons." The Secret Service rightly resists this manipulation: the yells of demonstrators are much less of a concern than the sticks to which their signs are stapled. It was White House staff members who sometimes had to be reminded of the meaning of the First Amendment. Demonstrators have been less of a concern in more recent times. Research is being done on a device that may be able to detect concealed weapons in a crowd.

America's lax gun control laws are a dismaying problem to the Secret Service. Fifty-millimeter rifles and ammunition can be legally sold and used: a bullet of that caliber can go right through a manhole cover. Readers must reflect on the fact that the availability of this kind of weaponry in America poses a grave threat to protectees and a grave challenge to the Secret Service in its protective mission.

On foreign trips, each stop presents a unique protective challenge. As described in chapter 16, the advance preparations are innumerable. The federal intelligence community (finally overcoming years of territorial jealousies) combines its resources. Is there a terrorist threat? Will the motorcade need a counterassault team, a heavily armored and equipped "war wagon"? Logistics are reviewed: Will the presidential limousine fit through the palace gates? (One of the president's several limousines will be flown abroad and tested). Is a bundle of roses to be thrust at the first lady? The welcoming committee will be informed that it can't be done. (Presidential protective detail chief Jim Rowley once caught such a bouquet being tossed toward the president's face: it was full of thorns.) Will a helicopter be used? (When Ike went to Greece, a helicopter trip was planned from Athens to the cruiser *Des Moines* offshore. Would its flotation gear work? The Secret Service dunked the helicopter to find out.)

Because some foreign nations—such as Canada, Japan, and the United Kingdom—do not approve of the carrying of weapons, even by law enforcement officers, special arrangements have to be negotiated each time a presidential visit is scheduled. When one host government raised too many objections, it was told to meet the Secret Service's minimum protective standards—or the president wouldn't be coming. The establishment of Secret Service offices overseas has diminished such tensions. As a knowledgeable special agent explained, "Our agent in Moscow not only knows the territory there, but he has also created close liaison arrangements with the host country security services. He makes that bridge from the service here to the right people over there. We work very closely with foreign nations' security and police forces."[31]

Training

The Secret Service puts an exceptional emphasis on training. Federal agencies collectively share the facilities at the Federal Law Enforcement Center in Glencoe, Georgia, and the Secret Service has its own facility—the James J. Rowley Training Center—in Beltsville, Maryland. A new Secret Service recruit first takes a week of ethics training, then goes through eight weeks at Glencoe, then ten weeks at Beltsville, where the program includes firearms practice, driver training, water rescue, dog handling, and training in countersniper teamwork. Besides training the service's own agents, the Rowley Center trains state and local law enforcement personnel, with whom the Secret Service always collaborates during presidential trips.

The center especially likes to show off its capabilities to the protectees themselves—giving them a sense, close up, of how the protective details do their work. When President and Mrs. Clinton visited the Rowley Center in 1997, for example, they were shown how a motorcade would respond to a rocket-propelled grenade attack. The president himself took the wheel of a car and spun it around in the 180-degree "J-turn" used in quick escapes.[32]

"Reacting to What Happened Yesterday"

It is a sad and ironic fact that security for the first family and others has come about only through tragedy. The Secret Service was created in 1865 to hunt counterfeiters, but only after President McKinley was assassinated, in 1901, was the service given the presidential protective function. After President Kennedy was killed, the Warren Commission found that the Secret Service's protective research arrangements were "seriously deficient" and excoriated the FBI's "unduly restrictive view of its responsibilities in preventive intelligence work."[33]

The Secret Service's protection was extended to presidential candidates in 1968, the day *after* Robert Kennedy was shot. Protection was extended to foreign visitors only after a 1970 incident in Chicago involving French president Georges Pompidou. Carter White House officials blocked the installation of magnetometers at White House entrances—reportedly claiming that it was "not politically acceptable"—until a man walked in with a gun and said, "Take me to the president!"

It took the bombing of our troop quarters in Beirut before the Commission of Fine Arts relented and allowed the bollards to be set up outside the White House vehicle entrances, and the gates themselves were heavily reinforced only after a man crashed through the old ones one Christmas morning. The closing of Pennsylvania Avenue—long recommended by security experts—occurred only after the bombing of a federal building in Oklahoma City. "That truck-bomb would have flattened the White House," said one Secret Service veteran.[34] Former Secret Service senior official Robert Snow grimly summed up: "Protection is reacting to what happened yesterday."[35]

The budget history of the Secret Service reflects these increasing demands: in 1963 its budget was $5.8 million; its request for fiscal year 2001 is $826.6 million.

The growing Secret Service responsibilities—and budget—are not always viewed warmly. In 1992, after he and others in a congressional delegation were allegedly mistreated at a bill-signing in Texas, Senator Daniel Patrick Moynihan read aloud on the Senate floor a letter he had sent to the secretary of the Treasury in which the senator claimed that the Secret Service was "arrogant and presumptuous . . . a disgrace and a danger, its fantastic budget . . . fantastically bloated." In an accompanying speech he stated that "we are creating a praetorian guard which at the very least comes between Congress and the presidency and at the very worst poses a threat to the quality of the American democracy. . . . [It is] ubiquitous, overlarge and too frequently inconsiderate."[36]

The "Protective Function Privilege"

The most recent issue concerning the Secret Service arose during the Monica Lewinsky scandal. Like all federal law enforcement officers, Secret Service agents are obligated to report to the attorney general any activity which they observe that is criminal. Under that obligation, should agents guarding the first family be required to answer questions about what they see and hear in the course of their protective duties? At the request of Independent Counsel Kenneth Starr, Secret Service agents were subpoenaed to testify before a grand jury. Deeply concerned, the director of the Secret Service persuaded the secretary of the Treasury and the attorney general to argue in court for a "protective function privilege" that would override the broader obligation to report criminal activity. It was argued that without that privilege, and fearing an invasion of privacy, a president might push agents aside, thus endangering the zone of protection around him.

The issue had actually arisen earlier; during the Watergate congressional hearings in 1973, President Nixon had issued an order to Secretary of the Treasury George Shultz: "I hereby direct that no officer or agent of the Secret Service shall give testimony to Congressional committees concerning matters observed or learned while performing protective functions for the President or in their duties at the White House."[37] In the 1998 case, former president Bush joined the secretary of the Treasury and the attorney general in advancing this argument, writing, "had I felt they [the agents] would be compelled to testify as to what they had seen or heard, no matter what the subject, I would not have felt comfortable having them close in."[38] Former presidents Ford and Carter, however, along with four former attorneys general, disagreed.

The decision of the U.S. District Court went against the government: Judge Norma Holloway Johnson ruled that "a protective function privilege would contradict the goal of . . . [having] executive branch employees report criminal activity by government officials. . . . If Congress now believes such a privilege is warranted, it, unlike this Court, is free to create one."[39] On appeal, a unanimous panel of the U.S. Court of Appeals for the D.C. Circuit upheld the district court's ruling: "While courts must listen with the utmost respect to the conclusions of those entrusted with responsibility for safeguarding the President, we must also assure ourselves that those conclusions rest upon solid facts and a realistic appraisal of the danger rather than vague fears extrapolated beyond any foreseeable threat." The appeals court "said the Secret Service had fallen short of proving the 'heavy burden' needed to justify the creation of a 'new protective function privilege.'"[40] The Supreme Court, by a 7 to 2 vote, denied *certiorari;* however, dissenting justice Stephen G. Breyer argued that "one could reasonably believe that the law should take special account of the obvious fact that serious physical harm to the president is a national calamity—by recognizing a special government privilege where needed to help avert that calamity."[41]

The Secret Service, the Treasury and Justice Departments, and the president will have to decide whether to propose legislation creating such a "protective function privilege" and what kind of language will be used to do so. President Clinton commented: "[This] will raise some serious questions and present a whole new array of problems for managing the Presidency and for the Secret Service managing their responsibility. And because previous people have understood that and cared enough about it, I don't think anybody has ever even considered doing this before. But we're living in a time which is without precedent, where actions are being taken without precedent, and we just have to live with the consequences."[42]

In the end, the Secret Service must be an adaptable outfit, and always a professional one. If the president rides, the agents will be on horseback; if the vice president jogs or enjoys superpowered speedboats, they will don sneakers or purchase 495-horsepower engines. They know that they must never recount to one president the privileged confidences of a predecessor— nor can an agent even do the president's bidding: "Please hold my coat for a second?" "Can you find me some small bills for the collection plate?" Kennedy, at Hyannisport, once spotted the agent outside his door. "Why stand out there?" he queried. "Come on in and watch the ball game with us." The answer was no; from the professionals' viewpoint, even new presidents need training.

The Correspondence Office

Write the president!

And people do—in the first six and one-half years of the Clinton administration, the president received 20,521,715 pieces of mail (including faxes), plus 3,876,105 e-mail messages. Typically, the mail count is much higher in the first year and drops in the later years of a presidency: the first-year Clinton total was approximately 8 million. Within a few months after publicizing the health care initiative, the Clintons had received 700,000 letters; more came in at a rate of 48,000 a day. Other yearly averages: Eisenhower, 700,000; Kennedy, 1,815,000; Johnson, 1,647,000; Nixon, 2,687,000; Ford, 2,381,000; Carter, 3,532,000; Reagan, 5,802,895; and Bush, 6,100,000.

Some letters come in foreign languages (these are sent to State for translation), a few in Braille (with help from the Department of Health and Human Services, these are answered in Braille). Visitors, especially children, leave notes behind after their White House tours.

And who answers them? A cadre of anonymous assistants? Unknown departmental subordinates in far-off corners of the capital? Not in the Clinton administration. A youngster named Chelsea Clinton once wrote to the president—and never received an answer. When Dad became president the mandate was issued: Each letter to the president would receive a reply—even if it was only an acknowledgement card—over the presidential signature. Faxes and e-mails were replied to via regular mail. If an incoming query concerned a policy matter, the correspondence unit would draft a reply that could be used as a model for responding to other letters on the same subject, and would then check it with the policy officers on the staff. If the questioner addressed a fast-breaking situation, the response would explain that any answer was being "overtaken by events."

In the Clinton White House a staff of 87 assistants, between 12 and 25 interns, and helpers from a pool of 774 volunteers (on rotating shifts) kept up with the deluge. But the mail-handling operation did not go on in isolation from the chief executive. In 1995 President Clinton told a youth group in Boston:

> In my correspondence operation, every week they pull out a certain number of letters that are either especially moving because of the personal stories involved or that represent a large number of letters I'm getting on a certain subject, so that even though I'm President and I've got, you know, millions of people writing to me all the time, I have a good feeling for what's going on. I also get a summary every week of how many letters came in, what the subjects were about, what people said, whether they were pro or con a certain issue. And I read the letters and sign them and in that way try to really stay in touch with what people are thinking.[43]

President Bush's staff secretary, James Cicconi, wrote a note to all the members of the Bush Correspondence Office, reminding them of the importance of careful mail handling. His note had an illustrative attachment: a 1939 letter to President Franklin Roosevelt. The letter, as Cicconi recalled, was messy, crudely typed, full of cross-outs and misspellings. Its author told the president of a theory he had, by means of which an explosive device of incredible magnitude could be created. An alert correspondence assistant pulled the letter out of what would ordinarily have been the "nut file," and sent it forward. It was signed: Albert Einstein.

The Correspondence Office has a number of component parts—among them Agency Liaison, the Comment Line, Electronic Mail, the First Lady's Correspondence, the Gift Office, the Greetings Office, Mail Analysis, Presidential Letters, Presidential Messages, and Student Correspondence.

Presidential Greetings

From sea to shining sea, Americans celebrate important passages in their lives: graduations, weddings, anniversaries, honors, special birthdays. They invite the president, as a kind of national pastor in chief, to be part of those celebrations. It has long been a tradition for the president and the first lady to respond, but that tradition has grown into a significant task for the Correspondence Office and its corps of public-spirited volunteers. A special room in the Old Executive Office Building, neatly equipped with minidesks and walls of cubbyholes, is "greetings central" for the "pastor's" nationwide "congregation."

Incoming requests are arranged by the date of the upcoming celebration and then sorted, by type of event, into dozens and dozens of labeled boxes: "Eagle Scout Awards," "101-and-up Birthdays," and so forth. Handsome printed cards from the president and the first lady are in orderly stacks, but the envelopes are always addressed by hand. (Those who are celebrating birthdays of 101 years and up receive letters.)

A cohort of volunteers cheerfully come on duty, day after day, penning the envelopes with stately script. The outgoing envelopes are then stashed in precisely the order in which they will be mailed, to ensure timely arrival.

Presidential Letters and Messages

If events, groups, or personages deserve greater recognition than a printed card bearing presidential greetings, letters or even specially drafted messages are furnished; these, too, are part of what can be called the pastoral role of the American presidency. Many of the 23,000 nonprofit organizations in the nation send in requests (for presidential greetings at their conventions, for example); they arrive at the rate of 750 a month. The more attention a presidential letter or message will attract, however, the greater the need for careful staff checking before the presidential signature is added.

There are rules and limits: none are sent to judges, for example, or to fund-raisers; commercial events are taboo. The White House counsel or the national security adviser must often review both the request and the message itself. Unfortunately, some individuals or groups try to manipulate the message tradition for selfish purposes. They are foiled only by meticulous and seasoned review (the two most recent staff members who have had the responsibility for preparing messages served eighteen and twenty-two years, respectively). Even the best screening efforts can fail, however: a message of greeting to a testimonial dinner for a mafioso was caught by President Johnson himself, just before he signed it.

The rules, of course, can be bent. A document that described the proprieties for messages under the Eisenhower administration had this paragraph near its end: "Because the White House is located on the growing fringe of precedent, and because the President is a human being—with a heart much bigger than protocol or policy—he can make exceptions to all the above rules and regulations. He can write a little girl who has lost her cat. He can write a golfer who can't control his slice. He can write anyone, anywhere, for any purpose—and the addressee is always delighted."[44]

On perhaps six hundred occasions each month, specially drafted greetings are dispatched to organizations or events that meet the criteria. In the Clinton administration, a staff of eight supported this contemporary extension of a long-observed presidential tradition.

The gracious presidential favor of yesterday, however, may have become the mere routine of today. A veteran of the message business asks the recurring question: Do messages that issue at a six-hundred-a-month clip signal "the ticky-tacky presidency"? Has the pastoral tradition become too "canned," too manufactured? An even more troubling question is raised at the same time: Has the auto-pen to too great an extent replaced the president's hand?

The Comment Line

As chief of state, the president is "president of all the people," say the textbooks, and it appears that more and more of the people themselves are discovering this axiom. By the 1970s the White House switchboard operators were becoming swamped with calls from the general public. A supplementary answering system was designed, and volunteers were invited to come into the White House to help answer the thousands of public queries. The idea worked: like other White House innovations, the Comment Line has been continued from presidency to presidency.

A separate telephone number—(202) 456-1111—leads directly to the Comment Line office. Some interest groups or radio stations urge their members or listeners to call the White House, and broadcast the Comment Line number. Twenty cubicles have been built into a ground floor room of the Old Executive Office Building, and most are staffed daily by over one hundred volunteers who donate one or two days a week of their time. On the nights of presidential speeches or press conferences, extra phones are set up, and volunteers from the Greetings Office join in to handle the avalanche of comments.

The calls average a thousand a day, with as few as five hundred or as many as several thousand. The monthly totals range from 14,000 to 54,000; in all of 1998, 332,453 calls were received.

Most of the callers comment on current issues, supporting or disagreeing with the president. "We are delighted to have your opinion," they are told, and the calls are carefully noted: from what state, on what issue, whether pro or con. Calls come in from Americans living abroad; foreigners will phone in as well. Both a daily and a weekly report are forwarded to the president, with copies to senior White House staff members—and it is this kind of assurance that most of the callers want. If the comment is particularly illuminating, the volunteer will write out a comment message and send it to the White House policy staff officer to whom it would be most useful.

Some callers ask questions—Why is the flag at half-staff today? Has the White House always been white?—but the volunteers diplomatically explain that their responsibility is to receive and relay comments, not to answer questions. A few calls threaten the president (the Secret Service handles those).

On some issues, hundreds of callers will use identical wording—evidence that a campaign is being mounted. Many of the callers ask to speak to the president; he *is* the White House, he is *their* president. "I gave my dollar to his campaign, surely he can talk with me!"

Quite a few of the calls are from people with personal problems. They may be elderly or lonely, confused at what they perceive as a complicated and impersonal society. They telephone the White House, and, fortunately, find themselves talking to a friendly voice. Some of their requests are simple: Who is their congressperson? What number can they call to report a lost social security card? The volunteers will give them basic referral information, but the cardinal rule is: Comment Line staffers are not there to offer callers advice on how to handle their problems. Nevertheless, if the caller seems desperate and if the emergency can be identified as legitimate (a few are recognized as "repeaters"), the volunteers, making no promises, write up a "hardship case" note, which is passed on to Agency Liaison (described in the next section). In each day, typically, several such cases are passed on.

Occasionally there are calls from people who are mentally ill; one volunteer commented that the number of such calls increased measurably when the moon was full. "I just talked to God!" some will say, or "to Jesus!" Several will be in tears, emotionally ravaged, "If you don't help me I am going to kill myself!"

Most of the callers, however, are citizens who telephone the White House in the good faith that they are letting the federal government know of their opinions and that their views may have an influence on government action.

Volunteers are given careful training that stresses the rules they need to follow. Current issues are summarized so that volunteers will be alert to the likelihood of questions on those subjects. Volunteers are also taught to anticipate the stress they will be under at times—handling the tears, the emotion, the calls from those who are having personal problems or are mentally ill.

The volunteers never give out even their first names, identifying themselves only with an "operator number." This somewhat impersonal technique had to be instituted after a person from California somehow discovered a Comment Line staffer's full name—and came straightaway to Washington from Beverly Hills looking for her. The workers don't say that they are volunteers, with the result that some citizens upbraid them: "Why are they paying you if you can't help me?"

Comment Line staff are proud of the service they render: "But it's not like mail!" exclaimed former Comment Line supervisor Judithanne Scourfield, "A caller is very much there—a real person with a real problem!"[45]

The Comment Line is a unique part of the pastoral role of the modern presidency.

Agency Liaison

Masked under the prosaic label of Agency Liaison, five staff members in a room in the Old Executive Office Building personify a particularly empathetic extension of the pastoral presidency. To them are given the hardship cases: those scrawled in letters, those referred from the Comment Line office. A Vietnam veteran will ask how to receive all of his or her service-connected benefits; a school will inquire about obtaining computers for classrooms;

an individual who needs a liver transplant wonders about medical insurance; someone who wants to start up a small business needs to know where a loan can be obtained. Where there is federal jurisdiction, Agency Liaison staff will refer cases like this to the right federal agency, which can investigate and possibly assist.

Some writers or callers have legal problems: if the person fits within the low-income guidelines, a referral will be made to the local Legal Services Corporation (which is federally funded). Others are elderly people, and the local agency on aging (also federally funded, in part) can be contacted by the agency liaison staff to see about assistance. Hundreds of desperate people write or call the president: for them he is the ultimate ombudsman. These are the toughest of all to handle: people in urgent need, men and women who are sick, jobless, being evicted, homeless; who have no food for hungry children. They call the White House, the nation's parsonage of last resort. Here the Agency Liaison staffers will refer the case to the local Salvation Army or will try to identify other possible sources of emergency assistance, such as churches, charities, or the local government.

Each case is registered into a computer, as is every departmental or White House action taken. The White House aides will often locate and telephone the individual citizens, to get more of their stories firsthand and to find out what efforts they have already made to help themselves.

Those who write repeatedly and those who are attempting to milk the system are easily identified, but the cases of real need are kept current until some answer is provided.

Since the Clinton administration took office, Agency Liaison has handled hundreds of thousands of cases.

The Gift Office

There was once a "black hole of Calcutta" in the White House itself. This was the term used to refer to the storage area underneath the Cabinet Room—where gifts to President Truman had piled up—"so many we didn't know what to do with them," one aide remembered.

Today the facilities are different, but the tradition of sending gifts to the president continues. To the same president who is "pastor," his "flock" is generous. Some 15,000 gifts flood into the White House each year; what can be accepted, however, is limited by law and by the Constitution itself.

It is the Gift Office that receives every incoming gift, registers it, judges its acceptability, arranges for the note of thanks, and sends the donation to its next destination. Five staff members handle this delicate assignment: one alumna of this office served for twenty years; another was on the White House staff from Calvin Coolidge to John F. Kennedy.

Gifts from foreign governments are considered to be presented to the nation rather than to the president personally. If they are of more than "minimal value" (currently defined as $250), they may be displayed temporarily in the White House but are then sent to the National Archives, to be part of a presidential library; to the Smithsonian Institution; to the Library of Congress; or to the Department of State, for use in its official functions. (In 1839, over the protests of the U.S. consul, a pair of lions from the emperor of Morocco were accepted, housed temporarily in one of the rooms of the consulate, and finally shipped to Philadelphia and auctioned off.) Foreign gifts of less than the minimal value may be kept by the recipient. The State Department annually makes public a list of gifts received from foreign governments. A few years ago the National Archives put on an exhibit of such gifts to the president and published a handsome photo album of especially noteworthy items, ranging from curiosities to real treasures.[46]

Gifts from private citizens arrive from everywhere in the world—but principally, of course, from American admirers. If a president has a well-known hobby, he is deluged with gifts to match it. Clinton received pieces of golf equipment by the hundreds; when he injured his knee, the mail was immediately replete with canes. An Arkansas admirer sent Clinton a sheet-metal sculpture of a razorback hog. The Reagans were sent horses and boots, the Fords skis and ski clothing; Johnson was given dozens of pairs of cowboy boots; Bush got boxes of jogging shoes and a sterling silver broccoli pin. Some private gifts are returned; if they are kept and are worth more than $100, they are reported to the Office of Government Ethics, which makes the list public.

If there are children or grandchildren in the president's immediate family, toys come in by the hundreds. In 1954, toy maker Louis Marx sent over eight hundred to Eisenhower for his grandchildren; they were donated to charities in Washington and to Secret Service agents who had kids.

Whoever he is, thousands of Americans regard their president with benevolence and affection—and without regard to politics. An elderly gentleman wills the president his cherished grandfather clock, an excited fisherman puts his prize catch on ice and sends it to the White House. (Unfortunately, all food is destroyed unless it comes from close friends.)

Less benevolent are gifts with a selfish purpose—for business promotion or advertising, for example—or that could give even the appearance of exploitation (an attempt to gain favor or to pretend that the donor "has a connection" with the White House). The Gift Office calls on the counsel to help spot donations that might cause embarrassment.

For the Gift Office, interwoven with never-ending judgments about laws, regulations, and proprieties, are threads of warmth and humor.

Staff members come back from foreign or domestic trips loaded down with presents that have been pressed into their hands. "Glad you visited our school today," said one donor, "Love from Andy." Which school? Who was Andy? Gift Office staffers act as sleuths so that the proper thank-you can be be sent.

A retired nun knitted President Ford a ski cap, which he kept. When she saw him wearing it, on a televison news clip, the donor was worried that it looked too tight. A letter came in with her further instructions: he should wet it and let it sit on his head until dry.

Among the hundreds of pets sent in (they are never destroyed, always donated elsewhere), one admirer sent Nixon a live rabbit. The Gift Office called the zoo: yes, they would take the bunny—but please let them know ahead of time when the White House van would come; if the rabbit got mixed up with their other small creatures used for food, it would get fed to the pythons.

Professional Support for Records Management

Every White House creates records—important in the present, to be sure, but even more important for the future, as the building blocks for presidential history. Even amid the first day's celebrations, a wise president will think of the last day's legacy: the empty file cabinets of the inaugural afternoon will, in four years, become the treasure vaults that contain the history of his presidency. In fact, the law requires this preservation.[47]

The Legal Mandates

In brief, the Presidential Records Act of 1978
—Requires the president to ensure that his "activities, deliberations, decisions and policies . . . are adequately documented and that such records are maintained."
—Insists that presidential and personal records be categorized and filed separately. *Presidential* is defined as those records—including those relating to his *or his staff's* political activities—that "relate to or have a direct effect upon the carrying out of constitutional, statutory, or other official or ceremonial duties of the President." *Personal* is defined as "diaries, journals or

other personal notes . . . not prepared . . . in the course of transacting government business" or as records that relate to "private political organizations . . . and having no relation" to the president's constitutional or statutory duties; also considered personal are diaries, journals, or other notes "relating exclusively to the President's own election to the . . . Presidency."

—Permits the president "to dispose of those of his Presidential records that no longer have administrative, historical, informational or evidentiary value" if he first consults the archivist and the archivist tells the president that he is not interested in them.

—Requires the president, if the archivist notifies Congress that he disagrees with the president and believes that the records "may be of special interest to the Congress," to give Congress sixty days' advance notice of the disposal schedule.

—Permits the president to deny public access to certain of his presidential records for up to twelve years after he leaves office, and to others for only five years.

The Presidential Records Act applies to the entire White House Office, including the Office of the Vice President and the domestic and economic councils. Court decisions have determined that the records of the Council of Economic Advisers; the National Security Council (NSC); and the director of the Office of Science, Technology, and Space Policy (when he is advising the president), are also presidential records.[48]

To carry out this statute faithfully, the White House relies on several trustworthy and highly professional resources for guidance and assistance. In addition to the executive clerk, described earlier in this chapter, there are three supporting elements to assist with the care and preservation of presidential papers.

Records Management

The White House Records Management office dates from the beginning of the twentieth century. The office reports to the staff secretary, and its current director and deputy director are both alumni of the National Archives and Records Administration (NARA). Traditionally, the members of the twenty-four-person Records Management staff, like those in the Residence and in the office of the executive clerk, are invited to stay on in the White House from administration to administration; a few have had three or four decades of White House service.

The responsibility of Records Management is to serve as a central file, managing the records of each current presidency for the daily use of the president and the White House policy units. These records, which will form the nucleus of the future presidential library, are preserved to ensure comprehensive documentation for history. From the very beginning, the creators of the records—the men and women of the White House policy units—need to understand the distinction between presidential and personal records and to be sensitive to the importance of maintaining them separately. Their specialized expertise enables the Records Management staffers to give advice and guidance.

The Records Management unit receives and files all documents subject to the Presidential Records Act, including internal memorandums, government reports, and public mail. All documents (other than classified papers) are optically scanned into the Records Management electronic storage system. They can then be searched, displayed, and printed—all without yanking out the original, which is retained in the Records Management files because of its historical value.

A correspondence review section within Records Management proofreads outgoing presidential correspondence before it is mailed.

Detailees from the National Archives

Several officers from the National Archives and Records Administration are detailed to the White House. They provide general assistance with records management, but their primary focus is the chief executive's future presidential library. There are three such detailees at the NSC; three more presidential-librarians-in-training are scheduled to be lent to the Clinton staff before January of 2001. A fourth National Archives detailee is regularly at the White House to capture, on the spot, those official public papers of the president that are destined for publication either in the *Weekly Compilation of Presidential Documents* or in NARA's *Federal Register.*

Senior officers of the Presidential Libraries Branch of the National Archives are in regular contact with the White House records management team, to provide professional assistance and support. In 1993, for example, archives experts prepared a "guidance package" for President Clinton and Vice President Gore that included the texts of the governing statutes and the established rules for separating presidential from personal documents; it also described any contingencies that might arise. "It was just strategic to get this information over there at the very beginning of the administration," explained Nancy Smith, the director of the Presidential Materials Branch of the National Archives.[49] The archives staff and the president very clearly share an objective: to fashion a future presidential library that is a complete and well-organized inheritance for the nation.

Yet another NARA detailee in the White House is Ellen McCathran, the presidential diarist. She started her work in 1975 and has been attached to the staff of the White House Office of Presidential Scheduling since 1977. Her job is "to provide a log of all the president's activities for future scholarly research . . . and a source document for legal matters":

> the only complete source of information on the president's activities and meetings. The log lists by time all activities of the president's day, including incoming and outgoing telephone calls (not his personal . . . calls . . . on his private line), visitors, meetings, conferences, announcements, signing ceremonies, recreational and social activities, and travel. The log identifies the president's physical location, individuals with the president (identified by professional title and organization if possible), the length of the meeting and subject matter or purpose of the activity. The diary is compiled of information obtained from source documents, including an Oval Office log kept by the personal aide, and the president's briefing papers. The log traditionally begins with . . . the president receiving a wake up call . . . or having breakfast and ending with him retiring for the evening. The log accounts for the president's time and activities on a 24-hour basis.[50]

Ms. McCathran's computer organizes the log: chronologically from all the source documents and alphabetically by the name of the person or the subject. If a request is made that a given person come to see the president, the log can be checked to see whether that person has been with the president before—and how often, and on what subject. If the president is to meet a foreign official on an overseas trip: Have they met before? In an Oval Office meeting held two years ago, was topic A discussed? The daily records are available at the touch of a button, through a tightly controlled access code. The diary is, of course, a principal guide for the presidential archives to come: the tracks leading into history for the retired president and for authors and scholars in the future.[51]

Direct Support from the National Archives

The White House complex is crammed with presidential and vice presidential staffers. What is in short supply is space—filing space. Since the Nixon administration, the National Archives and Records Administration has been making a fourth contribution to the White House: cubic footage for overflow storage of the current president's papers. (Part of this "courtesy storage space" is used to stash gifts to the current president from foreign chiefs of state, pending construction of the presidential library.)

Some 11,000 cubic feet of storage space was made available to the Clinton White House at the National Archives building downtown. The White House retained legal custody of the papers; the archives staff did just enough sorting to enable the White House to retrieve any of them at short notice. Some of these White House papers—four hundred boxes of records from the first lady's 1993–94 health care task force, for example—have already been made available to researchers, as was the collection of video recordings of Clinton's speeches. Others of these records are still privileged or classified.

Archives officers are proud of the professional support they give and are always there to remind the White House of the importance of good records management—especially in these times, when the practices of retaining preliminary drafts and taking notes have so withered under the heat of subpoenas and investigations. As Sharon Fawcett, director of the Presidential Libraries Branch of the National Archives, emphasized: "We want the White House officers to think about the future—from the very, very beginning. The other thing we want to help the White House do is to create the best possible records, the most extensive records possible. In this climate—in this era—this is a very, very difficult thing to do.[52]

The Executive Residence

"The White House" of pictures and tourists—the famous Executive Residence—has a problem: it may be famous for too much. Many competing uses strain its facilities and pressure its staff.

As a Physical Facility

The Residence is a home: for president and spouse, children, grandparents, grandchildren, guests, and pets (once including a pony). It is also a museum of American history, culture, and presidential furnishings (and has been given full accreditation as such by the American Association of Museums), a display center for paintings and furniture, a magnet for tourists, and a secure redoubt. The Residence has seen service as a wartime map and command post, a wedding chapel, a funeral parlor, a nursery, and a church. Today it is at once a backdrop for television productions, a press-conference auditorium, a concert hall, and banquet center. The White

House serves as a flower stall, overnight hotel, performing arts center, physical fitness emporium, Easter-egg-rolling yard, movie theater, heliport, parade ground, carpentry shop, art gallery, library, arboretum, clinic, office building, conference center, and sophisticated communications hub. (Some reports allege that it is a missile base as well, though officials there deny it.) The Clintons added a hot tub (from donated funds) next to the outdoor swimming pool and installed a putting green of natural turf and a jogging track.

The White House—that is, the fenced eighteen acres that contain the Residence, its West and East Wings, and the adjacent lawns, sits within the fifty-five acre President's Park, which is a large rectangle encompassing the Old Executive Office Building; the Treasury Building; the Ellipse (on the south); Sherman Park (on the east); the area to the west that surrounds the First Division Monument; and, to the north, the separate small rectangle of Lafayette Park. (The "White House complex"—the area in which the Secret Service controls access—includes the eighteen acres, the Old Executive Office Building, and the New Executive Office Building.)

Some unscrambling of jurisdictional threads will be useful here. President's Park is under the oversight of the National Park Service. An element of the National Park Service is the White House Liaison Office, which is responsible for

—Maintaining the grounds inside the White House fence.

—Maintaining the grounds of President's Park outside the White House fence.

—Operating the White House Visitor Center (located in the Department of Commerce building), which dispenses tickets to tourists.

—Operating the White House Museum Storage Facility, a separate building in College Park, Maryland. (The facility, which meets museum standards for storage, houses spare furnishings from the White House collection.)

—Doing repair and stabilization work on the White House furnishings collection.

—Operating a separate nursery and greenhouse for extra shrubs and plants and bringing them in for special events on the White House grounds.

—Providing architectural, design, and financial accounting services to the Executive Residence.

Maintenance of the East and West Wings of the White House, the Old Executive Office Building, the New Executive Office Building, and the Jackson Place office row is the responsibility of the Service Delivery Team of the General Services Administration (GSA). The interior of the Executive

Residence is maintained by the Residence staff, a segment of the White House staff.

There are actually twelve agencies and organizations that have some degree of control or oversight with respect to the White House.[53]

The Residence is white—and stays white longer—because of special research undertaken by what was then the National Bureau of Standards, in collaboration with the Duron Company, to develop a paint that adheres to sandstone. The repainting now needs to be done only every ten (instead of every four) years. There are five thousand trees and shrubs on the White House grounds, many planted by previous presidents; some belong to rare species.

As an Operating Institution

Can the Residence meet all the demands placed on it?

Its staff do their damnedest.

The full Residence staff numbers ninety-one. No staff now live in the Residence, nor are the employees there responsible for any of the president's out-of-town residences. The first family, of course, has overnight guests at the Residence, but visiting chiefs of state usually stay across the street—at Blair House, which is the official guest facility for international leaders and is managed and operated by the Department of State.

The chief usher (a thirty-year veteran of the White House), who has an immediate staff of seven, is the manager of the Executive Residence. While all those who work there serve at the pleasure of the president, they are proud of their tradition of being career professionals. There have been only five chief ushers since 1891; the average length of service on the Residence staff is twenty years, and two recent employees each served fifty years.

Close to the north foyer, the chief usher's mini-office is replete with noise-less reminders of both the present and the past. A digital locator box flashes the whereabouts of each member of the first family; computer terminals blink out the details of the fine arts collections, menus, supplies, and bud-get. But on the wall above the monitors hangs a piece of charred wood from the British fire of 1814.

In a dark workroom crammed with buckets and buckets of blooms, a florist and her staff of three, plus eleven part-timers, make up samples of arrange-ments for the first lady to inspect, then assemble stunning floral centerpieces for every variety of Residence event. All cut flowers are purchased directly from growers or wholesalers; many are flown in from special suppliers across the country. (One hot summer day the White House florist supervisor, anxious about the cooling capacity of the refrigerated trucks parked outside, turned the control dial way down—and the next morning found iced buckets holding solidly frozen blossoms. Emergency deliveries saved the day for the upcoming reception.) At Christmastime, up to ninety volunteers come in to help arrange the floral displays and decorate the Residence.

When a reception is given, the social secretary and the chief usher must determine ahead of time how the financial arrangements are to be handled. A state dinner for a foreign president is financed by the Department of State. Some events are hosted by the first family but sponsored—and reimbursed— by the outside organization involved (with interest and penalties charged for late payment). A third category—political receptions—must be paid for through an advance deposit from the sponsoring party's national committee. (It was in 1998 that Congress, irritated at the practice of very late reimbursements, imposed the advance-payment requirements and penalties for arrears.)[54]

The Residence's kitchens are in the hands of world-class chefs who, under the Clintons, featured American cuisine. A state dinner or other major affair will require perhaps fifty contract butlers and other part-time helpers to serve the State Dining Room's thirteen tables of ten (the thirteenth table is called Number 14)—or, as has often happened, a South Lawn outdoor sit-down dinner for as many as 1,370. This means erecting a huge tent (which may take three days to set up); filling it with 137 tables; and setting out, in all, 37,000 pieces of silver, glassware, and china.

Nineteen work-years of overtime are included in the Executive Residence's $16.4 million budget for fiscal year 2001, but many thousands of hours beyond that are gifts to the United States from a staff whose dedication is legendary. "When I hired them," commented one former supervisor, "I said, 'Don't plan on celebrating any anniversaries or birthdays with your family.'"[55] They have no job descriptions; the unpredictable is routine. Are the cut rosebuds not sufficiently unfolded? Some warm whiffs from a hair dryer will get them ready for the party. Does orange pollen from the lilies stain white uniforms? Fetch towels and shake out each bloom before the guests arrive.

Each Monday the chief usher holds a what-is-going-to-be-happening-this-week meeting among all the Residence staff units—to minimize surprises and ensure that everyone is working from the same event-calendar. In addition to the meeting, a within-the-mansion-only computer system keeps each segment of the Residence team posted on every event and on every last-minute change that might occur.

"The growing fringe of precedent" is everywhere in the White House, and the old mansion almost trembles under its new uses. The East Room floor, new in 1950, had been nearly worn through by thirty-seven million tourists by the time it was relaid in 1978. During a recent musicale, heretofore an occasion for decorum and calm, the chief usher counted twenty-seven two-person news teams with minicams.

For each press conference the technical crews monopolize the East Room, jamming the stately ballroom with mikes and lights; the hosting of a huge outdoor dinner means resodding the lawn; helicopter blades whoosh the petals off the spring flowers.

Can the new presidency preserve the old graciousness? The loyalties of the Residence staff run in two directions: to serve the current master and mistress of the White House, and at the same time to hold in trust a revered place that belongs to all the American generations.

THE CURATOR. Not only is the Residence the people's property, but most of its furnishings are as well. For nearly one hundred years (from 1808 to 1902), outgoing presidents or their families auctioned off their White House china and furniture—with the result that very few pieces of original White House furnishings are left. That practice finally ceased, and in 1961 a statute was enacted that guaranteed the preservation of White House furnishings.[56] Today, once any president declares a White House article to be "of historic or artistic interest," it becomes forever "inalienable" and may be used, displayed, or stored—but never sold. Every June, the law requires the National Park Service to undertake "a complete inventory" of all "plate, furniture and public property" in the White House. To perform this duty, Lyndon Johnson, in 1964, established a new staff position: the White House curator.[57]

There have been five curators since the post was established, and their mission has been much broader than to preserve what is there: they have gone on the prowl for some of the original paintings and pieces of furniture that should be added to the White House collections. On the East Coast of the United States, in England and in France, auctions, antique shops, and even private homes were visited and donors contacted; an "adopt-a-room" program was initiated for patriotic benefactors. Fourteen portraits of first ladies, for instance, had been missing; seven have now been acquired. One of the curators found a Dolley Madison portrait in a museum's basement; a painting by Gilbert Stuart of Mrs. John Quincy Adams was discovered in a private collection. One curator (who served for sixteen years) raised $7 million in cash and collected in-kind donations worth $15 million.[58] Today the White House has forty thousand pieces of furniture, china, silver, and other items in its inventory; most are in use in the Residence. "The princi-pal public rooms on the first floor" says the law, are of "museum character." The curator and a staff of four are there to help them remain so.

THE FAMILY THEATER. Like most other Americans, presidents enjoy relaxing at the movies—but absent a presidential box, a trip to the local cin-ema means unwanted disruption. The Family Theater was incorporated into the East Wing in 1942. When a union operator did not show up one night during the Roosevelt administration, a naval aide commandeered a substi-tute from the Navy—and started the practice of having a White House projectionist on call; one aide served for thirty-three years in that role. Groups of films are borrowed from the area's central booking service, and synopses are sent to the first family for their selection; the movies are shown in the White House or at Camp David. President Carter may hold the record for nights at the movies: he viewed 564 showings during his term.

THE WHITE HOUSE VISITORS OFFICE AND VISITOR CENTER. In a strik-ing mixture of traditions, Americans exalt the presidential office, but they own the president's home. His position is respected, but his house is open for visitors: every tourist who comes to Washington expects to walk through it. The White House is said to be the only home of a head of state, anywhere in the world, that is regularly open to the public free of charge.

The Visitors Office, a seven-person staff in the East Wing, is responsible for all the public admissions to the Residence. Invitees to formal state din-ners and similar functions are controlled by the social secretary, and entrants on official business are processed through the WAVES Center, described ear-lier. But tours for the public are the responsibility of the Visitors Office.

The tradition in which members of the public dropped by to shake hands with the president stopped with Hoover, but a new one began with Tru-man: fixed hours for self-guided public tours of the ground-level corridor and the "State floor" of the Residence. Still another practice started under Eisenhower: special guided tours of those areas at the beginning of the morning for both individuals and groups who are sponsored—in most cases—by members of Congress.

The self-guided public tours, available between 10 A.M. and noon, Tues-day through Saturday, are by ticket only, on a first-come, first-served basis. The tickets are free and are given out at the White House Visitor Center (a suite located in the Department of Commerce Building, on E Street, near the White House), beginning early on the same morning as the tour itself. Getting a ticket is a challenge for anyone who is not an early bird: during the peak spring and summer months the two to three thousand tickets are usually gone by eight o'clock in the morning. The tickets are timed, so that a visitor holding a ticket for 11:00 A.M. doesn't have to stand in line for three hours but can do other things until the specified admission time.

During the peak months, with tickets in such high demand, the Visitor Center has introduced a new practice: at five A.M. a park ranger patrols the line, taking down the names of visitors and the number of tickets each is requesting. The objectives are to prevent line-crashing and to determine when the day's supply will reach its limit, so that visitors beyond that limit will not have to wait in line needlessly. In the fall and winter months, no tickets are used for the public tours; visitors line up at the southeast gate.

Constituents may request individual tickets for the guided (sometimes called "congressional") tours from their senators' or representatives' offices; the White House Visitors Office also fills requests from members of Congress on a first-come, first-served basis until the daily allocation is exhausted. On these tours, specially trained tour officers from the Secret Service's Uniformed Division escort the appreciative contingents of visitors, explaining as they go the history of the famous State Rooms and of the White House collections.

Congressional requests for group tours must be approved by the director of the Visitors Office—a dauntingly uncomfortable decisionmaking area for the person in that job. The criterion is equitability: distributing the privilege fairly among the members of Congress, among representative groups of all kinds (veterans, students, civic associations, political groups), and among visitors from all corners of America. The Visitors Office processes forty thousand group tour tickets each year.

The White House Legislative and Political Affairs Offices, always eager to reward supporters, compete for space on the guided tours as well, although these demands add to the burden already shouldered by the Visitors Office staff. Even though political emnity is sometimes strong, rarely is any member of Congress cut off altogether. "You talk about doing all of this stuff politically versus serving the office of the president," recalled one veteran. "In my opinion you cannot divorce one from the other."[59]

Like other traditions described in this book, the practice of offering tours of the Residence presses against the very limits of what is possible—hopefully without degrading the experience itself. The public tours now average from 1.3 to 1.5 million people a year (Johnson let 2 million come through in 1964). The "congressional" tour for individuals has mushroomed from 150 to 1,300 participants a day; the daily group limit is 600. In addition, there are some special public touring occasions: thirty-two thousand kids and parents scrambled in for the Easter Egg Roll in 1999; the spring and fall garden tours attracted 20,000 each; at Christmas, 160,000 visitors came in to see the decorations.

Crowd-raising is another assignment for the Visitors Office; if an arrival ceremony for a head of state is planned on the South Lawn, several thousand admission cards will be distributed to federal agencies, congressional invitees, school groups, and friendly associations (for example, Future Farmers of America). The list may be six thousand names long; social security numbers are procured for each person, brief security checks made ahead of time.

Like other staff units described here, the Visitors Office labors on the thin edge between accommodating to the pressures of accumulated expectations and preserving the dignity of the presidential office. Staff members are torn between two laudable but nearly irreconcilable objectives: opening the opportunity to all who ask, yet making the visit to this cherished place a meaningful experience for each person. One director of the office formerly served at the National Gallery of Art—which, for special exhibits, offers shoulder-hung audiotape players with earphones; the tapes explain the paintings, in depth, at the leisure of the listener. Would that something similar could be done for White House visitors—but alas, the long queues of sightseers could then never be accommodated.

Then there is the equally stressful quandary of adapting the visiting schedule to the obviously constant needs of the folks whose house this is: the first family. While art galleries and museums are open all day, White House tours are in the mornings only—and if a prayer breakfast or other official event is on the calendar, there will be no tours that day at all.

Representatives of foreign governments have come to the Visitors Office to learn how the White House manages this massive enterprise, but no foreign nation has ever duplicated the White House arrangements. Parts of Buckingham Palace have been opened to the public—for a fee equivalent to $14—but only when the Queen is not in residence.

An anecdote illustrates the surprising variety of people encountered by the director of the Visitors Office: One morning the U.S. Marine Corps commandant brought in a group of Marine commandants from several foreign nations, including Britain. In her welcoming remarks to the group, the director told them the story of how General Ross and his British Marines burned the White House in August of 1814, then marched to the nearby U.S. Marine Corps headquarters to destroy the commandant's house there. An aide reportedly cautioned the general: "Better not burn *this* house—after we win this war, where will *you* be living?" The general concurred; the house was spared (and still stands today). The aide, who was killed in battle three days later, turned out to be an ancestor of the visiting British commandant.

THE COMMITTEE FOR THE PRESERVATION OF THE WHITE HOUSE. In the same executive order that created the position of White House curator, President Johnson established the Committee for the Preservation of the White House under the chairmanship of the director of the National Park Service. The members of the committee are distinguished citizens appointed by the president, along with the White House curator, the chief usher, the secretary of the Smithsonian Institution, the director of the National Gallery of Art, and the chairman of the Commission of Fine Arts. Among other things, the committee advises the president and the director of the National Park Service about what items "shall be used or displayed" at the White House. The first lady is honorary chair of the committee and takes part in its semiannual meetings.

THE WHITE HOUSE HISTORICAL ASSOCIATION. The White House Historical Association is a private, independent, nonprofit charitable institution. The association was formed in November of 1961 at the instigation of Jacqueline Kennedy, who wanted to improve the quality of published factual and historical information about the White House. By 2000, it had arranged for the publication of some twelve million copies of guidebooks and scholarly works.

The association's headquarters are on Jackson Place, and there are sales desks at the headquarters, in the Visitor Center, and (during tour periods) in the White House itself. The association manufactures and sells White House Christmas tree ornaments, producing a new one each year. Income from the ornaments is used for the association's publications program and for the acquisition of historical furnishings and other objects for the Executive Residence.

Support from the Office of Administration

In 1977, to make the White House staff appear smaller, President Carter transferred a group of Executive Office (including White House) administrative functions to a new, non–White-House "Office of Administration."

Payroll, accounting, purchasing, printing, computing, movers, and painters were thereby "subtracted" from the White House staff. The changeover was, however, largely on paper. Section 3(a) of Carter's original executive order specifies that "the Office of Administration shall, upon request, assist the White House Office by performing its role of providing those administrative services which are primarily in direct support of the President."[60] It is estimated that half of the Office of Administration (OA) staff is committed to meeting this requirement.

Dozens of professionals continue their former White House support duties while wearing hats labeled "OA." There are, for example, now three OA-managed libraries, with over 65,000 volumes and 1,000 journal titles. Two of the libraries are next door to the White House, in the Old Executive Office Building. One of the two, a law library, was opened in 1982 and is used constantly by the office of the White House counsel. The second, the main library in the Eisenhower Building, is a prime institutional resource for the White House. Although the members of the library staff do not undertake detailed research projects themselves, they can quickly point White House researchers toward the resources they need. A third OA library is in the New Executive Office Building.

The Conference Center

A Clinton innovation was the construction of a suite of five new conference rooms at number 726 in the Jackson Place row, across the street from the Old Executive Office Building (which had only five such rooms). Varying in size and connected to a closed-circuit TV system, the rooms were named for presidents Eisenhower, Jackson, Lincoln, Truman, and Wilson.

Having the Conference Center's entrance on Jackson Place obviated the necessity for arranging WAVES clearance—a significant convenience for conferees coming from offices outside the White House. These new conference rooms are testimony to the elevated pace of meetings in the modern White House—and to the shortage of square footage for personal offices. A special White House desk arranges for reservations for these rooms.

The White House Database

Upon taking office, the Clinton management and organization team was vexed to find that more than two dozen different name-files were being maintained in separate offices across the White House—for example, by the Correspondence Office; the Social Office; and the Offices of Cabinet Affairs, Intergovernmental Affairs, Political Affairs, and Public Liaison. All in all, there were some 300,000 entries: names, addresses, dates of birth, and social security numbers of everyone who had attended a White House social event, had been sent a letter from the president, or was on the list to receive a White House Christmas card. But the files were not compatible, not cross-referenced; indeed, some of them were not even computerized.

Efficiency proposal: consolidate the lists, set up a central and computerized White House database. Proposal adopted: the database—WhoDB—was created (at a cost of $656,688). To ensure that it was not misused, access was tightly controlled by the assistant for management and administration.[61] The White House counsel set rules for access and downloading: "Generally, the White House cannot provide data from the database to a non-federal entity or individual," wrote Deputy Counsel Cheryl Mills, in January of 1994.[62] Perhaps in ignorance of this ruling, a note from a 1996 campaign-era meeting recorded that "Harold [Ickes] and Debra Lee [of the Democratic National Committee (DNC)] want to make sure WhoDB is integrated w/DNC database—so we can share."[63] The political sharing idea was aborted.

The White House Staff Manual

As a helpful guide to new staff members and as a means of introducing rationality and transparency to White House administrative processes, the Clinton Office of Management and Administration prepared a Staff Manual: a 131-page booklet whose five sections set forth the "rules of the road" for White House employees.

Section A is a 54-page alphabetical listing of services, prescriptions, and practices: for example, how to book a conference room, arrange for a foreign visitor, use the Athletic Center (locker rooms, sauna, showers, and exercise machines—detailees and interns welcome), apply for observation seats at a presidential radio address. The manual warns: briefing memos for the president are due to the staff secretary at 4:00 P.M. the night before— and the Cabinet Room is to be used only by the president.

Section B describes each White House office in a brief paragraph; Section C contains twenty-six sample forms; Section D, in great detail, sets forth the legal and ethical regulations for White House employees, and Section E lists the thirty-one acronyms in use at the White House (for example, POTUS for the president, VPOTUS for . . . readers can guess). The manual concludes with a map of the White House vicinity. One certainly hopes that this manual will be kept up to date and passed on to each succeeding White House group.[64]

The GSA Service Delivery Team

Almost since the General Services Administration was created in 1949, it has had an office at the White House: the headquarters for what has become the 190-person Service Delivery Team, which maintains the East and West Wings of the White House; the Jackson Place townhouses; the Old and New Executive Office Buildings; and the Winder Building, on 17th Street—headquarters of the U.S. Trade Representative. (As noted earlier, the Residence and its grounds are the responsibility of the National Park Service.) The GSA team includes carpenters, electricians, painters, plumbers, air conditioning and elevator mechanics, and custodial staff.

The White House pays "rent" (currently $34 a square foot) to the GSA for a package of services: for example, a given office can be painted once every five years. If it orders services or equipment replacements above and beyond what's included in the package, the White House is charged extra. GSA makes no profit from this arrangement. In fact, it's the other way around: the White House, in effect, gets a subsidy.

Day-to-day coordination is essential: an informal steering committee made up of representatives from the GSA, the National Park Service, the chief usher's office, the Secret Service, and the Military Office meets monthly. (If the Oval Office is to be repainted, it must be done when the boss will be away, so that all the fumes will have dissipated.) The Service Delivery Team is part of the White House community; its technicians are invited to South Lawn arrival ceremonies and to the president's Christmas party.

One item the GSA will probably not replace: the seventy-eight-pound copper-covered ball, three feet in diameter, which—from 1885 to 1936, at 11:55 each morning—was manually hoisted up the flagpole atop the east central roofpoint of the Old Executive Office Building and slid down the flagpole for five minutes to signal "ball time"—that is, noon—to the White House neighborhood.[65]

The White House Branch of the U.S. Postal Service

To facilitate rapid dispatch of White House mail, the U.S. Postal Service maintains a twenty-one-person unit in the Old Executive Office building. The unit reports to the Correspondence Office and also acts as a regular post office for the convenience of those within the building.

The Telephone Service

In 1878 it was known as the Executive Mansion, and its newly installed telephone number was 1. More than a century later, the famous number— (202) 456-1414—receives many thousands of calls each day. Thanks, however, to a completely new White House telephone system—which includes direct dialing and voice mail—only about two thousand calls a day (more in crisis times) require personal operator assistance. Gone, since 1993, is the big old switchboard with holes and plugs: today there are only some fourteen operators on duty, in three shifts, in a suite in the basement of the Old Executive Office Building.

Sitting comfortably in upholstered cubicles, they tap a minimaze of electronic keys at their fingertips. What used to be a master list of ten thousand VIP phone numbers is now only five hundred—nor are the White House operators expected to spend time adding many new ones. And gone is the famed perquisite of White House senior staffers: having the White House telephone operators stop trains or delay planes on their behalf. (Staffers all carry cell phones or pagers now, and there are telephones on board both planes and trains.) Only the president is given the privilege of having calls put through to unlisted numbers.

The Telephone Office remains an entirely professional place; one of the operators is in her thirty-fifth year of service. New recruits get six months of training.

There are occasional humorous incidents. A seven-year-old girl named Maria called to explain to the sympathetic operators how tough her teacher was being on her. During the Reagan presidency, a gent who could mimic the Reagan voice astoundingly well called one night to say, "I am locked out; please have someone come and open up the back door for me!" When the switchboard was located on the second floor of the West Wing, the operators would sometimes watch over Kennedy toddler John-John when he was allowed to stroll in.

Crank calls, children's calls, president's calls—all part of the working day. One night after midnight the president's light went on; President Kennedy had one question: "Where can I find a can opener?"

The Photography Office

In their official hours, presidents may have note-takers to write down what is said and by whom—important as raw material for history. And then there is the presidential diarist, described earlier in this chapter, who records exactly how the president spends the minutes of each day.

Contemporary presidents have "visual diarists" as well: a staff of White House photographers who enrich the written record of each presidency by creating a photographic archive of all official presidential activities. They are White House employees, with the necessary security clearances to enter any Oval Office or Cabinet Room meeting; they are treated like "just another person in the room," and their job is to record photographically almost every meeting and every event involving the chief executive. If the meetings are recurrent, one shot will do; if new faces appear, the visitors will be captured on film. There is close collaboration with the diarist: matching names with pictures and pictures with names.

There was a National Park Service photographer on duty in Franklin Roosevelt's time (he stayed on through the Eisenhower years), but only in the more recent presidencies have photographers taken up the role of fully documenting the president's days. "The president would walk out of his elevator in the morning, and we'd be on his tail until he went back into the family quarters," explained an alumnus of the White House photo office. "We would review the private schedule the night before, and would assign one of our staff to cover every event of his day."[66] At major presidential events, the official photographers use a "zone" system: assistants are pre-positioned in the press stands while one photographer "comes and goes with the body."

After each photography session, the film is dropped into bags and developed at a laboratory at the WHCA facility at the Anacostia Naval Air Station. Digital disks are simply inserted into the computer in the Photography Office, conveniently located in the basement of the West Wing. Studying the computer screen, the photo staff select the best shot for preservation; an assistant in a second office in the Old Executive Office Building, working with National Archives professionals, builds and preserves the precisely documented photo file, which will end up in the future presidential library. The name, date, time, and place of each event—as well as the names of attending VIPs—are registered as well; the staffers of today or the historians of tomorrow can reach any photo record instantly. The photo archive is not for the future only: selected pictures are given to the White House "Webmaster," to be loaded each day into the White House Web site.

Presidential trips are prime subjects for the White House photographer; she and at least one professional assistant will accompany the presidential party. If the first lady is on the trip, four photographers will be on duty. When a trip event is scheduled, the photographers make it their business to be in the most strategic spot well in advance. Digital photos are instantly relayed back to the White House by satellite.

For international conferences of chiefs of state held overseas, the White House photo team used to set up shop and produce an exquisite photo album for presentation to each foreign head of state as the conference ended. Other governments, emulating the American preoccupation with photographic history, now bring their own photo crews with them. If the United States hosts the conference, however, as it did the G-8 summit meeting in Denver, the White House photo group will still assemble a set of gift albums.

The White House photographers have an artist's eye for the striking scene, the memorable setting—President Clinton arriving in New Zealand, for example, descending the stairway of *Air Force One* and being greeted by a disciplined swarm of half-naked Maori chieftains. "We go for the moment!" exclaimed photographic chief Sharon Farmer, who avoided posed scenes of any kind (unless the president specifically wanted them set up).

Of course, besides its primarily archival purposes, White House photography achieves some public relations objectives as well: the foreign ambassador who presents his credentials to the president receives a letter and an accompanying photograph; every White House corridor glows with dramatic shots of recent presidential events.

In the first six and one-half years of the Clinton presidency, the Photography Office used some 76,000 rolls of film. "Our purpose is to serve the American democracy by creating a visual record of its presidency," explained Farmer. "We are creating a legacy, not for public relations purposes, but as an archive for the future."

Her declaration is underscored by another set of pictures in the corridor immediately outside the Oval Office: the drawings of American Indians by nineteenth-century artist George Catlin, who traveled to the frontier in the early 1830s and whose portraits and illustrations are American history's unique portrayal of the native peoples, their leaders, and their cultures as they were at that particular time. He was a "visual diarist" then; the White House Photography Office is, in a certain sense, a George Catlin for the presidency of today.

The Travel Office

The White House Travel Office has functioned for many years to provide travel and communications services to White House and Executive Office staff traveling on official business. The office also—on a reimbursable basis—provides travel arrangements for members of the press corps who accompany the president on trips. These arrangements may include chartered air transportation, ground transportation, work space, and telephone services.

Because the president may travel on short notice, travel arrangements must sometimes be made only a few days or hours in advance. For the period

May 1992 through April 1993, the Travel Office disbursed about $7.7 million to pay for expenses related to press travel—all of which was reimbursed.[67]

The Volunteer Office

In President Clinton's words, "Most Americans have utterly no idea how many hundreds and hundreds of people volunteer at the White House, without which we could not do our jobs. . . . All over America, whenever someone comes up to me and tells me that they've had some contact from the White House that I know came because of a volunteer, I am once again grateful for what you do."[68]

A thousand men and women, many of them senior citizens, come into the White House on a part-time basis. They work from one to three days a week; the minimum commitment is sixteen hours a month. In 1998 volunteers put in over 200,000 hours for the White House; if they had been paid, the cost would have been $1.2 million. Other than a compulsory briefing on ethics (behavior in the White House, the use of White House stationery, etc.), volunteers receive very little orientation. They work in any of forty-five different offices, but most of them—some 775—serve in the Correspondence Office, helping to open and sort the millions of letters to the president that arrive annually.

One hundred rotate in and out of the first lady's office; another group serves in the social secretary's domain. They answer telephone calls on the Comment Line; they address the thousands of cards that the president and first lady send to Americans who are celebrating their hundredth birthdays, golden wedding anniversaries, and other special events. A volunteer who serves in that "greetings" office holds the seniority record: she has been a White House volunteer for twenty-nine years. Volunteers hand out programs at South Lawn receptions and help at the Easter Egg Roll. A few volunteers come in at 4:30 A.M. to help the Press Office assemble the news summary packets. Some volunteers are "floaters," assigned ad hoc as needs peak or diminish.

As of this writing, the oldest volunteer is a woman ninety-two years of age, who comes in every Monday. At Christmastime, ninety volunteers—some coming (at their own expense) from distant parts of the country—help "deck the halls" of the White House during a three-day, dawn-to-midnight decorating marathon. One couple, while trimming the White House Christmas tree in the mid-1980s, met, fell in love, courted, and later married; she continued to work at the White House, and he continued to be a volunteer. Another gentleman has come down from Nashua, New Hampshire, every year for twenty-five years. Volunteers in the first lady's correspondence office address the first family's 125,000 Christmas cards.[69]

The volunteers are given a "national agency check" by the Secret Service, then put on the access list with a daily "V-pass" for entry. A ruling by the Department of Justice's Office of Legal Counsel permits employees of non-profit or educational institutions or state, local, or tribal governments to become volunteers, and some of these men and women do professional work, helping to "write speeches, analyze policies and perform political chores." (Before 1997, some twenty-three of these "volunteers" were actually on the payroll of the Democratic National Committee, but this practice was stopped after objections from the House Appropriations Subcommittee.)[70]

The selection (from a long waiting list) of volunteers, their assignments, and the backup paperwork are handled by the White House Volunteer Office, a part of the Correspondence Office. Besides the pride they have in serving such a revered institution, the volunteers receive modest rewards: the Volunteer Office sponsors special local trips (for example, a behind-the-scenes tour of the National Archives or a lecture on the history and preservation of the Old Executive Office Building), and there are special thank-you appearances (for instance, by the president or the chief of staff). The president and first lady sponsor an annual Volunteer Appreciation Day in the Rose Garden. An informal newsletter, the *Volunteer Voice*—with articles written by volunteers themselves—is published and circulated by the Volunteer Office.

The nation, as well as the first family, can be grateful for these thousands of hours of public-spirited dedication. Said a senior White House aide: "We could not operate without the volunteers; there is no way around it."[71] Chief of Staff Podesta told them: "All of you are here because you care about your country, care about being involved, and believe in the powerful ways that government is at the heart of what it means to be an American."[72]

White House Fellows

In 1957 John Gardner, then president of the Carnegie Corporation, had an idea: "If we could take some of the best of our young people and put them in direct contact with the daily functions of government. . . ." He put the suggestion in a memorandum at the time, but nothing happened until 1964, when Lyndon Johnson (who, under Franklin Roosevelt, had been the head of the New Deal's Texas National Youth Administration), was bewailing "the gulf between youth and government." Gardner sent his memorandum to Johnson, who seized upon it and initiated the White House Fellows Program—an enterprise that is now a continuing and highly prized part of the White House environment.

Each year a call for applications goes out from the President's Commission on White House Fellowships: the commission seeks men and women who have already distinguished themselves, even though their careers may be at an early stage. Eight hundred may apply. Perhaps forty are winnowed out—to face, one by one, a panel of judges; between eleven and nineteen are selected as White House Fellows.

Appointed by the president to serve for one year in professional assignments, they work at the White House, in the vice president's office, in cabinet members' offices, and in other agencies. Their salaries, of nearly $70,000 a year, are paid by the agencies to which they are assigned; those Fellows who are assigned to the White House are attached to various agencies and then detailed to the White House, with the detailing agencies supplying their stipends.

As of this writing, some 535 talented young men and women have served as White House Fellows. Their ranks have included Colin Powell, Henry Cisneros, and author Doris Kearns Goodwin. Their service keeps alive a tradition—in President Johnson's words, "when the young men and women of America and their government belonged to each other—belonged to each other in fact and spirit."[73]

The Intern Program

In the summertime, the average age of the Washington population must take a nosedive: the town jumps with college-agers. Interns throng Capitol Hill and are also used throughout the executive branch—including the White House.

Summer interns were used in the White House as early as Gerald Ford's administration. Under President Reagan, about thirty young people joined the staff each year for the summer months. There was no centrally managed procedure; each White House office did its own recruitment.

In the Bush administration, the numbers climbed, and the White House Intern Office was created to handle the recruitment and selection, do the paperwork, and manage the assignments. Opportunities were opened up for both the fall and spring semesters, in addition to the summer, and between seventy and ninety interns were recruited for each of those three periods. The limit for an internship was ninety days (duty in the White House beyond that requires an expensive full-field FBI investigation).

The White House offices got used to having the extra personnel—and began to depend on having them. A three-quarter-day orientation program was instituted for their first day on the job: a security lecture, a list of do's and don'ts, points about conduct and dress, and instructions on the use of White House stationery. They were given packets of information: an organization chart of the White House, a map of whose office was where (interns were often sent on delivery missions). The assistant for management and administration addressed them.

In the Bush years, interns were not allowed in the East or West Wings without escort or special permission. "The minute you cross West Executive Avenue, the world changes," declared a former aide. According to one Bush veteran, most interns received college credit for their service, but they had to write a paper to get it. "There were several types of interns," recalled another. "Some were just doing it because their mothers or fathers wanted them to do it; some were serving because they truly believed in the administration, or a cause. Some were there just to get a chit on their resume or because they wanted to get into X law school. If we got the ones who truly cared, and wanted to make a difference, we were lucky."[74]

Their reward: being invited to arrival and departure ceremonies on the South Lawn and being in a "class picture" with the president. At the end of their tenure, some would apply for jobs on the staff; the Bush White House hired a dozen or more of them.

An enormous change took place in the Clinton administration. The regular staff was being cut by 25 percent, and the Intern Program exploded—from 250 a year to 1,000 during each of the early Clinton years. Four sessions were organized: two summer sessions, during which the interns worked full time; and fall and spring sessions (to coincide with their college semesters), when the interns worked at the White House three days a week. For the first several years of the administration, 250 interns were taken in for each of the four sessions. Interns could serve in any of thirty offices in the White House or in the Office of the Vice President; applicants were invited to list their top four preferences. (The separate Legal Intern Program might, during each session, take in up to five full-time interns who would work in the counsel's Office.)

Each applicant had to submit a resume and a college transcript, a one-page statement describing why he or she wanted to be a White House intern, a 150-word description of a "formative experience" or "greatest accomplishment," and a 500-word writing sample. All applicants were notified that there would be a security check and likely a drug test. The tiny Intern Office, consisting of the director and three interns, was swamped by thousands of applications. Those who applied were reminded that the White House could neither provide public funds nor seek private monies for them; applicants were simply given a list of "directories" to use in searching for their own financial support if they needed it.

The expenses of living in Washington ($30 a night in a local university dorm) had to be met from the applicants' own resources; as a result, those who actually joined the program in the early Clinton years tended to be well-off, and there were all too few minority entrants. In the later years, the Clinton White House cut back the annual numbers to six or seven hundred and tried much harder to build diversity into the intern classes. Whether the interns would receive college credit continued to be up to their home institutions.

Under the Clinton administration, the interns' White House orientation was minimal: a briefing on security (a "scare tactic," one of them called it) and reminders that they should dress "professionally." The story made the rounds that if the woman who was the senior overseer of the Intern Program spotted a too-short skirt, she would give it a downward yank as a warning. One young woman, in a hurry, came into the West Wing with bare shoulders; she was sent back to her office for her jacket. Clinton interns were permitted to work in both the East and West Wings.

For the very laudable purpose of facilitating effective internships, the Intern Office director drew up a guide for heads of White House offices: "Having an Intern in Your Office," which contained a section headed "Please appreciate your intern! Here is a list of ten things you can do to do that." In at least one office, an intern composed an internal briefing book describing how an intern should function in that unit, but that was an exception. The actual duties varied, of course, with each office and each young person's capabilities and energies.

Interns were invited to brown-bag luncheons, visits to other executive departments, and occasional lecture sessions in Presidential Hall (the new name for the auditorium in the Old Executive Office Building), where senior staff members met and talked with them and engaged in Q & A dialogues. One aide in the chief of staff's office mentioned that he would have to tell their intern: "I'm sorry you're not getting out to the Pentagon to hear the speakers, but I need help here until eleven o'clock tonight." To the author he added: "I like to see their side of it, but I lean more to the be-responsible-for-your-job side of things."[75]

What was true under Bush was true under Clinton as well: some interns wished to stay on at the White House as paid staffers—and were chosen for full-time employment there.

One former White House intern director remembers the welcome she gave to each incoming class: "You have the honor of being chosen to serve here; you will have the intellectual excitement of working in Washington, the special tingling sense which comes from being inside these walls. If that sense disappears, you don't belong here any more."[76]

Rewards for the Clinton interns, like those for their Bush predecessors, were much more psychological than material: being invited to an occasional South Lawn event; receiving a certificate, a mug, and the opportunity to purchase a T-shirt; being in a group picture with the president. (The T-shirt was imprinted with the presidential seal and the words *White House Intern, Summer 199–*. After the Lewinsky scandal, some interns were too embarrassed to wear it in public.) Oh yes, and a photo-op with Socks.

One senior Clinton aide gave his own views: "I think that to give young people a glimpse of government at that level is a great experience. I have talked with parents of interns who have told me that their child spent the most wonderful three months of his or her life here. Is it worth the risks that the Monica Lewinsky thing brings about? I would have to say no. I think it is a luxury, not a necessity. . . . All the interns I had were terrific— bright, energetic, inquisitive. But there was potential for abuse. The White House is a very small place."[77]

Mr. Clinton's sins with one young intern did not put a stop to his administration's intern program. It continued, and the author trusts that it will continue into the future.

The Jackson Place Hostelry for Former Presidents

The General Services Administration owns and rents to the White House a minihotel for former presidents, who may arrange to stay there, without charge, when they are in the city. This modest perquisite was initiated by President Nixon. The row house at 716 Jackson Place has a bedroom, a living room, a dining room, and a kitchen facility; the food is prepared by stewards from the White House Mess.

The White House, then, is not empty at the inaugural noon.

Throughout its expectant halls, in its foyers and kitchens, at its switchboards and guardposts, men and women are on duty who will serve tomorrow as they served yesterday. Some have walked taller in the mornings of two, three, or four decades: skilled, committed, and proud—to support the office which they honor and the House which they revere. They will continue to be unknown to their fellow Americans and some of them even to their president, who years later will depart, as they again remain. Their respectful loyalty is always transferred to each new chief executive, and president after president is rewarded by their service.

PART FOUR

White House Service in the Years Ahead

CHAPTER TWENTY-THREE

The Essence of White House Service: Looking to the Future

Today the attorney general presides over a department of 95,000 people. . . . [She] has a huge department to run and when the president needs her, the chances are she will be down on the Rio Grande looking at the fences or tightening up the immigration process. The whole government has grown to the point where the Cabinet departments, important as they are, have become what you might call outer-moons, and the president's need for an intimate personal staff, who used to be the Cabinet, today requires that he create his own.

LLOYD CUTLER

There is always the danger that impulsive, inexperienced aides, puffed up with the prestige of the White House—and emboldened by the absence of personal accountability—will seek to bully the main federal establishments into reckless, ill-considered or improper actions in the service of pet ideological or short-term political aims.

JEREMY RABKIN

My sense of reality was just altered. I started out being excited working for the president. Then I became arrogant, then I became grandiose.

DICK MORRIS

This volume, so far, has given the reader an encyclopedic look at "the White House Staff" of the recent past. From "inside the West Wing," it is now time to peer ahead. What can be said about the White House staff of the near future?

The White House Staff and the Cabinet

The epigraphs at the opening of the chapter give rise to the question: Are the White House staff and the cabinet necessarily antagonistic bodies? Is the staff brimming with "impulsive, inexperienced aides," "arrogant" and "grandiose" minions who ply their presidential trade, leaving the cabinet "outer-moons" out of the loop—or wondering, as former secretary of labor Robert Reich wrote, whether "there *is* a loop" at all? In other words, is staff-cabinet antipathy inevitable?

The anwer is yes and the answer is no.

First, as political scientist Charles Jones reminds us, "Presidents-elect enter the critical transition period in a physically and mentally exhausted state, typically dependent on an equally fatigued staff. . . . However competent on the campaign trail, their aides have been selected for a purpose that is weakly related to governing, if related at all." In 1992, "the lack of Washington-based executive experience among Clinton's advisers was not automatically compensated for by the energy of their youth." As one former aide put it, "The problem with the Carter administration was that there [were] too many people . . . for whom it was the best job they ever had. And that probably is true here [in the Clinton administration] too." Another asked: How can a president "discern [the] governing talent of staff who have never governed?" Jones quotes a Republican aide: "The attack by White House staff on cabinet is a source of bad government. And it is extremely pervasive. There is mutual contempt, but it is much stronger . . . contempt felt by White House staff for cabinet than vice versa. . . . The White House staff, by virtue of physical proximity, feels closer to the president. All White House staffs feel embattled and form deep kinds of bonds, an us-against-them mentality."[1]

Second, with these early mind-sets coloring the perspectives of some if not many of them, new White House staff members will next encounter one of the basic facts of contemporary governance: the reality that major public policy issues of presidential concern are inextricably scrambled across what were once well-defined cabinet jurisdictions. Preparing for the consequences of climate change, guarding against terrorism, meeting the challenges of economic disparity or racial discrimination, structuring future relations with Russia or China: no "lead" cabinet secretary can marshal the totality of the interagency staff work involved in exploring such issues—nor can even a group of cabinet secretaries inject into that staff work the president's own perspective as to what might be the most desirable solutions.

The preceding chapters have adduced many examples of what fifty years of organizational struggles have made clear: the strategic development, coordination, and articulation of major policy initiatives have now become centered in a large and active White House—likely a disquieting notion to the cabinet.

So, yes: there is inherent separateness—tension, in fact—between White House staff and cabinet. And in the past, real hostility—as in the cases of Henry Kissinger and William Rogers, Zbigniew Brzezinski and Cyrus Vance, Chief of Staff John Sununu and Environmental Protection Agency Administrator William Reilly, White House policy adviser Ira Magaziner and cabinet secretaries Lloyd Bentsen and Donna Shalala.

In Clinton's second term, however, the answer was no. And the reason was not organizational but personal. National security adviser Samuel "Sandy" Berger, domestic policy director Bruce Reed, economic policy assistants Robert Rubin and Gene Sperling and their top staff associates—to name the principal players—collapsed the stereotype described in the second and third epigraphs of this chapter. They kept policy development and coordination centralized in the White House but did so with such personal diplomacy and such sensitivity to departmental prerogatives that the traditional acrimony diminished, if not disappeared. Their channels of communication to the heads of the line departments were crammed with constant alerts and exchanges of even the most sensitive information. In their superintendence of interagency paperwork, in their presentations to the president, they prided themselves on personifying the role of honest broker: they did not use their White House positions to obtain an edge in the debates, but neither did they sacrifice their freedom to present their own views. The result: a White House staff and a cabinet that, in Clinton's last four years, worked well together.

Will this pattern hold true for the future? Will the centralization of policy control continue in the relatively cooperative pattern set during the Clinton years?

By no means necessarily. It is the author's belief that the process of centralization will not be reversed, but it is also his apprehension that this recent era of congenial relationships could vanish if arrogance and grandiosity were again to infect the psyche of junior—or senior—White House assistants.

The value of Jones's *Passages to the Presidency* is the advice to new presidents on how to make the transition from campaigning to governing—and on how to avoid the mistakes that have led to such bitterness between the cabinet and the White House in the past. The book stresses, for instance, that a president-elect should choose the White House staff first—to have them in place as the cabinet choices are made. A former Reagan and Bush adviser is quoted:

> I have never understood why presidents-elect are so enamored of this idea that cabinet officers matter. They don't matter. You can run a damn cabinet for months without a cabinet officer and nobody will ever know the difference. That's the least crucial item that should be on a presidential agenda. Instead, because of the symbolic value they spend enormous amounts of time on it. They spend very little time on the staff, or how the White House works. It always amazes me that presidents don't understand—even those that have been governors—how much of the real power and decisionmaking in government is in the White House operation.[2]

A critic of Clinton's 1992 transition added: "So much focus was put on the diversity and politically correct combinations of the makeup of the cabinet, whereas really the White House staff is where all the power resides. . . . These people, with whom really the essential power of governing will reside, were not told that they had any authority until well past the end of the transition."[3]

Dick Morris quotes President Clinton's own rueful retrospection: "I spent all my time before I took office choosing my Cabinet. . . . It's a great Cabinet. But I didn't spend the time I should have choosing my staff. I just reached out and took the people who had helped get me elected and put them on the staff. It was a mistake." Morris notes: "He [Clinton] would plead for more 'adults' in the White House."[4]

Organizing the Future White House Staff

The structure of the contemporary White House staff is not the mindless burgeoning of willy-nilly empire-building; it is a direct consequence of growing presidential needs—step by step, since the 1950s—to have certain tasks undertaken. Elements added to the White House by earlier presidents as useful innovations—the Advance, Intergovernmental Affairs, and Public Liaison Offices, the Situation Room, the daily news summary, the weekly Cabinet Report, the White House photographer, the Intern Program, for example—have now proven their worth and are standard White House functions. With more and more institutions reaching *in* to the presidency (interest groups, state and local officials, political coalitions), and affording additional avenues of persuasion, the White House has organized itself—and grown—to reach *out* to exploit those opportunities. As other authors have so well demonstrated, presidents put great store on "going public"; the "White House bubble machine" is a staff apparatus that no future president will forgo.[5] Governing, as Jones emphasizes, is taking on a style of continuing campaigning. *That is not going to change.*

Above all else, the centrality of the president's personal role in leading and coordinating the executive branch, detailed in parts 1 and 2 of this volume, has required the president to increase his own staff resources for policy development. The thirty-one cabinet departments and agencies are every chief executive's proud professional wellsprings, but their disparate capacities have to be marshaled and synchronized—a task that the Constitution itself implicitly assigns to the president.

The tighter and more interwoven the threads of policy issues become—throughout the entire national security community, across all the old boundary lines between "domestic" and "foreign"—the more influential and the more numerous may become the White House assistants who must struggle to accomplish the synchronization. The more centrifugal are the forces exerted by the inevitable cacophony outside the White House gates, the more potent will become the centripetal strength within: those offices described in chapter 21.

As political scientist Terry Moe wrote,

> Over time the built-in advantage of the White House will prevail: presidents will incrementally enhance its competence; problems and issues will be increasingly drawn into it for centralized coordination and control, expectations surrounding previous patterns will slowly break down, new expectations will form around a White House–centered system, and the new expectations will further accelerate the flow of problems and issues to the White House—thus enhancing the need for still greater White House competence.[6]

How much flexibility would a new president have to reorganize the White House? The quick answer would seem to be this: almost complete freedom. The Constitution mandates that there shall be a vice president; the law establishes (but does not require the president to use) the National Security Council and authorizes—but puts only a modest limit on the number of—highly paid staff. Is the rest a tabula rasa?

No. It is a concluding thesis of this book that most of the forty-six principal policy elements—and almost all of the fifty-one technical and support units—in the contemporary White House are so clearly indispensable to the modern presidency that they should be, and in fact are very likely to be, continued in the White House of the future. Not for reasons of tradition, not for reasons of patronage, but because the effectiveness of the presidential office itself depends on the presence of these staff institutions.

A new president certainly can shift the White House offices around somewhat, recombine some with others, decide on a different mechanism for coordinating domestic and international economic policy, pare down or perhaps even strengthen the NSC imperium, decrease (or, as Ike did, increase) the cohort of special assistants for special purposes. A new president will be free to negotiate different roles for the vice president and for the two spouses—but it is, frankly, doubtful that there would be a return to the Alben Barkley or Bess Truman models. Any incoming chief executive—Democrat or Republican—will certainly put new faces in all the policy positions, and he or she could sweep out all the long-termers in the professional posts; but only sheer stupidity would call for replacing, say, the White House telephone operators or the contingent of White House Communications Agency specialists.

Are there superfluous offices in the White House? Only if a president is willing to deprive himself of functions already being performed. While in theory a new president has a clean slate, outside the White House there are expectations that condition his choices. Governors, legislators, state party chiefs, interest groups, and local news media would be the first to decry an "isolated" presidency if the intergovernmental, legislative, political, public liaison, or communications staffs were abolished. Would a new president reduce the Residence staff (and the public tours, and the entertaining)? Cease holding international summits at Camp David? Instruct the first lady to be less active? Return the vice president to isolation on Capitol Hill? Make only the secretary of state the "vicar" of foreign policy? Stay at home more?

A new president might be tempted—but really cannot choose—to transfer the White House counsel's "just-us" function back to the attorney general, to use the House or Senate leaders of his party to manage his relationships with Congress, to delegate the political appointment process back to party headquarters.

In structure, then, the White House staff community is likely to be a continuing enterprise. Whatever changes a new president makes, he may have to make them appear sufficiently dramatic to support a claim that "reform" has taken place—but they should not be such as to diminish the powers of governance that the existing systems afford. It is the author's judgment that the "reformed" White House will look a great deal like the one already described in part 2.

The Size of the Future White House Staff

The structure of the institution may be reshuffled (even if only cosmetically), but can the actual number of staff be substantially reduced? As shown in chapter 21, there are over 5,900 men and women in what the author has defined as the White House staff community. Some 700 of them (aided by about 100 volunteers, 100 interns, and 5 White House Fellows) are in the policy offices of the White House. Where—and how much—reduction can be made?

President Clinton's promised "25 percent cut in the White House staff" was in several ways a failure. Of his touted 350-person "White House reduction," 245 were in Executive Office rather than White House units. The White House offices that bore the cuts were left to carry out their continuing responsibilities with fewer people—adding to the strain on the remaining employees and resulting in the heavy use of interns (an arrangement that had some successes and a few drawbacks).

The many White House incumbents and alumni whom the author interviewed were almost unanimous in their criticism of setting a fixed percentage as a reduction target. By 1997, the White House had finally conceded the error, telling the responsible House Appropriations subcommittee that "to meet the President's aggressive drug control strategy to which Congress agreed last year, and in order for the Counsel's Office to respond to requests for information from Congressional and other bodies, *it is no longer possible to maintain the 1993 staffing level* [emphasis added]."[7] Press Secretary Mike McCurry commented, "It sounds like there was more work to do than the downsizing would have allowed."[8]

A new president could, similarly, ordain that while the core functions would continue, their staffs must be smaller. He might pare his Public Liaison Office, cutting back its policy briefings, for instance, for the Business Roundtable or the Urban League. The president, however, needs the informed influence of just such groups in the halls of Congress. He could delegate subcabinet patronage to his cabinet members, shrinking his presidential personnel staff. President Carter tried that and recognized too late that he had given up too much authority.

The threat of terrorism leaves the president no choice but to require in-depth security support. The president's pastoral role—represented by mail, telephone calls, tourists, hardship cases, messages, cards, and gifts—nearly overwhelms the place. During his four years, for example, President Bush received 24.5 million letters. Does a future president expect fewer? In that same Correspondence Office that handles those letters and supports the nation's "pastor," the nearly eight hundred volunteers have been essential in keeping the staff's heads above the flood.

Size per se is not the true issue in the management of the White House. As former chief of staff Richard Cheney urged,

> I don't think we should place artificial constraints on the president. If the president says he needs five hundred people to do the job, give him five hundred; if he thinks he needs seven hundred, give him seven hundred. It's a minor price to pay for having a president who is the leader of the free world. . . . A trillion-dollar federal budget, 3.8 million federal civilian and military employees—we can afford to give the president of the United States however many persons he needs on his personal staff.[9]

"The president is the best judge of what he needs to do his job," observed a House Appropriations staff officer. "We give him what he asks for—and then, if he screws up, we can criticize him. We have made very, very few cuts in the White House Office requests."[10] (Of course, however large is the total number of people, the ring of power itself is smaller: in the Clinton second term there were only eighty White House staff officers with formal presidential commissions. Among these were the members of the senior circle: the heads of the forty-six major offices described in part 2. Even within that ring, there are, in every White House, a very few who are the president's most intimate associates.)

To be a countervailing magnet to the atomizing particles in the polities of the nation and the world, and to be the successful centralizer of the executive branch policy process, the American president needs and deserves all the personal staff resources he can control.

"Control" is the nub.

The limit on White House staff size is this: the point at which the president senses that he can no longer govern what the least of his staff do or say—and when, because they are not well governed, their relationships with department and agency heads leave the cabinet chieftains alienated and resentful. This limit can vary: it should not be an arbitrary, imposed figure. The limit on the size of the White House staff will depend, in great part, on the internal communications and disciplinary systems that the president and

Media Influence on the Public's View of the White House Staff

In recent years, the entertainment media have featured shows that throw an unflattering spotlight on the White House staff. In several motion pictures about the presidency, Hollywood has portrayed White House staff members as thoroughly evil conspirators. *Dave* depicts a malevolent chief of staff; *Clear and Present Danger* and *Murder at 1600* cast the national security adviser as a secret enemy of the president. *Wag the Dog* highlights the manipulations of presidential aides. *In the Line of Fire, The President's Daughter,* and *Air Force One* feature Secret Service agents who have poor judgment or are traitorous.

The West Wing, an NBC television series, is a much more realistic portrayal—although, in the author's judgment, it places overmuch emphasis on the staffers' preoccupation with their own personal problems. Nonetheless, it has given viewers a realistic sense of the contentiousness that precedes White House decisionmaking. Of course, the sordid truth of the real White House escapades—Watergate, Iran-Contra, and the Lewinsky scandal—only makes the cinematographic fictionalizations all the more believable.

Then there are the kiss-and-tell books: *Unlimited Access,* by Gary Aldrich; *Madhouse,* by Jeffrey Birnbaum; *Breaking Cover,* by Bill Gulley; *Inside the White House,* by Ronald Kessler; *For the Record,* by Donald Regan; *My Turn,* by Nancy Reagan; *At Reagan's Side,* by Helene von Damm; *All Too Human,* by George Stephanopoulos; *Behind the Oval Office,* by Richard Morris—and more. These volumes, while adding some raw material for history, bring forward the rivalries, jealousies, enmities, and weaknesses of White House staff colleagues. No wonder the public may have a low opinion of the place.

his chief of staff establish. In answer to a question from the author about White House staff size, former president Bush opined: "*Ring of Power* had it right the first time. It is staff organization and staff management that matter. In this regard, a strong Chief of Staff is very important."[11]

If information flows readily from the president through the chief of staff to senior staff and to midlevel officers, all of them can accurately reflect and relay the president's priorities, and a large staff is manageable. As the assistant cabinet secretary attending Eisenhower's cabinet meetings, the author could and did convey to other White House colleagues and to inquiring departmental experts the precise thrust and emphasis of the presidential decisions rendered in those sessions. If there is blockage in internal communications, however, the staff will lack direction.

It is not the number of staff, but their behavior that is key. If White House officers interpret their position as license to minimize consultation with departments or as opportunity to favor their own views when presenting issues to the president, their interdepartmental engagements will be no more than snarling matches—and the staff will be berated. If any of them, of highest or lowest status, let their egos get puffed up by the prestige of the "White House" title or the privileges of its environment, the traditional acrimony between "insiders" and "outsiders" will reappear—to bite them. If any of the two first couples or their staffs treat the experienced press as their enemies, the old battles will heat up—which the White House will lose. If overeager partisanship constantly overcomes the staff's willingness to work with congressional leaders of both parties, the historic tensions will surface—and the staff will be derided as excessive. If the concerns of governors are slighted and skeptical advocacy groups pushed aside, the staff will be excoriated for its haughtiness.

The issue is not how large is the White House staff—but how is it organized and how professionally does it conduct itself?

Accountability

Is the staff out of control?

The Iran-Contra escapade certainly gave the public the impression that some members of the White House staff were a freewheeling bunch, pursuing not the president's agenda but their own. It even appeared that some had interposed themselves—the president unknowing—between the chief executive and his line subordinates.

That impression is understandable but wrong. No major enterprise takes place in the White House neighborhood without the president's knowledge and consent. Those in the seniormost ring of the White House staff are close to the president, and he to them: their confidences intimately shared, the mutual respect intense. The chances that they would keep secrets from one another—especially they from him—are close to zero.[12]

The senior staff will constantly be the transmitters of the chief executive's wishes; on occasion they will use—or will be told to use—a directive ostensibly their own to mask the president's hidden hand. Some disgruntled recipients of such orders may mistakenly believe, or may choose to believe, that the instructions emanate not from the president's choice but from the staff's own arrogance. They, too, are wrong. "If Bob Haldeman tells you something, you are to consider it as a communication directly from me and to act on that basis," President Nixon once declared.[13] "If Ham or Stu or Jack calls on my behalf, take their word as coming directly from me," President Carter told his cabinet. "You have been overly reluctant to respond when the White House staff calls you."[14] For their part, rarely do senior staff need the kind of reminder President Johnson often gave: "You make sure you know what I think before you tell . . . [an outsider] what you think I think."[15]

It is the use by lower-ranking aides of the presidential "we" that most quickly provokes challenges to the staff's reliability. "If you have hundreds of people doing that, there is no way you can keep them out of mischief," commented Kennedy assistant Ted Sorensen.[16] Presidential scholar Richard Neustadt observed: "Only those who see the President repeatedly can grasp what he is driving at and help him or dispute him. Everybody else there is a menace to him. Not understanding, they spread wrong impressions. Keeping busy, they take their concerns for his."[17]

There is, however, a sharp, fast antidote to mischief-making by the more junior staff, a kind of pruning saw that operates to discipline the White House aide who tries to badger outsiders into believing that he is speaking for the chief executive. Should a query fired back to a more senior White House officer reveal that the original caller was not close to the presidential trunk, but out on a limb of his own, the saw cuts quickly, the limb is severed, and with it collapses the aide's credibility—if not his employment. Whenever cabinet officers, governors, ambassadors, or legislators hear "the White House calling," they may be tempted to test out the pruning-saw discipline through a call back to a more senior officer. At the White House, every midlevel or junior assistant soon learns that he or she operates under that sharp-toothed regimen.

How sharp? Johnson assistant Joseph Califano tells of the evening when he asked his associate, Lawrence Levinson, to pass on a presidential request to Secretary of Labor Willard Wirtz. The secretary doubted the authenticity of the younger aide's request and paid it no heed. The next morning, after explaining his hesitation to an irritated president, Wirtz received the following admonition: "If you get a call from anyone over here, if you get a call from the cleaning woman who mops the floors at three A.M. and she tells you the President wants you to do something, you do it!"[18] Johnson, however, followed a very different principle where Secretary of Defense Robert McNamara was concerned. In a 1965 interview Johnson declared: "I've told Bob McNamara if anybody calls him and says he speaks for me, let me have the name of that man right away and I'll fire him."[19]

Accountability—as in "The Buck Stops Here!"—does, however, end in one place: the Oval Office. A White House is organized, and behaves, exactly as the president prescribes: it will fit each chief executive's own style. If a Nixon insists that he be guarded—almost isolated—by a "Berlin Wall" of assistants, that is what will take place. If a Clinton, as in his early months, keeps his door open to staffers high and low, he will get just what he invites. The president makes the rules for White House staff functioning—and that includes the limits on access to his office. (He can also bend or break those rules—for a young intern, for example.)

The White House is the president's house. Accountability runs straight up the line. If the cabinet, the Congress, or the country are persistently offended by what a White House staff says and does, there is just one person in whose hands to heap their woe: the president of the United States. Ask not the White House staff to be what he is not. Should a president, fully informed, insist on unwise decisions, it is not they who will reverse him. Should he be malicious or dishonorable, it is only the more independent institutions of our nation—Congress, the courts, the press, not the White House staff—who must guard the Republic.

A "Passion for Anonymity"?

Louis Brownlow's 1936 prescription was the original maxim that was to govern the conduct of White House staff: they were to do their work behind the scenes, and stay out of the limelight.

Parts 1 and 2 of this volume catalogued the assignments that White House staff undertake: gathering information, developing and coordinating ideas for substantive programs, drafting policy option memos, making presentations to the president. These staff activities can breed tension—and possibly conflict—between White House staff and cabinet officers. Such potential polarities are inherent in the methods presidents now use to exercise their leadership over the executive branch.

While the tensions are unavoidable, they would be exacerbated many-fold—so went the old prescription—if a White House staff member were to appear in the newspapers or on television, because that would imply to the public that the staffer was the centerpoint of the action. These days, it seems, Louis Brownlow's hoary maxim is subject to revision. Not only have the development and the coordination of policy now become centered in the White House, but so has its articulation. To explain and defend administration policies, the president still "needs help"—but in a new mode. The same White House assistants who aided in shaping the policies are brought forward to play a central role in publicizing them. A White House communications veteran explained:

> The pressure that comes is: the *Today Show* has a huge audience, and they will come to you and say, "We would like somebody to speak on the president's views on *XYZ*." Do you know how many departments really know the president's views? You're down to the press secretary and maybe the chief of staff. You have the *Today Show*, and all three networks, plus Fox, plus CNN—all want somebody to appear, all want somebody out there. You've got only this one person, and they say, "Well, OK, if you won't put somebody out there, we'll put your opposition on." So, you're left with that terrible choice: Do you want to keep people anonymous, or do you want to defend your position?[20]

The limelight, therefore, now illumines a wider circle. Pictured at the Briefing Room podium will be not the press secretary but the National Security Council senior director for defense policy and arms control, to make a presentation on missile defense, and answer questions.[21]

The chief of staff appears on *Meet the Press*. The White House director of the National Economic Council is out front to rebut the opposition's tax cut plan. The national security adviser writes an op-ed column entitled "Don't Sell Clinton Short" and delivers a major foreign policy address to the Council on Foreign Relations criticizing the congressional "New Isolationists."[22] The *Washington Post Magazine* does an in-depth feature story on the first lady's chief of staff.[23] White House assistants are newsworthy, a fact now greeted with more interest than criticism. Some of the old requirement for anonymity is fading. . . .

The Unforgiving Ethical Standard

But not the intolerance for impropriety.

New recruits may chafe at the ethical demands of government service: conflict-of-interest statutes and financial disclosure mandates. At the White

House those are merely the minimums. The White House is a glass house, shot through with floodlights of scrutiny from a skeptical press and a hostile political opposition, watched by a changeable public. It is expected to be a model for the public service—and it cannot help but be attacked for even the least of peccadilloes. Its rules of conduct reflect its honored—and vulnerable—circumstance.

The basic ethical standard in the White House is so old and so clear that it comes as a surprise to see any staff officers falling afoul of the rule. Quite simply, the *appearance* of impropriety is itself the impropriety. Will a staffer's acceptance of favors from outsiders, for instance, in fact compromise his or her judgment? No matter; it will look that way—enough to fail the test. The "appearance" rule is not in any law: it is tougher than law. It is the unrelenting standard for men and women who serve near the presidency.

White House staff can have no agendas other than to help the president. Political, professional, and financial ambitions have to be put aside, or one runs the risk of using the office for personal gain and of putting selfish priorities ahead of presidential objectives—instead of the other way around.

Even after leaving the staff, White House officers are expected to adhere to the proprieties required by their continuing closeness to the president; some have disregarded such mandates, if not the conflict-of-interest rules themselves. Indictments and trials may lead to convictions; they certainly bring embarrassment to the presidents whose trust has been wounded.

Getting Some Help

Before launching any innovations, future White House managers need to know what it is they are reforming. How has the White House been operated in the past? It is of course the author's hope that this work will be of help here. Beyond professional writings of this sort, however, presidential public administration enters virgin territory. With few exceptions, post-election communication between incoming and outgoing White House staff members has been perfunctory at best. Transition briefings are provided for newcomers within the cabinet departments, but conversations among new and old White House office heads have often not gone much beyond handing over the floor plans.

Such communication gaps are harmful to good government. Between election and inauguration, therefore, private forums are needed in which newly designated staff leaders can put their inherent hesitations aside and give a hearing to the observations of those who have preceded them—whether of their own party or not. The White House of the future deserves the seeking rather than the rejection of the experience gained in the course of each presidency. Efforts have been planned in this direction—by the Pew Charitable Trusts and by some forward-looking career public administrators who have asked Congress to amend the Presidential Transition Act to authorize preinaugural orientation seminars for newly designated senior White House and cabinet appointees.[24]

Improved Facilities for the Future: *The Comprehensive Design Plan for the White House and President's Park*

In October of 1998, the National Park Service, together with eleven cooperating federal agencies and organizations, spoke up: "Most problems over the last 200 years have been addressed as they have arisen, or not at all, resulting in a piecemeal approach to implementing solutions. Also, problems occurring outside the [President's Park] area, such as surrounding urban land uses and traffic, are encroaching on the site, threatening its dignity and character."[25]

Headed by the Park Service—specifically its White House Liaison Office, and under the leadership of its director, James I. McDaniel—the collaborating agencies spent three years looking at the present and future needs of the White House and its environs. Working together, they produced the first-ever comprehensive plan: a 408-page compendium of proposals for halting the damage being done to the White House neighborhood and for protecting its special nature, while continuing to meet its unique and indispensable operating requirements. Several alternatives were set forth—including a "no-action" option.

The plan that the several agencies all prefer, briefly summarized, emphasizes "a pedestrian-oriented experience within the President's Park, with no surface parking and limited vehicular traffic": meaning a large parking garage out of sight underneath the Ellipse and a smaller one—for presidential motorcade and other VIP cars—under Pennsylvania Avenue. Efficient new underground facilities would also be provided under West Executive Avenue for "meetings and conferences . . . deliveries, storage for frequently used items, first family recreation activities and the news media."[26] The Visitor Center on E Street, where all tours would start, would be expanded to encompass a museum—including four video theaters and "new exhibits on the history of the White House and the American presidency"—and would be connected with the White House by an underground corridor and moving sidewalk. A "permanent events plaza" would be built in one segment of the Ellipse. The trashy souvenir vans would be outlawed (or "relocated to another downtown area"—to assuage the $1.4 million loss of the vendors' annual profits).

In the words of the plan's authors, "The *Comprehensive Design Plan* represents a consensus of hundreds of planners, architects, historians and ordinary citizens about how to protect and enhance one of the preeminent symbols of our democracy. Its priorities are clear: to make the White House more livable and more inspiring for the nation. Such an opportunity comes along rarely. Not to seize it would be impractical, insensitive and irresponsible. Now is the time to act."[27]

The next step involves consultations with the appropriate committees of Congress and may include taking soundings on the possibility of raising private monies to support elements of the plan that cannot be financed with public funds. One would also anticipate an expression of personal presidential support: it is, after all, his President's Park, now and into the future.

Conclusion

What of the future?

As Hamilton would remind us, the raucous pluralism of American society will long continue to be the frustrating environment of those who govern. In a world balancing between peace and the frequent use of force—and in a nation buffeted by competing prescriptions for the division of its resources—parties, legislators, cabinets, and presidents will forever be making their decisions in surroundings that are supercharged with advocacy and pressures.

Can anything "bring us together"?

John Gardner looks at the White House:

Whatever may be said for the parties and for Congress, the best hope of accomplishing the orchestration of conflicting interests, the building of coalitions and the forging of coherent national policy is the President. It is his natural role. He begins the process long before election as he seeks to put together the constituencies he needs. In this day of media-dominated campaigns, the coalition of constituencies may appear to be less needed to gain electoral victory; but it is as needed as ever if the President is to govern effectively after victory. The President's capacity to balance conflicting forces and forge coherent policy and action should be substantially strengthened.[28]

It is the thesis of this book that the modern White House staff is the necessary part of that strengthening.

After each presidential changeover, the alumni of the years just gone begin to draw together to recall—and celebrate—the unforgettable intensities they shared. Eisenhower administration veterans used to gather in reunion luncheons and dinners; the Judson Welliver Society includes all the speechwriters present and past; the 1600 Club welcomes the White House Communications Agency insiders. The Nixon domestic council staffers reunite annually. Every few months the February Group of Nixon-Ford alumni convenes, its national directory of names and addresses kept current, its newsletter chatty with nuggets about new promotions, new marriages, old memories.

Within weeks of inauguration, a new White House staff comes to reflect, as did its predecessor, the president's own policies, priorities, and style. The older core functions continue, juggled perhaps into different hierarchies, adorned with new labels. Faces change, fresh adjustments are made, practices fine-tuned. The White House staff then becomes no more and no less than what the chief executive allows it to be; the instructions it gives are his orders, the procedures it specifies the ones he desires.

The essence of White House service is not the notorious dishonor of a few, but the quiet honor of thousands. The newest staff intern remembers what the oldest White House veteran never forgets: John Adams's prayer inscribed over the fireplace in the State Dining Room: "I pray Heaven to bestow the best of blessings on this House and all that shall hereafter inhabit it. May none but honest and wise men ever rule under this roof."

That invocation reaches the entire White House staff community; few fail to be humbled by the sense of obligation that those words instill. Implied within them is a further admonition: whether high or low in the staff, even in the midst of partisanship, one's duty is not only to the ruler of the present but to the House of the future—to the president of today and to the presidency of tomorrow.

The true reward of White House service reaches beyond the excitement of the moment, is deeper than the seductive allure of the trappings of office.

The energetic and intellectually aggressive men and women who make up the White House staff are driven not so much by the thirst for fame in the present as by the prospect of nudging the future—of "hacking a few toe-holds on history," in the words of one.

A president is elected to effect a coherent program of change, battling all the while the incoherencies of the pluralism beyond the White House gates. The White House staff are his compatriots in this battle, tolerating the extreme personal pressures and accepting at least partial anonymity as lesser sacrifices for a larger goal.

Notes

Notes to Introduction

1. The author's inclusion of the National Security Council (NSC) as part of the White House staff is supported by the following language from a District of Columbia Court of Appeals decision: "The close working relationship between the NSC and the President indicates that the NSC is more like 'the President's immediate personal staff' than it is like an agency exercising authority, independent of the President" (United States Court of Appeals for the D.C. Circuit, case number 95-5057, *Scott Armstrong, et al., v. Executive Office of the President,* decided August 2, 1996, p. 25).

2. Measured by the number of hours worked in direct support of White House activities, nearly half of the Office of Administration is de facto White House staff (and is so counted in chapter 21).

3. The exceptions are some administrative personnel on the staff of the National Security Council.

4. *U.S. Code,* vol. 44, secs. 2201–7.

5. *U.S. Code,* vol. 44, secs. 2101–18, 2901–10, 3101–7, and 3301–24. See the discussion of these statutes in part 3. A court of appeals decision of May 24, 1985 *(Rushworth v. CEA),* affirmed an earlier district court decision conferring presidential records status on the papers of the Council of Economic Advisers, 762 F2d 1038 (1985).

6. For a catalogue of the occasions since 1970 when White House aides have in fact testified, see Louis Fisher, "White House Aides Testifying before Congress," *Presidential Studies Quarterly* 27, no. 1 (Winter 1997):139.

Notes to Chapter One

1. *Statistical Handbook of the United States, 1999,* 119th ed. (GPO, 1999).

2. Henry Kissinger, "America's Contra Muddle," *Washington Post,* July 28, 1987, p. A15.

3. Alexander Hamilton, "The Seventieth Federalist," in *The Federalist Papers of Hamilton, Madison, and Jay* (New York: Mentor Books, 1961), 427.

4. Lemuel A. Garrison, *The Making of a Ranger* (Sun Valley, Idaho: Institute of the American West, 1983), 304.

5. Quoted in "What Loyalty Can Mean to the Top Marine," *Washington Post,* July 3, 1986, p. A21.

6. R. W. Apple Jr., "A Lesson from Shultz," *New York Times,* December 9, 1986, p. 1.

Notes to Chapter Two

1. Joseph Califano, *A Presidential Nation* (W. W. Norton, 1975), 25.

2. *Papers Relating to the President's Departmental Reorganization Program: A Reference Compilation* (GPO, 1971), 11.

3. Louis Fisher and Ronald C. Moe, "Presidential Reorganization Authority: Is It Worth the Cost?" *Political Science Quarterly* (Summer 1981):316.

4. Califano, *Presidential Nation,* 52.

5. By act of Congress (Public Law 106-92), the Old Executive Office Building was given a new name: as of November 9, 1999, it became the Dwight D. Eisenhower Executive Office Building.

6. Henry M. Kissinger, *Years of Upheaval* (Boston: Little, Brown, 1982), 435.

7. Jimmy Carter, "Memorandum for Six Cabinet Heads," March 21, 1977, author's personal collection.

8. Background interview with author.

9. David Broder, *Washington Post,* March 29, 1978, p. A23.

10. Canady's House bill was H.R. 2128, 104th Cong., 1st sess. It was narrowly approved in a vote along party lines by a House Judiciary subcommittee but never came to the House floor.

11. A case particularly significant for affirmative action policy—*Adarand Constructors, Inc.* v. *Pena*—which involved the award of federal contracts, had been argued in the Supreme Court. The Court's opinion (115 S. Ct. 2097) was handed down just as the president's *Affirmative Action Review* was being completed and exactly one week before the presidential speech. The gravamen of the justices' diverse opinions added up to the imposition of stricter standards for *all* federal affirmative action programs but did not demand their cessation—a kind of "mend it but not end it" principle, quite consistent with the conclusions to which the president had just come. Nine days after the issuance of the president's directive, and his speech, Assistant Attorney General Walter Dellinger sent all agency general counsels a 38-page memorandum carefully explaining and analyzing the Court's decision. The texts of the *Affirmative Action Review,* of the president's directive, and of the Dellinger memorandum were bound together in a White House publication, *Affirmative Action Review—Report to the President,* of 1995.

12. Christopher Edley, interview with author, April 22, 1999.

13. Ibid.

14. Ibid.

15. William Jefferson Clinton, *Weekly Compilation of Presidential Documents* 31, no. 29 (July 24, 1995):1264–5.

16. Ibid., 1255–64.

Notes to Part Two introductory text

1. Hillary Clinton's New York State Senate bid is being handled not by the publicly funded first lady's office at the White House, but by a separate campaign staff supported entirely by nongovernment contributions.

2. Extract from a "letter" (number 62) by political satirist Seba Smith (whose pseudonym was Major Jack Downing). Dated August 17, 1833, the letter was printed in the Portland, Maine, *Daily Courier* and reprinted in *The Select Letters of Major Jack Downing* (Philadelphia, 1834), 160–63. The author acknowledges the assistance of John McDonough of the Manuscript Division of the Library of Congress.

Notes to Chapter Three

1. Background interview with author.

2. Brent Scowcroft, interview with author, Washington, D.C., January 11, 1999.

3. Background interview with author.

4. Ibid.

5. Billy Webster, interview with author, Spartanburg, S.C., October 6, 1998.

6. Background interview with author.

7. Background interview with author.

8. Ibid.

9. Ibid.

10. George Bush and Brent Scowcroft, *A World Transformed* (Alfred A. Knopf, 1998),
p. 100.

11. John Lancaster and Lee Hockstader, "Secret Efforts by U.S. Put Israel, Syria Closer to Pact," *Washington Post,* December 13, 1999, p. A1.

12. Scowcroft, interview.

13. Ibid.

14. Bush and Scowcroft, *World Transformed,* 60.

15. Ibid., 61.

16. Ibid., 62.

17. William Jefferson Clinton, *Weekly Compilation of Presidential Documents* 30, no. 7 (February 21, 1994):315.

18. Scowcroft, interview.

19. Walter Pincus, "Reconnaissance of Bosnia Goes On-Line," *Washington Post,* April 13, 1996, p. A24.

20. Scowcroft, interview.

21. Bob Woodward, *The Commanders* (Simon and Schuster, 1991), 364.

22. See Dana Priest, "The Commanders' War: Bombing by Committee," *Washington Post*, September 20, 1999, pp. A10, A11.

23. Senate Armed Services Committee, testimony of General Henry Shelton, October 14, 1999, *Committee Transcript*, p. 56.

24. Senate Armed Services Committee, testimony of Secretary of Defense William Cohen, October 14, 1999, *Committee Transcript*, pp. 65, 91.

25. Letter to author from former president George Bush, September 21, 1998.

26. Scowcroft, interview.

27. Richard Haass, interview with author, Washington, D.C., April 15, 1998.

28. Deputy White House Press Secretary Joe Lockhart, press briefing, March 8, 1997, p. 4.

29. Background interview with author.

30. Of *his* congressional relations officer, national security adviser Zbigniew Brzezinski said: "In a special category was my choice in 1978 for congressional liaison, Madeleine Albright. A close associate of Senator Muskie and an extremely able supporter of Democratic causes, Albright not only became a key NSC staffer but greatly reinforced the occasionally sputtering overall White House coordination with Congress." See *Power and Principle* (Farrar, Straus and Giroux, 1983), 76.

31. Bill Danvers, interview with author, Washington, D.C., January 6, 1998.

32. Report of the President's Special Review Board (GPO, February 26, 1987), pt. 4, p. 6.

33. Ibid., pt. 5, p. 6. The members of the review board were John Tower, Edmund Muskie, and Brent Scowcroft.

34. "An Interview with NSC Legal Adviser Alan Kreczko," *National Security Law Report* (October 1995):6.

35. Bush and Scowcroft, *World Transformed*. This quotation and the others here are from a lengthy, candid discussion of the speechwriting process laid out on pp. 48–55.

36. Ibid., 51. In the seven pages in which Bush and Scowcroft expand on this issue, there is not a single mention of the Department of State.

37. Background interview with author.

38. Ibid.

39. Background interview with author.

40. William Jefferson Clinton, "Commencement Address, U.S. Naval Academy," *Weekly Compilation of Presidential Documents* 34, no. 21 (May 25, 1998):944.

41. "Combating Terrorism: Presidential Decision Directive 62," White House fact sheet, May 22, 1998.

42. Tamraz, an oil financier, desperately wanted a personal appointment with President Clinton to get the president's support for an oil pipeline scheme in the Caucasus. Using old CIA contacts, Tamraz got an appointment with NSC staffer Sheila Heslin, who judged Tamraz to be totally disreputable. Tamraz then made contributions totaling more than $300,000 to the Democratic National Committee and related party campaigns and allegedly used the resulting influence to circumvent Heslin's negative recommendations and to wangle six reception and dinner invitations with the president. In the end, Tamraz's initiative was unsuccessful, but the incident exposed the need for stricter NSC policy control over proposals to have foreign

nationals meet with the president. (See Senate Committee on Governmental Affairs, *Investigations of Illegal or Improper Activities in Connection with 1996 Federal Election Campaigns,* vol. 2, chap. 21.) Foreign nationals who had private business interests and who had made heavy political contributions were also included among invitees to fund-raising coffees with the president, giving rise to suspicions that there was a quid pro quo involved and underscoring the same procedural weaknesses that had been revealed in the Tamraz incident. (See Senate Committee on Governmental Affairs, *Investigations of Illegal or Improper Activities,* vol. 1, pp. 205–23.)

43. The text of this six-page memorandum is included in Senate Committee on Governmental Affairs, *Investigations of Illegal or Improper Activities in Connection with 1996 Federal Election Campaigns,* vol. 1, pp. 760–5.

44. A few NSC employees, principally in the administration and records sections, are tenured civil servants—an exception in the White House bailiwick.

45. Elaine Sciolino, "Berger Manages a Welter of Crises in the Post-Cold-War White House," *New York Times,* May 18, 1998, p. A9.

Notes to Chapter Four

1. A principal reason for this 1985 consolidation was to afford incoming chief of staff Donald Regan a greater degree of control over the agendas of the councils. Bush chief of staff John Sununu continued the arrangement for the same reason. In addition, the secretary to the cabinet—who was the head of the Office of Cabinet Affairs—was considered more of a neutral broker, with respect to contentious issues, than the staff of the substantive policy offices of the White House.

2. Michael Weisskopf, "No Breakthrough in Clean Air Talks," *Washington Post,* February 24, 1990, p. A7.

3. George Bush, "Presidential Statement on Wetlands Preservation," *Weekly Compilation of Presidential Documents* 27, no. 33 (August 19, 1991):1127. The text of the revised interagency manual was published in the Federal Register of August 14, 1991.

4. Roger Porter, interview with author, Washington, D.C., April 28, 1999.

5. William Jefferson Clinton, "Executive Order 12859," *Weekly Compilation of Presidential Documents* 29, no. 33 (August 23, 1933):1638.

6. White House Fellows are exceptionally promising young men and women selected from business, government, the professions, the arts, and the academic world for one year of service in government agencies, including the White House. (See part 3.)

7. William Jefferson Clinton, "Memorandum on an Interagency Task Force on Nonprofits and Government, October 22, 1999," *Weekly Compilation of Presidential Documents* 35, no. 43 (November 1, 1999):2128.

8. Bill Galston, interview with author, College Park, Md., August 14, 1997.

9. Ibid.

10. Ibid.

11. William Jefferson Clinton, "State of the Union Message," *Weekly Compilation of Presidential Documents* 30, no. 4 (January 31, 1994):151.

12. Bruce Reed, interview with author, Washington, D.C., March 1, 1999.

13. William Jefferson Clinton, "Message to Congress Transmitting the Work and Responsibility Act of 1994," *Weekly Compilation of Presidential Documents* 30, no. 25 (1994):1320.

14. Reed, interview.

15. Two years later, on a separate issue—tobacco legislation—Reed and Chief of Staff Erskine Bowles would meet with thirty or forty members of Congress.

16. Reed, interview.

17. Carol Rasco, interview with author, Washington, D.C., September 18, 1997.

18. John Ehrlichman, telephone conversation with author, circa 1976.

19. Reed, interview.

Notes to Chapter Five

1. "Establishment of the President's Economic Policy Board, Executive Order 11808," September 30, 1974; quoted in Roger B. Porter, *Presidential Decision Making: The Economic Policy Board* (Cambridge University Press, 1980), 41.

2. Ibid., 82, 83.

3. Ibid., 84.

4. Robert Rubin, interview with author, New York City, August 9, 1999.

5. Ibid.

6. Gene Sperling, interview with author, Washington, D.C., August 17, 1999.

7. Ibid.

8. Ibid.

9. William Jefferson Clinton, "Statement on the Kyoto Protocol on Climate Change," *Weekly Compilation of Presidential Documents* 33, no. 50 (December 15, 1997):2017–8.

10. Rubin, interview.

11. Sperling, interview.

12. William Jefferson Clinton, "Remarks in the Globalization and Trade Sessions of the Democratic National Committee's Autumn Retreat on Amelia Island," *Weekly Compilation of Presidential Documents* 33, no. 45 (November 1, 1997):1707.

13. Sperling, interview.

Notes to Chapter Six

1. This and the other quotations in this paragraph are from several off-the-record interviews with the author.

2. In an interview with the author in Washington, D.C., on October 22, 1986, Mr. Cutler attributed this aphorism to former undersecretary of State George Ball.

3. Lloyd Cutler, letter to author, August 9, 1999.

4. Adams had telephoned the Federal Trade Commission (FTC) to inquire about a case before the commission involving an old friend of his from New Hampshire— a friend who had done many favors for and had given gifts to the Adams family, but who was now in trouble with the FTC. His call gave the appearance that undue influence was being put on the commission—an appearance that, in turn, placed

intense political pressure on the White House; the result was that Adams resigned.

5. "Standards of Conduct," *The White House Office Handbook* (February 1975), Tab E, p. E-7.

6. *U.S. Code*, vol. 18, sec. 202(a).

7. Other legal experts disagree with that opinion and with the reasoning of the Office of Government Ethics. See Gregory S. Walden, *On Best Behavior: The Clinton Admininstration and Ethics in Government* (Indianapolis: Hudson Institute, 1996), 20–1.

8. *Association of American Physicians and Surgeons, Inc., et al.* v. *Hillary Rodham Clinton et al.*, Civil Action no. 930-399 (RCL): declaration of Ira Magaziner, paragraph 5, lines 2–3 (March 3, 1993).

9. Ibid.; Judicial Order of December 18, 1997. The order was overturned on appeal.

10. Lloyd Cutler, letter to Congressman Frank Wolf, March 18, 1994, quoted in Walden, *Best Behavior,* 183.

11. Ibid., 184–6.

12. Executive Order 10939, May 5, 1961; Executive Order 11222, May 8, 1965; Executive Order 12674, April 12, 1989.

13. *United States* v. *Sun-Diamond Growers of California,* 98–131 of April 27, 1999.

14. See *Weekly Compilation of Presidential Documents* 30, no. 32 (August 15, 1994):1670.

15. William Jefferson Clinton, "Executive Order 12834," *Weekly Compilation of Presidential Documents* 29, no. 3 (January 25, 1993):77.

16. Geoffrey C. Hazard Jr., quoted in Stephen Barr, "Clinton's Ethics Rules: Balance or Barrier?" *Washington Post*, December 14, 1992, p. A21.

17. Griffin B. Bell, *Taking Care of the Law* (William Morrow, 1982), 42.

18. William Jefferson Clinton, "Statement on Signing the National Defense Authorization Act for Fiscal Year 2000," *Weekly Compilation of Presidential Documents* 35, no. 40 (October 5, 1999):1930.

19. Walter Dellinger, Memorandum for the Counsel to the President, "Presidential Authority to Decline to Execute Unconstitutional Statutes," November 2, 1994, p. 4.

20. See Frank B. Cross, "The Constitutional Legitimacy and Significance of Presidential 'Signing Statements,'" *Administrative Law Review* 40, no. 209 (1988).

21. Linda Greenhouse, "In Signing Bills, Reagan Tries to Write History," *New York Times,* December 9, 1986, p. B14.

22. A legislative veto is typically a provision in law that permits Congress to block an executive branch action by a resolution of one house or by a concurrent (two-house) resolution. Such resolutions do not come to the president for signature or veto.

23. United Nations Security Council Resolution 678 of November 1990. See George Bush and Brent Scowcroft, *A World Transformed* (Alfred A. Knopf, 1998), 414–5.

24. U.S. Constitution, amend. 25, secs. 3 and 4. Section 4 contains the added provision that some body other than the cabinet—that is, a majority of "such other

body as Congress may by law provide"—may take this declaratory action along with the vice president. Congress has never specified what other body this might be—an ambiguity of some concern to students of the presidency.

25. White Burkett Miller Center of Public Affairs, University of Virginia, *Report of the Miller Center Commission on Presidential Disability and the Twenty-Fifth Amendment* (Lanham, Md.: University Press of America, 1988), 7.

26. *Public Papers of the Presidents: Ronald Reagan, 1985* (GPO), 919.

27. *Washington Post*, June 14, 1993, p. A17.

28. Boyden Gray, interview with author, Washington, D.C., December 14, 1997.

29. U.S. Court of Appeals for the District of Columbia Circuit, Case 96-3124, *In re: Sealed Case*, decided June 17, 1997; 32, 33, and 35.

30. United States Court of Appeals for the Eighth Circuit, *In re: Grand Jury Subpoena Duces Tecum*, Case 96-4108, unsealed May 2, 1997, pp. 17 and 19.

31. *United States* v. *Haldeman*, 559 F.2nd 31 (D.C. Cir., 1976).

32. U.S. District Court for the District of Columbia, *In re: Grand Jury Proceedings*, 5F Supp. 2d 21, May 27, 1998, pp. 6, 7.

33. U.S. Court of Appeals for the District of Columbia Circuit, *In re: Bruce R. Lindsey (Grand Jury Testimony)*, Case 98-3060; decided July 27, 1998.

34. In the Supreme Court of the United States, October Term, 1996, *Office of the President* v. *Office of Independent Counsel et al.,* On Petition for a Writ of Certiorari to the United States Court of Appeals for the Eighth Circuit, June, 1997, p. 2.

35. Judy Mann, *Washington Post*, July 31, 1998, p. E3. The Paula Jones case is relevant here: the Supreme Court rejected the argument that a sitting president could be excused from participating in a civil lawsuit while he was still in office. The process of appealing that decision, however, ate up so much time that the proceedings were in fact delayed until after the 1996 election—a tactical if not a substantive "victory" for Mr. Clinton.

36. Lloyd Cutler, interview with author, Washington, D.C., December 4, 1997.

37. *U.S. Code*, vol. 18 (1913).

Notes to Chapter Seven

1. Quoted in Charles O. Jones, *Passages to the Presidency: From Campaigning to Governing* (Brookings, 1998), 62.

2. Nick Calio, interview with author, Washington, D.C., August 4, 1998.

3. Ibid.

4. Ibid.

5. Pat Griffin, interview with author, Washington, D.C., September 24, 1997.

6. Background interview with author.

7. Ibid.

8. Ibid.

9. Griffin, interview.

10. Mack McLarty, interview with author, Washington, D.C., October 5, 1998.

11. Griffin, interview.

12. Except, as mentioned earlier, in cases of criminal investigations.

13. Griffin, interview.

14. Timothy J. Keating, interview with author, Washington, D.C., February 15, 1998.

15. Calio, interview.

16. Keating, interview.

17. Ibid.

18. Calio, interview.

19. Keating, interview.

20. Griffin, interview.

21. Keating, interview.

22. Timothy J. Keating, interview with author, March 15, 1997.

23. Griffin, interview.

24. Calio, interview.

25. Griffin, interview.

26. Keating, interview.

27. Calio, interview.

28. Griffin, interview.

29. John Hilley, interview with author, December 18, 1998.

30. Ibid.

31. Quoted in Dom Bonafede, "Carter's Relationship with Congress: Making a Mountain out of a Moorehill," *National Journal,* March 28, 1977, p. 459.

Notes to Chapter Eight

1. Quoted in John Kennedy, "Mike McCurry's About-Face," *George,* March 1999, p. 75.

2. Quoted in Jay Gatsby, "Jay Gatsby in the Oval Office—A Critical Look at Clinton's Sixth Year," *Public Affairs Report* (July 1998):6.

3. Quoted in Kenneth T. Walsh, *Feeding the Beast: The White House versus the Press* (Random House, 1996), 235.

4. Gatsby, "Gatsby in the Oval Office."

5. Lesley Stahl, *Reporting Live* (Simon and Schuster, 1999), 56.

6. Walsh, *Feeding the Beast*, p. 7.

7. Ibid., 35.

8. Stahl, *Reporting Live,* 43.

9. Quoted in Charles O. Jones, *Passages to the Presidency: From Campaigning to Governing* (Brookings, 1998), 143.

10. David Gergen, interview with author, Arlington, Va., March 26, 1998.

11. Marlin Fitzwater, *Call the Briefing! Reagan and Bush, Sam and Helen: A Decade with Presidents and the Press* (Times Books, 1995), 144.

12. Lorraine Voles, interview with author, Washington, D.C., March 14, 1998.

13. Neel Lattimore, interview with author, Washington, D.C., October 30, 1998.

14. Fitzwater, *Call the Briefing,* 209.

15. Howard Kurtz, *Spin Cycle* (Free Press, 1998), 66–7.

16. Ibid., 45.

17. David von Drehle, "President Clinton, Winding Down," *Washington Post,* June 26, 1999, pp. C1, C5.

18. Both Greenstein and Kumar were quoted in John F. Harris, "The Snooze Conference," *Washington Post,* April 20, 1995, pp. D1, D2.

19. Kurtz, *Spin Cycle,* 28.

20. Ibid., 36.

21. Quoted in Howard Kurtz, "The Full Retort: Joe Lockhart, Pressing the President's Point," *Washington Post,* January 18, 1999, p. C4.

22. Howard Paster, "Centralized System for News Media Inquiries," *Washington Post,* January 6, 1993, p. A15.

23. For a penetrating and brilliant in-depth discussion of contemporary White House press and communications strategy, tactics, and operations, see Martha Joynt Kumar, *Wired for Sound and Pictures: The President and White House Communications Operations* (Johns Hopkins University Press, forthcoming). The author acknowledges with thanks the value of being able to examine two advance chapters of this unique work.

24. Quoted in Howard Kurtz, "White House Aide Sent to Somalia to Deal with Press," *Washington Post,* October 14, 1993, p. A22.

25. Ibid.

26. R. Jeffrey Smith, "Washington's 'Bermuda Triangle of News,'" *Washington Post,* May 31, 1996, p. A21.

27. Kurtz, *Spin Cycle,* 43–4.

28. Ibid., 208–11.

29. Mary Ellen Glynn, interview with author, Washington, D.C., August 4, 1998.

30. Background interview with author.

Notes to Chapter Nine

1. William Jefferson Clinton, "Interview with Larry King," *Weekly Compilation of Presidential Documents* 29, no. 29 (July 26, 1993):1397–8.

2. Marlin Fitzpatrick, *Call the Briefing* (Times Books, 1995), 325.

3. Mary Ellen Glynn, interview with author, Washington, D.C., August 4, 1998.

4. Donald Baer, interview with author, Washington, D.C., April 7, 1998.

5. John F. Harris, "Another Budgetary Sound Bite," *Washington Post,* January 6, 1999, p. A8.

6. Sidney Blumenthal, "Letter from Washington: The Syndicated Presidency," *New Yorker,* April 5, 1993, 42ff.

7. Howard Kurtz, "Inaugurating a Talk-Show Presidency," *Washington Post,* February 12, 1993, p. A4.

8. Kenneth T. Walsh, *Feeding the Beast* (Random House, 1996), 130.

9. Howard Kurtz, *Spin Cycle* (Free Press, 1998), 144.

10. Baer, interview.

11. Background interview with author.

12. William Jefferson Clinton, "Interview with the Arizona Media," "Interview with the California Media," *Weekly Compilation of Presidential Documents* 29, no. 31 (August 9, 1993):1507–21.

13. Charles Babington, "Clinton Urges a New Web of Giving," *Washington Post,* October 23, 1999, p. A16.

14. Howard Kurtz, "Clinton to Field Questions Live in First Online Chat by a President," *Washington Post*, October 30, 1999, p. A9.

15. William Jefferson Clinton, "Remarks in an Online Townhall Meeting," *Weekly Compilation of Presidential Documents* 35, no. 45 (November 15, 1999).

16. Charles Babington, "President Goes a Step Further in Online Chat," *Washington Post*, November 9, 1999, p. A10.

17. Kevin Moran, interview with author, Washington, D.C., May 10, 1999.

18. Blumenthal, "The Syndicated Presidency," 44.

19. Barrie Tron, interview with author, Washington, D.C., March 28, 1999.

20. Blumenthal, "The Syndicated Presidency."

21. Steve Silverman, interviews with author, Washington, D.C., November 24, 1997, and New York City, September 2, 1998.

22. Robert B. Reich, *Locked in the Cabinet* (Knopf, 1997), 108–9.

23. David Broder, in a conversation with the author on February 26, 1993, following the appearance of Broder's op-ed column "Beware the 'Trust' Deficit," *Washington Post*, February 24, 1993, p. A19.

24. As described in Kurtz, *Spin Cycle*, 262–4.

25. Lloyd Grove, "All Noisy on the Budget Front," *Washington Post*, July 31, 1993, pp. D1, D5.

26. Greg Lawler, interview with author, Bethesda, Md., September 11, 1997.

27. David Gergen, interview with author, Arlington, Va., March 26, 1998.

28. Leon Panetta, telephone interview with author, November 23, 1998.

29. Don Baer, interview with author, Washington, D.C., March 26, 1998.

30. Background interview with author.

Notes to Chapter Ten

1. Background interview with author.

2. Richard Morris, *Behind the Oval Office: Winning the Presidency in the Nineties* (Random House, 1997), 245.

3. Background interview with author.

4. James C. Humes, *Confessions of a White House Ghostwriter* (Washington, D.C.: Regnery Publishing, 1997), 9.

5. David Kusnet, interview with author, Washington, D.C., September 8, 1997.

6. Background interview with author.

7. David Shipley, interview with author, New York, N.Y., September 2, 1998.

8. Theodore C. Sorensen, "Dearth of Eloquence at the Top," *Chicago Tribune*, August 12, 1979, p. 18.

9. Carol Gelderman, *All the President's Words: The Bully Pulpit and the Creation of the Virtual Presidency* (New York: Walker and Company, 1997), 177.

10. George Stephanopoulos, *All Too Human: A Political Education* (Boston: Little, Brown, 1999), 365.

11. Christopher Edley, interview with author, Cambridge, Mass., April 22, 1999.

12. Kusnet, interview.

13. Ibid.

14. Chriss Winston, interview with author, Pomfret, Md., October 20, 1998.

15. William Jefferson Clinton, "Remarks at a Democratic Congressional and Senate Campaign Committee Dinner in Beverly Hills, California," *Weekly Compilation of Presidential Documents* 35, no. 20 (May 24, 1999):909–15.

16. Kusnet, interview.

17. Background interview with author.

18. Dick Morris, *Behind the Oval Office: Getting Reelected against All Odds* (Los Angeles: Renaissance Books, 1999).

19. The triad were "Address before a Joint Session of the Congress on the State of the Union," *Weekly Compilation of Presidential Documents* 31, no. 4 (January 30, 1995):96 (see Morris, 497); "Remarks and a Question-and-Answer Session with the American Society of Newspaper Editors, Dallas, Texas," *Weekly Compilation of Presidential Documents* 31, no. 14 (April 10, 1995):560 (see Morris, *Getting Reelected against All Odds,* 367); "Address to the Nation on the Plan to Balance the Budget," *Weekly Compilation of Presidential Documents* 31, no. 24 (June 19, 1995):1051 (see Morris, 439).

20. Kusnet, interview.

21. Melanne Verveer, interview with author, Washington, D.C., February 25, 1999.

22. Lissa Muscatine, interview with author, Bethesda, Md., September 29, 1998.

23. Background interview with author.

Notes to Chapter Eleven

1. Background interview with author.

2. Bobbie Kilberg, President Bush's public liaison director, quoting a well-remembered comment by Mr. Bush.

3. *U.S. Code,* vol. 18 (1913).

4. William Jefferson Clinton, "Remarks to the Congressional Asian Pacific American Caucus Institute Dinner," *Weekly Compilation of Presidential Documents* 31, no. 20 (May 22, 1995):856.

5. Steve Hilton, interview with author, Washington, D.C., June 11, 1998.

6. Bobbie Kilberg, interview with author, Herndon, Va., September 11, 1997.

7. Audrey Haynes, interview with author, Washington, D.C., February 5, 1999.

8. Ibid.

9. William Jefferson Clinton, "Address before a Joint Session of the Congress on the State of the Union," *Weekly Compilation of Presidential Documents* 35, no. 3 (January 25, 1999):81.

10. William Jefferson Clinton, "Remarks to the Women's Economic Leadership Forum," *Weekly Compilation of Presidential Documents* 33, no. 14, (April 7, 1997):461–6.

11. White House Office for Women's Initiatives and Outreach, "President Clinton and Vice President Gore: Supporting Women and Families," fact sheet, March 1999. Noncareer SES jobs are Senior Executive Service positions that are filled by political appointees on a patronage basis rather than on a strictly merit or career basis. Schedule C jobs are positions in the middle or upper-middle ranks of the civil service that have been identified as handling "policy or confidential" matters and

are therefore exempted from civil service standards and filled on a political basis. For a full discussion of patronage positions in the executive branch, and the White House role in controlling them, see chapter 15.

12. Haynes, interview.

13. Hilton, interview.

14. Mary Beth Cahill, interview with author, Washington, D.C., July 20, 1999.

15. Hilton, interview.

Notes to Chapter Twelve

1. Billy Webster, interview with author, Spartanburg, S.C., October 6, 1998.

2. Frederick Ryan, interview with author, Washington, D.C., February 18, 1987.

3. Marcia Hale, interview with author, Washington, D.C., September 23, 1998.

4. Kathy Super, interview with author, McLean, Va., August 28, 1998.

5. Webster, interview.

6. Ibid.

7. Leon Panetta, telephone interview with author, November 23, 1998.

8. Super, interview.

9. Webster, interview.

10. Andrew Card, interview with author, Washington, D.C., August 29, 1997.

11. Super, interview.

12. Webster, interview.

13. Ibid.

14. Ibid.

15. Ibid.

16. Lucie Naphin, interview with author, Washington, D.C., August 25, 1998.

Notes to Chapter Thirteen

1. An intensely challenging and complicated area of public policy that is a part of the White House intergovernmental affairs universe—coordinating the government's relationship with the 558 federally recognized Native American tribes—is not included in this chapter. The Clinton White House assigned this responsibility to an officer who, while reporting directly to the chief of staff, handled this subject area as a special project. It will be described in chapter 17. (In a future White House, however, this responsibility may revert to the IGA Office, where it was located under President Bush.)

2. In practical terms, the Big Seven are really six: the Council of State Governments, the National Association of Counties, the National Conference of State Legislatures, the National Governors Association, the National League of Cities, and the U.S. Conference of Mayors. The International City/County Management Association has fewer matters of business with the White House, in part because it represents appointed rather than elected officials.

3. Ray Scheppach, interview with author, Washington, D.C., October 7, 1998.

4. Lanny Griffith, interview with author, Washington, D.C., October 19, 1998.

5. Marcia Hale, interview with author, Washington, D.C., September 23, 1998.

6. Scheppach, interview.

7. Background interview with author.

8. Griffith, interview.

9. Background interview with author.

10. Hale, interview.

11. Griffith, interview.

12. Hale, interview.

13. Ronald Reagan, "Executive Order 12612," *Public Papers of the Presidents: Ronald Reagan, 1987* (GPO), 2:1235.

14. William Jefferson Clinton, "Enhancing the Intergovernmental Partnership," *Weekly Compilation of Presidential Documents* 29, no. 43 (November 1, 1993):2177.

15. David Broder, "Executive Order Urged Consulting, but Didn't," *Washington Post*, July 16, 1998, p. A15.

16. William Jefferson Clinton, "Executive Order 13083," *Weekly Compilation of Presidential Documents* 34, no. 20 (May 18, 1998):866–9.

17. William Jefferson Clinton, "Executive Order 13095," *Weekly Compilation of Presidential Documents* 34, no. 32 (August 10, 1998): 1570.

18. William Jefferson Clinton, "Executive Order 13132," *Weekly Compilation of Presidential Documents* 35, no. 31 (August 9, 1999):1557.

19. Big Seven, letter to the president of August 3, 1999.

20. Background interview with author.

21. *Catalogue of Federal Domestic Assistance*, published semiannually by the General Services Administration and available from the Government Printing Office.

Notes to Chapter Fourteen

1. The 1993–94 Clinton consultants, reportedly because they were so intimately involved in White House deliberations, were considered "special government employees" within the meaning of 18 U.S.C. 208 and were made subject to the conflict-of-interest laws and required to file financial disclosure reports—as was Dick Morris. The consultants whom President Clinton has used since 1995, not having such continuous and "intimate access to Clinton," have not been made subject to these requirements, even though they have many business commitments in addition to those at the White House. See Peter Baker, "White House Isn't Asking Image Advisers to Reveal Assets or Disclose Other Clients," *Washington Post*, May 19, 1997, p. A8.

2. The degree of President Clinton's concern about, and personal immersion in, the actual designing of polls is evident in these two observations by Dick Morris: "In our Arkansas days together, Clinton would spend hours reviewing each detail of a questionnaire before we gave it to the interviewers to field. Surely now that he was president, his review would be more cursory. That's what I thought. . . . But after two hours of reviewing each question, I realized that Bill Clinton's need for the micromanagement of polling had not lessened as his responsibilities had increased [p. 10]. . . . After hours of carefully reviewing each question on the poll, haggling with me over every word, and adding dozens of extra questions, the president then

demanded immediate poll data [p. 85]. See Morris, *Behind the Oval Office: Getting Reelected against All Odds* (Los Angeles: Renaissance Books, 1999).

3. See Bradley Patterson, *The Ring of Power: The White House Staff and Its Expanding Role in Government* (Basic Books, 1988), ch. 17.

4. Background interview with author.

5. James Wray, interview with author, Washington, D.C., September 14, 1998.

6. Quoted in Kathryn Dunn Tenpas, "Institutional Politics: The White House Office of Political Affairs," *Presidential Studies Quarterly* (Spring 1996):512.

7. Ibid., 513.

8. Kathryn Dunn Tenpas, "Promoting President Clinton's Policy Agenda: DNC as Presidential Lobbyist," *American Review of Politics* 17 (Fall/Winter 1996):286.

9. Mary Matalin and James Carville with Peter Knobler, *All's Fair* (Random House, 1994), p. 50; quoted in Herbert S. Parmet, *George Bush: The Life of a Lone Star Yankee* (Scribner, 1997), p. 429.

10. Tenpas, "DNC as Presidential Lobbyist," 287.

11. Joseph Velasquez, interview with author, Washington, D.C., September 11, 1998.

12. Ibid.

13. Ibid.

14. Ibid.

15. Ibid.

16. Ibid.

17. Senate Committee on Government Affairs, *Investigation of Illegal or Improper Activities in Connection with 1996 Federal Election Campaigns, Final Report*, 105th Cong., 2nd sess., March 10, 1999, 1:367.

18. Ibid, 131.

19. Quoted in John F. Harris and Peter Baker, "Ickes Release of Papers Surprised White House," *Washington Post*, February 27, 1997, p. A16.

20. See the table—including Dole's $117,671,328—in Ira Chinoy, "In Presidential Race, TV Ads Were Biggest '96 Loss by Far," *Washington Post*, March 31, 1997, p. A19.

21. President and Mrs. Bush entertained 273 overnight guests at the White House. Some, but not all, were major contributors; many were personal friends, and a few were celebrities—such as Johnny Carson, the Reverend Billy Graham, and the Oak Ridge Boys. See Don Balz and Charles R. Babcock, "Heavy Hitters Are Light on Bush's Overnight List," *Washington Post*, February 27, 1997, p. A17.

22. Quoted in Fred Wertheimer, "Unless We Ban Soft Money," *Washington Post*, August 10, 1997, p. C7.

23. William Jefferson Clinton, press conference, reprinted in *Washington Post*, March 8, 1997, p. A11.

24. John F. Harris and Peter Baker, "'Mistakes Were Made,' Clinton Says of Gifts," *Washington Post*, January 27, 1997, p. A1.

25. Clinton, press conference, *Washington Post*.

26. A statement issued by DNC chairman Donald Fowler included the following: "Our donor program corresponds in significant detail to every donor program used by both political parties since Dwight Eisenhower was president. . . . President Clin-

ton has been a leader in the fight for campaign finance reform. But until the system is changed, we will not unilaterally disarm." Quoted in Tom Raum, "Democrats Defend Perks for Big Donors," *Washington Post*, July 7, 1995, p. A4. But in a later *Post* story, Shawn La Franiere and Susan Schmidt comment, "Ickes's actions underscore questions about whether the White House failed to keep the proper distance between official and political business in the fund-raising frenzy of the last election" ("White House Denies Ickes Broke Law Sending Memo on DNC Gifts," *Washington Post*, February 5, 1997, p. A2). Readers should also study Elizabeth Drew, "A Gourmet's Guide to the Campaign Finance Stew: How to Tell What Smells Fishy from What Really Stinks," an article in the *Washington Post*, March 23, 1997, p. C1.

27. Kathryn Dunn Tenpas, "Campaigning to Govern: Political Consultants as Presidential Advisers" (paper presented at the annual meeting of the American Political Science Association, Boston, Mass., September 6, 1998), 18.

28. Ibid., 6.

29. Two books have described that period: both emphasize, and one of them evaluates, the consultants' unusually privy relationship to the seat of power. See Bob Woodward, *The Agenda* (Simon and Schuster, 1994); and Elizabeth Drew, *On The Edge: The Clinton Presidency* (Simon and Schuster, 1994).

30. Drew, *On the Edge,* 124.

31. James P. Pfiffner, *The Modern Presidency,* 3d ed. (Boston: Bedford, 2000), 80.

32. Dick Morris, *Behind the Oval Office: Winning the Presidency in the Nineties* (Random House, 1997).

33. Ibid, p. 87.

34. Ibid., 144.

35. Ibid., 143.

36. Tenpas, "Campaigning to Govern," 5.

37. Chinoy, "TV Ads Were Biggest Loss," table, p. A19.

38. Morris, *Winning the Presidency,* 9.

39. Ibid., 183.

40. Ibid., 10.

41. Ibid., 84, 338.

42. Ibid., 300.

43. Bruce Reed, interview with author, Washington, D.C., March 1, 1999.

44. Background interview with author.

45. Charles O. Jones, *Passages to the Presidency: From Campaigning to Governing* (Brookings, 1998), 109.

46. Morris, *Getting Reelected against All Odds.*

47. Ibid., 350.

48. Quoted in Donnie Radcliffe, "The Notable Nofziger," *Washington Post,* April 12, 1981, p. L8.

Notes to Chapter Fifteen

1. At the other end of Pennsylvania Avenue is another patronage universe—different and independent from this one, and very large: the staff of the Congress.

2. The list that follows includes paid positions only. Unpaid interns and volunteers are discussed in part 3.

3. There are a very few career employees on the staff of the National Security Council, principally in the administrative and record-keeping sections—a rarity in the White House bailiwick.

4. See part 3.

5. *Obstacle Course: The Report of the Twentieth Century Fund Task Force on the Presidential Appointment Process* (New York: Twentieth Century Fund Press, 1996), 9.

6. Ibid., 17.

7. House Subcommittee on Government Management, Information, and Technology, *Presidential Transition Act Amendments of 1999*, 106th Cong., 1st sess., testimony of Paul Light, October 13, 1999.

8. Public Law 88-277 (March 4, 1964).

9. Quoted in Charles O. Jones, *Passages to the Presidency: From Campaigning to Governing* (Brookings, 1998), 73.

10. Ibid., 127.

11. Background interview with author.

12. See Sharon La Franiere and Lena H. Sun, "DNC Urged Jobs for Fund-Raisers," *Washington Post*, April 15, 1997, p. A4.

13. Although it is never true in fact, it is being assumed here, for convenience, that all 868 federal judgeships are filled when the president leaves office.

14. See part 3—in particular, the section on the White House Military Office.

15. Chase Untermeyer, interview with author, Washington, D.C., September 4, 1997.

16. Richard M. Nixon, *The Memoirs of Richard Nixon* (Warner Books, 1978), 2:285.

17. Bob Nash, interview with author, Washington, D.C., March 17, 1999.

18. Constance Horner, interview with author, Washington, D.C., September 29, 1997.

19. Untermeyer, interview.

20. Ibid.

21. Hamilton Jordan, "What Not to Do," *Washington Post*, November 9, 1992, p. A21.

22. Nash, interview.

23. Frederick W. Wackerle, quoted in Jay Matthews, "Are There ANY Skeletons in Your Closet?" *Washington Post*, May 2, 1995, p. D1.

24. Paper from Dwight Ink and others in support of an amendment to the Presidential Transition Act of 1963, Spring, 1999 (author's private collection).

25. Horner, interview.

26. Nash, interview. For a brief account of the decidedly indelicate ways that the Carter and Reagan administrations tried to evaluate political subordinates, see Bradley Patterson, *The Ring of Power: The White House Staff and Its Expanding Role in Government* (Basic Books, 1988), 256.

27. Miller Center of Public Affairs, *Improving the Process of Appointing Federal Judges: A Report of the Miller Center Commission on the Selection of Federal Judges* (Charlottesville: University of Virginia, Miller Center of Public Affairs, 1996), 5.

28. Ibid., 8.

29. Ibid.

30. Task Force on Federal Judicial Selection of the Citizens for Independent Courts, *Justice Held Hostage: Politics and Selecting Federal Judges,* final prepublication manuscript (Washington, D.C.: September 29, 1999), 10, 11, and table 3. (Former White House counsel Lloyd Cutler is a co-chair of the Citizens for Independent Courts.)

31. It is beyond the scope of this book to delve into the delays that have plagued Senate confirmation of some of President Clinton's judicial and ambassadorial nominees. Suffice it to say that many of these cases got caught between the personal-political grindstones of the president and the Senate committee chairs, then became the subjects of tendentious negotiations.

32. William Jefferson Clinton, "Remarks Announcing the Withdrawal of the Nomination of Lani Guinier and an Exchange with Reporters," *Weekly Compilation of Presidential Documents* 29, no. 22 (June 3, 1993):1028.

33. A fifth treatise, *Thickening Government: Federal Hierarchy and the Diffusion of Accountability,* by Brookings Institution scholar Paul Light, criticizes the growth of the *layers* of government, "whether occupied by careerists or appointees" (Brookings, 1995).

34. Untermeyer and Horner, interviews.

35. Edwin Feulner, "One Veto the GOP Ought to Support," *Washington Post,* September 13, 1995, p. A19. (Feulner is president of the Heritage Foundation.)

36. Mention should be made of a 1999–2000 project, funded by the Pew Charitable Trusts, to "provide relief to presidential nominees in filling out forms and learning about the vagaries of the appointment process." The Presidential Appointments Project "will prepare a software package with an accompanying online manual that nominees can easily download from the Project's Web site onto their computers and fill out for return to the several relevant federal agencies seeking information. [The project] . . . will furnish a narrative walk-through of the nomination process with its individual steps laid out, accompanied by supporting information identifying and describing each stage."

Notes to Chapter Sixteen

1. The quoted information in this chapter comes from three principal sources: (1) lengthy and detailed interviews that the author conducted with the heads or senior members of the White House Advance Office—Red Caveney and Ron Walker from the Nixon administration; John Keller from the Bush administration; and Dan Rosenthal, Paige Reffe, and Aviva Steinberg from the Clinton administration (where possible, the particular source for a quotation has been indicated); (2) background interviews with a number of additional persons, including several American diplomats (these interviews provided the author with factual information, such as the figures given here, accounts of personal experiences, and judgments about methods and objectives); (3) White House advance and orientation manuals from several presidencies. The author is deeply indebted to the men and women who so graciously shared their experiences, opinions, and information with him, as well as to the Advance Offices for the opportunity to examine the manuals.

2. For the first several years of his administration, President Clinton combined

the Advance Office with the Office of Presidential Scheduling. Later the Advance Office was made a separate entity.

3. Paige Reffe, interview with author, Washington, D.C., September 25, 1997.

4. John Keller, interview with author, Alexandria, Va., September 2, 1997.

5. Advance Manual.

6. Background interview with author.

7. Advance Manual.

8. Ibid.

9. Ibid.

10. Background interview with author.

11. Ibid.

12. CBS newswoman Susan Zirinsky, quoted in Martin Schram, *The Great American Video Game: Presidential Politics in the Television Age* (William Morrow, 1987), 57.

13. Schram, *Great American Video Game*, 57.

14. Dan Rosenthal, interview with author, Washington, D.C., October 28, 1997.

15. Advance Manual.

16. Ibid.

17. Ibid.

18. Ibid.

19. Ibid.

20. Background interview with author.

21. Ibid.

22. Advance Manual.

23. Dan Rosenthal and Aviva Steinberg, director and deputy director of the Advance Office, respectively; interview with author, Washington, D.C., September 9, 1998. Both Rosenthal and Steinberg advanced the China trip.

24. Ibid.

25. Ibid.

26. Ibid.

27. Ibid.

28. Ibid.

29. Ibid.

30. Ibid.

31. Ibid.

32. Red Caveney, interview with author, New York, N.Y., spring 1987.

33. Advance Manual.

Notes to Chapter Seventeen

1. Christopher H. Forman Jr., "AIDS and the Limits of Czardom," *Brookings Review* (Summer 1993).

2. Forman, "Limits of Czardom."

3. William Jefferson Clinton, "Remarks on the Appointment of Kristine M. Gebbie as AIDS Policy Coordinator and an Exchange with Reporters," *Weekly Compilation of Presidential Documents* 29, no. 25 (June 25, 1993):1168. For

some of the language from the President's remarks, see the second epigraph to this chapter.

4. The important difference between these two institutions is delineated in the Introduction to this book.

5. *U.S. Code,* vol. 21, sec. 1501 et seq.

6. Don Colburn, "The Woman Who Would Not Be Czar," Health Section, *Washington Post,* July 26, 1994, p. 7.

7. Ibid.

8. Sandy Thurman, interview by Diane Rehm, *Diane Rehm Show,* radio broadcast, June 5, 1998.

9. Sandy Thurman, interview with author, Washington, D.C., June 21, 1999.

10. Office of National AIDS Policy, *Report on the Presidential Mission,* July 19, 1999.

11. Thurman, interview.

12. Thurman, *Diane Rehm Show.*

13. Thurman, interview.

14. William Jefferson Clinton, "Opening Remarks at the White House Conference on Climate Change," *Weekly Compilation of Presidential Documents* 33, no. 41 (October 13, 1997):1493.

15. The language used here to describe the initiatives is taken from this fact sheet, a copy of which is in the author's personal collection.

16. William Jefferson Clinton, "Message to the Congress Transmitting an Account of Federal Agency Climate Change Programs and Activities," *Weekly Compilation of Presidential Documents* 35, no. 16 (April 26, 1999):685

17. William Jefferson Clinton, "Executive Order 13123," *Weekly Compilation of Presidential Documents* 35, no. 22 (June 7, 1999): 1021.

18. William Jefferson Clinton, "Executive Order 13073," *Weekly Compilation of Presidential Documents* 34, no. 6 (February 9, 1998):198–9.

19. William Jefferson Clinton, *Weekly Compilation of Presidential Documents* 34, no. 43 (October 26, 1998):2078–9.

20. Senate Special Committee on the Year 2000 Technology Problem, 105th Cong., 1st sess., testimony of John Koskinen, July 29, 1999.

21. Ibid.

22. President's Initiative on Race, *The Advisory Board's Report to the President: One America in the 21st Century—Forging a New Future* (GPO, September 1998), 1.

23. Ibid., 94–5.

24. President's Initiative for One America, *Pathways to One America in the 21st Century: Promising Practices for Racial Reconciliation* (GPO, 1999), introductory letter from Ben Johnson.

25. See Howard Kurtz, "Gore to Announce Plans to Hike Budget for Civil Rights by 15%," *Washington Post,* January 18, 1999, p. A7.

26. Lynn Cutler, interview with author, Washington, D.C., August 17, 1999.

27. National Academy of Public Administration, *Coping with Catastrophe: Building an Emergency Management System to Meet People's Needs in Natural and Manmade Disasters* (Washington, D.C.: NAPA, February, 1993), 8.

28. H.R. 1685, 105th Cong., 1st sess.

29. Dan Morgan, "Alice Rivlin's Budget Dream," *Washington Post,* January 1, 1993, p. A17.

30. *Washington Post,* December 7, 1993, p. A4; Al Kamen, "In the Loop," *Washington Post,* December 20, 1993, p. A23.

31. Guy Gugliotta, "Lone Bureacratic Island under Fire from Territories," *Washington Post,* April 26, 1994, p. A13.

32. Peter Perl, "President, Hill, Must Provide Leadership, Rights Panel Says," *Washington Post,* January 17, 1995, p. A1.

33. There is a subgroup of special appointees who may look like White House czars but, in the author's opinion, are not: special envoys, designated by the president, whom he sends on tough missions abroad. William Gray for Haiti, George Mitchell for Ireland, and Richard Beattie for Cyprus come to mind. Although the special envoys reported to both the secretary of state and the president, they don't fit into the "czar" category within the meaning of this chapter: they were not physically located within the White House perimeter and the very special focus of each was limited to one country abroad.

Notes to Chapter Eighteen

1. *Association of American Physicians and Surgeons, Inc., et al.* v. *Hillary Rodham Clinton,* United States Court of Appeals for the District of Columbia Circuit, case numbers 93-5086 and 93-5092, June 22, 1993, p. 11.

2. Carl Sferrazza Anthony, *First Ladies: The Saga of the Presidents' Wives and Their Power,* 2 vols. (William Morrow, 1990–91).

3. A detailed examination of Mrs. Clinton's Senate candidacy is outside the purview of this book.

4. Haynes Johnson and David Broder, *The System* (Boston: Little, Brown, 1996), 100.

5. In view of a lawsuit filed on February 24, 1993, by the Association of American Physicians and Surgeons alleging that the task force and the working groups were "advisory committees" for purposes of the Federal Advisory Committee Act— and thus had to make all their papers public—Mrs. Clinton did not actually chair task force meetings after that date. (The task force was eventually found not subject to that act, but it did release more than 250 boxes of its papers.)

6. George Stephanopoulos, *All Too Human: A Political Education* (Boston: Little, Brown, 1999), 198.

7. Eleanor Roosevelt appeared before Congress twice: once during the Depression, to speak about the plight of migrant workers; and once during World War II, to speak about slum-housing conditions. Rosalyn Carter testified in 1970 about mental health issues. (Research credit here goes to Johnson and Broder, *The System,* 182.)

8. Johnson and Broder, *The System,* 183, 185.

9. Ibid., 176.

10. Ibid., 101.

11. Ibid., 176.

12. Ibid., 183.

13. Ibid., 176.

14. Ibid., 324.

15. Ibid., 462.

16. Stephanopoulos, *All Too Human,* 301.

17. Melanne Verveer, interview with author, Washington, D.C., February 25, 1999.

18. See William Jefferson Clinton, *Weekly Compilation of Presidential Documents* 32, no. 51 (December 23, 1996):2512–4.

19. William Jefferson Clinton, "Remarks upon Signing Public Law 105-89," *Weekly Compilation of Presidential Documents* 33, no. 47 (November 19, 1997):1863–4.

20. See William Jefferson Clinton, "Remarks during the Morning Session of the White House Conference on Child Care," *Weekly Compilation of Presidential Documents* 33, no. 43 (October 27, 1997):1634–41.

21. William Jefferson Clinton, "Remarks Announcing Proposed Legislation on Child Care," *Weekly Compilation of Presidential Documents* 34, no. 2 (January 12, 1998):12–5.

22. David A. Vise, "Hillary Clinton Steps Up Effort to Help D.C.," *Washington Post,* December 18, 1996, p. A1.

23. David A. Vise, "Hillary Clinton Makes D.C. Advocate Debut," *Washington Post,* December 20, 1996, pp. C1, C6.

24. William Jefferson Clinton, "Remarks Announcing the District of Columbia College Reading Tutor Initiative," *Weekly Compilation of Presidential Documents* 33, no. 8 (February 24, 1997):220–5.

25. Quoted from a copy of the first lady's letter that was given to the author.

26. The quotations are from William Jefferson Clinton, "Executive Order 13072," *Weekly Compilation of Presidential Documents* 34, no. 6 (February 9, 1998) and from several fact sheets distributed by the White House Millennium Council.

27. Hillary Rodham Clinton, "Memorandum for the President," April 18, 1999, author's personal collection.

28. Hillary Rodham Clinton, "First Lady Hillary Rodham Clinton's Remarks to the United Nations Fourth World Conference on Women, Beijing, China," White House press release, September 5, 1998.

29. Melanne Verveer, interview with author, Washington, D.C., February 25, 1999.

30. William Jefferson Clinton, *Weekly Compilation of Presidential Documents* 35, no. 5 (February 8, 1999):193.

31. Verveer, interview.

32. Distinguished political scientists Louis Brownlow, Robert Merriam, and Luther Gulick were the members of the President's Committee on Administrative Management (colloquially known as the Brownlow Committee), which, at the end of 1936, told Franklin Roosevelt that "the president needs help" and recommended that Roosevelt strengthen his staff resources and build a small and self-effacing White House staff.

33. Public Law 95-570, 95th Cong., 2nd sess. (November 2, 1978), sec. 105(e).

34. Neel Lattimore, interview with author, Washington, D.C., October 10, 1998.

35. Verveer, interview.

36. Lissa Muscatine, interview with author, Bethesda, Md., September 19, 1998.

37. Judith Ann Stock, interview with author, Washington, D.C., May 8, 1998.

38. Ibid.

39. Ibid.

40. Roxanne Roberts and David Montgomery, "The ABC's of the A List," *Washington Post,* April 14, 1999, p. C11.

41. Dwight Cramer, interview with author, Bethesda, Md., July 29, 1998.

42. Verveer, interview.

43. Lynne Duke, "First Lady Says She's Definitely in Senate Race," *Washington Post,* November 24, 1999, p. A1.

44. Quoted in Duke, "First Lady in Senate Race," p. A4.

45. Judy Mann, "First Lady Should Have Second Thoughts," *Washington Post,* December 1, 1999, p. C15.

Notes to Chapter Nineteen

1. *A Heartbeat Away: Report of the Twentieth Century Fund Task Force on the Vice Presidency* (New York: Priority Press Publications, 1988), 12.

2. Public Law 95-570, 95th Cong., 2nd sess. (November 2, 1978), sec. 106(a).

3. George H. W. Bush, letter and attachments to author, September 21, 1998.

4. William Kristol, interview with author, Washington, D.C., August 13, 1998.

5. In addition to the vice president, who chaired the council, the council's members were the secretaries of Treasury and Commerce, the attorney general, the chair of the Council of Economic Advisers, the director of the Office of Management and Budget, and the White House chief of staff. There were several interwoven issues with respect to the council: (1) whether the president and the OMB even had the authority in the first place to review agency regulations that were promulgated pursuant to statute; (2) whether the council's leadership was stacked against the environmental perspective; and (3) whether the council itself was a "back door" to the presidency for pro-business and antiregulatory interests.

6. Dan Quayle, *Standing Firm: A Vice Presidential Memoir* (HarperCollins, 1994), 135–40. See also Bob Woodward, *The Commanders* (Simon and Schuster, 1991), 146–53.

7. Quoted in Herbert S. Parmet, *George Bush: The Life of a Lone Star Yankee* (Scribner, 1997), 486.

8. Bush, letter and attachments to author.

9. Quoted in Cindy Skrzycki, "The Tekkie on the Ticket," *Washington Post,* October 18, 1992, p. H1.

10. William Jefferson Clinton, "Remarks Announcing the Initiative to Streamline Government," *Weekly Compilation of Presidential Documents* 29, no. 9 (March 3, 1993):350.

11. William Jefferson Clinton, "Vancouver Declaration: Joint Statements of the Presidents of the United States and the Russian Federation," *Weekly Compilation of Presidential Documents* 29, no. 14 (April 12, 1993):546.

12. William Jefferson Clinton, "Remarks and an Exchange with Reporters on Immigration Policy," *Weekly Compilation of Presidential Documents* 29, no. 30 (August 2, 1993):1460.

13. William Jefferson Clinton, "Memorandum Establishing the President's Community Enterprise Board," *Weekly Compilation of Presidential Documents* 29, no. 36 (September 13, 1993):1716–7.

14. William Jefferson Clinton, "Executive Order 12866," *Weekly Compilation of Presidential Documents* 29, no. 39 (October 3, 1993):1925.

15. Jim Hoagland, "Al Gore's New Assignment," *Washington Post*, November 9, 1993, p. A19.

16. Todd Robberson, "In Mexico, Gore Stresses Goal of Democracy," *Washington Post*, December 2, 1993, p. A37.

17. R. Jeffrey Smith, "Gore Presses Kohl on Aid to Russia," *Washington Post*, December 19, 1993, p. A44.

18. Sandra Sugamara, "Gore to Urge Phone, Cable Deregulation," *Washington Post*, December 21, 1993, p. D1.

19. R. Jeffrey Smith, "Gore's Central Asia Trip Keeps Him on Route to Broader Foreign Policy Role," *Washington Post*, December 22, 1993, p. A26.

20. Frank Swoboda, "Gore to Meet with Top Leaders in Reconciliation Effort," *Washington Post*, February 16, 1994, p. D4.

21. William Jefferson Clinton, "Memorandum on the Ounce of Prevention Council," *Weekly Compilation of Presidential Documents* 30, no. 37 (September 19, 1994):1762.

22. *Washington Post* (September 8, 1994).

23. William Jefferson Clinton, "Memorandum on Supporting the Role of Father in Families," *Weekly Compilation of Presidential Documents* 31, no. 25 (June 26, 1995):1077–8.

24. Charles Aldinger, "Gore Vows Defeat of Drug Cartels," *Washington Post*, July 26, 1995, p. A6.

25. William Jefferson Clinton, "Remarks to the White House Community Empowerment Conference," *Weekly Compilation of Presidential Documents* 31, no. 30 (July 31, 1995):1303.

26. Lynne Duke, "U.S., S. Africa Establish Broader Economic Ties," *Washington Post*, December 6, 1995, p. A31.

27. R. Jeffrey Smith, "Counter-Terrorism to Be Olympic Event for U.S.," *Washington Post*, April 23, 1996, p. A9.

28. William Jefferson Clinton, "Executive Order 13015," *Weekly Compilation of Presidential Documents* 32, no. 34 (August 26, 1996):1489.

29. William Jefferson Clinton, "Executive Order 13017," *Weekly Compilation of Presidential Documents* 32, no. 36 (September 9, 1996):1659–60.

30. William Jefferson Clinton, "Memorandum on Electronic Commerce," *Weekly Compilation of Presidential Documents* 33, no. 27 (July 7, 1997):1006–12.

31. John Lancaster, "U.S. Role as Arms Merchant to Kuwait Faces Challenges by China," *Washington Post*, July 15, 1997, p. A14.

32. William Jefferson Clinton, "Remarks Announcing a New Initiative to Protect Youth from Tobacco," *Weekly Compilation of Presidential Documents* 33, no. 38 (September 22, 1997):1352–6.

33. William Jefferson Clinton, "Joint Statement on U.S.–Kazakhstan Relations, November 18, 1997," *Weekly Compilation of Presidential Documents* 33, no. 47 (November 24, 1997):1853.

34. William Jefferson Clinton, "Memorandum on Streamlining the Granting of Waivers," *Weekly Compilation of Presidential Documents* 34, no. 17 (April 27, 1998):686.

35. Thomas W. Lippman, "Gore Tour Fuels Hope for Talks," *Washington Post,* May 4, 1998, p. A1.

36. William Jefferson Clinton, "Remarks on the Next Generation COPS Initiative in Alexandria, Virginia, January 4, 1999," *Weekly Compilation of Presidential Documents* 35, no. 2 (January 18, 1999):52–4.

37. Nora Boustany, "Diplomatic Dispatches," *Washington Post,* February 26, 1999, p. A24.

38. Greg Simon, interview with author, Washington, D.C., April 15, 1998.

39. Lorraine Vales, interview with author, Washington, D.C., March 14, 1998.

40. Bruce Reed, interview with author, Washington, D.C., March 1, 1999.

41. Dick Morris, *Behind the Oval Office: Getting Reelected against All Odds* (Los Angeles: Renaissance Press, 1997), 124.

42. Simon, interview.

43. Ibid.

44. For a concise history and overview of what this initiative is doing and has done, see John Kamensky, *The National Partnership for Reinventing Government: A Brief History* (January, 1999); Kamensky's report is also available on the Internet at *http://www.npr.gov. whoweare/history2.html.*

45. Albert Gore, "Memorandum to the Heads of Departments and Agencies," October 18, 1997, author's private collection.

46. Simon, interview.

47. Morris, *Getting Reelected against All Odds,* 119.

48. Simon, interview.

49. Ibid.

50. Ceci Connolly, "Most Involved Vice President Disengages," *Washington Post,* November 22, 1999, pp. A1, A6, A7.

51. Ibid.

Notes to Chapter Twenty

1. Bob Woodward and David S. Broder, "Guardian of the Quayle Image," *Washington Post,* January 18, 1992, pp. A1, A12, A13.

2. Public Law 101-354, 101st Cong., 2nd sess. (August 10, 1990).

3. Megan Rosenfeld, "Marilyn Quayle, Settling In," *Washington Post,* November 24, 1989, p. B9.

4. Ibid.

5. This account was zestfully related to the author by Mr. Natsios during a telephone conversation in the fall of 1999.

6. Ibid.

7. Marilyn Quayle and Nancy Northcott, *Embrace the Serpent* (Crown, 1992).

8. Denise Balzano, interview with author, McLean, Va., April 29, 1999.

9. William Jefferson Clinton, "Remarks on Signing the Departments of Veterans Affairs and Housing and Urban Development and Independent Agencies Appropriations Act," *Weekly Compilation of Presidential Documents* 32, no. 39

(September 30, 1996):1875. The fiscal year 1997 appropriations act for Health and Human Services and the Veterans Administration is Public Law 104-204, 104th Cong., 2nd sess. (September 26, 1996).

10. William Jefferson Clinton, "Executive Order 12848," *Weekly Compilation of Presidential Documents* 29, no. 20 (May 24, 1993):909–10.

11. Spencer Rich, "Panel Votes to Expand Mental Health Benefits," *Washington Post,* May 18, 1994, p. A10.

12. William Jefferson Clinton, "Statement on Signing the Telecommunications Act of 1996," *Weekly Compilation of Presidential Documents* 32, no. 6 (February 12, 1996): 218–20.

13. William Jefferson Clinton, "Remarks at the Children's Television Conference," *Weekly Compilation of Presidential Documents* 32, no. 31 (August 5, 1996):1363.

14. Skila Harris, interview with author, Washington, D.C., September 24, 1997.

15. William Jefferson Clinton, "Address before a Joint Session of Congress on the State of the Union," *Weekly Compilation of Presidential Documents* 33, no. 6 (February 10, 1997):139.

16. Tipper Gore, letter published in the *Washington Post,* Health Section, April 7, 1998, p. 4.

17. William Jefferson Clinton, *Weekly Compilation of Presidential Documents* 34, no. 18 (May 4, 1998):732.

18. William Jefferson Clinton, *Weekly Compilation of Presidential Documents* 34, no. 45 (November 9, 1998):2258.

19. The transcript of this November 10, 1998, telephone conversation was published in the *Weekly Compilation of Presidential Documents* 34, no. 46 (November 16, 1998):2291–2.

20. William Jefferson Clinton, "The President's Radio Address," *Weekly Compilation of Presidential Documents* 34, no. 47 (November 23, 1998):2317–8.

21. William Jefferson Clinton, "Remarks on the White House Conference on Mental Health," *Weekly Compilation of Presidential Documents* 35, no. 23 (June 14, 1999):1052.

22. *Picture This* (Broadway Books, 1996); *The Way Home: Ending Homelessness in America* (Harry Abrams, 1999).

23. Tipper Gore with Beth Berselli, "Tipper's Photo Finish," *Washington Post,* November 30, 1999.

24. Public Law 95-570, 95th Cong., 2nd sess., secs. 106(a)(2), 106(c).

25. Audrey Haynes, interview with author, Washington, D.C., February 5, 1999.

26. William Jefferson Clinton, "Remarks at a Democratic National Committee Dinner," *Weekly Compilation of Presidential Documents* 35, no. 3 (January 25, 1999):70–1.

Notes to Chapter Twenty-One

1. The back door referred to here is in the northeast quadrant of the Oval Office. A completely separate west door leads to the president's study, bathroom, and private dining room—where the escapades with Ms. Lewinsky took place.

2. Lloyd Grove, "Guardians at the Gate," *Washington Post*, September 16, 1998, p. D3.

3. Stephen Goodin and Andrew Friendly, interview with author, Washington, D.C., January 17, 1998.

4. Ibid.

5. Ibid.

6. Andrew Friendly, quoted in Peter Baker, "The President's Loyal Shadow," *Washington Post*, December 29, 1997, p. A15.

7. Steve Bull, interview with author, Washington, D.C., July 25, 1986.

8. Baker, "The President's Loyal Shadow."

9. Gooding and Friendly, interview.

10. Ibid.

11. Gooding and Friendly, interview.

12. Baker, "The President's Loyal Shadow."

13. For a more detailed description of Ike's use of the cabinet, see Bradley Patterson, *The Ring of Power: The White House Staff and Its Expanding Role in Government* (Basic Books, 1988), 27–33; Patterson, "An Overview of the White House," in *Portraits of American Presidents,* ed. Kenneth W. Thompson (Lanham, Md.: University Press of America, 1984), 3:113–41.

14. Edith Holiday, interview with author, Washington, D.C., September 16, 1998.

15. Steve Danzansky, interview with author, Boston, Mass., April 23, 1998.

16. See Patterson, *Ring of Power,* 50–3.

17. Thurgood Marshall Jr., interview with author, Washington, D.C., November 24, 1997.

18. Background interview with author.

19. Danzansky, interview.

20. Christine Varney, interview with author, Washington, D.C., December 16, 1997.

21. Background interview with author.

22. Steve Silverman, interview with author, Washington, D.C., September 2, 1998.

23. Ibid.

24. Varney, interview.

25. Background interview with author.

26. Well, perhaps not. Note the following July 5, 1993, entry in the memoir of Robert Reich, former secretary of labor: "I'm losing confidence that my memos are getting to B. And even when they are, a fair number leak to the press. I ask Hillary for advice. 'Send them to *me,*' she says. 'I'll make sure they get to him. Use blank sheets of paper without any letterhead or other identifying characteristics. Just the date and your initials.' Now I have my own loop." Robert B. Reich, *Locked in the Cabinet* (Alfred A. Knopf, 1997), 180.

27. Todd Stern, interview with author, Washington, D.C., January 26, 1999.

28. Ibid.

29. Ibid.

30. Ibid.

31. Creating the Office of Administration helped Carter to claim that his White

House staff was smaller; actually, it freed up several White House positions that could then be assigned for policy instead of administrative tasks.

32. Background interview with author.

33. General Accounting Office, *Presidential Travel: Costs and Accounting for the President's 1998 Trips to Africa, Chile, and China*, GAO/NSIAD-99-164, September 21, 1999, p. 3.

34. In February of 1992, the House Post Office and Civil Service Committee, led by Congressman Paul Kanjorski, undertook an election-year vendetta against the Bush White House. Question after question was flung at the weary testifiers (a sample: "How many floral arrangements, invitations, banners, streamers, balloons, and other decorative items were used for each event at the White House or at the residence of the Vice President during 1991?"); thousands of pages were generated in response.

35. If a president regularly spends time at oceanfront property (as did Nixon and Bush, for example), another contributing agency is added to the list: the Department of Transportation's Coast Guard.

36. Derivation of this figure: the fiscal year 2001 budget amount was $7,165,000, which finances 60 positions at an average cost of $119,416. Added to that amount was the value of approximately 130 detailees and experts, also at $119,416 each.

37. See endnote 2 of the Introduction (p. 437) and the brief description of the OA's functions in part 3 (pp. 403–04).

38. The author's personal estimate includes $59,000,000 for the White House Communications Agency; that figure is based on the 1996 audit hearings. See House Committee on Government Reform and Oversight, *Hearings before the Subcommittee on National Security, International Affairs, and Criminal Justice* 104th Cong., 2nd sess. (May 16, 1996; June 13, 1996). Consider, for example, the Department of Defense costs for just three international presidential trips in 1998— $60,559,490—as reported in General Accounting Office, *Presidential Travel*.

39. This figure is the author's own estimate of salaries, expenses, and procurement. The U.S. Secret Service does not make public the budget figures for its presidential or vice presidential protective functions; however, the total Secret Service budget for fiscal year 2001 is $826.6 million. In the early summer of 1999, the Secret Service moved into a new headquarters building in downtown Washington; the cost of that building is not included here.

40. This figure, 70 percent of the Service Delivery Team's total annual cost of $13,500,000, is based on an estimate of the person-hours committed to the direct support of White House building maintenance.

41. An estimate of the salaries, expenses, and equipment costs for this unit of some twenty-one persons.

42. This figure represents the cost of the Office of the President's Commission on White House Fellowships. Those fellows who are assigned to the White House have their salaries paid by various federal agencies; those agencies then assign them to the White House as detailees. These salaries are included in the figures for the detailees in item 15, rather than in item 12. Part 3 of this volume includes a description of the White House Fellows program.

43. This is the author's personal estimate. Consider, for example, the Department

of State costs for just three international presidential trips in 1998—$8,588,747—as reported in General Accounting Office, *Presidential Travel*.

44. Based on figures drawn from the latest available Report of the Director of the Office of Administration to Congress, December 24, 1998. The total given here represents 12,857 person-days at $250 per day. After 180 days of service, the White House reimburses the home agencies of the respective detailees, as required by section 112 of Public Law 95-570. These reimbursement costs are reflected separately in items 1, 2, and 3 of the budget.

45. Still absent from this total are (1) the costs to the FBI for security investigations of White House employees and (2) the costs to several other agencies (for example, Commerce, Energy, Justice, Labor, Transportation, the Agency for International Development, the Customs Service, the Immigration and Naturalization Service, and the Overseas Private Investment Corporation) for their support of presidential trips. (See General Accounting Office, *Presidential Travel*.)

46. Public Law 95-570.

47. *National Security Act of 1947, U.S. Statutes at Large* 61 (1947): 497.

48. The assistant to the president for management and administration controls the budgets and staffs of all Executive Office units except the Office of Management and Budget and the U.S. Trade Representative.

49. Public Law 95-570, sec. 112. One tactic that the White House uses to escape the reimbursement obligation is to arrange for a detailee to be on duty in the White House for the final 180 days of one fiscal year and then for the first 180 days of the next.

50. Public Law 105-61, 105th Cong., 4th sess. (October 10, 1997), sec. 618(a). Section 618(b) of this statute exempts the national security and intelligence agencies from the provisions of section 618(a).

51. Public Law 95-570, sec. 113.

52. Public Law 103-270, 105th Cong., 4th sess., sec. 6.

53. Consultants, experts, and detailees are not listed separately but have been included in the staff numbers for the various White House offices to which they are assigned.

54. See endnote 1 of the Introduction (p. 437) and the brief description of the OA's functions in part 3 (pp. 403–04).

55. As noted earlier, the Secret Service does not make public any figures for its presidential or vice presidential protective functions. This figure is the author's estimate of the number of Secret Service personnel based in Washington who directly handle presidential and vice presidential protection. It includes the Uniformed Division (that is, the White House police), the technical security and protective research units, a portion of the training staff, and the presidential and vice presidential details. These details are of course, augmented when the chief executive and the vice president travel. In 2000, additional protective details (beyond this estimate) will be created to cover major presidential candidates.

56. This number represents 70 percent of the total Service Delivery Team staff of 190.

57. James P. Pfiffner, "The President's Chief of Staff: Lessons Learned," *Presidential Studies Quarterly* 23, no. 1 (Winter 1993):77.

58. Quoted in Charles O. Jones, *Passages to the Presidency: From Campaigning to Governing* (Brookings, 1998), 105.

59. Leon Panetta, telephone interview with author, November 23, 1998.

60. Ibid.

61. Background interview with author.

62. George Bush, letter to author, September 21, 1998.

63. John Podesta, interview with author, Washington, D.C., July 9, 1999.

64. Ibid.

65. Erskine Bowles, interview with author, New York, N.Y., July 15, 1999.

66. *Five Presidents on the Presidency,* CBS News, 1973, quoted in Fred I. Greenstein, *The Hidden-Hand Presidency* (Basic Books, 1982), 43.

67. Bob Haldeman, *The Ends of Power* (New York Times Books, 1978), 112.

68. Joseph Califano, *A Presidential Nation* (Norton, 1975), 45.

69. Reich, *Locked in the Cabinet,* 179.

70. Podesta, interview.

71. Kevin Moran, interview with author, Washington, D.C., May 10, 1999.

Notes to Chapter Twenty-Two

1. "The Office of the Executive Clerk," White House fact sheet, January 1993, author's personal collection.

2. George Bush, *My Life in Letters and Other Writings* (Scribner, 1999); quoted in Scott Sherman, *Washington Post Book Review,* November 21, 1999, p. 13.

3. Evan P. Aurand, Naval Aide to President Eisenhower, Oral History 127, Columbia Oral History Project, Eisenhower Library, p. 4. Used with permission.

4. Background interview with author.

5. See House Committee on Government Reform and Oversight, *Hearings before the Subcommittee on National Security, International Affairs, and Criminal Justice,* 104th Cong., 2nd sess., May 16, 1996; June 13, 1996. Among those testifying was Colonel Joseph J. Simmons IV, commander of the WHCA.

6. Background interview with author.

7. R. S. Robins and H. Rothschild, "Doctors for the President," *New York Times,* April 7, 1981, p. 25.

8. William Safire, "The Operating Room," *New York Times,* January 5, 1987.

9. White Burkett Miller Center of Public Affairs, University of Virginia, *Report of the Miller Center Commission on Presidential Disability and the Twenty-Fifth Amendment* (Lanham, Md.: University Press of America, 1988), 25.

10. Ibid., p. 26.

11. Robert E. Gilbert, *The Mortal Presidency: Illness and Anguish in the White House* (New York: Fordham University Press, 1998), 275.

12. *Disability in U.S. Presidents: Report, Recommendations and Commentaries by the Working Group* (Winston-Salem, N.C.: Bowman Gray Scientific Press, 1997), app. 2, p. 22.

13. W. Dale Nelson, "A Secret Sanctuary," *Maryland Magazine,* February 1996, pp. 38–43. Nelson mentions that the camp "had been part of the Catoctin Recreational Demonstration Area, showpiece of a New Deal program to turn poor

farmland into playgrounds for city dwellers. Families of government workers in Washington camped out in it. It cost $18,650 to adapt it for FDR's use."

14. Ibid.

15. Quoted in Lynne Duke, "Clinton Chats with Reagan, Visits Suburban Mall," *Washington Post*, November 28, 1992, p. A7.

16. See Robert Reich, *Locked in the Cabinet* (Alfred A. Knopf, 1997), 46–51.

17. The author's recollection of a statement made several times by President Eisenhower during cabinet evaluations of the annual "Operation Alert" exercise.

18. Background interview with author.

19. *U.S. Code,* vol. 18, sec. 3056(a).

20. Quoted in Maria Fernandez, "Secret Service Fires Flare to Warn Pilot Away from White House," *Washington Post*, January 16, 1999, p. A5.

21. Don Phillips, "White House Overflights Breach Strict Security Zone," *Washington Post*, September 21, 1998, p. A12.

22. Philip H. Melanson, *The Politics of Protection: The U.S. Secret Service in the Terrorist Age* (Praeger, 1986), 95, 97–8.

23. See U.S. Senate, *Final Report of the Committee on Governmental Affairs,* March 10, 1998, 1:769–71, 437–69, 826–30; 3:4366–8.

24. Robert A. Fein and Bryan Vossekuil for the National Institute of Justice, *Intelligence Threat Assessment Investigations: A Guide for State and Local Law Enforcement Officials* (U.S. Department of Justice, Office of Justice Programs, July 1998).

25. Ibid.

26. Background interview with author.

27. Ibid.

28. Ibid.

29. Ibid.

30. Lou Cannon, *Washington Post*, May 20, 1985, p. A2.

31. James Mackin, interview with author, Washington, D.C., April 28, 1999.

32. "Clintons Enjoy Secret Service Demonstration," *Washington Post*, October 5, 1997, p. A10.

33. Miriam Ottenburg, "Time to Revise Security Plans," *Washington Evening Star*, September 28, 1964.

34. Background interview with author.

35. Robert Snow, interview with author, Annandale, Va., January 27, 1998.

36. Daniel Patrick Moynihan, "Wretched Excess," *Washington Post*, February 9, 1992, p. B7.

37. *Public Papers of the Presidents: Richard Nixon, 1973* (GPO, 1975), 647.

38. "Bush's Letters Opposing Agents' Forced Testimony," *New York Times*, April 25, 1998, p. A8.

39. Quoted in Peter Baker, "Secret Service Officers Told to Testify on Clinton," *Washington Post*, May 23, 1998, p. A14.

40. Susan Schmidt, "Starr Wins Appeal in Privilege Dispute," *Washington Post*, July 8, 1998, p. A1.

41. Quoted in Joan Biskupic, "Court Lets Stand Rulings on Secret Service, Lawyers' Testimony," *Washington Post*, November 10, 1998, p. A4.

42. William Jefferson Clinton, "Remarks of May 22, 1998," *Weekly Compilation of Presidential Documents* 34, no. 21 (May 25, 1998):950.

43. William Jefferson Clinton, "Remarks of January 31, 1995," *Weekly Compilation of Presidential Documents* 31, no. 5 (February 6, 1995):162.

44. Frederic E. Fox, "The Pastoral Duties of the President," undated memorandum, author's personal collection.

45. Judithanne Scourfield, telephone interview with author, Fall 1999.

46. National Archives and Records Administration and the White House Historical Association, *Tokens and Treasures: Gifts to Twelve Presidents* (Washington, D.C.: National Archives Trust Fund and the White House Historical Association, 1996).

47. *Presidential Records Act, U.S. Code*, vol. 44, sec. 2201 et seq.

48. The papers of the Council on Environmental Quality, the Office of Administration, the Office of Management and Budget, and the U.S. Trade Representative are not presidential records but federal records and are governed by the Federal Records Act, *U.S. Code*, vol. 44, sec. 3101 et seq. Despite the fact that the papers of the vice president come under the definition of presidential records, they are not commingled with the papers of the president but are kept separately. If a vice president never becomes president, his papers may be preserved elsewhere at a place of his choosing; if he wishes, the vice president may donate his papers to the presidential library of the president with whom he served.

49. Nancy Smith, director of the Presidential Materials Branch, and Sharon Fawcett, director of the Presidential Libraries Branch, both of the National Archives and Records Administration; interview with author, Washington, D.C., January 20, 1999.

50. U.S. Senate, *Final Report of the Committee on Governmental Affairs,* deposition of Ellen McCathran (March 10, 1998), 3:4418.

51. The question, of course, will be raised in readers' minds whether the diarist knew of Monica Lewinsky's visits to the Oval Office area. It is clear that in composing the diary, the diarist is totally dependent on the information that comes to her from her regular sources: the presidential aide, the Secret Service, the telephone operators, the president's secretary, and so forth. The system worked on those days, as it worked every day. Ms. McCathran's detailed account was given to the grand jury and is not publicly available.

52. Sharon Fawcett, interview with author, Washington, D.C., January 20, 1999.

53. Those just mentioned plus nine others: the Advisory Committee on Historic Preservation, the Commission of Fine Arts, the Committee for the Preservation of the White House, the Department of the Treasury, the District of Columbia, the Executive Office of the President, the National Capital Planning Commission, the U.S. Secret Service, and the White House Military Office.

54. Public Law 105-277, 105th Cong., 1st sess., sec. 101(h).

55. Background interview with author.

56. Public Law 87-286, 87th Cong., 1st sess. (September 22, 1961).

57. Lyndon B. Johnson, Executive Order 11145, *U.S. Code,* title 3 (March 7, 1964), 256–7.

58. Background interview with author.

59. Ibid.

60. Jimmy Carter, Executive Order 12028 (December 12, 1977).

61. The following description of the consolidated database was given to the House Appropriations Subcommittee in 1997: "White House offices and employees who interact with outside individuals and organizations use the database as a tool to record relevant contact information, develop lists, and plan for future events. There are fields for name, address, telephone number, region, issues of particular interest, Social Security number, and date of birth. Other fields include the industrial, governmental or professional field with which an individual is associated, marital status, contacts with the President and other principals, and, for an individual attending a White House event, special assistance needs. The Social Office, the primary user of WhoDB, uses the system to manage events, including creating invitation lists, generating lists to clear guests into the Complex, tracking attendance at White House events, and producing RSVP and gate lists, etc. Access to WhoDB is password-protected, and only a limited number of White House employees with an official need have been granted access." Hearings of the House Appropriations Subcommittee on the Treasury, Postal Service and General Government, 105th Cong., 1st sess., *Part 3, Executive Office of the President and Funds Appropriated to the President for Fiscal Year 1998* (GPO, 1997), 203, 205–6.

62. Quoted in John Harris and Sharon La Franiere, "Clinton Aides Shared Data with DNC," *Washington Post*, January 31, 1997, p. A1.

63. Quoted in Guy Gugliotta, "Lawmaker Suggests Obstruction in Late Delivery of Memo on White House Database," *Washington Post*, October 31, 1997, p. A8.

64. The Staff Manual was the brainchild of Jodie Torkelson, assistant to President Clinton for management and administration; Torkelson was aided first by Frank Reeder, director of the Office of Administration, and later by Cheryl Mills, associate counsel.

65. General Services Administration, *The Executive Office Building*, Historical Study 3 (GPO, 1973), 74–5.

66. Sharon Farmer, interview with author, Washington, D.C., Fall 1999.

67. This description is based on General Accounting Office, *White House Travel Office Operations*, GAO-94-132 (May 1994), 4.

68. William Jefferson Clinton, "Remarks to the White House Volunteers," *Weekly Compilation of Presidential Documents* 35, no. 16 (April 26, 1999):687–8.

69. The cost of presidential Christmas cards is typically borne by the national committee of the party of the president.

70. See Charles R. Babcock, "White House 'Volunteers' Were Paid by DNC," *Washington Post*, February 20, 1997, p. A4; Stephen Barr, "White House Lists 41 'Volunteers' Paid by Others," *Washington Post*, March 12, 1997, p. A10. See also Hearings of the House Appropriations Subcommittee on the Treasury, Postal Service and General Government, *Part 3, Executive Office of the President*, 222.

71. Background interview with author.

72. Quoted in *Volunteer Voice* 49, no. 23 (August 1999):2.

73. Quoted in Sarah Booth Conroy, "Chronicles: Following Up on Fellows," *Washington Post*, October 9, 1995, p. C2.

74. Background interview with author.

75. Ibid.
76. Ibid.
77. Ibid.

Notes to Chapter Twenty-Three

1. The quotations in this paragraph are from Charles O. Jones, *Passages to the Presidency: From Campaigning to Governing* (Brookings, 1998), 107, 50, 106, 107 and 112, respectively.

2. Ibid., 104–5.

3. Ibid., 157.

4. Dick Morris, *Behind the Oval Office: Winning the Presidency in the Nineties* (Random House, 1997), 98.

5. See Samuel Kernell, *Going Public* (Washington, D.C.: CQ Press, 1986); and Martha Joynt Kumar, *Wired for Sound and Pictures: The President and White House Communications Operations* (Johns Hopkins University Press, forthcoming).

6. Terry M. Moe, "The Politicized Presidency," in *The New Direction in American Politics,* ed. John E. Chubb and Paul E. Peterson (Brookings, 1985), 244–5.

7. Hearings of the House Appropriations Subcommittee on the Treasury, Postal Service and General Government, 105th Cong., 1st sess., *Part 3, Executive Office of the President and Funds Appropriated to the President for Fiscal Year 1998* (GPO, 1997), 221.

8. *Washington Post*, February 21, 1997, p. A19.

9. Richard Cheney, interview with author, Washington, D.C., April 27, 1987.

10. Background interview with author.

11. Letter to the author from former president George Bush, September 21, 1998. *Ring of Power* was the author's earlier book about the organization and functioning of the White House staff (Basic Books, 1988); now out of print.

12. Although national security adviser Admiral John Poindexter testified to a congressional committee that he did not tell the president about the NSC staff's diversion of funds to aid the Nicaraguan contras, all the author's past experience at the White House makes him unable to give credence to that story. Even the committee itself commented, "Preempting a decision by the President to provide political deniability—which Poindexter testified that he did—was totally uncharacteristic for a naval officer schooled in the chain of command." See *Report of the Congressional Committees Investigating the Iran-Contra Affair,* 100th Cong., 1st sess. (GPO, November 1987), 272.

13. H. R. Haldeman, interview with author, Santa Barbara, California, April 16, 1986.

14. Joseph Califano, *Governing America* (Simon and Schuster, 1981), 411.

15. Ibid., 50.

16. Quoted in Samuel Kernell and Samuel Popkin, eds., *Chief of Staff: Twenty-Five Years of Managing the Presidency* (Berkeley: University of California Press, 1986), 106.

17. Richard Neustadt, "Presidential Leadership: The Clerk against the Preacher,"

in *Problems and Prospects of Presidential Leadership,* ed. James Sterling Young (Lanham, Md.: University Press of America, 1982), 1:33.

18. Califano, *Governing America,* 412.

19. "An Interview with LBJ," *Newsweek,* August 2, 1965.

20. David Gergen, interview with author, Arlington, Va., March 26, 1998.

21. Bradley Graham, "Missile Defense Accord Brings Discord," *Washington Post,* March 25, 1997, p. A4.

22. See the *Washington Post,* September 5, 1999, p. B7; and Samuel Berger, "New Isolationists, Old Fallacies," excerpted in the *Washington Post,* October 31, 1999, p. B3.

23. Karen Bell, "Matter of Principle," *Washington Post Magazine,* November 23, 1997, p. 19.

24. See Francine Kiefer, "Smoothing the Bumps to the White House," *Christian Science Monitor,* January 21, 2000, p. 3.

25. *Comprehensive Design Plan and Draft Environmental Impact Statement for the White House and President's Park* (Department of the Interior, National Park Service, October, 1998), 1.

26. Ibid.

27. *Comprehensive Design Plan Summary* (Department of the Interior, National Park Service, 1998), 24.

28. John W. Gardner, *Toward a Pluralistic but Coherent Society* (Queeenstown, Md.: Aspen Institute for Humanistic Studies, 1980), 20–1.

Index